KU-338-539

Key Contemporary Thinkers

Published

Jeremy Ahearne, *Michel de Certeau: Interpretation and its Other*
Peter Burke, *The French Historical Revolution: The Annales School
1929–1989*
Colin Davis, *Levinas: An Introduction*
Simon Evnine, *Donald Davidson*
Kate and Edward Fullbrook, *Simone de Beauvoir: A Critical
Introduction*
Andrew Gamble, *Hayek: The Iron Cage of Liberty*
Philip Hansen, *Hannah Arendt: Politics, History and Citizenship*
Sean Homer, *Fredric Jameson: Marxism, Hermeneutics,
Postmodernism*
Christopher Hookway, *Quine: Language, Experience and Reality*
Simon Jarvis, *Adorno*
Douglas Kellner, *Jean Baudrillard: From Marxism to Post-Modernism
and Beyond*
Chandran Kukathas and Phillip Pettit, *Rawls: A Theory of Justice
and its Critics*
Lois McNay, *Foucault: A Critical Introduction*
Philip Manning, *Erving Goffman and Modern Sociology*
Michael Moriarty, *Roland Barthes*
William Outhwaite, *Habermas: A Critical Introduction*
John Preston, *Feyerabend: Philosophy, Science and Society*
Susan Sellers, *Hélène Cixous: Authorship, Autobiography and Love*
Georgia Warnke, *Gadamer: Hermeneutics, Tradition and Reason*
Jonathan Wolff, *Robert Nozick: Property, Justice and the Minimal
State*

Forthcoming

Alison Ainley, *Irigaray*
Maria Baghramian, *Hilary Putnam*
Sara Beardsworth, *Kristeva*
Michael Caesar, *Umberto Eco*
James Carey, *Innis and McLuhan*
Thomas D'Andrea, *Alasdair MacIntyre*
Eric Dunning, *Norbert Elias*
Jocelyn Dunphy, *Paul Ricoeur*
Graeme Gilloch, *Walter Benjamin*
Christina Howells, *Derrida*

Paul Kelly, *Ronald Dworkin*
Valerie Kennedy, *Edward Said*
Carl Levy, *Antonio Gramsci*
Harold Noonan, *Frege*
Wes Sharrock and Rupert Read, *Kuhn*
David Silverman, *Sacks*
Nick Smith, *Charles Taylor*
Geoff Stokes, *Popper: Politics, Epistemology and Method*
Nicholas Walker, *Heidegger*
James Williams, *Lyotard*

ADORNO

A Critical Introduction

Simon Jarvis

Polity Press

Copyright © Simon Jarvis 1998

The right of Simon Jarvis to be identified as author of this work has been asserted in accordance with the Copyright, Designs and Patents Act 1988.

First published in 1998 by Polity Press
in association with Blackwell Publishers Ltd.

Reprinted 2002

Editorial office:
Polity Press
65 Bridge Street
Cambridge CB2 1UR, UK

Marketing and production:
Blackwell Publishers
108 Cowley Road
Oxford OX4 1JF, UK

All rights reserved. Except for the quotation of short passages for the purposes of criticism and review, no part of this publication may be reproduced, stored in a retrieval system, or transmitted, in any form or by any means, electronic, mechanical, photocopying, recording or otherwise, without the prior permission of the publisher.

Except in the United States of America, this book is sold subject to the condition that it shall not, by way of trade or otherwise, be lent, re-sold, hired out, or otherwise circulated without the publisher's prior consent in any form of binding or cover other than that in which it is published and without a similar condition including this condition being imposed on the subsequent purchaser.

ISBN 0–7456–1178–8
ISBN 0–7456–1179–6 (pbk)

A catalogue record for this book is available from the British Library.

Typeset in Palatino 10.5/12pt Photoprint, Torquay
Printed in Great Britain by Athenæum Press Ltd, Gateshead, Tyne & Wear

This book is printed on acid-free paper.

Contents

Acknowledgements

I thank the Master and Fellows of Sidney Sussex College, Cambridge, the Fellowships and Studentships Committee of the University of Newcastle-upon-Tyne, the Warden and Fellows of Robinson College, Cambridge, and the Master and Fellows of Fitzwilliam College, Cambridge, for supporting my research. I would also like to thank my parents and the following friends and colleagues for their support and advice during the writing of this book: Lillian Alweiss, Fenella Cannell, Katerina Deligiorgi, Haydn Downey, Gordon Finlayson, Yoram Gorlizki, Ian Hunt, Tim Jarvis, Garry Kelly, William Large, Nigel Mapp, Rod Mengham, Simon Parker, Chris Thornhill. I am deeply indebted to the thought and remarks of Jay Bernstein and the late Gillian Rose. Almost every line in this book has at some time during the past decade been argued over with two friends in particular. Drew Milne's opposition has been true friendship. Nicholas Walker has been an incomparably generous friend and teacher. This book is dedicated to him.

Abbreviations and a Note on Translations

FfM	Frankfurt am Main

Works by Adorno

GS	*Gesammelte Schriften* (23 vols, FfM: Suhrkamp, 1970–). The following texts have their own abbreviations for more readily recognizable reference:
AT	*Ästhetische Theorie* (GS 7)
DA	*Dialektik der Aufklärung* (GS 3)
DS	*Drei Studien zu Hegel* (GS 5)
K	*Kierkegaard. Konstruktion des Ästhetischen* (GS 2)
ME	*Zur Metakritik der Erkenntnistheorie* (GS 5)
MM	*Minima Moralia* (GS 4)
ND	*Negative Dialektik* (GS 6)
NzL	*Noten zur Literatur* (GS 11)
PhT	*Philosophische Terminologie* (FfM: Suhrkamp, 1973–4)
PnM	*Philosophie der neuen Musik* (GS 12)
VEET	*Vorlesung zur Einleitung in die Erkenntnistheorie 1957–8* (FfM: Junius, n.d.)
VESoz	*Vorlesung zur Einleitung in die Soziologie* (FfM: Junius, 1973)
VA	*Vorlesung zur Ästhetik 1967–8* (Zürich: H. Mayer Nachfolger, 1973)
Briefwechsel	Theodor W. Adorno / Walter Benjamin, *Briefwechsel 1928–1940*, ed. Henri Lonitz (FfM: Suhrkamp, 1994)

Translations

Translations from Adorno's German are generally my own except where otherwise stated or in the case of translations by Jephcott, Livingstone and

Walker. Provision of my own version does not necessarily imply a criticism of the existing translation. References to English translations are given for convenience, except in the case of the English translation of *Philosophy of Modern Music*, and of some articles. Readers with no German should note that these translations are often inaccurate; and that Ashton's version of *Negative Dialectics* contains serious flaws, in particular the translation of *Tausch* (exchange) as 'barter', and of *Vermittlung* (mediation) as 'indirectness' or 'transmission'.

Ashton	*Negative Dialectics*, tr. E. B. Ashton (London: Routledge, 1973)
Cumming	*Dialectic of Enlightenment*, tr. John Cumming (New York: Seabury Press, 1972)
Domingo	*Against Epistemology* (tr. of **ME**), tr. Willis Domingo (Oxford: Blackwell, 1982)
Hullot-Kentor	*Aesthetic Theory*, tr. Robert Hullot-Kentor (London: Athlone, 1997)
Hullot-Kentor	*Kierkegaard: Construction of the Aesthetic*, tr. Robert Hullot-Kentor (Minneapolis: University of Minnesota Press, 1989)
Jephcott	*Minima Moralia*, tr. E. F. N. Jephcott (London: New Left Books, 1974)
Jephcott	*Mahler*, tr. E. F. N. Jephcott (Chicago: University of Chicago Press, 1992)
Livingstone	*Quasi una Fantasia*, tr. Rodney Livingstone (London: Verso, 1992)
Livingstone	*In Search of Wagner*, tr. Rodney Livingstone (London: Verso, 1981)
Nicholsen	*Notes to Literature*, tr. Shierry Weber Nicholsen (2 vols, New York: Columbia University Press, 1991–2)
Nicholsen	*Hegel: Three Studies*, tr. Shierry Weber Nicholsen (Cambridge, Mass.: MIT Press, 1993)
Weber	*Prisms*, tr. Samuel and Shierry Weber (Cambridge, Mass.: MIT Press, 1981)

Other works

BT	Martin Heidegger, *Being and Time*, tr. John MacQuarrie and Edward Robinson (Oxford: Blackwell, 1962)
Kemp Smith	*Immanuel Kant's Critique of Pure Reason*, tr. Norman Kemp Smith (London: Macmillan, 1933)
KPM	Martin Heidegger, *Kant and the Problem of Metaphysics*, tr. Richard Taft (Bloomington and Indianapolis: Indiana University Press, 1990)
KrV **A**	Immanuel Kant, *Kritik der reinen Vernunft*, 1st edn (Riga, 1781)
KrV **B**	*Kritik der reinen Vernunft*, 2nd edn (Riga, 1787)
SZ	Martin Heidegger, *Sein und Zeit*, 16th edn (Tübingen: Max Niemeyer, 1986)

Introduction

Why read Adorno today? Many people probably first encounter Adorno through one of the small group of aphorisms for which he has become famous. 'After Auschwitz all culture, including its urgent critique, is garbage.' 'The splinter in your eye is the best magnifying glass.' 'The whole is the false.' Taken together and out of their contexts, aphorisms like this can give a rather misleading picture of Adorno. Hastily read, Adorno can look like a pessimistic elitist who belongs to a lost age of mandarin modernism – a thinker with little illumination to offer in our own apparently very different historical circumstances.

It is the aim of this book to explain why Adorno's work still matters today. Why does Adorno remain such a powerful force in fields as different as philosophy, musicology and social theory? One reason is the startling inner coherence of his thought. Adorno illuminated an extraordinary range of subjects in his lifetime – from dialectical logic to newspaper astrology columns, from the authoritarian personality to sonata form, from the syntax of poetry to the Hollywood studio system. Yet despite this, the central motifs of his thought remain remarkably stable from the time of his two early manifestos – 'The Actuality of Philosophy' and 'The Idea of Natural History' – through to his two late masterpieces – *Negative Dialectics* and *Aesthetic Theory*. His thought deepens and broadens immeasurably through his lifetime, but he is preoccupied with certain fundamental questions throughout his career: What is the relationship between power and rationality? Can there ever be a kind of thinking which does not live off the suffering of others, or which does not suppress or conceal the injustice which it lives off? If so, how? Can we imagine a world in which one's joy does not depend upon another's woe? Or are we inescapably locked into a life in which every pleasure is bought at the cost of someone else's suffering – to the extent that we cannot even imagine a world without this injustice?

What is most remarkable about Adorno's work is that these questions are implicitly present even when he is investigating matters of the minutest detail. Adorno focuses on the slightest particulars of cultural objects – the material shape and layout of books, the syntax and punctuation of poetry, the performance history of classical music. But he does this, not out of some encyclopaedic desire to collect all the available information, but because he believes that if we really can interpret these minute particulars with sufficient determination and rigour they will tell us something about the whole world from which they emerge. The expression on a face, the type-face of a book, the precise intonation of a violinist may be the smallest details, and so the easiest to miss, but they are for just this reason not the least, but the most important matters. As soon as we say that some small detail or other is just an accident, all that we have done is to give up trying to interpret it. The best way to start answering the big questions is with the small details. Even an apparently indifferent object such as the astrology column of the *Los Angeles Times* is a cipher of the human experience which it buries and falsifies. If we scrutinize it attentively, rigorously and imaginatively enough it will begin to speak. This would be the aim of Adorno's thought – to decipher in a tone of voice or in an unfamiliar turn of phrase the entire prehistory which has made these details possible. It may be, strange as the idea initially seems, that if we are ever to interpret our own social experience, we need to start with just those particulars which are usually written off as insignificant details.

Anyone attempting to explain this body of thought faces some unusual difficulties. Adorno believes that style is inseparable from content in philosophical and social-critical thought. It is obvious that the meaning of a sentence depends not only upon which words it has in it but upon the order in which these words are placed; but for Adorno it is no less the case that the meaning of a paragraph depends upon the order of the sentences in it, that the meaning of a work depends upon the arrangement of its chapters, and that the meaning of a life's work can depend upon the relation of different works to each other. What this means is that it is unusually hard to pick and choose in Adorno's work – to select out arguments which still work and to discard those which do not – because all Adorno's arguments have something like a systematic relationship to each other. They share a philosophical idiom which gives his work its internal coherence. If we lop off the bits which look difficult or obsolete – the engagement with Hegelian idealism, say – we can find that even apparently unconnected aspects of Adorno's work, like his social theory or music criticism, suddenly make no sense.

It is hard to explicate such a body of work without doing some violence to it, but if the explicator is to do more than simply provide a stuffed replica of the original, it has to be attempted. This book, therefore, is an attempt to separate out for the purpose of analysis all the key arguments in Adorno's work. For this reason it is best read in conjunction with some of Adorno's own work. This introductory chapter surveys the development of Adorno's thought over the course of his life, as well as sketching the intellectual and institutional contexts from which his thought emerged. It also offers a preview of some key concepts and the stage at which they entered Adorno's thought: *immanent critique, utopian negativity, metacritique, instrumental reason,* the ideas of the *double character of language, negative dialectic* and the notion that works of art have a *truth-content.*

The early years: 'immanent' critique and utopian negativity

When Adorno was born in 1903 it was as Theodor Wiesengrund (the name which he later adopted was the maiden name of his mother, who had been a successful singer before her marriage). The history of Adorno's name carries in miniature something of his own history: Adorno was known as 'Wiesengrund' or 'Wiesengrund-Adorno' until 1938, when Friedrich Pollock asked him to drop 'Wiesengrund' because there were too many Jewish names amongst the members of the Institute for Social Research, in exile from Hitler's Germany.[1] His was a relatively wealthy background and his early studies were undisturbed by financial distress. His philosophical interests began early: he studied Kant with Siegfried Kracauer and began reading the work of the young Georg Lukács and Ernst Bloch shortly after the First World War. He befriended many of the leading left-leaning thinkers and critics of

his generation, amongst whom Walter Benjamin and Max Horkheimer were to remain close friends. He lived in Vienna for a time
in the mid-1920s, where he studied composition with Alban Berg
and attended Karl Kraus's lectures with him; it was not until the
mid-1930s that Adorno finally renounced composition in favour of
philosophy and social and cultural criticism.[2] His early academic
work was supervised by Hans Cornelius, a complex figure with
professional interests in chemistry, psychology and art. Cornelius's
philosophical thought was concerned with the theory of knowledge in general. In his *Transcendentale Systematik* (1916), Cornelius
set out a theory of the conditions making possible all valid
knowledge as such, offering a broadly Kantian approach which
discarded the more metaphysically ambitious features of Kant's
thought. Cornelius attempted to derive all the conditions of the
possibility of scientifically valid judgements from the requirement
that our experience should be a single unified whole.[3] Adorno
declared that Cornelius's transcendental idealism was the basis for
the approach taken by 'The concept of the unconscious'.[4] It is an
attempt to provide an account of the concept of the unconscious
through a reading of Kant and Freud, written for presentation as a
Habilitationsschrift, a publication conferring on the author the *venia
legendi*, the right to teach in the German university system. In the
event the text was withdrawn before it could be examined, on the
advice of Cornelius himself. Save for some of its closing reflections,
which announce a quite un-Cornelian interest in the social content
of philosophical concepts, Cornelius's work is presupposed as a
theoretical basis throughout. This work and the short study of
Husserl which preceded it represented false starts in Adorno's
academic career. Adorno had curbed his philosophical imagination
in order to satisfy what he perceived as insuperable institutional
requirements; yet Cornelius insisted on the dissertation's being
withdrawn precisely because it showed so little originality.[5]

Adorno was in many respects dissatisfied with Cornelius's
work, which he found excessively dry and abstract.[6] But Cornelius
was himself only a rather minor representative of the neo-Kantian
philosophical climate dominant in Germany in the early years of
the century. At the close of the nineteenth century thinkers such as
Wilhelm Dilthey and Georg Simmel had insisted that, despite their
impressive success, the natural sciences could not provide a model
for all forms of intellectual inquiry. Wilhelm Windelband proposed
an influential distinction. The method of the natural sciences, he
suggested, was to gather particular examples under general laws.

In this sense the natural sciences were 'nomothetic' – they put forward general laws. But the humanities could not borrow this method, because cultural and historical phenomena were irreducibly and qualitatively individual. Historical inquiry was 'idiographic', an interpretation of quite individual events and circumstances which could not be assembled under so-called laws.[7] A very broad range of philosophers, sociologists, historians and historical economists accordingly began to look not to the natural sciences but to classical German philosophy, and particularly to Immanuel Kant, for their theoretical foundations.

Adorno's torn attitude towards Kant gives a good idea of the direction of his early thought in general. On the one hand, there was the abstract, epistemological Kant represented by Cornelius. Yet at the age of sixteen, he was already imbibing a different Kant from the later film critic and social theorist Siegfried Kracauer. Kracauer had already taught Adorno to regard Kant's *Critique of Pure Reason* as more than a general theory about how valid scientific judgements were possible. Kracauer's Kant was also deeply interested in questions which looked to many at the time like obsolete metaphysics – questions about what kind of meaning we could attach to the ideas of God, of a free will, or of the immortality of the soul. More importantly, Kracauer saw the internal contradictions of Kant's thought not as mistakes, but as symptoms of wider social and historical conflicts. In some respects, all Adorno's thought can be understood as working through this tension – between a wish to get beyond the emptiness and abstractness of much contemporary philosophy, and a wish to retain its logical rigour. Kracauer's teaching was important here, because it allowed Adorno to begin to see that the abstractness of philosophy was closely connected to certain central features of social experience in modernity – so that abstractness could not simply be got rid of by an act of will.[8]

This insight explains the direction which Adorno began to take after the failure of 'The concept of the unconscious'. In his inaugural lecture as a *Privatdozent* (junior university teacher), 'The Actuality of Philosophy', Adorno presented for the first time a programme of philosophical interpretation of startling originality.[9] He suggested that philosophy should regard itself as a kind of interpretation. Instead of attempting to become so abstract and general that nothing could escape its net, that is, philosophy should start out from the interpretation of minute particulars. Increasingly he began to think of this way of writing philosophy as what he came to call an *immanent critique*. 'Immanent' means 'remaining within'. An immanent critique is one which 'remains within' what it criticizes. Whereas a 'transcendent' critique, a critique from outside, first establishes its own principles, and then uses them as a yardstick by which to criticize other theories, immanent critique starts out from the principles of the work under discussion itself. It uses the internal contradictions of a body of work to criticize that work in its own terms. Immanent critique is thus not only a criticism of individual arguments, but also of the way those arguments fit together within a body of philosophical work. It is interested in what Adorno calls the 'truth-content' of entire works and authorships, which are more than the sum of their parts. Unlike most 'critiques', that is, it is not so much trying to score a victory over the work criticized, as to understand the significance of the particular kinds of contradiction present in a given body of such work – in particular, to understand what these contradictions tell us about the social experience out of which the work was written. For example, Adorno's immanent critique of Kant's thought points to certain contradictions in the way Kant uses the concept of 'experience'. But the point is not to argue that Kant was 'wrong' in any simple way. Instead the point is to show how Kant's very philosophical honesty and intelligence lead him to contradictions which tell us something important about the way modern social experience itself is structured. The 'abstractness' of Kant's thought is not so much an error as a testimony to the increasingly 'abstract' quality of modern experience itself.

Adorno began, then, to develop a practice of philosophical writing in which the truth-content of his own thought remains partly implicit, residing partly in the way his explicit criticisms of earlier thinkers are organized. Adorno's immanent critique, for that reason, is not really a method of interpretation which is worked out in advance and then applied identically to all philosophical texts, regardless of the differences between those texts. Instead, it uses a critique of concepts to get to a critique of the real experience which is already sedimented in those concepts. Because, Adorno suggests, concepts always carry buried within them, even when they look entirely abstract, the traces of bodily pleasure or suffering, fear or desire, critically interpreting conceptual contradictions can be a way of critically interpreting our real social experience.

Such work, connecting what was apparently most abstractly philosophical with the concretely social and political, was hard to undertake in the German academia of the 1920s. The difficulties which might be expected are indicated by the fact that none of the three thinkers by whom Adorno was most strongly influenced – Ernst Bloch, the young Georg Lukács and Walter Benjamin – was an established academic. Few of Adorno's mentors liked his inaugural lecture. Even Kracauer thought its explicit use of terms like 'materialist dialectic' tactically ill-advised.[10] None the less, the liberal environment of the University of Frankfurt am Main, where the first ever Institute with a predominantly Marxist programme had recently been established, looked like a promising place in which to continue this work. The Institute for Social Research opened in 1924 in Frankfurt am Main. It was financed by Felix Weil, the Marxist son of a grain millionaire, who wished, according to one contemporary, 'to create a foundation similar to the Marx–Engels Institute in Moscow . . . and one day to present it to a German Soviet Republic'.[11] Under the leadership of its first director Carl Grünberg the Institute was preoccupied primarily with a Marxist approach to issues in political economy (Friedrich Pollock and Henryk Grossmann were especially prominent contributors), with Marx–Engels scholarship, and with the history of the labour movement. At this stage the Institute's journal was called the 'Journal for the History of Socialism and of the Workers' Movement'.[12] When Horkheimer took over the directorship of the Institute in 1930, its commitment to Marxism remained no less forceful. But Horkheimer (who, unlike Grünberg, was philosophically trained) had a keen appreciation of Marxism's ineradicable debt to classical German philosophy and believed that philosophy needed to be allocated a more central place in the Institute's work.

Adorno had revealed with his inaugural lecture that he was a genuinely autonomous thinker. He appeared to stand, at the age of only twenty-seven, on the verge of a brilliant academic career in Germany. He began lecturing on a wide range of topics, from Bacon, Descartes, Hobbes and Locke to Hegel's philosophy of history, Simmel, Husserl and problems in aesthetics.[13]

One central feature of Adorno's thinking which is already evident in his early philosophical programme is his *utopian negativity*. A decisive influence on the early Adorno in this respect was Ernst Bloch's *Spirit of Utopia*. It offered an imaginative and apocalyptic account of philosophical and cultural life in early twentieth-century Europe. For Bloch most modern thought was marked both

by its 'rootlessness' or 'homelessness' and by its essentially 'contemplative' approach.[14] Bloch aimed at a kind of thinking which,
instead of pretending to be detached from human needs and
desires, placed them at its centre. He insisted that thought could
not be detached from human interests and wishes, not simply in
the sense that all thought serves some interest, but also in the less
trivial sense that only the activity of wishing and imagining makes
contemplation possible.[15] Knowledge was now to be understood
not simply as a contemplative description of what exists, but as an
imaginative and active striving towards what *is not yet*.

Adorno's own thinking was deeply influenced by Bloch's Marxist utopianism: in his own work he attempted to provide a more
philosophically rigorous account of Bloch's utopian thinking. But
as Adorno came to understand it, utopia could only be addressed
negatively. In order to see why, it is helpful to look at another
important early influence on Adorno's thought, the work of Georg
Lukács. Lukács's early *Theory of the Novel*, a book which Adorno
greatly admired, had offered a tragic theory of modernity.[16] But
Lukács's involvement in revolutionary political activity after the
war transformed his theoretical approach. He saw that Marxism's
attempts to shed its philosophical shell had in many respects
resulted, not in an escape from philosophy, but simply in a relapse
into more naive philosophical positions. Reflection on the relation
between theory and practice, for example, had sunk to a low
philosophical level, with the political consequence that revolutionary practice seemed to be faced with a choice between passive
determinism and naive voluntarism.[17] Lukács argued that the
argument could not be settled on these terms because this abstract
opposition was itself bound up in the all-pervasive 'reification' of
human life, thought and culture under the capitalist mode of
production. In their 'reified' form social institutions and processes
come to appear as though they are autonomously self-directing.
Human practice comes to serve this reified social process rather
than to direct it. It becomes pseudo-practice, 'contemplative' practice.[18] At the same time theoretical activity is governed by a
division of intellectual labour. Philosophy, for example, becomes a
department for grounding the other departments; sociology
searches for 'purely sociological' objects. The result is that theory
becomes blind to the social totality and incapable of theorizing this
totality. Its sight can only be restored from the perspective of a
praxis – the revolutionary praxis of the proletariat – dedicated to
overcoming the capitalist mode of production.[19]

The deep influence of Lukács's theory of reification on Adorno – despite his later criticisms of Lukács – indicates why Adorno came to think that philosophy and social theory could only address utopia negatively and implicitly rather than positively and explicitly. The social theorist could not pretend that he or she was speaking from some place outside society. If Lukács's theory of reification was correct, any blueprint for the good or just society could hardly be more than an ideological product of one branch of the division of intellectual labour. But Adorno found Lukács's own solution to this problem, the idea that the proletariat were a cognitively privileged collective subject of history, unsatisfactory. Adorno's utopian negativity, instead, works through immanent critique. It cannot provide a blueprint for what the good life would be like, but only examines what our 'damaged' life is like. It hopes to interpret this damaged life with sufficient attention and imagination to allow intimations of a possible, undamaged life to show through.

It was to this kind of project that Adorno turned in his second attempt to produce a *Habilitationsschrift*. Working as an assistant to the Christian socialist Paul Tillich, Adorno submitted in 1931 a study of Kierkegaard. Horkheimer and Tillich granted Adorno his *Habilitation*, despite Horkheimer's reservations about the book's apparently theological approach.[20]

Horkheimer's early conception of the Institute's work was in part an interdisciplinary and collaborative one.[21] The obstacles placed in the way of a materialist theory of society by the division of intellectual labour were to be overcome by criticizing the presuppositions of this division, and by interdisciplinary and collaborative work. Horkheimer, who had himself undergone psychoanalysis, was interested in the contributions which Freud's thought might make to a materialist theory of society. Erich Fromm worked on psychoanalysis with a view to elaborating its possible contributions to social theory. At the same time Horkheimer insisted, unusually, that artistic and cultural production could not be written off as spheres of secondary importance to social theory. Accordingly, new personnel were drawn into the Institute's orbit: a young student of Martin Heidegger's, Herbert Marcuse, worked on philosophical issues confronted by social theory; Leo Löwenthal prepared literary-critical studies from an ideology-critical viewpoint. Friedrich Pollock and Henryk Grossmann continued to contribute work in political economy. Adorno was seen at first as

the Institute's musical expert rather than as its guiding philosophical spirit. These workers were brought together in the service of a
materialism requiring the interdisciplinary 'unification of philosophy and science'.[22] Horkheimer's thought was a decisive factor in
Adorno's intellectual development. From him Adorno learned an
exacting scepticism about the good intentions of social theory.
More than any other single figure, Horkheimer was responsible for
the materialist dimension of Adorno's thought, its continual concern to weigh thinking against the bodily experience of suffering
or desire which thinking was all too liable to conceal or suppress.

Adorno's own work, however, continued to follow a trajectory
strongly independent of Horkheimer's. The crucial influence on
Adorno's study of Kierkegaard was the philosopher and philolo-
gist Walter Benjamin, and in particular Benjamin's own failed
Habilitationsschrift, *The Origin of the German Play of Lamentation*. The
work offered an interpretation of German Baroque drama which is
both philological and philosophical. Its own significance, however,
extended well beyond this task. Benjamin contrasts *Trauerspiel* and
'allegory' with tragedy. They are manifestations of a post-tragic
modernity. Benjamin's critique of allegory implies nothing less
than a critique of modernity itself. The relationship between
signifier and signified in allegory is arbitrary. 'Any person, any
object, any relationship can mean absolutely anything else. With
this possibility a destructive, but just verdict is passed on the
profane world: it is characterized as a world in which the detail is
of no importance.'[23] Benjamin holds it against the modern world,
that is, not against allegory, that anything can be made to stand for
absolutely anything else. This is how things will be in a world
imprisoned in immanence, a world 'denied direct access to a
beyond'.[24] Anything can be made to stand for anything else only
because nothing is absolute. Without a perspective outside this
'context of guilt' or 'natural history' the context cannot be interpreted.[25] This is why Benjamin insists that a critical understanding
of the *Trauerspiel* in its extreme, allegorical form is possible only
from the higher domain of theology.[26]

Many of the central motifs of Adorno's thought, some of which
we have already met, and some of which we shall meet later in this
study, derive directly from this encounter with Benjamin. Like
Benjamin, Adorno thinks of the modern world as a 'context of
immanence' which has placed a prohibition on thinking the absolute. Both think of philosophy as interpreting minute particulars

with the aid of 'constellations' of concepts. But Adorno's immanent critique works differently from the theological approach of the early Benjamin. The fact that a particular phenomenon is uninterpretable without access to a 'beyond' does not give us the right to assume that perspective ourselves. The theological motifs in Adorno's thought are always negative. It is a central concern of Adorno's that they should never become an appeal to an immediate or positive transcendence. In Benjamin's early thought their status is more ambiguous.

Exile: 'metacritique' and the dialectic of enlightenment

When Hitler came to power in Germany in 1933 Adorno was quite unprepared for the collapse of his plans. Liberal and socialist academics were gradually forced into resignation and exile. Although Adorno's father had been an assimilated Jew and his mother a Catholic, he would not after 1933 have been able even to teach music in Germany, except to 'non-Aryans'.[27] The Institute for Social Research was closed by the National Socialists on 13 March 1933; its leading thinkers left after various periods of delay for the United States. Adorno, however, was not at this period a paid employee of the Institute and left instead for England with Gretel Karplus, in an attempt to find academic employment there. Although in Germany Adorno had already qualified for the right to teach in a university (the *venia legendi*), this did not help him to find comparable work elsewhere. His attempts to submit the Kierkegaard book for a parallel qualification in Vienna failed because the academic assigned to assess Adorno's merit judged that 'only the quotations are of any interest.' When asked for his advice about Adorno's qualifications for a British post Ernst Cassirer replied that Adorno's work was obscure and could not be unreservedly recommended.[28] Instead Adorno, still dependent on the financial support of his parents, was obliged to settle for affiliation as a doctoral student at Merton College, Oxford.

These years spent 'as it were locked up in a quite alien land' saw Adorno developing and deepening the programme set out in his early philosophical manifestoes in a variety of directions.[29] His two main projects were an intensive study of Husserl which later appeared as his *Metacritique of Epistemology*, and work towards a study of Wagner, as well as publications for the Institute's journal, the *Zeitschrift für Sozialforschung* (Journal for Social Research) (sometimes, as in the case of his ferocious article on jazz, under the pseudonym Hektor Rottweiler) which continued to be published in German from the Institute's new base affiliated to Columbia University, New York. Adorno's role in the Institute's journal during the 1930s was still primarily as a social theorist of music. His work on Wagner (published in full in 1952) and on most aspects of musical composition, reception and production, began to show that the approach of immanent critique need not be restricted to philosophical texts but could also be used to illuminate art. Increasingly, Adorno began to feel the need to show that works of art were not merely decorative or entertaining, but that they had a cognitive content or 'truth-content', an implicit kind of truth which philosophical criticism could interpret. It was with this idea of the 'truth-content' of works of art that his last work, *Aesthetic Theory* (1970) was to be preoccupied.

It was in the work towards the Husserl book – initially conceived as a possible Oxford DPhil. thesis but not published until 1956 – that the mature form of Adorno's thought began decisively to emerge. This was Adorno's most extensive attempt to date to justify in detail his belief that even those philosophical texts which were apparently most abstract necessarily contained sedimented within them the traces of the social experience which had made them possible. In particular, it is in this study that Adorno begins to put into practice the idea of a *metacritique*. Whereas epistemological critique asks what categories make experience possible, metacritique asks what experiences make the epistemological categories possible. The social-critical content of the book, rather than being presented as background information, was extrapolated from the account of key Husserlian categories. The book was also a practical demonstration of Adorno's conviction that the only way to break out of the prevailing abstractness of philosophical thought was through an immanent critique of the most advanced forms of logic and epistemology. Many of the central preoccupations of the later *Dialectic of Enlightenment* are already present in embryo in the work on Husserl.

In 1937 Adorno was invited to come to America to head a programme of sociological research into radio listeners with Paul Lazarsfeld.[30] From this time forth the debate in which he had long been engaged with Horkheimer, the Institute's director, began to develop into a full collaboration, the closest intellectual relationship of his life. Horkheimer was increasingly persuaded by Adorno's arguments that the reunification of philosophy with

material research was further off than he had thought. Positivism
was radically irreconcilable with a theory whose primary interest
was in social change. Its ahistorical appeal to raw facts, and its
construction of alleged laws from such data, took past and present
experience as though it were legislative for future experience. It
was thus already dependent on metaphysical presuppositions.
Research conducted along such lines could not straightforwardly
be 'reunified' with philosophy. Two important articles, Horkheimer's own 'Critical and Traditional Theory' (1937) and Marcuse's 'On the Concept of Essence' (1936, in his *Negations*) took the
opposition between this new programme of 'critical theory of
society' and positivism to be central to the Institute's work.

Horkheimer remained no less preoccupied with philosophy's
social and ideological content than he had always been. Now,
however, he became increasingly persuaded by Adorno's belief
that this social content had to be understood from the inside out,
rather than being externally researched and then used as a yardstick against which to assess philosophy's ideological content or
truth-content. Social experience could not be unreflectively 'added
on' from research whose own theoretical formulations were themselves unsatisfactory. Neither Adorno nor Horkheimer took this to
mean that philosophical criticism was the only kind of work which
need go on in the Institute. Yet they did become increasingly
unhappy with any belief on the part of expert political economists
such as Pollock that philosophy could be left to the philosophers.
Horkheimer eventually decided that the 'materialist' or 'dialectical' logic on which he had originally intended to collaborate with
Herbert Marcuse could best be completed with Adorno's help.
Throughout the latter half of the decade Adorno and Horkheimer
were engaged in the simultaneous study of the classical problems
of philosophy and materialist social theory.[31]

From this plan for a dialectical logic emerged the most celebrated work of the so-called 'Frankfurt School', *Dialectic of Enlightenment*. Initially published in mimeograph in 1944 under the title
Philosophical Fragments, the book has proved both controversial and
influential ever since. Its meaning and even its subject matter are
still matters of dispute, but the book consists of several complementary studies – of the concept of enlightenment, of *The
Odyssey*, of Sade, of the culture industry, and of anti-semitism –
each of which explores aspects of the history of rationality. The
central argument is that reason has become irrational precisely
because of its attempt to expel every non-rational moment from

itself. In this way, reason becomes incapable of understanding what makes rationality itself possible, the non-rational element which reason depends upon. The consequence is a kind of rationality which is a tool, blindly applied without any real capacity either to reflect on the ends to which it is applied, or to recognize the particular qualities of the objects to which it is applied. Adorno and Horkheimer call this unreflective rationality *instrumental reason*. The theory of instrumental reason became a central motif of critical theory from this point onwards. Adorno and Horkheimer suggested that the instrumentalization of reason went together with an increasingly absolute separation between the language of 'art' and the language of 'science'. The former became something with no cognitive content, merely image-like; the latter became something with no mimetic similarity with what it classified, a pure sign. This separation of the language of art and the language of science is what Adorno often later referred to as the *double character of language* in modernity.

The climate of social science in the United States in the 1930s and 1940s, however, meant that the innovative philosophical core of critical theory was not the face it most openly presented to the world. Horkheimer was anxious to secure for the Institute the recognition and financial support of American universities, where social science research was largely conducted along lines imitative of the natural sciences. Accordingly collaborative empirical projects bound to pre-formed goals absorbed much of the Institute's time and effort. Adorno collaborated with Paul Lazarsfeld, himself an emigré but by now a solid citizen of Anglophone social science, who reported of Adorno that 'he behaves so foreign that I feel like a member of the Mayflower Society. When you talk to him, however, he has an enormous amount of interesting ideas.' He later informed Adorno that one of the latter's draft memoranda was 'definitely below the standards of intellectual cleanliness, discipline and responsibility which have to be requested from anyone active in academic work.'[32] Adorno in his turn referred to his experience *'du côté de chez Lazarsfeld'* as one which required 'the theoretical elimination of all meaning'. He concluded that 'we are no more capable of understanding them than they are of understanding us.'[33] Collaborations with such figures produced some interesting work, and Adorno later praised aspects of American academic life;[34] but they had the consequence that Anglophone discussion of critical theory was for long focused on less characteristic products such as the collaborative *Studies in the Authoritarian*

Personality (1950), and remained largely ignorant of its philosophical programme.

The genuinely important fruit of Adorno's encounter with America – apart from the collaborative *Dialectic of Enlightenment* – was his masterpiece *Minima Moralia: Reflections from Damaged Life* (1951). The work is intimately informed by Adorno's experience of exile in America. It consists of 153 brief essays or long aphorisms which offer perhaps Adorno's most successful realization of the idea of 'micrological' thinking. Most of the essays begin from some moment of contemporary experience which is an instance of damaged life. In each case, Adorno's interpretations of these moments make surprising connections which show how their significance extends far beyond their immediate context to illuminate the systematic transformation or distortion of modern human experience: one essay, 'Tough Baby', moves from the film image of the 'handsome dinner-jacketed figure returning late to his bachelor flat, switching on the indirect lighting and mixing himself a whisky and soda' to an analysis of the psychological foundations of totalitarianism.

The Frankfurt years: aesthetic theory and negative dialectic

After the war the left-wing German emigrés were scattered. Bertolt Brecht and Ernst Bloch were in East Germany; Marcuse, Franz Neumann and Karl Wittfogel all eventually found jobs in American universities; and Adorno and Horkheimer returned to the new Federal Republic where the Institute was once again allied with the University of Frankfurt. Adorno was now securely installed as the head (with Horkheimer) of the Institute and as a professor at the University of Frankfurt am Main. Adorno became less and less involved in empirical sociological work and more and more preoccupied with elaborating the theoretical foundations of his thought. A series of lecture courses, most of which remain unpublished but which are gradually appearing in a new critical edition, allowed him to develop his own philosophical position through a rereading of the tradition of German philosophy, in particular of Kant, Hegel, Marx, Nietzsche and Heidegger.

This period has sometimes been seen as one of political and intellectual retrenchment.[35] Many younger disciples of critical theory were disappointed by what seemed to them Adorno's and

Horkheimer's increasingly quietistic attitude towards political practice. In 1968 the Institute was the target for radical student protest. The Institute, and Adorno in particular, were charged with a betrayal of Marxism and of the proletariat. When asked to cancel his lecture on Goethe's *Iphigenie* as a protest at the murder of an Iranian student, Adorno refused.[36] At one point Adorno called the police to clear university premises of an occupying force of students. These events left him severely shaken; he died not long afterwards. Yet if the post-war years were an institutionally troubled period for critical theory, they were also the years in which some of the deepest and most enduring works left by critical theory, Adorno's *Negative Dialectics*, *Aesthetic Theory* and his late social-critical essays, were written, and in which a second generation of critical theorists, led by Jürgen Habermas, emerged. In the last two decades of Adorno's life a series of studies of major importance – as well as collections of Adorno's musical and literary criticism – appeared one after the other. Especially important were his *Three Studies of Hegel* (1957), which began to prepare the way for a final articulation of the goal to which all Adorno's thought had been tending – a materialist dialectic.

This was delivered in *Negative Dialectics* (1966). Adorno's 'negative' dialectic was an attempt to exemplify a materialist thinking which could avoid the naturalistic or sociological dogmatism which Adorno thought all previous materialisms had fallen into – with the result that such materialisms had offered some unexamined and quite abstract category such as 'matter' or 'nature' or 'history' or 'society' as though it represented an immediate given, a point at which theoretical enquiry simply had to stop. 'Negative' dialectic was deeply indebted to Hegel's dialectic, but differed from it above all in not claiming already to have gained successful access to absolute truth. For Adorno, the possibility of such access was dependent upon the possibility of a change in our social experience. Negative dialectic was thus an attempt to criticize the obstacles – real and conceptual – impeding our possible access to the absolute, rather than a claim to have achieved such access.

At the same time, Adorno was also preoccupied with his last major work, *Aesthetic Theory*, which remained unfinished at his death and which was published posthumously in 1970. In *Aesthetic Theory*, Adorno attempted what was in many ways a counterpart to *Negative Dialectics*. That work had developed Adorno's long-standing conviction that the conceptual language of cognition, of 'science', necessarily contained reference to the social experience which had made it possible; *Aesthetic Theory*, conversely, argued that art and aesthetic experience had a cognitive content. The book attempts to make explicit through philosophical interpretation the cognitive content or 'truth-content' which is implicit in works of art. In doing so it provides an unparalleled resource for an aesthetics which is neither formalist nor relativist.

These two late major works are undoubtedly Adorno's most important. They investigate in depth problems which had often been rather compressedly or obliquely addressed in his earlier work. Unfortunately, however, they have not always been well understood in the Anglophone world. This is partly because of the inadequacy of the existing translations (a new translation of *Aesthetic Theory*, however, has recently appeared). But it is also because of the relative unfamiliarity, especially amongst social theorists, musicologists and literary critics – but also even amongst philosophers – of the tradition of classical German philosophy whose language and idiom forms the very element of Adorno's thought. Unfortunately, there is no short-cut through this obstacle. To introduce Adorno's thought is also to introduce the philosophical tradition in which he writes.

The structure of this book

From this point onwards, therefore, this book is organized analytically rather than narratively. It falls roughly into three parts. The first three chapters are all concerned with different aspects of Adorno's work as a critical theorist of society. Adorno's social theory is introduced by looking at what is perhaps the central work of first-generation Critical Theory – *Dialectic of Enlightenment* – and attempting an explanation of some of its central theses: in particular, the claims that 'enlightenment reverts to mythology', that 'myth is already enlightenment', and that 'the history of civilization is the introversion of sacrifice.' It also considers some of the most significant recent objections which have been made to the work. This is followed by a chapter on Adorno's 'critical theory of society' as a whole, contextualizing it through an account of Adorno's criticisms of Durkheim and Weber, explaining the unusual nature of Adorno's appropriation of Marx, and examining its consequences for his thought about substantive issues such as the theories of commodity fetishism, of surplus-value, of class, of 'monopoly' capitalism and fascism. The first part of the book closes with a discussion of Adorno's theory of 'the culture industry', suggesting that this theory cannot really be understood as an elitist attack on 'popular' culture, before going on to relate the account of the 'culture industry' to Adorno's account of the impact of commodity fetishism and to the psychoanalytic aspects of his social theory. This part of the book closes with an evaluation of the strengths and weaknesses of Adorno's social theory.

There follow two chapters on Adorno's aesthetic theory. The first of these explains the peculiar character of what Adorno meant by an 'aesthetic theory', by comparing it with the classical German tradition in aesthetics out of which it emerges – and in particular with Kant and Hegel. It shows how Adorno defended his idea that works of art could be said to have a 'truth-content' which depended on their 'language-character', and considers some objections to the way in which Adorno formulates this idea. The chapter closes with an explanation of Adorno's idea that art represents the 'social antithesis of society'. It is followed by a chapter in which I consider some examples of Adorno's aesthetic theory at work in his music criticism and in his literary criticism. By a close engagement with Adorno's interpretations of Beethoven, Bach and Schoenberg, and with his readings of the essay form, Hölderlin's later hymns and the poetry of Gottfried Benn, I try to show what Adorno meant by suggesting that the socially critical character of works of art resides in their form.

Finally, in the last three chapters, I turn to Adorno's work on epistemology and metaphysics. In chapter 6 I explain the concepts of metacritique and negative dialectic, and introduce some of Adorno's most fundamental philosophical convictions through an account of his metacritique of Kant. The following chapter discusses Adorno's idea that 'constellations' of concepts might go beyond classificatory thinking, and shows how this idea is related to his account of a 'priority of the object' and to his ideas about the relationship between theory and practice in critical thought. The last chapter considers the difficult problem of Adorno's relationship to metaphysics, showing why Adorno thinks that some of the most influential attempts to rid thinking of metaphysical presuppositions have failed, and what alternatives he himself offers.

Each main part of the book has two aims. The first is to give a clear account of Adorno's key arguments in each area of his intellectual activity. The second is to examine the justifications for these arguments, and to consider the criticisms which have been made of them, so as to indicate what relevance Adorno's ideas have today – a question which I pursue in the conclusion, which compares Adorno's work with some more recent theoretical and philosophical developments, notably with the 'second-generation' critical theory of Jürgen Habermas, Albrecht Wellmer and others, and with deconstruction.

1

The Dialectic of Enlightenment

Introduction

Adorno and Horkheimer's *Dialectic of Enlightenment* is, on first reading, a bewildering book. The reader is confronted with what look like a series of wild generalizations barely susceptible to empirical confirmation, claims which are not followed by a leisurely marshalling of evidence, but rather by further equally ambitious claims: 'Myth is already enlightenment'; 'Enlightenment reverts to mythology'; 'The history of civilization is the introversion of sacrifice'. A few thinly sown references to often out-of-date historical and anthropological sources do little to cheer the reader up. It looks as though the book is an outlandish survival of the nineteenth-century genre of speculative universal history – except that this time the story runs not from barbarism to civilization but in the other direction.

In order to get anywhere in reading the book it is essential to have some sense of what it is and is not trying to do. First of all, it is not an attempt to write a kind of encyclopaedia of human history and culture. It is not trying to add up chunks of knowledge from history, social anthropology, psychoanalysis and so on, and then to give them a philosophical gloss. Nor is it an attempt to write a single 'grand narrative' of historical progress or decline. Instead, the title the book was given when it first appeared in a mimeographed edition of 1944 – *Philosophical Fragments* – gives two important clues to what the book is.[1] It is *philosophical* in the sense that it is fundamentally concerned with how we can think today. Instead of telling a story, which would start from some distant and inevitably hypothetical 'origin' and then eventually arrive in the twentieth century, the book starts out from where we are now, from the assumptions about concepts and about the world which we habitually deploy, very often without recognizing that we are making these assumptions. It sets out to give an account of how we got to these assumptions, but it does this by working back from these assumptions themselves. It asks: what must have happened for our thinking to have become what it is? Secondly, the book is not some impermeable system but a group of *fragments*. Each of the essays approaches linked questions from a series of different angles.

It may be useful here to think a little more about this idea of the book as a series of fragments or essays, and how it is related to the more scientific ways in which social and political thought has usually wanted to understand itself in the twentieth century. In his introduction to *The Positivist Dispute in German Sociology* Adorno insisted that

> Amongst the moments which must remain common to philosophy and sociology if both are not to decline – the former to contentlessness, the latter to conceptlessness – one of the most important is that both contain something not wholly transformable into science. In both, nothing is meant entirely literally, neither *statement of fact* nor pure validity . . . This not entirely literal element bears witness to the tense non-identity of appearance and essence. Emphatic cognition's refusal to bid an absolute farewell to art does not push it into irrationalism. The scientistic adult mockery of 'thought-music' only serves to drown out the creaking of the filing cabinets in which the questionnaires are stored away – the sound of the enterprise of pure literalness.[2]

At this stage, there is much that will probably be unclear to many readers in this account of how philosophical social thought is to be written. Adorno suggests that the idea of social theory as a science aims at a perfectly literal language, in which there would be nothing equivocal or figurative, and in which the ideal style would be one which exactly replicated the facts discovered. Adorno questions the usefulness of this ideal – but not because he thinks that facts do not matter, or that it is more important for social thinking to be 'imaginative' in some undefined way, nor because he thinks that we can never really get at the truth about social experience. What he is suggesting, instead, is that the qualitative specificity of social experience is actually more likely to go missing in social science when it attempts to be absolutely literal in its presentation of its results. Without a certain self-reflective cunning in its deployment of concepts, social science is likely to end up without any concepts worthy of the name. It ends up, not in fact interpreting the experience it claims to be investigating, but rather classifying it. For Adorno, then, careful attention to 'style' is in fact essential to providing an interpretation of the 'content'.

None of this excuses Adorno, of course, from the need to come up with a properly supported defence of the particular claims which he makes. But it does indicate why one procedure that could be used to explain Adorno's work – to declare the fixed meaning of some 'key terms' and then to show how these key terms get put together – is not likely to be of very much help in understanding what is going on in a work like *Dialectic of Enlightenment*. Instead, thinking a little about the form of the work may be the best way into an understanding of its ambitious claims, and, in particular, may be the best way of understanding why one of the most widespread readings of the book – the idea that it is a polemic 'against' enlightenment – is misguided.

Dialectic of Enlightenment is not a narrative, although it certainly contains narrative passages. Instead it is composed 'correctively', to elaborate 'two theses: myth is already enlightenment; and enlightenment reverts to mythology.'[3] 'Ancient' and 'modern' do not designate given and radically separate categories, but are concepts which each rely on their counterpart if they are to have any meaning at all. Modern society, which provides us with our very idea of what the new is, is also the oldest, the society with the longest history behind it. Ancient society, conversely, can only be explicated from a modern standpoint, through concepts and categories which, since they are ours, cannot avoid being modern.

Adorno's and Horkheimer's 'two theses' demand to be read in conjunction with each other. If we only hear the second, 'enlightenment reverts to mythology', it is easy to arrive at a misreading of the work in which the authors are understood to be saying that enlightenment is a bad thing. Adorno and Horkheimer do not want to *reverse* enlightenment. They are not, for example, suggesting that power and knowledge are identical, but, instead, are asking how knowledge might become the dissolution of domination.[4] The point is that positivistic and rationalistic conceptions of enlightenment are not enlightened *enough*. They present us with an idea of reason which is actually mythical, rather than fully rational, because it suppresses, rather than reflecting on, its own relation to myth and tradition.[5] Conversely, Adorno and Horkheimer suggest that myth is itself already a kind of rationality, a way of ordering, classifying and controlling the world.

Adorno and Horkheimer repeatedly direct attention to this double perspective. A closer look at two particular passages may indicate something of its impact on the book's rhetorical organization. The first is from the extended reading of the *Odyssey*, 'Odysseus, or Myth and Enlightenment':

> The test Penelope puts her husband to concerns the immovable position of the marriage bed; her husband had based it on an olive tree round which he had built the room itself – the olive tree being the symbol of [the unity of] sex and property. Penelope's moving artifice is to speak as if the bed could be moved from its position: furious, her husband answers her with a detailed account of his longlasting piece of woodwork. He is the prototypical bourgeois – the with-it hobbyist. His do-it-yourself effort is an imitation of the actual labor of a craftsman, from which, in the framework of differentiated conditions of property ownership, he has long been necessarily excluded. He enjoys this for the freedom to do what is really superfluous as far as he is concerned confirms his power of disposal over those who have to work in order to live.[6]

The second passage is from 'The Culture Industry: Enlightenment as Mass Deception':

> No medieval builder can have scrutinized the subjects for church windows more suspiciously than the studio hierarchy scrutinizes a work by Balzac or Hugo before finally approving it. No medieval theologian could have determined the degree of the torment to be suffered by the damned in accordance with divine love more meticulously than the producers of shoddy epics calculate the torture to be undergone by the hero or the exact point to which the leading lady's hemline shall be raised. The explicit and implicit, exoteric and esoteric catalog of the forbidden and tolerated is so extensive that it not only defines the area of freedom but is all-powerful inside it.[7]

These passages are in fact examples of the oldest literary means for registering the gap between ancient and modern: burlesque and mock-heroic. The first passage is burlesque: that is, an ancient hero is made comical by being bathetically redescribed in the unheroic terms of modern life – Odysseus as the home woodworker. The second passage, conversely, is mock-heroic: modern life is made comical through a description in terms of a more ancient and solemn order – the film producer as medieval theologian. But the bathos redounds upon the ancient as well as upon the modern. The account of the culture industry, that is, is as much about pre-modern myth and unfreedom as it is about Hollywood. The reading of the *Odyssey* is as much about modern rationality and its organization of work and leisure as it is about Homer.

The point of this kind of 'serious play' is to overcome a choice of two different kinds of evils which arise when we try to consider the relation between our own experience and its history. Unhistorical humanism too easily takes Homer as the agent of a timeless human truth no less relevant now than it has always been. Radical historicism, conversely, insists on the absolute incommensurability of archaic Greece with modern life: we are to purge our approach of late twentieth-century presuppositions and replace them with the authentic world-view of archaic Greece. Each is internally circular. If Homer's truths are timeless, we need not go to Homer for them; but if they are radically incommensurable, then we bar in advance the very access we claim to seek. Adorno and Horkheimer's serious play allows us instead to recognize the identity and difference of the ancient and the modern. When Odysseus is described as a woodworking hobbyist, or the producer's dictates as theological dogma, the shock registers our recognition both of the similarity of the terms compared and of the gulf between them. The point is to make visible both how domination persists even in what are taken as neutral or simply methodological forms of modern rationality, and how what is often taken as archaic sheer domination is already itself a form of rationality. This 'corrective' form has the advantage of allowing Adorno and Horkheimer to admit that all rationality to date has been entangled in some way with social domination and the domination of nature, while opening a space for them to suggest that, none the less, reason does not have to be like this.

Enlightenment reverts to mythology

Adorno and Horkheimer do not use the term 'enlightenment' primarily to designate a historical period running from Descartes to Kant. Instead they use it to refer to a series of related intellectual and practical operations which are presented as demythologizing, secularizing or disenchanting some mythical, religious or magical representation of the world. The protest of Xenophanes against the projection of human qualities on to the gods is, in this sense, no less typical of 'enlightenment' than, say, Helvétius's materialism or early twentieth-century logical atomism. Early philosophers protest that anthropomorphic religion projects a merely subjective meaning on to the worshipped object; analogously, modern positivists protest that a concept such as that of 'essence' is mystical, a subjective fiction. 'Unity is the slogan from Parmenides to Russell. The destruction of gods and qualities alike is insisted upon.'[8] Adorno and Horkheimer see the history of thought, that is, as an ever-increasing scepticism about any claims for access to a 'transcendent' content or meaning, that is, to a content or meaning lying outside thought itself. All invocations of anything which might transcend thought in this way are progressively regarded as being mere poetry, thought's own fictions. In this way thought turns itself into a 'context of pure immanence', pure inside-ness, in which 'Nothing at all may remain outside.'[9]

Paradoxically, Adorno and Horkheimer suggest that it is by just this process of radical rationalization that 'enlightenment reverts to mythology.' In order to escape the charge that it is merely subjective, thought sets itself the task of replicating what exists – with no hidden extras. Thought is to confine itself to the facts, which are thus the point at which thought comes to a halt. The question as to whether these facts might *change* is ruled out by enlightened thought as a pseudo-problem. Everything which is, is thus presented as a kind of fate, no less unalterable and uninterrogable than mythical fate itself. Yet the effect of this drive for complete objectivity is, in the event, a solipsism, an inability to get outside the thinker at all. Enlightenment insists that if knowledge is really going to be knowledge of an object, it must not be contaminated by anything subjective. But its reflex scepticism leads it in practice to claim that any 'object' actually invoked is in fact a fiction of the subject. The relentless demand for objectivity, that is, has the paradoxical result of liquidating all knowledge which really concerns the object. The demand that nothing can be allowed to stand outside thought becomes, Adorno and Horkheimer argue, the severest limitation on thought of all: 'the world as a gigantic analytic judgement'.[10] Because of this, thought becomes unable to understand what it depends upon, unable to imagine that it is not entirely self-sufficient.

'Enlightenment', then, is used by Adorno and Horkheimer as a way of referring to any operation of sceptical demythologization as such. One of the most important of such operations, in their view, affects language itself. They suggest that modern rationality has progressively confined language to two equally one-sided functions: 'As a system of signs, language is required to resign itself to calculation in order to know nature, and must discard the claim to be like nature. As image, it is required to resign itself to copying in order to be nature entire, and must discard the claim to know nature.'[11] Adorno thinks that this division has not yet become complete – indeed that it could not become complete without making thinking itself impossible. The justifications for this belief will need more discussion later, but for now it needs to be noted that this way of talking about the progressive separation of discursive from mimetic language is really a way of understanding the developing separation of art from science in western, and particularly in modern, rationality. Scientific work which does not confine itself to discursive language will be understood as a mere fiction; art which does not confine itself to mimesis will be thought of as inartistically encroaching upon scientific territory. Of course, the picture is a great deal more complicated than this very sweeping outline suggests, and it will need more discussion when Adorno's theory of art is considered later.

One obvious objection to the whole series of ideas outlined here is that they present an impossibly generalized account of 'enlightenment', one so generalized that it is impossible to test. This kind of objection, significantly, is itself an example of what Adorno and Horkheimer mean by 'enlightenment'. Finally even the concept of enlightenment itself is regarded as a piece of 'animistic magic', a wild generalization, or a 'myth', because only the absolutely particular is thought to be real. This provides a good example of what the authors mean by suggesting that 'what is' becomes construed as fate. No real changes can ever really be understood to have taken place because the conceptual vocabulary which might be used to refer to the major historical transformations of human life is anathematized as 'wild generalization'. Of course this does not mean that we can allow ourselves whatever generalizations we like. Instead it is intended to indicate that the specificity of social experience is not necessarily best understood by a posture of automatic scepticism towards all general concepts; there is no thinking without concepts, and thinking which pretends otherwise only delivers itself to unexamined presuppositions. The account of 'enlightenment', it needs emphasizing once again, is not an account of a historical period, however broad, but an attempt to decipher the prehistory of our own instrumental rationality, that is, a rationality which carries on the same regardless of its object.

Enlightenment as domination of nature

Adorno and Horkheimer argue that this developing sceptical demythologization is not just an intellectual process, but accompanies a more practical development – the conversion of nature into manipulable material. The criterion of whether knowledge is scientific is in fact a pragmatic or procedural one: can its experimental procedures be made to *work* on exemplary material? The material which serves as an example in any given cognition is not known in its own complex individuality, but, instead, as a representative of something else (cf. chapter 6 below). Mimesis, a cognitive attempt to be like the object, is thus progressively replaced by identification, thought's attempt to subsume and classify the object. Mimesis is subsequently confined to the realm of art, and thought which does not turn itself into classificatory identification is reproached with being no better than a fiction. Nothing remains sacred, so that everything can be worked on, consumed, and exchanged. Nothing is to be beyond thought; nothing is to be beyond price.[12]

This domination of nature, however, is not a socially innocent resource. Adorno and Horkheimer take mastery over nature to be indissolubly entangled not only with mastery over human nature, the repression of impulse, but also with mastery over other humans. Adorno and Horkheimer use the stratagem which Odysseus used to pass the sirens as a picture for the way in which the domination of nature goes together with self-domination and social domination. Odysseus plugs the ears of his crew so that they cannot hear the sirens; he has himself lashed to the mast so that he can hear the sirens but cannot move. Freedom from the blind compulsion of nature does not, in the event, remove compulsion altogether; instead it is won at the cost of self-blinding social and psychological compulsion. Odysseus, the master, is also mastered and self-mastered. Domination over nature is paid for with the naturalization of social domination. Power over nature, the real advance of human freedom, is paid for with impotent subjection to the social divisions and domination which grant that power.[13]

A striking feature of this kind of analysis of the entanglement of power and rationality is the extent to which domination is argued to be coeval with sociality. The capitalist mode of production and the 'administered life' of late capitalism, for example, are newly totalized forms of this entanglement, not its origin.[14] Class domination appears with the division of labour, most archaically, with a division between intellectual or spiritual labour and manual labour: there is class domination before there is capitalist class domination. The category of the subject appears with conscious mastery over impulse and over other subjects; there are subjects before there are bourgeois subjects. Accordingly, an end to capitalism and its property relations, difficult enough as this already is to imagine, might not of itself secure an end to domination.[15]

The internalization of sacrifice

Adorno and Horkheimer take some care to remind the reader that there is no route 'back' from the dialectic of enlightenment; it is not suggested, as it were, that instead of lashing ourselves to the mast we should dash ourselves on the rock. Because 'myth is already enlightenment' Adorno and Horkheimer do not believe that there was a time 'before' domination. What enlightened thought represents as sheer myth or superstition, rather, is already a form of cognition.

In the light of twentieth-century social anthropology the idea that magic is a cognitive practice, or that ancient religion and cosmology themselves contain rational criticisms of animist or other forms of religion might appear obvious to the point of banality. Their local force can be better seen in an intellectual-historical context. Adorno and Horkheimer are distinguishing their own argument from the one-sided reception of Nietzsche by twentieth-century irrationalists – a reception which continues to be influential over social theory today. They point out that such writers have adopted only Nietzsche's attack on the nihilistic element in the enlightenment and have converted it into a glorification of an immediate coercion.[16] The argument is thus organized so as to emphasize its difference from this kind of anti-enlightenment stance. What it glorifies as immediate pre-rational social relations in fact already anticipate the features of that modern rationality which they despise.

Ludwig Klages's work *The Spirit [Der Geist] as the Antagonist of the Soul* is an important instance.[17] Klages attempted to show that 'The essence of the "historical" process of humanity (also called "progress") is the triumphantly progressing struggle of the mind against life, with the (however only) logically foreseeable aim of

the annihilation of the latter.'[18] He appealed to sacrifice as a form
of exchange without mediation, in which the individual is sub-
merged in the collective, and cannot be distinguished from it. For
Klages, archaic reciprocity represents a purely immediate form of
social exchange in which social relations are not concealed and
which requires (indeed which allows) no reflection on the part of
social actors.[19]

Adorno and Horkheimer, by contrast, insist that all exchange to
date has involved at least a partial concealment of social relations.
This, however, is only one aspect of the exposition of incipient
features of enlightened rationality in sacrifice. Adorno and Horkheimer make the further startling claim that 'The history of civilisation is the history of the introversion of sacrifice.'[20] This means
nothing less than that the whole nexus which Adorno, as we shall
see later, characterizes under the headings of commodity fetishism,
subsumptive thinking, the constitution of the subject, and class
division together with its ideological concealment, is already anticipated in sacrificial substitution. The sacrifice already treats its
object as a representative, not as an individual: whereas in magic
'there is specific representation. What happens to the enemy's
spear, hair or name, also happens to the individual', the sacrificial
animal, by contrast, 'is slaughtered *instead of* the god'.[21]

Sacrifice thus, firstly, already anticipates commodity exchange,
because in it one object or creature may be substituted for another
incommensurable with it.[22] Secondly, sacrifice is already a form of
classificatory thinking, a thinking which seeks to say not what
something is, but what it comes under, of what it is a representative or an example – and what, therefore, it is not itself. Thirdly,
sacrifice anticipates the constitution of the subject. In the sacrifice
the victim is deceptively promised immortality; the ego 'owes its
existence to the sacrifice of the present moment to the future'.[23] The
sacrificial structure of substitution thus comes to govern the structure of the self. Sacrifice is internalized, as 'self-sacrifice'. But this
self-sacrifice is as deceptive as literal sacrifice. Just as sacrifice
deceptively promises the victim that he or she will become immortal, so self-sacrifice deceptively promises the ego that by sacrificing
the present moment it can preserve itself indefinitely.

The point of this claim that 'the history of civilisation is the
history of the introversion of sacrifice' is not only to show up the
way in which a supposedly archaic violence remains present in
civility – 'the smoke of the sacrificial altar turns into the whole-
some smoke of the fireside'[24] – but also to show up the rationality

and the lack of immediacy in sacrifice. Sacrifice does not represent those transparent social relations for which Klages is nostalgic, because it comes together with a division of labour between priests and those who are not priests. Accordingly, it contains deceit, ideology, non-transparency, from the beginning. It already takes the form of the deception by manipulative substitution of the god who is allegedly worshipped in it.

If 'sacrifice' is opposed to the still more archaic 'mimesis' and 'magic', however, perhaps these latter correspond to social transparency and to non-identificatory rationality? If we may not be nostalgic for sacrifice, perhaps we may be nostalgic for magic and mimesis? This would be a misconstruction. Magic and mimesis are themselves cognitive practices, rational attempts to control nature.[25] As such they too exhibit not pure irrationality, but the incipient entanglement of rationality and domination. Adorno and Horkheimer do indeed argue that magic and mimesis do not yet conceal this domination by claiming to have themselves constituted, produced or legislated over those external powers which they seek to ward off or invoke. Nor do they yet treat what is spelled or imitated as a representative rather than as an individual.[26] Domination is thus not yet internalized and mystified. Magic and mimesis, that is, represent a stage before the unity of the subject, but not before rationality or before domination.

Two important consequences follow from all this. First of all, there is no time 'before' domination which could be restored or returned to by reversing sceptical disenchantment. The critical force of the account of rationality's entanglement with domination does not rely on an appeal to a time when this entanglement supposedly did not prevail, but, rather, on the possibility that reason might change. Secondly, domination would in any case be no *better* for not being concealed. Adorno has no sympathy with the argument that at least naked coercion is 'honest'. Hatred of social complexity and of the middleman, the mediating agent who embodies that complexity – a hatred which is at work, for example, in fascist protests against usury – is one of the symptoms which Adorno diagnoses rather than his recommended cure.[27] The fact that rationality is entangled with domination partly conceals domination; yet only this entanglement, despite its deceptiveness, makes the idea of freedom from domination even imaginable.

Adorno and Horkheimer's account of mimesis and magic, then, is corrective rather than nostalgic. It suggests, not that there was a time before domination, but that rationality's entanglement with domin ation has changed qualitatively. This demonstration aims to make imaginable the idea that this entanglement need not be a necessary condition of any experience whatever – by showing that the manner of this entanglement itself has changed.

Self-sacrifice and self-preservation

The self-preservation of the ego, for Adorno and Horkheimer, is not only internalized sacrifice, but also, at a wider level, is still a kind of mimesis. Identificatory thinking is not only opposed to mimesis: indeed, such thinking 'is itself mimesis: mimesis of what is dead'.[28] What does this astonishing claim mean? Mimesis, for Adorno, it needs to be borne in mind, is not the attempt to make a copy of nature but the attempt to become like nature in order to ward off what is feared; but what remains to be feared when instrumental reason has apparently brought a feared nature under control? Death is an inextinguishable reminder of the nature in culture. The whole nexus of self-preservatory thought and action, Adorno and Horkheimer suggest, mimics death, strives to become inorganic, object-like in its attempt to ward off death. Self-preservation has thus become intimately entangled with self-destructiveness. Individual psychological self-destructiveness and collective (military-industrial) self-destructiveness are alike interpreted by Adorno as this kind of desperate miscarried self-preservation, a mimesis of what is dead. (In chapter 2 it will be seen how Adorno further specifies this argument through an account of the changing technical composition of capital in late-capitalist society.)

By this point readers will wish to draw breath and ask some awkward questions. In particular, if it is true that 'without a moment of compulsion there could be no thinking of any kind', how could internalized self-sacrifice be brought to an end without this making thinking itself impossible?[29] If the introversion of sacrifice is part and parcel of self-preservation, in what sense is the notion of life without sacrifice even minimally thinkable? Joel Whitebook has recently formulated some of these difficulties in an especially incisive way through an account of the psychoanalytic aspects of the *Dialectic of Enlightenment*.[30] He draws an instructive contrast between the later Marcuse's utopianism in *Eros and Civilization* and the *Dialectic of Enlightenment*. For Marcuse, the classic psychoanalytic formulation of the reality principle – the necessary postponement of gratification – was based on the idea that resources would always be scarce. Because the forces of production have now reached a level of development where scarcity could be abolished, given the right change in the relations of production, Freud's reality principle has been revealed as historically limited. Universal lasting gratification could thus be realized in the contemporary world, given the right change in the relations of production. Marcuse, indeed, was led by the logic of his praise of lasting gratification to an attack on human finitude itself: 'the fatal enemy of lasting gratification is *time*, the inner finiteness, the brevity of all conditions. The idea of integral human liberation therefore necessarily contains the vision of the struggle against time.'[31]

Some salient differences between the later Marcuse's utopianism and Adorno and Horkheimer's utopian negativity should already be apparent. Adorno does not think that the abolition of finitude would lead to utopia, but rather the reverse – that a change for the better would depend upon the possibility that the spirit could come to *accept* its own finitude, its own conditionedness. The model of such a thinking, then, is not the absence of any differentiation whatever, immersion in indistinct lasting gratification, but reconciliation, and in particular the 'coercionless synthesis of a manifold'. Adorno asks us to try to imagine a situation, that is, in which thinking would not be the sacrifice of particulars to universals, but rather the unsealing of the non-conceptual by means of concepts (a more detailed account of what this might mean in practice is given in chapter 7).

This idea of thinking as the coercionless synthesis of a manifold has itself appeared to be part of the problem to some of Adorno's critics, because they fear that Adorno really allows for the possibility of such coercionless synthesis only in the work of art, and that his thinking consequently relies on an aestheticized idea of reason. As Josef Früchtl has shown, however, there are many different figures for the notion of a coercionless synthesis in Adorno's work, by no means all of them confined to the artwork, and some directly psychoanalytic.[32] The account of the double character of language given in the *Dialectic of Enlightenment*, however, should in any case already allow us to contest such an interpretation. It is crucial to this account that the separation between language as image and language as sign has not yet become absolute.[33] Adorno's case is not, then, that 'purely discursive thinking' 'ought' to be deplored because of its coercive classification of particulars under universals; it is that *purely* discursive thinking, absolute literalness, is not even thinkable. Language itself already provides the model for a coercionless synthesis. This idea is not a retreat from a discursive to an aesthetic use of language; it rests, instead, upon the idea that pure discursivity, absolute literalness, is itself a chimera.

We can begin to see, then, how the resources to supply White-book's desideratum – 'a concept of the noncoercive integration of the self' – may already be present in the *Dialectic of Enlightenment* itself.[34] It is just such a concept which is aimed at in Adorno's hope for a *reconciliation* between culture and nature – as contrasted with a hope either for the final triumph or destruction of culture, or for a merging of nature and culture into an undifferentiated unity. This is a hope for a reconciliation of nature and culture within the individual as well as on a broader historical level. The idea of such a reconciliation is not simply a wish, however. It is grounded in the fact that the concepts of 'pure' nature and 'pure' culture respectively are unthinkable.

As Whitebook suggests, Adorno and Horkheimer do not think that the collapse of the ego, of internalized sacrifice, would by itself be any kind of emancipation from coercion, given that the world itself remains coercive. This would be a false reconciliation. Even the delusive ideal of secure ego-integration in an antagonistic world is preferable to such a false reconciliation. But for Adorno and Horkheimer a non-coercive integration of the self could never be realized in an objectively antagonistic society.

Adorno and Horkheimer's account of the internalization of sacrifice thus claims, as Whitebook correctly notes, to be aporetic (that is to say, it admits to being contradictory, but claims that the contradiction is necessary rather than accidental).[35] It offers a theory of how this internalization has happened, yet does not think that this theory can of itself provide an escape from it. Escaping from the internalization of sacrifice would require more than a new theory of social experience – it would require a change in social experience and its structures itself. The decisive question is whether this contradiction is necessary or whether it is self-inflicted. But in order to answer this question, we need to consider a whole series of further difficulties connected with the meta-historical ambition of Adorno and Horkheimer's account.

The concept of domination

Adorno and Horkheimer's argument is clearly extraordinarily ambitious, as any attempt to establish what rationality shares 'from

Parmenides to Russell' is likely to be. There are several obvious difficulties with it. In particular, the concept of domination (*Herrschaft*) remains unclear.[36] This is not a defect which could be removed simply by defining 'domination'. It is, rather, a structural feature of the kind of argument that is being undertaken. Let us consider the argument in the context of earlier equally ambitious attempts in the philosophical tradition to understand the relation between rationality and domination in human sociation. For Rousseau, human sociation begins with a contract, which is then preserved and protected by socially legitimated domination.[37] For Nietzsche, conversely, human sociation begins with domination, an attack of the strong on the weak; the idea of social right is a ruse of the dominated.[38] For Hegel's account of social 'recognition', however, rationality is entangled with domination. It is still more mythical to posit a pure or originary domination than to posit a pure or originary communication.[39]

Adorno and Horkheimer's is not a vulgar-Nietzschean argument. It does not posit domination as a first from which all else is derived, and for which political argument can only be a deceptive cover. Instead Adorno and Horkheimer want not only to show up, like Nietzsche, the extent to which whatever is presented as pure or disinterested rationality is entangled with domination, but also, like Hegel, the distorted rationality implicit in whatever is presented as sheer irrational coercion.

This has two consequences. Firstly, since there is no domination unmediated by rationality, 'pure' domination cannot be defined. Secondly, since there is no rationality (yet) wholly free of domination, domination is not (yet) wholly intelligible. To claim that domination had been made wholly intelligible, or that domination must necessarily be intelligible, would be to claim access to a rationality free from domination. In the terms of our earlier discussion, it would offer a false reconciliation of subject and object. It is just Adorno and Horkheimer's point that if rationality remains oblivious to the domination with which it is entangled, a real end to domination is less rather than more likely. The rationalistic insistence that no element of unclarity can be allowed to remain in the concept of domination is a critical instance of such oblivion. Adorno's argument risks scepticism, then, but only because to rule all sceptical moments out of court would be to declare that the world is now rational. The element of opacity in the concept of domination, that is, testifies to a real opacity in

petrified social relations. There is no reason to believe any reassur-
ances to the contrary which are based primarily on the fact that
this opacity is inconvenient for social theory.

This response, however, does not deal with all the criticisms
which have been levelled at the account of domination and rationality given in the *Dialectic of Enlightenment*. Subsequent criticism
has complained not merely of the opacity of the concept of
domination, but also of the way in which social power is conceptually modelled on mastery over nature (*Naturbeherrschung*).[40]
Such a modelling, on the account developed by Axel Honneth, has
serious consequences. Firstly, it leads to what Honneth regards as
the paradoxical disappearance of the properly social itself, conceived of as 'intersubjectivity', from Adorno's later theory of
society. Secondly, it is linked to what Honneth takes to be the
supplanting of the individual disciplines of empirical social inquiry by a philosophy which is, increasingly, aesthetically conceived. The second charge is addressed later in this chapter. At this
point, though, the charge that Adorno conflates natural and social
domination needs to be addressed, along with the accompanying
charge that his later social theory lacks a category of social
intersubjectivity.

Honneth argues that 'Adorno and Horkheimer are so strongly
fixated on the model of the instrumental control of nature, which is
the real interest of their philosophy of history, that they also want
to conceive the manner of functioning of intra-social domination
according to this model.'[41] The central impulse of the *Dialectic of
Enlightenment* is towards the possibility of a reconciliation of
culture and nature. On Adorno's account, such a reconciliation
would only be possible if cultural idealism could be relinquished,
if the notion that human culture is *radically* separate from, or
constitutive of, what it distinguishes from itself as nature, could be
given up. To insist upon a separation, whether as a description of
the world or only for the purposes of analysis, between a 'sphere
of social action in general',[42] and a pre- or asocial natural world,
reinforces culturalism. For a materialist theory, to dominate other
humans – since humans are not pure culture – is *already* domination of nature as well as social domination, not social domination
instead of or 'modelled upon' domination of nature. Only a theory
which itself presupposes mastery of nature can regard intersubjectivity as a separate sphere which has somehow separated
itself from the natural. To fix a separation between 'domination of

nature' and 'social domination' is to fix a separation between the
categories of 'society' and 'nature' themselves.

The conflict between Honneth's idea of a critical theory and
Adorno's and Horkheimer's, then, cannot be contained at the level
of a conflict about the proper thematic content of such a theory, but
goes right down to their respective philosophical presuppositions,
which cannot be sidelined as 'methodological' considerations.[43] It
reflects the broader conflict between first- and second-generation
critical theory, even though Honneth is not simply an orthodox
representative of the latter. Honneth's critical theory develops 'a
model of social conflict grounded in a theory of communication':
the theory of communication is the grounding element, the model
of social conflict is what is grounded.[44] Adorno and Horkheimer
develop instead, as has been shown above, a theory of the entanglement of communication and domination, which could not be
'grounded' in a theory of communication. A materialist theory of
intersubjectivity cannot accept a fixated separation, even a
methodological or procedural one, between a theory of communication and a model of social conflict. The category of the subject
is ineliminable from theories of intersubjectivity, and any account
of domination which is grounded in a notion of intersubjectivity
will be no less idealist than one grounded in subjectivity:

> If speculation on the state of reconciliation were permitted, neither the
> undifferentiated unity of subject and object nor their antithetical hostility
> would be conceivable in it; rather, a communication between differ-
> entiated elements. Only then would the concept of communication, as an
> objective concept, come into view. The existing concept is so infamous
> because it betrays the best there is, the potential for an agreement
> between people and things, to an interchange between subjects according
> to the requirements of subjective reason. In its proper place, even
> epistemologically, the relationship of subject and object would lie in the
> realization of peace among men as well as between men and their
> Other.[45]

Whether it is at all possible to escape from idealism, on the other
hand, is a question the answer to which Adorno by no means takes
for granted, since on his own account such an escape cannot be
effected by an act of will, but would itself be bound up with the
possibility of a change in our natural-historical experience. Clearly
Adorno does not take critical theory to be in possession of immediate access to a 'nature' freed from cultural mediation. But any
theory which aims at materialism cannot install fixed separations –

even if procedural or methodological – between nature and culture, or between communication and domination.

A philosophy of history?

A further apparent difficulty with the argument is its complex relation to a philosophy of history.

Adorno and Horkheimer might be thought guilty of providing a monological account of history whereby information about non-capitalist societies can be identified with a primitive stage of a unilinear historical development. Clearly this objection cannot be lightly dismissed. When Mauss and Hubert's *General Theory of Magic* is used to describe a cognitive practice in which the unity of the subject is 'not yet' presupposed, an evolutionary or teleological schema seems implied.[46]

This complexity of this issue means that some kind of clarification about what is meant by a 'philosophy of history', and about whether it is possible to avoid having such a philosophy, is needed. A much fuller account of Adorno's complex relation to Hegel will be necessary later, but for the moment the relation of the dialectic of enlightenment to a philosophy of history can be illuminated through his reflections on the way the problem of history is thought about by Hegel and Marx.[47] Adorno resists a fully teleological view of history, in which the course of history is taken as the activity of a single historical world-spirit moving towards its complete self-realization. This is how he interprets this aspect of Hegel's philosophy of history and the associated concept of a world-spirit – although Adorno emphasizes that Hegel is far from being the complacent ,apologist for historical progress for whom he is often mistaken.[48] Yet at the same time he is not satisfied with the presentation of history as sheer discontinuity, as though there were no connection whatsoever between different 'epochs'; or as though monad-like 'cultures' could be presented in their sheer individuality without a concept of culture in general.

Adorno compares Hegel's philosophy of history with Marx's and Engels's criticisms of it. In *The Holy Family* Marx and Engels rejected any personification of historical process:

> *History* does nothing: it does not 'possess monstrous wealth'; it does not 'fight battles'! Rather it is human beings, actual, living human beings who do all this, who 'possess' and 'fight'. It is not 'history' that uses human beings as a means in order to bring about its own ends, as though

it were a separate person; rather history itself is nothing but the activity
of human beings pursuing their own ends.[49]

These claims are true in the obvious sense that history would be
nothing at all without particular human beings. 'History' becomes
a myth as soon as it is represented as some kind of independent
external power over them. But the personification of history is not
just a mistake, because the attribution of these processes to the
abstraction, History, reflects the real abstractions from particular
individuals which have been taking place in exchange and social-
ization for millennia. The petrified social relations of capitalist
society, for example, are relations which individual human beings
have indeed made, and which would be nothing at all without
those human beings, yet they are also relations in which human
beings can no longer recognize their own work, which appear to
have taken on a rather solid life of their own. These relations then
in their turn have all the appearance of externally coercing and
remaking those very human beings whose product they are supposed to be.[50]

Adorno argues, then, that 'Universal history must be construed
and denied',[51] or, as he also puts the matter, that 'history is the
unity of continuity and discontinuity.'[52] What do these apparent
paradoxes mean? Firstly, the endorsement of totality in universal
history is false, but it nevertheless reflects a real totalization in
natural-historical experience. The ever more energetic appeals to
the irreducible specificity of non-capitalist 'cultures', for example,
as though they were isolated monads utterly discontinuous and
qualitatively incommensurable with capitalism and the forms of
rationality associated with it, are accompanied, for Adorno, by the
ever more powerful entanglement of such cultures in a global
nexus of exchange-value. The more such 'cultures' in fact surrender their discontinuity with global capitalism, the more furi-
ously is their supposedly absolute cultural difference insisted
upon.[53]

Insistences on sheer discontinuity, then, whether positivist or
postmodern, turn out to be no less metaphysical than a teleological
insistence on historically unified progress. If the latter presents
history as governed by a kind of secularized deity, the former
confronts us with a sheer facticity which arbitrarily cuts off all
further inquiry. In order to preserve such sheer discontinuity the
connectedness of what is presented as a pure monad (whether an

individual 'culture' or an individual 'epoch') with elements out-side it must be suppressed.

The *Dialectic of Enlightenment* needs to be understood as a simultaneous construction and denial of universal history. It is not built on the fantasy of the certain arrival of a better world. Instead it aims against the closure of the possibility of new historical experience which it sees both in an affirmative metaphysic of history and in the mythical redundance and invariance of pos-itivist historiography. The work rejects the pessimistic theory that human nature is irrevocably founded on domination. But it also rejects the cultural idealist denial that there can be anything natural in social life, the insistence that social life is cultural 'all the way down'.

Once more this furnishes a critical point of Adorno's engage-ment with the Marxist tradition. For Marx, Adorno notes, 'Econ-omics has primacy over domination; domination may not be deduced otherwise than economically'.[54] Adorno's attitude to this aspect of Marx's thought is equivocal. He regards the thesis of the priority of economic relations over domination as a remnant of idealism in historical materialism. Power must be shown to be the result of particular relations of production – to be socially pro-duced – so that we can believe that the end of those relations will also be the end of domination. Adorno can even remark, provoc-atively, that the interest at stake here is 'the deification of history, even for the atheistic Hegelians Marx and Engels'.[55] Adorno, conversely, is inclined to concede that all human life to date has been entangled with domination. But it is merely redundant to claim that such a concession makes this domination legitimate. The fact that domination 'is' reports on experience and cannot be converted into a law.

It has become clear from an analysis comparing the 1944 mimeo-graph of the *Philosophical Fragments* with the first printed *Dialectic of Enlightenment* of 1947 that a startling number of very direct changes in vocabulary were introduced in order to indicate that no priority of economics over politics could be read into the work. *Kapitalismus* can thus disappear entirely at one place; *Kapital* becomes *Wirtschaft* (business); *Monopol* (monopoly), a central cat-egory of the Institute's thought on the structure of late capitalism, is replaced by a wide variety of terms, from *Trusts* and *Konzerne* to, in one instance, *Faschismus*. These changes can of course in part be explained by a reasonable tactical caution in the anti-communist atmosphere of the post-war United States – as Alfred Schmidt observed, the name Marx occurs only once in the book, and then only in the phrase Marx Brothers[56] – but they all tend, also, to underscore the text's difference from any thesis of the primacy of economics.[57]

What the changes do not represent is any absolute farewell to Marx; as Adorno acknowledges, this way of construing the relationship between the categories of nature and history has its own model in another aspect of Marx's thought. Marx's insistence that 'History can be considered from two sides, the history of nature and the history of mankind. Yet there is no separating the two sides; as long as human beings exist, natural and human history will condition each other'[58] is the model for Adorno's non-dogmatic materialism. Adorno concludes in a closely related remark that 'The traditional antithesis of nature and history is both true and false; true, in so far as it expresses what the moment of nature underwent; false, in so far as it apologetically recapitulates, by conceptual reconstruction, history's concealment of its own natural growth [*Naturwüchsigkeit*].'[59] This remark contains in embryo Adorno's entire negative philosophy of history. Philosophy of history cannot be escaped by appeals to sheer historical or geographical discontinuity. Such appeals remain more metaphysical than their intended target.

The contemporary relevance of the *Dialectic of Enlightenment*

Even where the non-teleological character of the *Dialectic of Enlightenment* is recognized, however, its relationship to a philosophy of history has still continued to cause concern. In an article on 'The contemporary relevance of the *Dialectic of Enlightenment*', Herbert Schnädelbach has provided one of the most penetrating of such criticisms of the work, and his objections to it are worth considering in some detail because they are informed by a close engagement with its philosophical and social-critical presuppositions.[60] Schnädelbach, reasonably, asks whether it is enough 'to say over and over again that Adorno and Horkheimer, unlike other critics of enlightenment, held fast to the goals of enlightenment; does this really suffice to stop their analyses providing more grist to the postmodern mill of counter-enlightenment?'[61] For Schnädelbach the difficulty is not one which can be settled simply by demonstrating enough good will towards the unrealized goals of enlightenment on Adorno and Horkheimer's part; rather, it lies in the genre to which their argument itself belongs. This is not any straightforward historical narrative, Schnädelbach argues, but rather what he calls a 'social myth': 'Horkheimer and Adorno do not simply want to write the history of civilization itself, but rather they tell the story of something which interprets and explains this history itself: the history of this history, the true history of the historical, the always still current primordial history [*Urgeschichte*].'[62]

The *Dialectic of Enlightenment* can thus be understood as a further contribution to a tradition of philosophical accounts of the nature of human sociation itself from Rousseau to Hegel, Marx and Freud.[63] Such 'social myths', Schnädelbach argues, are necessarily a 'narrativism'.[64] They inevitably end, that is, by providing us, not with a theory of human sociation, but with a story about it. The tendency for the *dialectic* of enlightenment to be replaced with a *dynamic* in which social life is tendentially becoming 'more and more' administered and commodified, and reason is becoming 'more and more' identitarian and instrumental, could thus from a viewpoint like Schnädelbach's be seen as just what we should expect from a social myth with culturalistic presuppositions. Schnädelbach is arguing, then, that the materialist aspects of Adorno and Horkheimer's thought, whose aim is precisely to bring cultural idealism to an end, necessarily conflict with the narrative aspects of its form, which must needs imply culturalistic presuppositions: 'in so far as the *Dialectic of Enlightenment* is narratively organized . . . it cannot be saved. As a social myth which wishes to enlighten us about the enlightenment, it only confirms the aporia: "Just as myths already complete enlightenment, so enlightenment, with each step it takes, becomes more deeply entangled in mythology." '[65] Schnädelbach insists, instead, that such dialectic can only be formulated theoretically, not narratively, and must be formulated not as a philosophy of history, but as social theory.[66]

This brings us once again to the difficulty which we came up against in considering Whitebook's objections. Are the contradictions which the *Dialectic of Enlightenment* exhibits really necessary contradictions, 'aporias', or are they instead, as Schnädelbach suggests, the result of the authors' own failure to recognize the fact that there are some norms which simply cannot be radically historicized? Could these contradictions in fact be avoided by separating out such non-historicizable norms?

Because *Dialectic of Enlightenment* exhibits, rather than liquidating, these contradictions, a defence of it will need to show that given criticisms of it in fact fall more helplessly, because more unconsciously, into contradiction themselves. Schnädelbach's criticisms of the *Dialectic of Enlightenment* rest upon a position which Adorno's materialist dialectic would certainly regard as dogmatic. Schnädelbach complains that 'the "contradictions" in the "thing itself" [*Sache selbst*], of which Adorno used to speak, are not logical phenomena, but rather antagonisms . . .'[67] But this posits a clean break between thought and being. On the one hand we have the rational theorist, who ought to be free of all contradiction, on the other the a-rational matter which is to be theorized. We are confronted in the very language of Schnädelbach's criticisms by the repetition around which the *Dialectic of Enlightenment* is constructed. Unilateral declarations of independence from metaphysics end up not in the least freed from metaphysics, but simply deploying metaphysical identifications and oppositions in an insufficiently thematized form.

Schnädelbach's presuppositions are connected to the way he understands the generic status of *Dialectic of Enlightenment*. In his account the work is made to sound something like an account of historicity, a 'history of the historical' to which actual historical particulars would be merely contingent. From Schnädelbach's perspective, this is doubtless a generous way of understanding the work, because otherwise we should have simply to dismiss it along with Westermarck, Kirfel and Glotz as a partially informed and syncretic universal history. But is this quite the choice which interpretation of this text really faces? Were Schnädelbach's interpretation of the work as a 'history of the historical' adequate, subsequent historical developments would be unlikely to affect the authors' view of its validity; but their later comments on their own work show that they in fact took the historical variability of its truth-content very seriously indeed.[68] The interpretation set out by Schnädelbach implies a much more abstract relationship to empirical enquiry than is actually operative here.

Like Adorno's social thought in general, then, the *Dialectic of Enlightenment* needs to be conceived of not as the liquidation of empirical 'facts' from some higher or more primordial domain of wisdom, by means of an originary 'social myth', but instead as a 'rebellion of experience against empiricism'. It is partly a way of trying to understand, that is, how it has come about that social-scientific empiricism, a programme of social science whose whole point was to do justice to the specificity of social experience, has usually ended up giving a very abstract account of social experience indeed. The next two chapters consider some of the means by which Adorno attempted, by contrast, to formulate a 'critical' theory of society. Such a theory hoped to place concrete social experience at its centre, yet without abandoning the wish to interpret and understand such experience, rather than merely to classify it.

2

A Critical Theory of Society

The concept of society

The approach developed in the *Dialectic of Enlightenment* must clearly have far-reaching consequences for any social criticism. We can see this if we confront it with sociology's most elementary question. What is society? One kind of approach might say that if we cannot answer this question with a definition, the concept of 'society' should be jettisoned – that, to put the argument at its most nominalistic, there is 'no such thing as society'.[1] On this interpretation it is the term 'society' itself which is mystifying, a last remnant of metaphysics, and meaningful research would have to dispense with such unhelpful abstractions until a clear definition could be given. Adorno agrees with one aspect of this criticism. Society, he agrees, is not a thing. Yet, despite this, the concept cannot be dispensed with. 'Society' resists summary definition not because too little work has been put into coming up with a clear concept of it, but because what the concept refers to cannot be presumed in advance to be wholly knowable.

Adorno regards modern capitalism as progressively self-totalizing. Just as the motto of 'enlightened' thought is that 'nothing shall remain outside', that nothing can be taken as a limit to thought, so the motto of what Adorno often refers to as 'exchange society' is that nothing shall remain outside it, that no value shall resist commensurability with exchange-value. Just as the dictum that nothing shall remain outside thought makes thought unable to see any limits to its own self-sufficiency, so the impulse that

nothing shall remain unsocialized confers an element of unintelligible transcendence on society itself.

Adorno argues that the result is that 'Society is both intelligible
and unintelligible.'[2] What is the force of this paradox? In his essay
'Society', Adorno explains it through a discussion of the contrast
between the two most significant sociologists of the early twentieth
century, Max Weber and Émile Durkheim. From the contrast
between Durkheim and Weber, Adorno develops a way of formulating his own sociological interests:

> Action within bourgeois society, as rationality, is indeed objectively, to a
> great extent, just as much 'understandable' [*verstehbar*] as it is motivated.
> The generation of Max Weber and Dilthey rightly reminded us of this.
> But their ideal of understanding [*Verstehensideal*] was one-sided in that it
> excluded that element in society which is contrary to identification by the
> understanding subject. This was the point of Durkheim's rule that social
> facts should be treated like things, that the attempt to understand them
> should be renounced in principle. He would not let himself be talked out
> of his awareness that society impacts upon each individual primarily as
> something non-identical, as 'compulsion'. In this sense reflection on
> society begins where its comprehensibility [*Verstehbarkeit*] ends . . . [but]
> The antithesis to Weber remains just as partial as his thesis, because it
> comes to rest in incomprehensibility just as Weber does on the postulate
> of comprehensibility. Instead of this, the task would be to understand the
> incomprehensibility which distorts relations between humans into non-
> transparent self-sufficient relations. Sociology today would need to un-
> derstand the incomprehensible, the entry of humanity into inhumanity.[3]

Durkheim and Weber are interpreted here within the context of the
need to construe and deny the philosophy of history which we
examined in chapter 1. Each is invoked correctively against the
other. Weber argued that social institutions and processes had to be
understood through the subjective self-understanding of individuals participating in them, without whom these processes
would be nothing at all. The merit of this approach, for Adorno, is
its refusal to present social relations which are historical and
produced as though they were simply objects 'given' to sociological study in the same way that data are arguably given to
natural science. The difficulty with it is that Weber underestimated
the extent to which in modern society social relations take on a life
of their own. Under capitalism, and especially, as we shall see,
under late capitalism, social relations, which are indeed made by
human individuals and which would be nothing without those
individuals, have taken on an apparently autonomous and objective existence. It is indeed illusory to think that social relations

could be presented as wholly autonomous from the relating individuals. Yet the autonomy of social relations is not simply a
mistake, but a 'real illusion'. Social relations are no longer interpretable as the sum of the subjects participating in and making
them.

Durkheim's contribution, against Weber, is to point to this. The
merit of his approach is that it testifies to the real preponderance of
petrified social relations over individuals. Durkheim 'brought to
light, voluntarily or not, the extent to which the old spell still
imprisons modern humanity'.[4] Yet Durkheim, conversely, pays
insufficient attention to the illusory character of the objectivity of
social relations. Although, as Adorno notes, Durkheim was well
aware that collective forms would be nothing at all without the
individuals who constitute them, it is nevertheless the case that he
attributes powers and capacities abstracted from the individual to
the collective and then presents them as prior to the individual.[5]
Adorno's criticism is that Durkheim converts such preponderance
of the collective into an invariant. His sociology lacks any distinction between 'what a society truly is, and how it appears to itself',
because it equates the collectivity of social values with their
objectivity.[6]

To this extent, then, Weber's sociology can be described as 'more
enlightened' than Durkheim's in that it 'testified both in its method
and in its content to the disenchantment of the world, whilst
Durkheim and his school . . . weave the magic once again'.[7]
Weber's sociology retains a greater sense of how existing social
relations have emerged historically than does Durkheim's and,
consequently, a greater sense of how they might change. Yet
Durkheim's sociology indicates as Weber's cannot the extent to
which enlightenment itself and the world which it has apparently
disenchanted remain under a spell. Sociology must neither presuppose the interpretability of society nor presuppose its non-
interpretability; both presuppositions are equally dogmatic.

Adorno's somewhat schematic antithesis between Durkheim
and Weber provides an orientation in his own social-critical
thought. In particular, it is the context for Adorno's attitude
towards the question of sociology's scientific status. Is it possible to
speak of sociological 'laws'? Adorno repeatedly, and perhaps
surprisingly, rejects the neo-Kantian distinction (to which Weber, as
an adherent of Rickert's, held) between the 'nomothetic' natural
sciences, concerned with organizing appearances under laws, and
the 'idiographic' human sciences, concerned with specifying

unique particulars not susceptible to subsumption under laws.[8] Yet talk of sociological laws is false to the extent that it posits a domain of 'purely' sociological phenomena which are to be the object of sociology. As Adorno points out, there is no such thing as an object which is in itself 'purely' sociological; all phenomena have non-sociological aspects, and any demand for purely sociological objects presents the procedural requirements of social scientists as though they were, instead, a feature of the material itself. Hence Adorno's claim that in Durkheim's work 'the panegyrist of the division of labour was himself its victim'.[9]

Whilst Weber, conversely, was sharply aware of the restrictions as well as the freedoms accompanying the 'formally free' division of labour characteristic of capitalist societies, he was a strong, if stoical, advocate of scientific professionalism and of the autonomy of sociology.[10] To this extent, Adorno continues, sociology which claims a fully autonomous status remains in practice dogmatic, whatever its explicit epistemological position, because its object is pre-formed by its own methodological self-definition.[11] Adorno, by contrast, agrees with Durkheim and Weber that the conversion of social theory into a professional discipline cannot be ignored (otherwise social inquiry would become merely impressionistic); but he insists, against them, that professional procedures cannot be taken as setting the limits of what social theory may and may not look into (otherwise critical reflection would be extinguished altogether).

The consequences of this position on sociology's scientific status can be seen in Adorno's attitude to the idea of a sociological methodology. Both Durkheim and Weber were deeply concerned to ground sociology as an independent discipline with its own autonomous and methodological canons. Sociology tries to guarantee its autonomy by renouncing philosophy in favour of methodology. This attempt, however, delivers it to insufficiently reflective philosophical positions. In particular both Weber and Durkheim fall back behind Kant's critical overcoming of the choice between rationalism and scepticism and behind Hegel's dialectical understanding of the relation between 'is' and 'ought' (see chapters 6 and 7 below), or, in Weberian terms, the relation between fact and value.

For Weber sociological method must strive for value-freedom. Fact-problems and value-problems are 'absolutely heterogeneous'.[12] But the insistence on the separation between fact and value is, as Weber himself concedes, a value, a regulative ideal which sets

up a morality of method: 'even though the moral law [to distinguish between empirical statements of fact and value-
judgements] is perfectly unfulfillable, it is nonetheless "imposed"
as a duty'.[13] For Durkheim, conversely, fact and value are identified in the discovery of 'moral facts'. In a revealing passage from
introductory lectures in sociology which he gave in 1968, Adorno
recognized the danger of regarding the criticism of a complete
separation of fact from value as a pretext for installing arbitrarily
chosen, dogmatic values: his students, he warns, are not to think

> that I would like to fall back into a dogmatic hypostasis of some kind of
> universal anthropological values. This is as far from my position as is the
> Weberian position on the other side; rather, the Kantian proposition that
> the critical way alone remains open seems to me to be of greater
> relevance, even with reference to the so-called problem of values.[14]

Adorno is not wholly hostile to Weber's insistence on the separation of fact from value. Weber's insistence on the separation of 'is'
and 'ought' is aimed against the tendency (especially prevalent
amongst German historians of his generation) to regard what 'is'
as something which therefore 'ought' to be.[15] Kant's 'critical way',
to which Adorno refers here, was intended to get beyond both
rationalist and sceptical varieties of dogmatism: that is, both the
presupposition that the world *must* be intelligible and the presupposition that it *must* be unintelligible. In this sense, Adorno is
suggesting that Weber's dogmatism is to presuppose the intelligibility of society and social process; Durkheim's to presuppose that
they are ultimately inexplicable givens.

Instead, Adorno follows a 'critical' path. Sociological thought
must proceed through the criticism of sociological concepts and of
the social experience embedded in them. Neither a radical separation nor a radical identification of fact and value is satisfactory.
Instead, the aim of a critical social theory is to allow the entanglement of fact with value to become visible, by showing up both the
way in which tacit valuations are present in all apparently purely
factual description, and the way in which apparently pure valuations always presuppose descriptive models.

Marx and the critique of political economy

This sort of consideration may induce a certain amount of im-
patience: never mind why Adorno thought Durkheim and Weber

were wrong, what did he think himself? Before rushing to give a summary of Adorno's opinions, however, a little more considera-tion needs to be given to the difficulty of settling on any un-equivocal method for social theory, because without such consideration Adorno's substantive views will appear merely dogmatic.

Whilst Adorno deploys a contrast between Durkheim and Weber to show what each in his view lacks, he thinks that they both share the methodological dogmatism of 'autonomous' sociology – prior-ities of sociological method, that is, are mistaken for features of social experience itself. Yet because the involuntary dogmatism of sociological method is not simply a mistake, it cannot be removed simply by substituting a 'good' method, materialist or otherwise, for a bad one. The problem lies not so much in the goodness or badness of the method but in the fixated separation of 'method' from 'material'. Although Marx provides the model for Adorno's criticisms of Durkheim and Weber, then, it cannot be a question for Adorno of providing a superior and Marxist method, even a 'dialectical method', for sociology. Any method posited in advance of its object would already in fact be idealist, however strident its claims to materialism.

Marx sometimes writes of a 'dialectical method',[16] and of freeing the materialist 'kernel' of such a method from the idealist 'shell' in which it supposedly remains trapped in Hegel's thought.[17] Yet it would be mistaken to think of Marx's method as wholly separable from, and externally applied to, an inert 'material'. This is clear enough from the form of a work like *Capital*. No methodology for *Capital* is set out in advance. Marx regards his method not as something prepared in advance and then simply applied to an inert 'material', but as developing out of the material itself. This distance from methodologism orientates Adorno's reception of Marx. Adorno's approach to Marx's substantive theses can be understood only in the light of it.

Adorno's interpretation of Marx starts out from a deep aware-ness of the centrality of the Hegelian inheritance to Marx's work. If this inheritance is cast off as an idealist survival, many of the most elementary features of Marx's work make no sense. Yet he also takes very seriously Marx's critique of Hegel, and his claim to be a materialist thinker. Adorno does not think that Marx has infallibly succeeded in this attempt; at one point he compares the dogmatic limitations of Marx's attempt to go beyond idealism with those of Kierkegaard and Feuerbach.[18] Yet more often Adorno's account of

Marx emphasizes the difference between Marx's thought and positivistic or epistemological materialism. His discussions with Horkheimer in the late 1930s and early 1940s are preoccupied with this question above all: what differentiates a materialist dialectic, or historical materialism, from dogmatic materialism?[19] Adorno emphasizes Marx's self-description as a *critic* of political economy rather than as a political economist.[20] Marx refuses both radically to separate 'is' from 'ought' and straightforwardly to identify what 'is' with what 'ought to be'. He attacked the 'critical criticism' of the left Hegelians and the utopian socialism of Proudhon alike for relying on an empty 'ought', an empty set of moral demands which are left without any connection to social experience. Classical political economy, by contrast, illegitimately presents a deductive account of how political economy ought ideally to work, an account which starts out from definitions of basic concepts such as the commodity, the division of labour, exchange-value, and so on, and from hypothetical situations in which these are imagined in ideal action, as though these analyses possessed synthetic status – as though, that is, they told us how economic life, factically and historically, *has* worked.

Far from suggesting that what Marx does is simply to cut out this prescriptive element from political economy, and trying to provide an account which is sheerly descriptive, Adorno suggests that Marx takes this prescriptive element as his starting point. The categories of Marxist political economy, then, are not simply descriptive. They must be understood with this entanglement of description and prescription, fact and value, in mind. Adorno's words in one of the discussions he had with Horkheimer in the 1930s when working towards the *Philosophical Fragments* are significant:

> The meaning of Marx's economics is much rather that he starts out from just that element in bourgeois political economy which is more than descriptive (fair exchange). And that he shows that the society which develops on the basis of such principles contradicts these principles, whilst the realization of these principles would supersede [*aufheben*] the form of society itself. Marx does not want to show, as it were, positivistically, according to which laws exchange is 'now actually' conditioned; rather he takes from bourgeois society the measures of legality which it has itself constituted, shows that bourgeois society cannot fulfil them, and retains this measure at the same time as a negative expression of a right constitution of society. This is just what we need to do with respect to bourgeois categories like that of the individual.[21]

Adorno regards Marx's critique of political economy as an immanent, not a transcendent critique. It does not start out by prescribing its values and then judging supposedly 'brute' facts against them. Rather, it brings to light the prescriptiveness which is already present in the apparently purely descriptive categories of bourgeois political economy. It judges such a political economy and the society which it describes by the light of political economy's own concealed and unfulfilled prescriptions.[22] Because the categories of classical political economy are themselves not in fact purely abstract or arbitrary, but contain sedimented within them real social experience, a critique which follows through the logic of those categories will at the same time be a critique of our real but changeable society.

This interpretation of Marx's work as an immanent critique of political economy does not imply an indifference to the wealth of Marx's empirical research. But it does mean that Marx's categories cannot be received as purely descriptive ones. It follows that what is of most value in Marx's thought, for Adorno, is not an adherence to every last substantive tenet, but the continuation of Marx's critique of bourgeois political-economic categories. This is all the more the case because Marx himself offers a historical materialism, not a perennial philosophy or a synchronic sociology. The object of a historical materialism changes; historical materialism will therefore also change.

It is true, then, that Adorno emphasizes the critical Marx and places less emphasis on Marx's substantive theses. He did not simply discard Marx's belief that a true theory of social relations was possible from the standpoint of a revolutionary 'universal class'. Unlike Lukács, however, he did not identify such a perspective with that of the revolutionary proletariat. For Adorno a true 'universal' could never, by the logic of the concept itself, refer to any particular class but only to the end of class, to the possibility of a reconciled society – the view from what is referred to at the end of *Minima Moralia* as 'the standpoint of redemption'.[23] This standpoint, it is important to insist, is not a teleologically grounded and necessary but a negatively implied and possible perspective. There is no 'subject' of history, individual or collective, whose consciousness could ground true theory. Accordingly there is no unequivocally true consciousness either. Instead truth is glimpsed in the determinate negation of what is false. True theory would only be fully possible given freedom from subjectivity. Since such a

view can self-evidently only be disclosed negatively for any subject, however, it is itself an immanently entangled, rather than a
theoretically transcendent or practically privileged one. In other
words, as *Negative Dialectics* later specifies, it is no longer a
'standpoint' at all.[24]

Does this imply that Adorno's Marxism has become a method or
a 'search for style'?[25] Clearly Adorno would be unhappy with any
such result (cf. chapter 6 below). If Marx's substantive insights
were regarded as irrelevant to a dialectical-materialist method
which could be extracted from his work and then applied to any
material whatever, such a 'method' would in any case no longer be
dialectical. Adorno's immanent critique differs from Marx's critique of political economy not by discarding all Marx's substantive
claims, but to the extent that its object also now differs. The
critique of political economy and ideology must be reconsidered in
the light of changed circumstances. Adorno emphasizes certain
aspects of Marx's critique of political economy – those which he
considers continue to have the greatest critical force in these
changed circumstances – at the expense of others.

Commodity fetishism

In that section of *Capital* entitled 'The Fetishism of the Commodity
and its Secret' Marx analysed the form which exchange takes in
capitalist society. He provided a theory of commodity exchange as
simultaneous identification and misidentification. Its logical model
is the account of abstract identification given in Hegel's *Logic*
(cf. chapter 6). In the commodity exchange disparate and incommensurable use-values are represented as abstractly identical
exchange-values. None of the qualities of what is exchanged is
expressed in the exchange. An abstract identification is made
between two non-identical objects. Non-identical and unequal
relations between people are thus misrecognized as though they
were identical and equal relations between things. The unequal
relation between the owner of the means of production and the
wage-labourer lacking such means, for example, is expressed as an
equal and identical relation between the abstractly quantified work
of the wage-labourer and the money paid by the owner.

The result is that exchange-value comes to appear as though it
were not the result of human labour, but an inherent property of
the commodity itself. The social characteristics of human labour

take on the appearance of 'objective characteristics of the products of labour themselves, as the socio-natural properties of these things'.[26] Marx called this illusory autonomy of the commodity 'commodity fetishism'. A 'fetish' is an inanimate object invested with autonomous magical or divine powers by its worshipper. Marx argues that the commodity in commodity exchange is in a parallel way invested with an illusory autonomy.[27]

The implications of this theory of commodity exchange as simultaneous identification and misidentification are extensive. Marx's critique of the form which exchange takes in a commodity society implies a critique of the way in which the participants in such a society habitually act within it and understand it. A form of exchange and social organization which has arisen historically takes on the appearance of a natural series of equivalences demanded by commodities themselves. The social, cultural and intellectual consequences of commodity fetishism, however, were not fully explained by Marx. Lukács's chapter on 'Reification and the Consciousness of the Proletariat' in *History and Class Consciousness* offered such an account. Lukács used the term 'reification' to refer to the extension of commodity fetishism to all human consciousness and activity in a society where the commodity form has become 'the universal structuring principle' (modern capitalist society).[28] He conducted this exposition in the light of Weber's thesis of capitalist accounting's requirement of the predictable calculability of economic and political circumstances.[29]

In Lukács's view, the effects of such reification could hardly be overestimated. All human capacities, including consciousness, become 'reified'. Commodified abstract labour, like all commodities, takes on an illusory autonomy of its own. Human activity, as commodified labour, becomes a 'contemplative' activity in the service of an apparently autonomous exchange-value.[30] This applies also to intellectual labour. The autonomy which individual intellectual disciplines such as jurisprudence or sociology strive for is interpreted by Lukács as just this kind of illusory autonomy.[31] They follow their own delusively self-grounding methodologies rather than the historically varying material itself. Practice is thus de-practicalized; theory becomes formal and unhistorical. The illusory autonomy of individual disciplines is not, however, a mistake, testifying for example to the stupidity of the thinkers in question. It is inseparable from the fate of consciousness in a society universally structured by the commodity form.

Lukács's theory, though, clearly entails an internal problem. If the consequences of reification extend to all consciousness, how can reification itself be known? Here Lukács introduces a distinction between the consciousness of the capitalist and the consciousness of the collective of wage-labourers, the proletariat. Both experience the effects of reification. But the capitalist mistakes himself, contemplatively, for the subject of reification, as controlling reification and its consequences.[32] Conversely, 'in every aspect of daily life in which the individual worker imagines himself to be the subject of his own life he finds this to be an illusion that is destroyed by the immediacy of his own existence.'[33] However, this does not mean that the consciousness of individual wage-labourers effortlessly escapes reification. A contemplative acceptance of a position as the object of reified social processes is no less contemplative and therefore no less reified than a self-misrecognition as the subject of them. Non-reified consciousness is inseparable from the collective practical orientation of a revolutionary proletariat towards the overcoming of the capitalist mode of production.[34] On these conditions only does the proletariat become 'the identical subject-object of the history of society'.[35] Lukács's account implies as its own condition of possibility that such a moment is at hand as a 'real possibility'.

In Adorno's work, by contrast, the revolutionary consciousness of the proletariat has no special epistemological status. This is not simply because Adorno's assessment of the chances for successful proletarian revolution is less optimistic than Lukács's, but, more fundamentally, because of his doubts about granting a privileged epistemological role to any kind of practice, and, in particular, to a collective subject of history. Adorno demurs from the speculative identification of theory and practice present in Lukács's account (cf. chapter 7 below). Equally, Adorno is suspicious of Lukács's notion of a self-identical subject-object of history. Adorno's criticism of both aspects is linked. Both, he suspects, posit a final identity of thought with its objects. Materialist thought, for Adorno, on the contrary, would be a recognition that thinking is not identical with its objects.

Nevertheless Adorno was deeply influenced by Lukács's account of the social, cultural and intellectual consequences of commodity fetishism. He especially emphasizes the implication that these consequences become more firmly embedded in the lives of modern human beings as more and more use-values become commodified and expressed in terms of exchange-value. All access to use-value – to anything which might be described as 'real' or 'natural' need – is now mediated by exchange-value. Adorno expresses this by saying that production has become the production of exchange-value for its own sake.[36] The primary object of consumption in the commodity is no longer its use-value (even if we could now know in any immediate way what that is, mediated as all our consciousness and sensations are by commodity fetishism) but its exchange-value. Because Adorno accepts that the commodity form is a 'structuring principle' of modern society, he regards attempts to invoke an immediate access to use-value as an ideological cover for the way in which all human activity is mediated by commodity exchange.

Adorno's admiration for Marx's chapter on the fetishism of commodities and its secret in *Capital*, which he ranked with the most important analyses of classical German philosophy, has not always been shared. It has been much less central to later traditions of Marxism in the west than to Lukács and Adorno; for very different reasons, Althusserian Marxism and Anglophone rational choice Marxism have found the idea much more problematic than did Adorno; and it has sometimes been thought that Adorno's debt to Lukács's much more generalized use of the notion of commodity fetishism is responsible for a supposed overestimation of the role of culture and a failure to appreciate the significance of more fundamental aspects of Marx's thought, particularly the idea of the double character of labour and the theory of surplus value. As far as the Anglophone reception is concerned, part of the problem here has simply been the unavailability in translation of some crucial essays; the remainder of this chapter shows how seriously Adorno in fact engaged with these aspects of Marx's thought, and some reasons for Adorno's commitment to the account of commodity fetishism will be considered later in the light of this account.

Class, class consciousness and crises under late capitalism

The distinction between the capitalist's experience of reification and that of the proletariat, as we have seen, has a much less important place in Adorno's thought than in Lukács's or Marx's. Adorno does not lack a concept of class, however. In an important and too little known essay of 1942, 'Reflections on the theory of class', he defends Marx's categories of class and class consciousness against the charge that they were simply obsolete, yet considers the obstacles to their immediate application to contemporary society.[37] In order to be understood, this aspect of Adorno's thought needs to be placed in the context of the debate over Marx's theory of crisis amongst political economists and historians associated with the Institute for Social Research in the 1930s.

Marx's theory of crisis was based on an opposition between 'forces of production' and 'relations of production'. By 'forces of production' were understood both the productive capacities inherent in the living labour of workers and those capacities made available by technological development. By the 'relations of production' were understood the social framework of exchange, distribution and consumption within which production was organized. Marx argued that when the relations of production came to form a restraint on the full development of the forces of production, a revolutionary crisis would develop in which the existing relations of production – in particular the alienation of producers from the means of production – would be overthrown. Marx believed that the forces of production were economically more fundamental than the relations of production, so that a conflict between the two would end in the dissolution of the existing relations of production and the formation of new relations of production more favourable to the unfettered development of the forces of production.[38]

Marx's theory of crisis had been a central topic of disagreement amongst German Marxists in the early years of the century. 'Social democrat' (SPD) Marxists such as Rudolf Hilferding argued that capitalism had shown itself quite capable of forestalling structural crisis.[39] The economist Otto Bauer developed Marx's schematic account of the reproduction of the means of production and consumption in vol. 2 of *Capital* to argue that capitalist accumulation could continue indefinitely without precipitating a terminal crisis.[40] The communist (KPD) Marxist Rosa Luxemburg, on the other hand, argued that the dependence of capitalist accumulation on 'non-capitalist areas' meant that such accumulation would reach a final limit at which the capitalist mode of production would be overthrown.[41] The argument was important to the diverging SPD and KPD programmes. A demonstration of capitalism's resilience could be used to argue for a constitutionalist socialism; a demonstration of the objective necessity of its collapse could be used to argue for its revolutionary overthrow.

Amongst political economists closely or loosely associated with the Institute for Social Research differing views of Marx's theory of crisis prevailed. Henryk Grossmann argued that Marx's theory of value could not be separated from his theory of collapse in the way that SPD Marxists such as Rudolf Hilferding had suggested. He argued that without a theory of collapse Marx's theory of value had no content. For Grossmann, the collapse of capitalist society remained objectively necessary. Unlike Luxemburg, however, Grossmann did not take such collapse to be a consequence of capitalism's dependence on 'non-capitalist areas'. Instead, he argued that Marx's reproduction schemes had been misunderstood. Marx had provisionally assumed, for the sake of analysis, a stable process of social reproduction. This had been misinterpreted as a proof that capitalist accumulation really does proceed harmoniously. Grossmann argued that if the consequences of Bauer's reproduction schemes were taken further, it could be shown that the rate of profit would necessarily diminish to such an extent that capitalist accumulation became impossible.[42]

Friedrich Pollock, however, took a different view. Pollock argued that the concentration of capital in the hands of cartels and monopolies had fundamentally altered the competitive character of capitalism. Such concentration meant that those productive forces which required massive investment and large-scale planning for their full development ('electricity, railways, etc.')[43] could now be released. The relations of production need no longer form a fatal restraint on the forces of production. Accordingly Pollock argued that the current crisis could 'be overcome by capitalistic means and that "monopolistic" capitalism is capable of surviving beyond the foreseeable future'.[44] The necessary condition of this survival was a far closer co-operation of state power and concentrated capital than had previously been the case. In monopoly capitalism political administration and economic activity had become far more closely entangled than had previously been the case.

Grossmann's emphasis on the non-descriptive status of Marx's political economy is one which we have seen above to be of central importance to Adorno's Marxism. But, at a substantive level, he found Pollock's emphasis on capitalism's resilience more persuasive.[45] Adorno emphasizes that for Marx it is the relationship to the means of production – whether an individual has these means at his or her disposal or whether he or she is alienated from them – which specifies class. Adorno rejected both attempts to replace qualitative concepts of class with quantificatory status classifications based on average living standards and attempts to define class through class consciousness.[46] From the standpoint of an objective concept of class, the concentration of capital must necessarily increase, rather than diminish, class antagonism.

Yet Adorno was reluctant – unlike many Marxists – to regard the decline in proletarian class consciousness as irrelevant to the concept of class itself.[47] Instead he regarded it as a symptom of a change in the organization of capitalism. This meant not that social antagonism had weakened, but only that it had become less visible as antagonism: 'The ruling class disappears behind the concentration of capital.'[48] Adorno did not see this concealment of antagonism as a mere trick, easily seen through. Instead it also had consequences for Marxist theory itself. Political and cultural institutions could no longer be understood as merely 'superstructural', a second-order reflection of economic phenomena, had this ever been possible.[49] Late capitalism presents us with an 'administered world' in which political domination and capitalist production are indissolubly intertwined, despite the persistence of real social antagonism.

The consequences for the concept of class are aporetic:

> This makes it necessary to consider the concept of class closely enough so that it is both preserved and changed. Preserved: because the distinction between exploiters and exploited not only persists undiminished but grows in compulsion and fixity. Changed: because the oppressed, today in accordance with the forecast of theory the overwhelming majority of humanity, cannot experience themselves as a class.[50]

The 'overwhelming majority of humanity' is not 'oppressed' in the sense that it is progressively immiserated, but in the sense of Marx's theory of classes, that it does not own the means for its production. Adorno does not regard Marx's doctrine of immiseration as a historical prediction. Instead it refers to the consequences of the autonomous course of the economic mechanism of competition posited by liberal economics, an autonomous course which has been modified by monopoly capitalism. 'The modifying circumstances are extraterritorial to the system of political economy, but central in the history of domination.'[51]

Here we come to the crux of Adorno's simultaneous preservation and revision of Marx's theory of classes. It is undertaken from the perspective opened by the *Dialectic of Enlightenment*'s suspension of any absolute opposition between ancient and modern or between pre-capitalist and capitalist society. Marx's account of exchange already indicated that an archaic injustice – the monopoly over the means of production – underlies apparently free and equitable exchange. The idea that the era of high capitalism was one of free competition was thus always illusory. In the 'administered world' of late capitalism, however, the coercive element in a world of free competition amongst capitalists and freely alienable labour becomes structurally overwhelming.

The importance of such a development for historical materialism cannot be ignored. It prompts Adorno to reconsider the relationship between power and needs in the critique of political economy. Domination is not identical with alienation. There can be power without private property; there can be domination without alienation. An end to alienation would not necessarily end domination. This is a central motif of Adorno's thought. He places little emphasis upon the concept of alienation; he criticizes its overuse.[52] For many critics, Adorno's distance from economism pushes him into a Nietzschean revision of Marxism in which an opaque and supra-historical concept of 'domination' reproduces itself in social and political forms merely contingent to it. Some aspects of a defence against this charge have been addressed above; more are considered below.

Forces of production and relations of production

Any assertion that late capitalism presents 'a world in which competition has actually been eliminated'[53] might prompt the suspicion that Adorno's Marxism rests on a simple historical error. Adorno's preservation and revision of Marx rests less on provocative exaggerations of this kind, however, than on the argument that the relationship between the forces of production and the relations of production has changed since Marx. This relationship is most explicitly discussed in the late essay 'Late Capitalism or Industrial Society?' Adorno's position differs from Marx's in a number of ways. Adorno remains convinced that productive forces have developed to such an extent that were it not for petrified social relations, the world *could* be delivered from the catastrophe of repeated mass death by starvation: 'Even in the poorest lands none would need any longer to die of hunger.'[54] For Adorno the evidence that the forces and relations of production are not at present in harmony is this glaring fact: millions starve whilst food is stockpiled or deliberately destroyed. However nothing can apparently be done about this. Marx's belief in a historically necessary primacy of the forces of production was too optimistic. The relations of production show no sign of collapsing. The relations of production have not only petrified still further since Marx's time; they are also preponderant over the forces of production, which increasingly come to serve those relations rather than *vice versa*.[55]

Secondly, Adorno places a different emphasis from Marx's on an unleashing of productive forces. He is more concerned than Marx to indicate the possibility that the development of productive forces might free us not only *for* production, but also *from* production. He is interested as much in the unleashing of human beings from production as in the unleashing of productive forces (cf. chapter 7 below).

Finally, Adorno points out that the opposition between forces of production and relations of production is itself not an absolute. No primacy of the forces of production over the relations of production can be posited, since the forces of production are themselves mediated through and through by these relations. Rather, Adorno suggests, whilst the belief 'that the forces of production and the relations of production are today one and the same, and that society can therefore be construed without further ado from productive forces' is not true, it 'is the current form of socially necessary illusion'.[56] The illusion is socially necessary because 'moments of the social process which earlier were separated from each other, living human beings included, are brought under a kind of lowest common denominator. Material production, distribution, consumption are administered together.'[57] This lowest common denominator is the production of exchange-value for its own sake. Yet it remains an illusion because it remains the case that use-values – including the concrete labour which is commodified as abstract labour under a capitalist mode of production – are misidentified in exchange-value.

The advocates of understanding contemporary society as 'industrial society' rather than as 'late capitalism' take this 'socially necessary illusion' for reality. Adorno, however, makes the suggestion that contemporary society is industrial society in its forces of production and late capitalism in its relations of production.[58] Since the relations of production retain their preponderance over the forces of production, however, a Marxist understanding of the autonomy of these relations as a real illusion remains a more pertinent one. The concept of capitalism cannot be dispensed with, despite the difficulty of applying certain aspects of a Marxist account of capitalism to contemporary society.

These are difficulties which have their own consequences for sociological method. Adorno thinks that late capitalism presents the illusion that use-value and exchange-value are identical, and that the forces and relations of production are in harmony – that is, put less technically, the illusion that the production of exchange-value for its own sake is necessary, and the illusion that the existing relations of production are the best framework for it. It is tempting to think that this could be put right by setting out a theory of natural economy, of production-for-need. But for Adorno, this is more difficult than might be supposed. Because the forces of production are today mediated through and through by the relations of production, because use-value is mediated through and through by exchange-value, access to these would depend on the alterability of those petrified relations, of the production of exchange-value for its own sake. The only sociological access to the forces of production would be through a criticism of the petrified relations; a criticism which could itself only be fully successful on the condition of their real demise.

Late capitalism and fascism

The consequences of the dispute over monopoly capital become especially acute when the account of fascism elaborated by the Institute and Adorno's role in shaping this account are considered. As Michael Wilson has pointed out, it is scarcely possible to talk of a unified 'theory of fascism' amongst the Institute's members.[59] Friedrich Pollock developed his earlier reflections into a theory of National Socialism as 'state capitalism'. For Pollock, the role of political change, and the National Socialist party in particular, in developing German monopoly capitalism was a central one. Political manipulation did not merely mask 'true' economic interests, it changed them. The disaster of fascism could not therefore be fully understood from economic premises.[60]

Franz Neumann's comprehensive study *Behemoth: The Structure and Practice of National Socialism* (1942), although it described the

German economy as a 'totalitarian monopolistic economy', insisted that 'state capitalism' was an oxymoron and that competition had by no means been abolished in Germany.[61] Neumann
continued to insist, accordingly, that the triumph of ideology was
by no means total in Germany. Indeed, he believed that at the time
of writing there were signs that the mass of German workers were
on the point of recognizing National Socialist ideology as 'bunk'.
Whether these signs were deceptive or not, National Socialism's
self-presentation as a charismatic or magical order was an illusion
which must eventually be dispelled because '[t]he process of
production is not magical, it is rational. Changes in the process
of production . . . do not just happen, they are man-made.'[62]

Adorno had criticisms of both accounts. In a letter to Horkheimer criticizing an early outline of Pollock's article, Adorno
complained of Pollock's 'undialectical assumption that a non-
antagonistic economy might be possible in an antagonistic society'.[63] Yet Neumann's distinction between rational interests and
magical delusion was unlikely to find favour in so blunt a form
with the future co-author of the *Dialectic of Enlightenment*. In
discussions with Horkheimer Adorno referred to Neumann's approach as one for which both had little sympathy. None the less, in
a 1969 lecture course Adorno recommended *Behemoth* to his students as the most satisfactory available interpretation of National
Socialism.[64]

Adorno's early lack of sympathy for Neumann's work is under-
standable. For Adorno, the power of National Socialist ideology
was a real illusion. Neumann overestimated its illusory character,
and thus risked presenting National Socialism as a glorified confidence trick. At the same time Neumann emphasized the distinction between the western capitalist democracies and Germany's
'totalitarian monopolistic' capitalism. This aspect of Neumann's
account of fascism was also highly unattractive to Adorno, because
of its potentially self-exculpatory function. Adorno was less interested in a political theory of the difference between fascism and
democracy than in understanding the characteristics of late capitalism in general, in fascism and in the 'culture industry' of the
western democracies alike. The latter was continually interpreted
from the viewpoint of its immanent potential for fascism; at times
the two are apparently identified. It is with some shock that the
contemporary reader notes that almost all the features of Adorno's
account of fascist propaganda – together with their social and

psychological preconditions – are replicated in his account of the culture industry.

Adorno was not so foolish as to be unable to tell the difference between the mass extermination of Jews, on the one hand, and elements of implicit anti-semitism in American proto-fascism, on the other. Adorno's account of his American experience points to the importance of the anti-authoritarian aspects of American culture in averting any triumph of fascism in America.[65] His emphasis on the affinities between the culture industry and fascism is directed against the complacent assumption that fascism is a uniquely German disorder, has nothing to do with capitalism, and 'could never happen here'.

The differences between Neumann's and Adorno's accounts of fascism are well indicated by their contrasting approaches to anti-semitism. Both concur in seeing anti-semitism as a grotesquely distorted form of anti-capitalism. In this distortion anti-capitalism is reduced to a hostility to the sphere of circulation as such; surplus-value is misrecognized as a product of sharp practice in circulation; Jews are equated with finance capital.[66] But whereas Neumann emphasizes the roots of this distorted anti-capitalism in the anti-capitalist economics of German thinkers such as Friedrich List, Adorno emphasizes the connections between anti-semitic anti-capitalism and late capitalism itself.[67] Anti-semitism cannot be fully explained, as Neumann's account tends to explain it, from the deliberate distortion and displacement of objective economic interests. Nor, conversely, could anti-semitic propaganda be in the least effective if there were not already powerful tendencies to receive it at work.[68]

For Adorno, anti-semitic anti-capitalism is a pathological extension of the logic of late capitalism itself, with its associated dialectic of enlightenment. On the one hand, the fear and hatred aroused by the non-transparency of social relations is revenged on mediators, on those (the Jews) who are taken to epitomize the sphere of circulation itself, as though their mediation were itself the reason for society's lack of transparency. On the other, all claims to a qualitative difference transcending exchange are regarded as obsolete and anti-egalitarian. This egalitarian assault on obstinate particularity turns into a secular fundamentalism.

> No matter what the Jews may really be like in themselves, their image, as that of the defeated people, bears the features of which totalitarian domination must be the deadly enemy: happiness without power, wages without work, a home without frontiers, religion without myth . . .

Reconciliation is the highest notion of Judaism, and expectation [*Erwartung*] is its whole meaning; from the incapacity for expectation springs the paranoiac form of reaction to it.[69]

Judaism hopes for happiness without power and so is an intolerable reminder of the possible living happiness of which late capitalism has made sacrifice. Adorno interprets anti-semitism as a pathological expression of late capitalism's desire to liquidate the possibility of a radically different world.

It is clear that Adorno's thought does undergo a shift of emphasis on this topic, and one well marked by his changing attitude to Neumann's work. In a preface to the 1969 edition of *Dialectic of Enlightenment* Adorno and Horkheimer remarked that 'today it is more a question of preserving freedom, and of extending and developing it, instead – however indirectly – of accelerating the advance toward an administered world.'[70] What this prefatory note marks is an awareness of the dangers implicit in any critique of capitalism's 'merely legal' or 'merely formal' freedom. The *Dialectic of Enlightenment* was already conceived of as an immanent critique of normative legal concepts which fail to correspond with their objects, not as an external attack on them in favour of sheer concretion. Throughout *Negative Dialectics*, Adorno is aware that left-wing criticisms of liberal concepts of freedom may participate in the demise of the very concept of freedom without in any way hastening the arrival of the 'substantive' freedom for which they hope. The jurist Neumann already regarded some of the left critics of the Weimar constitution – themselves influenced by the National Socialist philosopher of law Carl Schmitt – as a case in point.[71] Adorno's willingness to present the demise of the rule of law in Nazi Germany[72] as less significant than the supposedly common advance of monopoly capitalism in Germany and the West alike is provocative; it is nevertheless a significant weakness of his early account not only of fascism, but also of capitalism.

Essence, appearance and ideology

Adorno's Marxism is sometimes thought of as a Nietzschean revision of Marx.[73] This interpretation is associated with the charge that Adorno aestheticizes or culturalizes Marxism (and, in some versions, that he is an anti-enlightenment thinker). In discussions with exiled German Marxists in the 1930s and 1940s Adorno regularly took the position that certain aspects of Nietzsche's thought were of more critical force in changed circumstances than a devoted adherence to every tenet of Marxian theory. Whereas figures such as Pollock and Günther Anders continually objected that Nietzsche's critique of culture addressed superstructural, not fundamental matters, Adorno was reluctant to relegate the critique of culture to a subsidiary role.[74]

Adorno credited Nietzsche with an insight into the potentially coercive function of a primacy of practice based on 'true needs' in socialist thought; and into the fact that domination was not identical with economic exploitation:

> The migration of domination into human beings themselves means that human beings have no other needs than those prescribed for them by an invisible domination. Nietzsche's taboo-like disinclination to examine all questions bound up with material existence has all the bad aspects it could possibly have, but it also shows his awareness that there is something wrong with the concept of a totalized praxis.[75]

Nietzsche is selectively reinterpreted from a position informed by Adorno's own Marxism. The production of exchange-value for its own sake, Adorno suggests, not only means that false needs are continually created, but also makes it increasingly difficult to say just where the distinction between true and false needs lies. Nietzsche's polemical description of socialism, 'a flock without a shepherd', which Adorno quoted repeatedly,[76] is reinterpreted not only as a proleptic vision of the culture industry but also as an insight into how internalized domination might still persist even in a society which meets all 'true needs'. Adorno does not dwell on his many differences from Nietzsche in these discussions, since his colleagues are largely convinced that Nietzsche has nothing to teach Marxism.

Yet Adorno's differences from Nietzsche are of critical significance. They are best understood in the light of his theory of ideology. In his 'Contribution to the Theory of Ideology', Adorno stated 'the dialectical problem of ideologies: that these are indeed false consciousness, but that they are nevertheless not only false'.[77] Adorno argued that 'total' theories of ideology such as Pareto's had failed to recognize this aspect of ideology:

> We can only talk meaningfully about ideology in so far as something spiritual [ein Geistiges] comes forward from the social process as independent, substantial and with its own claim. Its untruth is always the price of just this separation, the denial of its social ground. But its truth-moment also adheres to this independence, to a consciousness which is

more than the mere impression of what exists, and which therefore strives to penetrate what exists. Today the characteristic mark of ideologies is the absence of this independence, rather than a deceptive claim to independence.[78]

For Adorno, then, freedom, humanity and justice might be ideologies in so far as they came with a claim to be unconditioned or ideal. To label these ideas as mere 'ideologies' today, however, testifies only to 'rage against whatever might refer to the possibility of something better, even in a spiritual [*geistiges*] reflection, however powerless'.[79]

The notion that ideology has a truth-moment may sound paradoxical, but it is closely tied to Adorno's reflection on the relationship between prescription and description, 'is' and 'ought'. Concepts such as freedom, humanity and justice are what Adorno calls 'emphatic' concepts in the sense that they are ineliminably both prescriptive and descriptive.[80] Nowhere can we point to an example of a free human being; yet the judgement that human beings are free, because it deploys an emphatic concept, carries an implicit prescriptive truth along with its descriptive incorrectness. For some moral theories, if such a premise were granted, the next step would be to separate out the prescriptive truth from the descriptive mistake and to keep them clearly separated: this human being is not free, but ought to be so. Adorno is deeply informed by the Hegelian argument (chapter 6) that any such radical separation leaves us with empty moral prescriptions which have no relation to anything we can describe. His salient point in his defence of supposedly 'ideological' universals, however, is against the possibility of using this kind of argument as a means of removing the normative element from 'emphatic' concepts altogether. A wholesale demand for the liquidation of prescription defeats itself because it is itself prescriptive. Such demands end by telling us that we ought not to say 'ought'.

What Adorno is reflecting on in his 'Contribution to the Theory of Ideology' is the phenomenon of the ageing of the central concepts of enlightened political thought. The most pressing target of *Dialectic of Enlightenment* is not a naive faith in progress or in historical necessity but what Adorno and Horkheimer take as an equally blind faith in the merely existent, in the impossibility of change. In his essay on Karl Mannheim's sociology of knowledge, Adorno remarks that the most prevalent form of philistinism today is not a crude faith in progress, but an undifferentiated cynicism appealing to an unalterable natural human baseness.[81] The typical form of ideology in late capitalism, for Adorno, is the redundant conversion of what is already described as existing into an imperative: a parody of the injunction: 'become what you are!'[82] Adorno also puts the same point by saying that in such ideology the distinction between appearance and essence has been abolished. Social appearance, the second nature of petrified social relations, is taken for the essence of society, for all there is or can ever be. For epistemological positivism the notion of essence is a metaphysical relic which must be liquidated; appearance is what there is.[83] For sociological positivism the corollary is that an objective concept of society is a metaphysical relic.[84]

Nietzsche, like the positivists, attacks any idea of a separation between appearance and essence. He mocks those who invoke it as 'Hinterweltler' ('backworldsmen'; the word is a play on Hinterwäldler, 'backwoodsmen'), trusting in another and better world behind this one.[85] Adorno admits that invocations of an essence absolutely separate from appearance are self-confuting; like Hegel, he believes that 'essence must appear'.[86] Yet he also resists the abolition of the concept of essence, or the identification of essence and appearance.[87] These non-Nietzschean emphases become especially clear in Adorno's later work; in discussions with Horkheimer in 1939 the view was already expressed that 'for the positivists there is no distinction between essence and appearance; for us the distinction is constitutive.'[88] Metaphysics is not to be 'overcome'; rather, its current 'solidarity' – in the hour of its demise – with the possibility of materialism is to be demonstrated (cf. chapter 8).

These different attitudes to the problem of essence and appearance are closely related to central divergences in Nietzsche's and Adorno's respective accounts of culture and society. Nietzsche's 'transvaluation of values' does not hope for the end of domination. Rather it regards such hopes as sentimental, and looks instead towards the honest recognition, and even the celebration, of a domination with which all our values must needs be entangled. Adorno's thought is, instead, that the domination in rationality and in sociability could only really be fully recognized if domination itself were to come to an end.

After Marx

What can a social theory which is so closely, if complicatedly, related to Marx have to tell us today? More than might at first be thought, perhaps. Adorno admitted in *Negative Dialectics* that 'Marx charged around in the epistemological categories like a bull in a china shop'; the way in which early Anglophone reception of Adorno's work was almost obsessively concerned with his relationship to Marx and Freud has fortunately been supplemented in recent years by a more patient interest in the contexts of Adorno's thought in classical German philosophy. But in recent years, and especially since the death of Eastern-bloc Marxism-Leninism, Marx has in any case been more and more flexibly and carefully read and treated less and less as a kind of social *Summa Theologica*.

Adorno's social thought is notable for this kind of non-doctrinal reading of Marx from the outset. None the less, there are still several aspects of it which look problematic from both Marxist and non-Marxist perspectives. It is here that we might return to the question of how viable a commitment to the notion of commodity fetishism still is. The doubts raised by deconstructive commentators are among the more important here. Jacques Derrida, for example, has cautiously described Marx's theory of exchange-value as 'pre-deconstructive'.[89] The theory appears to rest on an appeal to the possibility of finally freeing transparent and living social relations from their concealment by non-living and inert objects, whereas Derrida's double readings, through their attention to the border-category of the 'spectral', the ghostlike, would display the difficulty of finally separating out the living from the non-living.

Derrida has hit on an important point here, because as Michel Henry's remarkable book about Marx argued long ago, the distinction between the living and the non-living is indeed far more fundamental to Marx than any distinction between 'consciousness' and 'being'.[90] It is also one of the few categorical oppositions which Adorno makes little attempt to place in question; an appeal to the need to protect living experience from becoming 'dead', 'lifeless' or 'petrified' is one of his favoured topics. But whereas the importance of this distinction finally drove a figure like Erich Fromm into a Manichean view of the world as a battle between life-loving 'biophiles' and death-fixated 'necrophiles', Adorno attempts to understand the merging of the living and the non-living as a real illusion, that is as an illusion which cannot be dispelled simply by recognizing it as such.[91]

Adorno's continual recourse to a strong distinction between the living and the non-living, however, indicates an important difference from deconstructive thought about Marx. If it is thought through in the context of the approach to myth developed in the *Dialectic of Enlightenment*, it provides some resources for a way of thinking about commodity fetishism which does not depend upon a dogmatic appeal to social transparency. Commodity fetishism is a model of the way in which enlightenment reverts to mythology: commodity exchange looks like the most sceptically disenchanted social relationship there could be, but the chapter on fetishes shows why the exchangers are not so undeluded as they think themselves.

We can appreciate the importance of the distinction between the living and the non-living to Adorno's thought in slightly more detail if we look at one particular issue, the question of surplus value and its relationship to living labour. In *Capital* Marx had set out to explain how surplus value (whether in the form of profit, rent or interest) is produced. Marx argued that the value of commodities was determined by the labour-time socially necessary for their production. The value of the commodity of labour-power was accordingly determined by the labour-time socially necessary for the subsistence of the worker. Surplus value arose from the double character of labour as concrete and abstract labour. Labour-power, bought by the capitalist like any other commodity, was in fact unlike any other commodity because it was alive and capable of producing further commodities. Paid for at the rate of subsistence, it would nevertheless, given a sufficiently extended working day, produce surplus exchange-value beyond the value of the wage paid. Surplus value could only be extracted from living labour. In any given sum of capital Marx therefore distinguished the constant capital invested in the means of production from the variable capital invested in living labour. The rate of surplus value was not to be calculated with reference to all capital invested, but only with reference to variable capital.[92]

Marx had argued, and Henryk Grossmann had re-emphasized, that capitalist accumulation tended to bring about a change in the composition of capital.[93] The rapid technical development of the means of production in a capitalist economy tended to increase the proportion of constant capital with respect to variable capital. Adorno argued that this could not leave the extraction of surplus value from living labour unaffected:

> The theory of surplus value was supposed to explain class relations and the growth of class antagonism objectively and economically. Yet once the advantage of living labour, from which alone according to its concept surplus value is derived, tends to sink through the extent of technical

progress – through industrialization, in fact – to a marginal value, the centre-piece [*Kernstück*], the theory of surplus value, is affected by this.[94]

The contemporary difficulty of expounding an objective theory of surplus value, furthermore, leads to 'prohibitive difficulties in grounding the formation of classes'.[95] An objective theory of the production of value and of class struggle should also furnish a clear theory of ideological misrepresentations of value and class.

For Adorno, the insuperable difficulties at present lying in the way of an objective theory of value are bound up with the current impossibility of distinguishing true from false needs. Not all subjectively experienced 'need' can be endorsed as real need. Capitalist production mystifies all needs as though exchange-value were their measure; yet this mystification cannot be overcome by a dogmatic distinction between needs and wants. For similar reasons it is no longer possible dogmatically to identify the 'real' interests of workers and chalk up a failure to follow these real interests to ideological mystification.[96]

This aspect of Adorno's thought was a recurrent sticking-point in his relations with fellow members of the Institute for Social Research. In a July 1942 seminar on the theory of needs Pollock candidly declared the aesthetic and cultural desires which were of such importance to Adorno to be false needs: 'Do people really worry about higher things so long as they are full?'[97] Adorno considered that such views rested on a positive anthropology, a theory of human nature, in which those needs natural to human beings could be distinguished from merely cultural and hence artificial 'needs'. No distinction between human nature and human culture, however, can yet be posited. In a conversation with the German anthropologist Arnold Gehlen, Adorno emphasized his belief that 'to say what "man" is is absolutely impossible.'[98] The only possible anthropology in mass society is a 'negative anthropology'[99] or a 'dialectical anthropology'.[100] Even such an apparent lowest common denominator as a 'will to live' cannot be presupposed as a universal feature of human nature.

In a section of *Minima Moralia* headed 'Novissimum organum' Adorno outlines a theory of the increasing 'organic composition' of human beings. Adorno argued that the 'change in the technical composition of capital' argued for by Marx was 'prolonged within those encompassed, and indeed constituted, by the technological demands of the production process':

That which determines subjects as means of production and not as living purposes, increases with the proportion of machines to variable capital . . . Its consummate organization demands the coordination of people that are dead. The will to live finds itself dependent on the denial of the will to live: self-preservation annuls all life in subjectivity. Compared to this, all the achievements of adaptation, all the acts of conformity described by social psychology and cultural anthropology are mere epiphenomena.[101]

Here the thesis of the *Dialectic of Enlightenment* that modern rationality is 'mimesis of what is dead' is more explicitly worked through with reference to the capitalist mode of production. The more thoroughly developed the means of production and its associated division of labour, the less living labour can set its own goals: the less, indeed, living labour is living. The shift in the proportion of constant and variable capital is extended into the proportion of living and dead elements in the individuals. A social psychology posits a prior individual 'affected' by social development.[102] Adorno argues that petrified social relations have already entered into what individuals are. When 'Life in the late capitalist era' is described as 'a constant initiation rite'[103] the emphasis falls on 'constant'. Unlike a literal initiation rite, this initiation rite is not one which once completed allows a secure place within social relations, but one which must be undergone again and again, because the threat of expulsion is renewed again and again.[104] It is this negative or dialectical anthropology of late capitalism which is worked out in Adorno's theory of the culture industry, and it is to this theory that we must now turn.

3

The Culture Industry

Introduction

When Bertolt Brecht was briefly involved in the theoretical discussion groups organized in American exile by the Institute for Social Research he described their general tendency thus: 'je mehr iceboxes, desto weniger huxley' – 'the more iceboxes, the less Huxley'.[1] To Brecht, that is, the discussions sounded like a variation on a familiar lament over the commercially induced decline of high culture. Adorno's attack on the 'culture industry' – particularly the study of jazz which he produced in the early 1930s under the apt pseudonym of Hektor Rottweiler – has been one of the most consistently irritating aspects of his *oeuvre*, and has seemed to many to testify to an unappealing elitism.

Adorno's work on radio, film, astrology, and leisure time in general as forms of 'administered life' has sometimes, then, been understood as an attack on 'popular culture'. This interpretation in some cases results from a conflation of the term 'culture industry' with 'popular culture'. For Adorno, culture is only genuinely 'popular' when it is produced by those designated in such a term as the 'people', rather than merely consumed by them. The expression 'culture industry' is chosen instead to emphasize that 'The customer is not king, as the culture industry would have us believe, not its subject but its object.'[2] Adorno's complaint against the culture industry is as much that it wrecks and distorts popular culture as that it wrecks and distorts high art. The purity of high art in the face of the culture industry is already an ideological illusion:

Light art has been the shadow of autonomous art. It is the social bad conscience of serious art. The truth which the latter necessarily lacked because of its social premises gives the other the semblance of legitimacy. The division itself is the truth: it does at least express the negativity of the culture which the different spheres constitute. Least of all can the antithesis be reconciled by absorbing light into serious art, or vice versa. But that is what the culture industry attempts. The eccentricity of the circus, peepshow and brothel is as embarrassing to it as that of Schoenberg and Karl Kraus.[3]

Two kinds of cultural product fail to fit in with the culture industry. In each case the productive labour involved is imperfectly commodified. On one side, that popular culture which remains recalcitrant to centralized production and distribution; on the other, that advanced autonomous art which 'has renounced consumption'.[4] Adorno's own work paid much greater attention to the latter.

The culture industry offers a false reconciliation of this opposition. The opposition is glossed over rather than genuinely reconciled in what has since come to be called 'crossover' culture. The division between serious and light art is not 'the truth' in the sense that it should be affirmed as a justly universal feature of human culture, but in the sense that it does not attempt to efface the real antagonism between the two. The division could only truthfully end with the end of social antagonism. This is the force of Adorno's well-known declaration in a letter to Benjamin that serious art and light art are 'torn halves of an integral freedom, to which however they do not add up'.[5]

Commodified light art and commodified autonomous art alike offer instances of the experience of the culture industry from the side of production and from the side of consumption. The fetishism of commodities causes a relation between people to appear in the form of a property of a thing, expressed as its exchange-value. Adorno argues that the real object of consumption in late capitalism is not, as consumers believe, the use-value of a product, but its exchange-value. The counterpart to this fetishism of cultural commodities is a 'regression' of the attention of their consumers.[6]

This notion of 'regression' is partly informed by psychoanalytical categories. It is not primarily deduced from a change in consciousness, however, but from the advancing production of exchange-value for its own sake. The actual qualities of the cultural product – the structural form of a musical work, for example – are of less and less relevance to its consumption the more consumption comes to be focused on exchange-value. Accordingly attention becomes less inclined to notice the qualities of the product itself and more inclined to become fixated upon some single aspect characterizing it as 'unique'. Such pseudo-uniqueness allows consumers to misunderstand their consumption of exchange-value for its own sake as though it were the consumption of an irreplaceable use-value.

The culture industry thus generates a world of false specificity in which the advertised uniqueness of the individual product – the distinctive individual voice of a new poet, the inimitable style of a star conductor, or the sheer personality of a chat-show host – needs to be foregrounded by the relentless sameness of a whole range of the product's other qualities, from diction to typeface.[7] This theory of pseudo-specificity is one reason why Adorno is unconvinced that mass-cultural products are irreducibly specific. To give too much credence to such claims to individual distinctiveness, he fears, would be to renounce the central task of cultural criticism, an understanding of the real homogeneity behind this illusory diversity. It would be to confuse the illusory pluralism of competing products with a real pluralism of human freedoms.

The complaint that Adorno's account of the culture industry lacks discrimination, however, is only one of the criticisms levelled against it. Much subsequent work has emphasized that whilst mass culture may not be popularly produced in the literal sense, the meanings and significance of cultural commodities are to an important extent produced by their consumers rather than pre-determined by their producers.[8] Adorno's account of a 'regression' stands accused of misrepresenting culture's consumers as the passive and thoughtless dupes of its producers. If Adorno's theory of the culture industry presented us with dupes on the one hand and conspirators on the other it would indeed be trivial, because the trick would only need to be exposed to be brought to an end. Adorno emphasizes, instead, that 'This is the triumph of advertising in the culture industry: the compulsive mimesis of cultural commodities by consumers who at the same time see through them.'[9] 'Seeing through' the culture industry's products – in the manner of 'ironic' devotees of soap opera – is not the same as seeing through, still less dispelling, the systematic illusion which is the culture industry itself.

The culture industry, then, is not a piece of sharp business practice but a 'constant initiation rite'. Its apparently irresistible character is a real illusion: an illusion because these social relations are humanly made and remakeable, yet real because such relations really have become petrified. The energetic participation of consumers in the culture industry testifies not to their foolishness but to their well-founded sense that they will be punished with social exclusion for a failure to keep up with cultural production: 'Looking good, make-up, the desperately strained smile of eternal youth which only cracks momentarily in the angry twitching of the wrinkles of the brow, all this bounty is dispensed by the personnel manager under threat of the stick.'[10] Adorno does not regard mass culture as comically trivial or epiphenomenal in comparison with serious art. It is not merely 'mass deception' but 'enlightenment as mass deception', to be taken every bit as seriously as the disenchanting rationality of which it is the distorted and mythical fulfilment: 'For centuries society has been preparing for Victor Mature and Mickey Rooney. By destroying they come to fulfil.'[11] The bathos of this claim could not be more seriously meant.

Adorno's account of the culture industry's consumers, then, by no means regards them as its inert victims. The culture industry could hardly be so successful without the avid participation of consumers. Indeed, he emphasizes the extent to which cultural consumption has become sheer hard work. Despite the rigorous separation of production and consumption, leisure in late capitalism becomes pseudo-activity, a form of ersatz labour:

> Amusement under late capitalism is the prolongation of work. It is sought after as an escape from the mechanized work process, and to recruit strength in order to be able to cope with it again. But at the same time mechanization has such power over a man's leisure and happiness, and so profoundly determines the manufacture of amusement goods, that his experiences are inevitably after-images of the work process itself . . . What happens at work, in the factory or in the office, can only be escaped from by approximation to it in one's leisure time. All amusement suffers from this incurable malady. Pleasure hardens into boredom because, if it is to remain pleasure, it must not demand any effort and therefore moves rigorously in the worn grooves of association.[12]

Under late capitalism it costs less effort to extend habits of mechanical activity into leisure time than it does to bring such mechanical activity to a halt. This goes both for intellectual and manual labour. For Adorno, the hobbyist's 'curiosity' is positivism at play.[13] The listener with an encyclopaedic recall of available recorded performances but with little understanding of the music which can be heard on them is the leisure counterpart, as it were, of the professional bibliographer cataloguing textual variants with a labour out of all proportion to their conceivable interest. The rigorously disciplined activity of modern sport mimics closely supervised and controlled physical labour.[14] Any intimation of the possibility of genuinely spontaneous self-activity must be erased. Even leisure activities requiring the most strenuous exertion are less tiring than play which might intimate the possibility of a different life. Even leisure time becomes an image of the production for its own sake which rules in the sphere of production. This is the point of Adorno's early aphorism on the jitterbug: 'For people to be transformed into insects they require as much energy as might well suffice to transform them into human beings.'[15]

Such a theory of leisure as ersatz labour, of course, does not propose that the culture industry's consumers primarily determine the significance of the cultural products which they consume. Adorno's emphasis, like Lukács's in *History and Class Consciousness*, falls on the way in which human activity in a late-capitalist society is pseudo-praxis, 'contemplative' praxis.[16] At its bleakest the theory complains that that reification has already become complete.[17] Were this true, not only would critical thought no longer be possible, but human social life itself would come to an end. Accordingly complaints that 'Life does not live',[18] that living activity has been completely replaced by abstract labour, are not literal. To make such complaints excites immediate resistance on the part of the living. This is just what Adorno hopes they will do. Towards the end of his life Adorno came increasingly to emphasize this point, and even to refer to 'real interests' which might resist the transfiguration of existing circumstances into fate. In a radio broadcast of 1969 he discussed the way in which 'What the culture industry presents people with in their free time . . . is indeed consumed and accepted, but with a kind of reservation':

> It is obvious that the integration of consciousness and free time has not yet completely succeeded. The real interests of individuals are still strong enough to resist, within certain limits, total inclusion. That would concur with the social prediction that a society, whose inherent contradictions persist undiminished, cannot be totally integrated even in consciousness. Society cannot have it all its own way, especially in free time, which does indeed lay claim to people, but by its very nature cannot claim them totally without pushing them over the edge. I shall refrain from spelling out the consequences; but I think that we can here glimpse a chance of maturity (*Mündigkeit*), which might just eventually help to turn free time into freedom proper.[19]

One who is *unmündig* is a minor, not yet legally autonomous. In an interview with Hellmut Becker Adorno quoted Kant's essay 'What is Enlightenment?' to clarify his use of this term. 'Enlightenment is humanity's departure from its self-incurred immaturity [*Unmündigkeit*]. Immaturity is the incapacity to use one's reason without the direction of another . . . Sapere aude! have the courage to use your *own* understanding, is therefore the chosen maxim of enlightenment.'[20] It may initially be surprising to hear one of the authors of the *Dialectic of Enlightenment* declaring that 'this forthright program of Kant's is extraordinarily relevant today.'[21] As we have seen, however, the hope of that work was already not to reverse enlightenment but to encourage enlightenment to become enlightened about itself. Once thought's autonomy is turned into an absolute, it becomes delusory; yet without some resistance to sheer heteronomy thought cannot even begin to reflect on what conditions it.

The 'politics' of mass culture

Adorno's critique of the culture industry, then, differs from an elitist defence of high art in its recognition that both 'high' and 'popular' culture are transformed and mutilated by their commodity character under monopoly capitalism. But even those who have recognized this have, nevertheless, sometimes wanted to point to an imbalance in Adorno's treatment of high and mass culture.

It is instructive to contrast Adorno's account of mass culture with that offered by his friend Walter Benjamin. In his essay on 'The Work of Art in the Age of its Technical Reproducibility', Benjamin offered a more optimistic account of the potential offered by the 'developmental tendencies of art under present conditions of production' than that given by Adorno. Whereas Adorno emphasized the impact of structural changes in the social totality in the era of monopoly capitalism upon cultural production and consumption, Benjamin's essay paid more attention to the influence of technical advances in the ways works of art were themselves produced and reproduced: to advances in lithography, photography and film. For Benjamin 'that which is disturbed in the age of the work of art's technical reproducibility is its aura . . . The technique of reproduction, to offer a general formulation, frees what is reproduced from the domain of tradition.'[22] There was thus a secularizing potential implicit in the technical reproducibility of the work of art: works of art were less and less able to appear as unique and auratic cultic objects. The technical reproducibility of works of art marked their separation from the inflexibly hierarchical domain of ritual.[23]

Benjamin regarded technically reproducible art forms, freed from their connection with ritual, as offering certain new possibilities. Like Adorno, he admitted that in some respects technically reproducible art had simply replaced one kind of superstitious veneration with another: 'the cult of the film star . . . conserves the magic of the personality, which has long since ceased to consist in anything other than the ersatz [*fauligen*] magic of its commodity character.'[24] But unlike Adorno, he also believed that film allowed just those shock techniques of fragmentation which aroused a widespread hostility in modernist auratic works of art to be accepted by a mass audience: '[t]he technical reproducibility of the work of art alters the relationship of the masses to art. The most reactionary of attitudes to, for example, a Picasso, is converted into the most progressive of attitudes to, for example, a Chaplin.'[25] From Benjamin's perspective the fact that 'a receptive stance in the cinema does not require attentiveness' was an asset of the cinema rather than a defect because it assisted in the suppression of the cultic elements of the work of art.[26] 'Reception in a state of distraction' was the characteristic stance of the cultural consumer in the age of the technical reproducibility of works of art, and the film was its characteristic and largely laudable medium.

Adorno's objections to Benjamin's account were both substantive and theoretical. On a substantive level, he believed that Benjamin not only overestimated the degree of formal shock and experimentation at work in the contemporary mass-market film,[27] but was also deeply mistaken in regarding the 'distracted' response of the film-going public as a politically 'progressive' development.[28] For Adorno, such a response only confirmed all the more thoroughly Benjamin's own insight into the replacement of the artwork as a literal cultic fetish with the pseudo-magic of the commodity fetish. On a broader theoretical level, Adorno questioned Benjamin's emphasis on production techniques rather than on mode of production. For Adorno the critical factor in the emancipation of art from ritual was the commodity character of cultural production and consumption. The rise of autonomous art (cf. chapter 5), in which Adorno too saw both uses and disadvantages, was intimately connected with its commodity character. Adorno insisted that contemporary high art was no less intimately

and systematically transformed in its material and technical particulars by the loss of aura consequent upon the commodity
character of culture under a capitalist mode of production than
were more obviously modern forms such as film.[29]

Nevertheless, Adorno's response leaves some questions open.
Adorno suggested to Benjamin that the necessary counterpart of
his analysis of film would be an account of Mallarmé, whom
Benjamin had mentioned as the first thoroughgoing representative
of art for art's sake, which could investigate the technical consequences of the commodity character for advanced autonomous
art.[30] But the suggestion might easily be returned to Adorno in
reverse: if Schoenberg and the Hollywood film are equally 'torn
halves of an integral freedom, to which however they do not add
up', why is it that the latter has no elements of any truth-content?
As Albrecht Wellmer points out, the same letter makes clear that
Adorno does not discern any freedom in mass art, but *only*
reification and ideology.[31] Wellmer, instead wishes to explore the
subjectively emancipatory power of some aspects of mass culture
through a defence of what he takes to be Benjamin's notion of
technicized mass art as a 'counterpoison [*Gegengift*] to the psychological destruction of human beings in industrial society',[32] and
suggests that 'rock music as "industrial folk music" '[33] would form
a test case. The argument, with its preference for the term 'industrial society' rather than 'late capitalism', indicates Wellmer's
distance from Adorno's premises. For Adorno any notion of mass
culture as a meliorative remedy for the psychological damage
inflicted by capitalism would severely underestimate how radically late capitalism transforms human life. Culture cannot perform this function, and, were it able to, would in any case only
make things worse in the long run by pacifying, rather than
manifesting, social antagonism.

The absence to which Wellmer points, of any real consideration
of the possible truth-content of mass culture on Adorno's part, is
real enough. It could not, however, be supplied by an appeal to
mass culture as replacement tradition: the idea of rock music as
'industrial folk music' only indicates how pertinent Adorno's
criticisms of false spontaneity still are. Nor need it imply a
fundamental revision of Adorno's notion of the truth-content of
cultural products itself (as I suggest in chapter 4). Instead it would
mean a greater attention to the possible truth-content of some
mass-cultural products. It is possible, after all, that the repetitiveness and ugliness of some such products are no more immediately

indicative of a 'regression' in cultural production and consumption than are discord or serial technique in contemporary art music. The work of a figure such as Mark E. Smith, who turns the repetitiveness and banality of rock music against itself, might, for example, suggest the need for a reconsideration here, since this is just the procedure which Adorno so much admired in a writer such as Karl Kraus but which he appears to have considered little in analysing mass culture (and which in any case had fewer mass-cultural exponents in the decades when Adorno produced most of his work on mass culture).

Psychoanalysis and society

Adorno lays the more emphasis on the intimations of *Mündigkeit*, the autonomous attempt to 'think for oneself' which are present in 'free time', because he takes the characteristic psychological con-stitution of individual subjects under late capitalism to be an *Ichschwäche*, ego-weakness, and a consequent unwillingness to think for oneself. This thesis – like Adorno's idea of a 'regression' in the attention of cultural consumers – raises the question of Adorno's complex relation to Freudian psychoanalysis.

The Institute's psychoanalytic specialist in its earlier stages was Erich Fromm. Fromm published a series of articles in which he attempted to specify the relations between psychoanalysis and historical materialism. In 'The Method and Function of an Analytic Social Psychology' Fromm argued that psychoanalysis was itself both historical – because 'it seeks to understand the drive structure through the understanding of life history' – and materialist, because it started not from ideas or theories but from sexual drives.[34] In Fromm's envisaged social psychology the drive for self-preservation, the basis of Marx's historical materialism, would have primacy, not because it was in some quantitative way 'stronger' than the sexual drives, but because it was less modifi-able, not postponable and therefore not subject to repression or to remaining unconscious for long periods. Social psychology would therefore have a twofold task. At a basal level it would 'provide a more comprehensive knowledge of one of those factors that is operative in the social process: the nature of man himself'.[35] At a superstructural level it would 'show how the economic situation is transformed into ideology via man's drives'.[36] In a subsequent essay Fromm began to indicate the results obtainable by such procedures when he identified the 'spirit of capitalism' with the 'anal character'.[37]

It should already be clear how little of Fromm's envisaged social psychology could be acceptable to Adorno. For Adorno no theory of human nature was currently possible; no absolute distinction between a material base and an ideological superstructure could be drawn; and both the services promised on behalf of such a social psychology by Fromm were therefore delusive. In his essay 'Revisionist Psychoanalysis' Adorno rejects Karen Horney's social psychology, a body of work closely informed by Fromm's attempt to press Freud into the service of an integrated social psychology. Adorno argues that the attempts of revisionist psychology to counter what are taken as pessimistic or deterministic elements in Freud in the name of a more progressive social psychology – the moment of biologism in his thought, his emphasis on the compulsion to repeat, the central role of childhood memories – have in fact shorn it of its materialist moments and left it less rather than more capable of furnishing social insight. In a phrase strikingly reminiscent of his suggestion that Marx and Engels were 'enemies of utopia for the sake of its realization', Adorno argues that Freud's pessimism serves the end of domination better than the normative sentiment of Horney: Freud 'makes himself as hard as the petrified relations, in order to break them'.[38]

A whole series of Freudian motifs testify for Adorno in a more critical way to the compulsion-character of contemporary society than their social-psychological replacements. In particular Horney's fundamental conviction, that character is not determined so much by sexual conflicts as by the imprint of culture, loses the radicalism of psychoanalysis's focus on libido as something pre-social, a focus by which 'the point at which the social principle of domination coincides with the psychological principle of the repression of drives'.[39] Similarly Horney's elevation of the integrated personality, of 'love' over sexuality and of genital sexuality over misdirected libido smuggles in normative criteria of psychological health as though they were descriptive. At the basis of Horney's normative revisionism, Adorno argues, lies an implicit prescription that 'love should also be psychologically what it is becoming socially anyway, an exchange of equivalents. The question remains whether love, which transcends the circle of prevailing exchange-relationships, does not necessarily contain that moment of hopelessness which the revisionists want to drive out.'[40] Adorno places Freud in the tradition of those pessimistic bourgeois thinkers who

were declared in the *Dialectic of Enlightenment* to serve enlightenment better than its partisans. When it is complained that
'critical theory does not escape Freud's impasse in which social-
ization leads to its own destruction'[41] this is partially accurate, but
not a decisive objection, because Adorno is not sure that social-
ization will *not* lead to its own destruction. Any theory of society
which assumes that it *cannot* will be functionalist, whether voluntarily or not.

Adorno's essay on Horney indicates the nature and limits of
Adorno's own interest in Freud. Freud cannot yield a viable
anthropology; still less can psychoanalytic therapy be endorsed;
nor can psychoanalysis simply be inserted within sociology to
produce a social psychology, whether of Fromm's or of Talcott
Parsons's variety.[42] Adorno did not, however, join the ranks of
those who have reproached Freud's psychoanalysis for presupposing the category of the individual and for an insufficient attention
to historicity. He retained a lifelong suspicion of analytic therapy
on the grounds that the hope of individual cures for suffering
rooted in social antagonism could only be delusory. But his scepticism about the 'primacy of the economic' made him more rather
than less interested in the social-critical potential of Freudian
psychoanalysis. Adorno argues that the split between pysche and
society is ideology when it is presented as a natural invariant, but
that it nevertheless testifies to a real social separation. The relative
autonomy of psychoanalytic accounts of personality-formation
remains in force for so long as the real split between individuals
and petrified social relations.

Nevertheless the scope of such a relative autonomy for psychoanalysis in Adorno's own work is limited. Psychoanalytic insights
are deployed in tension with a critical theory of society, a theory
whose parameters are decisively given not by Freud but by the
account of the relationship between culture and nature, and later
that of the relationship between identity and the non-identical,
developed in Adorno's own work. This makes Adorno's confident
application of psychoanalytic categories the more perplexing.
Fromm's diagnosis of the spirit of capitalism as the anal character
emphasizes the formation of a strong ego as a central feature of the
bourgeois individual and was restricted in its application to the
bourgeoisie. Adorno, by contrast, does not provide a class-based
social psychology. Instead the theory of exchange is mobilized as
the framework for an account of the psychological constitution of
individuals as such under late capitalism.

Adorno argues that the shift from high to late capitalism has been accompanied by a shift in the psychological constitution of the individual. The typical characteristic of the individual under late capitalism is not a strong ego but 'ego-weakness' and narcissism. Odysseus is the model for the formation of the ego in the *Dialectic of Enlightenment*. His persisting 'I' makes a 'sacrifice of the moment' and preserves itself by the desires it has repressed. Under late capitalism, however, self-preservation only appears possible by mimetic adaptation to what is dead, to the expression of all use-values as exchange-values. The more obvious it becomes that the economic basis of any individual's life is liable to annihilation, and the more real economic initiative is concentrated with the concentration of capital, the more the individual seeks to identify with and adapt to capital. For capital, however, the individual's self-preservation is not in itself a matter of any importance.

The tension between super-ego, ego and id which Adorno takes as paradigmatic for the individual in the age of high capitalism is replaced in late capitalism by a false reconciliation between ego and id.[43] The false reconciliation is a parody of a genuine reconciliation of ego and id, which would only be possible with the end of structural social antagonism. Formal courtesy is replaced by a false spontaneity which is supposed to be 'more free' but is rather the reverse. Energetic self-preservation is replaced by the indissociable entanglement of self-preservation and self-destruction. Instead of internalizing and thus both mediating and concealing domination as the strong ego does, the ego-weak and narcissistic personality is ready to respond to *direct* domination at a moment's notice. Self-preservation under late capitalism is intimately entangled with self-destructiveness.

Self-destructiveness, accordingly, cannot be seen as a mere dysfunction which therapy could alleviate. It is rather the desperate and miscarried form of self-preservation in a society which lives by destroying, by its negativity. Auschwitz and Hiroshima announce the possibility that this entanglement of self-preservation and self-destructiveness may yet finish off the species entirely. This is a 'regression', a direct celebration of the archaic moment which in any case survived mediatedly in high capitalism; but the regression cannot simply be attributed to sick or inadequate individuals. It is in this sense that Adorno can continually apply the category of 'regression' in *Negative Dialectics* as a social category, not primarily as a description of the psychological constitution of an individual.[44] The self-destructive, masochistic and narcissistic qualities of the modern individual are at their most striking in fascism, Adorno thinks, but are also characteristic of late capitalism in general.

The strong ego and the possibility which it holds out for autonomy of thought and action is thus more positively evaluated in Adorno's negative anthropology than in Fromm's earlier social psychology.[45] Indeed, the less optimistic Adorno becomes about the possibility of revolutionary or even progressive collective practice, the more important the elements of resistance offered by the strong ego become to him. Adorno does not simply celebrate the strong ego. He never loses sight of the repression, domination and untruth constitutive of it.[46] His use of the categories of 'ego' and 'id' is, indeed, strongly informed by his philosophical account of thought itself. Thought is ineliminably coercive, but needs this coercion to think how coercion might come to an end in more than thought alone (chapter 7). Adorno's hope remains a reconciliation of ego and id; their unreconciled antagonism in the strong ego serves their true reconciliation better than their false reconciliation in ego-weakness and narcissism.

Adorno's use of psychoanalytic categories raises as many problems as it solves. Some of the difficulties with it are external, in the sense that they address what Adorno does not say. Adorno has no elaborated theory of kinship and gender. The attempts to deal with sexual oppression in his work are improvised applications of a theory of domination in general.[47] Moreover, just that psychological normativity which Adorno elsewhere resists – in his polemic against Horney's emphasis on genital sexuality, for example – resurfaces through his account of ego-weakness. The remark that 'Totality and homosexuality belong together'[48] is not of course meant to say that homosexuals are totalitarians, but to point to the ersatz virility of fascists as conditioned by fear of the very 'effeminacy' against which fascism rages. Yet such a remark itself depends upon the prior identification of homosexuality with narcissism and ego-weakness.[49]

At a more general level, ego-weakness is not argued to be universal under late capitalism (indeed a strong ego is implied, somewhat disconcertingly, to be a necessary condition of critical theory) but rather typical. Such a characterization leaves open the question of why some individuals are ego-weak and others less so. Indeed Adorno must leave this question open. Not only is he reluctant to impose a class-based social psychology upon relatively autonomous psychoanalytical thought; his theory of class is in any case aporetic and so could not provide the basis for a class-based social psychology.

The most extensive attempts to answer such questions come in the work for which Adorno was long best known in the English-speaking world, his contributions to *Studies in the Authoritarian Personality*. Like all the work which Adorno undertook in collaboration with American sociologists, the book bears the marks of a compromise not only with positivism but also with American political conditions. In the 'Introduction' we hear that the understanding of fascism is a priority because 'no politico-social trend imposes a graver threat to our traditional values and institutions.'[50] In this project a series of questionnaires were developed which were to give an idea of the psychological traits of those most likely to have sympathy for authoritarian politics. The questionnaires did indeed display more subtlety than some contemporary questionnaire-based sociology, in that they attempted to disclose such attitudes by linked groups of indirect questions rather than by a single series of direct questions. The final 'F-scale' was developed by including indirect questions about more general social, cultural and sexual attitudes on questionnaires assessing the 'A-S' [anti-semitism] and 'E' [ethnocentrism] quotients of those questioned. Once general rules of correlation between answers to these indirect questions and responses to the direct questions had been established, the indirect questions were asked without any direct 'A-S' or 'E' questions.[51] The hope of this procedure was that concealed or even unconscious anti-semitism and ethnocentrism which might be denied when asked about directly might be revealed through response to the indirect questions.[52] The irreconcilability of such a procedure with Adorno's critique of classificatory thinking will be evident. The collective introduction announces that '[i]t is to be suspected that [those who would not co-operate with questioning] were more antidemocratic than the average of their group.'[53] It is hard to imagine Adorno himself submitting to such questioning with much patience.

Despite Adorno's hostility to the idea of a syncretic social psychology, then, there are clear limits to the application of psychoanalytic categories in his work. Little 'autonomy', however relative, is in the event granted to psychoanalysis. Instead the parameters for the application of psychoanalytic categories are clearly set by Adorno's own theory of society. From the point of view of a practising analyst, Adorno takes concepts which are meaningful only in the context of individual case histories and turns them into a negative anthropology. Adorno's defence is that it is not he who has abstracted from the individuals, but the unceasing conversion of concrete into abstract labour. The psycho-analytic categories are to help us understand the negativity of this process of abstraction itself. The condition of understanding mental suffering today would be precisely that what appears unintelligibly idiosyncratic in it could be understood through what is discounted as banally universal and therefore of no relevance.

The rebellion of experience against empiricism

The weaknesses of Adorno's social thought need to be spelt out candidly. His social psychology, especially in such semi-empirical ventures as *The Authoritarian Personality*, is the weakest aspect of his work. This is partly the result of the absence of any fully elaborated account of sex and gender, a problem which is not helped by Adorno's apparent lack of interest in, for example, the comparative anthropology of kinship structures. The speculative anthropology of the *Dialectic of Enlightenment* remains deeply suggestive, but is also undeniably hampered not only by its reliance on questionable empirical sources, but also the way in which these sources are recruited for support with a much less careful attention to the difficult relationship between philosophical criticism and social theory than when Adorno is thinking about Marx or Weber.

Other difficulties can be seen in Adorno's relation to political economy and in his account of capitalism. Adorno is too influenced by the distinction developed by the Institute's economists between 'high' capitalism and 'monopoly' capitalism. This distinction relied on an assumption which turns out not to have been fully historically confirmed in any simple way, that 'market' competition would tend to decline even in capitalist economies because of the development of natural monopolies. The distinction produces especially implausible results in his social psychology and also causes problems for his account of fascism. Still more broadly, his account of capitalism is hampered by the absence of any serious and sustained empirical interest in non-capitalist societies. His theory of exchange, for example, not only takes no account of the most important contribution to the topic this century, Marcel Mauss's essay on *The Gift: The Form and Reason for*

Exchange in Archaic Societies, but shows little developed under-standing of the political economy of non-capitalist and pre-capitalist societies.

These, of course, are not defects which could be remedied by just adding in the relevant bodies of work. In any case much of this work rests on methodological and philosophical presuppositions and political positions which Adorno would have wanted to question. Had Adorno devoted any sustained attention to Mauss's theory of exchange, for example, it is certain that he would have wanted to question its recommendations for buttressing social solidarity: 'a good but moderate blend of reality and the ideal'. Instead the weaknesses discussed above are closely connected to Adorno's conviction that the globalization of capitalist economy had made non-capitalist societies epistemologically inaccessible in the same way as it had made it impossible to construct a theory of natural economy or 'true needs'. All social understanding today, his work implies, must route itself through an account of late capitalism on pain of misrecognizing the way in which it is itself determined by its position within a self-globalizing capitalist society.

The stance of Adorno's social and cultural criticism towards positivism remains a decisive consideration in assessing its value today. Given their weaknesses, it is hard to suggest that the substantive theses of Adorno's social thought constitute its most lasting significant contribution to social theory. What is perhaps more significant is his reconsideration of the relation between social theory and philosophical criticism, a reconsideration on which I shall have more to say in the later chapters of this book. Sociology has its origins in a farewell to metaphysics in favour of a professional division of intellectual labour; a farewell which Adorno, however, persuasively shows has not really been accom-plished.

The problem, therefore, needs to be understood in the context of the Institute's changing approach to the division of intellectual labour as a whole. The idea of 'The Present Situation of Social Philosophy and the Tasks of an Institute of Social Research' set out by Max Horkheimer in the early 1930s differed significantly in emphasis from the programme of his later essay 'Traditional and Critical Theory'. The major difference concerned the relationship of 'critical theory' or 'philosophy' to the individual positive dis-ciplines. For the earlier Horkheimer, what needed emphasis was materialist theory's capacity to reinterpret the results of individual disciplines in a way which could free them from the limitedness of perspective imposed by the division of intellectual labour framing them. Nevertheless theory, if it was to remain materialist, could not add anything of its own to these elements. A theory declaring its independence from the individual scientific disciplines was bound to relapse into metaphysics. The programme thus retains a syncretic aspect; no more emphasis is placed on the critique of expertise deformed by divisions of intellectual labour than on the informative assembly of such expertise.

Later in the decade Horkheimer's 'Traditional and critical theory' placed much greater emphasis on the criticism of positivism not merely as limited but as false through and through. This shift in emphasis testifies to Horkheimer's own autonomous development but also to the strong influence of Adorno's (and Marcuse's) philosophical work. In Adorno and Horkheimer's discussions in 1939 prior to the composition of the *Dialectic of Enlightenment* Adorno again and again argues that the concept of a sheerly given brute fact, positivity, represents merely the point at which theory stops thinking (chapter 8).[54] No fact is in truth 'brute'; no fact can even be presented without any mediation by concepts. Yet nothing is further from Adorno's mind than to take this as an excuse for dispensing thought from the need constantly to collide with social and historical particularity. Adorno memorably described his critique of positivism as 'the rebellion of experience against empiricism'.[55] Positivism is objected to because it is 'more metaphysical than metaphysics'.[56] When the fact is taken as a 'brute fact', a given before which thought must simply come to a halt, the changing features of what is and what has been are mystified into timeless invariance. Positivism is criticized not because it pays too much attention to experience, but because it is not attentive *enough*. Reports on present and past experience are construed as 'laws' and allowed to legislate over future experience. The putative pure description of positivism carries an ineliminable prescriptive moment within it. Positivism becomes the liquidation of the new, of the possibility that the facts might change.

Adorno wishes to renounce an idealist 'attempt to grasp the totality of the real in determinations of thought'. Yet he is also allergic to any insulation of philosophy from the special sciences, of thinking from knowing. The unconscious philosophical presuppositions of positivism, meanwhile, are turned against positivism with the aid of arguments drawn from Kant and Hegel. Faced with this series of aporias, some commentators have pointed to the virtues of Horkheimer's more interdisciplinary and less fundamentally philosophical initial project.[57] The danger of work conducted along such lines is that it will fall into a mechanical syncretism. The contrary danger is hollow mimicry of Adorno's negative dialectic which makes of it a self-insulation of thinking from knowing and misknowing.

Adorno's social and cultural criticism has suffered from being thought of as standing in an abstractly polemical opposition to 'empiricism' and 'positivism'. Central to the value of this work today is the seriousness with which Adorno took the task of doing justice to that concrete historical experience of which empiricism already believes itself to be in secure possession. The 'frozen waste of abstractions' must be crossed, not because it is a kingdom of higher wisdom from which mere facts can be scorned, but because the liquidation of philosophical reflection which has been the condition of empiricist sociology has so often merely delivered empiricism to still cruder abstractions. Yet only if critical theory can renew the rebellion of experience against empiricism, rather than freezing to a method or an idiolect by which experience is always already discounted, has it a future. Many of the resources it can offer towards such a renewal are present in Adorno's work on aesthetic theory, and it is to this that we must now turn.

4

Art, Truth and Ideology

The idea of an 'aesthetic theory'

For some twentieth-century thinkers aesthetics has seemed a discipline of subsidiary importance. It is regarded as heavily dependent on prior epistemological and metaphysical presuppositions and hence as secondary to epistemological or metaphysical inquiry. Its significance for Adorno's thought, however, can scarcely be overestimated. This is because of the way in which, as we have seen Adorno and Horkheimer arguing in *Dialectic of Enlightenment*, art has been systematically separated from science in the language of modern rationality. Adorno wants aesthetic theory to challenge this separation by showing that art has a cognitive content, albeit a content which cannot in any simple way be extracted in a series of propositions. This chapter looks in more detail at what it could mean to speak of art as having a cognitive content with a non-propositional character.

Adorno's 'aesthetic theory', however, is more than a theory of the cognitive character of art in general. It retains a strong interest in particular aesthetic experience, in particular works of art, and in a critique and renewal of the traditional categories of aesthetics. It attempts to understand art as essentially historical, whilst retaining a strong interest in aesthetic valuation, in the ideas of the 'beauty' and, more unusually, of the 'truth-content' of works of art.

An aesthetic theory, thus conceived, is rather different from what is usually understood under the rubric of 'aesthetics'. Adorno wanted to use a thought of Friedrich Schlegel's as the epigraph for his unfinished and posthumously published *Aesthetic Theory*: 'Philosophy of art usually lacks one of two things: either the philosophy or the art.'[1] Most writing on aesthetics and on works of art, this aphorism suggests, present us with a disabling gulf. On the one hand, philosophical aesthetics tends to reduce works of art to the role of a series of examples of its own general tenets. It thereby misses what is unique in any individual work of art; misses, indeed, just what makes it a work of art. Art history, on the other hand, presents us with an empirically rich treatment of particular works of art, yet one whose evaluations can tend to be opportunistic rather than philosophically stringent. All Adorno's writing on art might be understood as an attempt to produce a philosophy of art which lacks neither the philosophy nor the art.

The title *Aesthetic Theory* is intended to distinguish Adorno's work both from formal aesthetics and from art history. Adorno does not think that philosophy can any longer provide either prescriptive maxims for the production of works of art, or an account of some invariant laws of aesthetic judgement or aesthetic experience. For many philosophical traditions, of course, this would simply be to say that aesthetics as such is no longer possible. But for Adorno, if philosophy of any kind is to be possible today it needs to be able to understand as true, good or beautiful – as well as false, bad or ugly – something which has come into being historically.

This indicates how ambitious Adorno's aesthetic theory is. It offers to give a philosophically stringent account of art and of aesthetic judgement and experience. Yet it hopes to do this without losing its immersion in the minutest details of works of art themselves. Indeed, on Adorno's account it can only do this if it does not sacrifice such immersion. As Adorno himself recognizes, however, the gulf between art history and philosophical aesthetics is not simply a result of the short-sightedness of aestheticians or art historians. It is a division of intellectual labour; and Adorno is highly sensitive to the possibility that an attempt to overcome such divisions of labour by an act of will may result in a failure to make any worthwhile contribution to anything. The unique significance of Adorno's work on art lies in the unparalleled determination with which it dashes itself against this apparently natural and irresistible opposition. But this also means that nothing like a portable methodology for musicology or literary criticism, nor invariant criteria of aesthetic judgement, can be got out of it and then 'applied' at will to 'material' elsewhere.

The dissatisfaction with a choice between formalist aesthetics and art history, of course, is by no means entirely original to Adorno. It had been a central emphasis of Hegel's aesthetics, in particular. Adorno does not think that there can be a fresh start from first principles in aesthetic theory any more than he thinks that there can be such a fresh start in epistemology and metaphysics or in sociology; some of his aesthetic thought is therefore organized through a criticism of previous work. In order to understand how Adorno's aesthetic theory works, then, it will be necessary to give an account of its relation to the German tradition in aesthetics, and particularly to Kant and Hegel. A useful preliminary account of Adorno's relation to that tradition can be found in *Aesthetic Theory*: 'Subjective and objective aesthetics, as counterpoles, are equally to be criticized by a dialectical aesthetics: the former, because it is either transcendentally abstract or contingently dependent on the taste of individuals; the latter because it misrecognizes the objective mediatedness of art through the subject.'[2] What Adorno means here should become clear through his account of what can be characterized, although these labels are rather crude, as Kant's broadly 'subjective' aesthetics and Hegel's broadly 'objective' aesthetics. Here it needs to be noted that Adorno is not suggesting that these two approaches should be added together. Instead he is attempting to formulate a different kind of aesthetics, one which would be materialist, but without relying on a philosophically naive and dogmatic appeal to brute givenness, to what is 'just out there'. This is a difficult aim to fulfil, and Adorno's approach to it cannot be wholly understood without some idea of what he means by materialism in general (cf. chapters 6, 7 and 8).

Transcendental aesthetics: art and aesthetic judgement

The significance of Kant's third critique, the *Critique of Judgement* (or, more literally, of 'judgement-power')[3] for German aesthetics generally and for Adorno's aesthetics in particular can hardly be overestimated. It is a work of bewildering richness; only those aspects of most significance for Adorno's thought can be considered here.

A central aim of Kant's critique of pure reason was to show a path beyond the bad choice between dogmatic rationalism and sceptical empiricism – a 'critical' path which would provide an account of the conditions of the possibility of experience. An analogous aim is pursued in the *Critique of Judgement*. At the heart of Kant's aesthetics is the suspension of a bad choice between empiricist and rationalist aesthetics. Rationalist aesthetics presents beauty as though it were a quality of the object itself, dependent on its geometric or other properties, without any reference to subjective experience. For rationalist aesthetics, it would be possible to *demonstrate* to a sceptic that an object he or she found ugly was beautiful. Kant argues, against such views, that 'there can be no rule by which someone could be compelled to acknowledge that something is beautiful. No one can use reasons or principles to talk us into a judgement on whether some garment, house or flower is beautiful.'[4] Yet equally, against empiricist theories of taste, he insists that beauty is not reducible to subjective gratification. If it were, the judgement that a representation is beautiful would have no evaluative content at all, but would simply be a report on the speaker's sensations.

Kant suggests, instead, that pure judgements of taste 'must involve a claim to subjective universality'.[5] They are *subjective* because the judgement that an object is beautiful is not a cognitive judgement. Unlike a scientific judgement it cannot be proved objectively or made binding for others. Yet they are *universal* because the claim that an object is beautiful carries within it a claim to universal assent. Kant is arguing that there is a crucial difference between a judgement that 'this painting is beautiful' and a judgement that 'this painting makes me feel good'. The judgement of taste, unlike a report on experience, must claim universal assent, even though it cannot compel such assent.

Kant argues that 'only the liking involved in taste for the beautiful is disinterested and *free*.'[6] Our liking for what gratifies us is unfree because compelled by the interest of sensation; our liking for what is morally right is also unfree because compelled by an interest of reason.[7] Our liking for the beautiful, however, is 'a pleasure which alone is universally communicable although not based on concepts'.[8] If it were based on concepts, like a cognitive judgement, it would not be 'subjective'; if it were not universally communicable, like a feeling of gratification, it would not be 'universal'.

This raises the problem of how there can be 'disinterested delight'; of how a sensation can be universally communicable. This liking must rest on some element which is not a concept and yet which is universally shared a priori. Kant finds this basis in the interplay of the subjective conditions for the possibility of cognition as such.[9] Knowledge is universally demonstrable. It follows that the cognitive conditions for the possibility of knowledge must be universally communicable. The interplay of our ability to combine a manifold in intuition (imagination) and of our ability to bring this manifold under a concept (understanding), that is, must be universally communicable.[10] In our liking for the beautiful, a representation awakens this interplay of the conditions for cognition in general, yet no particular cognitive judgement is made. Kant takes this argument to have shown that we do have an a priori basis for presupposing a universally communicable feeling – or *sensus communis* – and to have shown it, not by resort to merely empirical observation, but from a transcendental argument about the conditions of the possibility of experience themselves.

Whilst 'an objective principle of taste is impossible',[11] then, Kant does think we can say that the beautiful must awaken the free play of the cognitive powers.[12] This requirement allows him to comment on various formal features of works of art, and even to present an order of rank for the various fine arts in the 'deduction' of the *Critique of Judgement*. What differentiates these arguments from an 'objective principle of taste', for Kant, is that they are arrived at not dogmatically or empirically, but through an account of the conditions of possibility of aesthetic judgement. Kant concludes that:

> Fine art must be free art in a double sense: it must be free in the sense of not being a mercenary occupation and hence a kind of labor, whose magnitude can be judged, exacted or paid for according to a certain standard; but fine art must also be free in the sense that, though the mind is occupying itself, yet it feels satisfied and aroused (independently of any pay) without looking to some other purpose.[13]

Kant's view of judgements of taste has important consequences for his theory of artistic production. Aesthetics has been stripped of its prescriptive content. This means not only that aesthetics cannot lay down a priori principles for judging beauty, but also that it cannot prescribe how beautiful works of art are to be produced. This distinguishes aesthetics from moral theory. Yet if there are *no* rules governing artistic production, how can it be distinguished from any other kind of empirical and interested action determined by inclination? 'There is no science of the beautiful',[14] yet 'a product can never be called art unless it is preceded by a rule.'[15] It is at this juncture that Kant introduces his theory of genius. Genius is a talent for production which is not itself governed by any rule or precedent and yet sets the rule for other productions. In genius, it is 'nature in the subject (and through the attunement of his powers) that gives the rule to art'.[16] It is impossible for aesthetics to usurp the place of genius and make rules for the production of beauty.

Kant thus suspends the archaic argument as to whether the function of the work of art is to please or to instruct, or some combination of both. Instead, he introduces the new idea that 'Beauty is an object's form of *purposiveness* insofar as it is perceived in the object *without the presentation of a purpose.*'[17] This raises the possibility that the idea of a 'function' might already be an inappropriate way to think about artistic production; that the beauty of works of art might depend precisely on the impossibility of assigning any fixed function to them.

Kantian aesthetics has been discussed at such length because certain of its central achievements are regarded as irreversible by Adorno. His critique of Kantian aesthetics is always sensitive to the possibility that the attempt to go 'beyond' Kant may lead to a relapse into positions already refuted by Kant. Kant's critique of rationalist aesthetics, Adorno thinks, remains in force against all attempts to stipulate timeless rules for the production or judgement of beauty. He regards Kant's critique of sceptical theories of taste as equally irreversible.[18] At the same time, the idea that the work of art cannot easily be prescribed a function is of pivotal importance to Adorno, who radicalizes it in his own paradox that 'in so far as a social function may be predicated of works of art, it is the function of having no function.'[19] Adorno continually appeals to these central motifs of Kantian aesthetics against positions which he thinks are varieties of rationalist or sceptical accounts – against the thesis that works of art should serve political praxis, for example, or, conversely, against the thesis that works of art are commodities like any other.

Yet Adorno also wishes to deploy Kantian criticism against aspects of Kant's own thought. Adorno's criticisms centre on the role of the transcendental subject in Kant's aesthetics. Adorno recognizes that it is not sufficient to complain that Kant's aesthetics is subjectivist. Adorno sees the *Critique of Judgement*, instead, as undertaking to rescue objectivity in aesthetic judgement from sceptical relativism. It does this through an account of what even a sceptical account of aesthetic judgement cannot help presupposing. 'Kant would like, analogously to the critique of reason, to ground aesthetic objectivity through the subject, not to replace the former with the latter.'[20] But Adorno regards the need to give a transcendental account as producing a series of contradictions. Interest, for example, must be excluded, otherwise Kant's account of the judgement of taste will not be properly transcendental; and yet '[e]ven Kant is obliged . . . to take into consideration the existing ontic individual, to a greater extent than is compatible with the idea of a transcendental subject' since '[t]here is no delight without living individuals whom the object pleases . . .'[21] This results in the central oxymoron of Kant's aesthetics: 'disinterested delight', a 'pleasure without pleasure'.[22]

Despite the fact that Kant's attempt is to rescue objectivity in aesthetics through a transcendental account, then, he considers the work of art 'only in relation to the one who contemplates or produces it'.[23] The central problem with this in Adorno's view is the way in which it fails to consider the possibility that the work of art or natural appearance may be beautiful – or, as we shall see later, may have a 'truth-content' – in itself. As Adorno recognizes, from a Kantian viewpoint such a demand could be taken simply as a relapse into the mistake of rationalist aesthetics, because it would violate Kant's insistence that the judgement of taste provides 'absolutely no cognition . . . of the object'.[24] But Adorno's point is not to posit such beauty as sheer objectivity, devoid of any reference to the subject. Instead it is linked to his insistence that works of art have a cognitive content. Works of art, for Adorno, are not merely inert objects, valued or known by the subject; rather, they have themselves a subjective moment because they are themselves cognitive, attempts to know.

Adorno sees that Kant's account of the relationship between art and cognition is aporetic. On the one hand, beauty is that which 'pleases universally without a concept'; with this, art seems to be resigned to the side of the extra-logical. Yet at the same time Kant treats the judgement of taste as a subjective *universal*, not merely as a report on subjective experience, and thereby implies that there is something in the work of art which is susceptible to universal logical judgement.[25] In Adorno's view this aporetic approach to the relation between art and cognition is to Kant's credit, because it registers a tension which Adorno believes is part and parcel of the artwork itself, a tension between its discursively rational and its mimetic components. None the less, the fact that Kant considers works of art only in relation to the contemplating or producing subject leaves him unable to interpret the cognitive element in works of art themselves. This cognitive element, in Adorno's view, cannot be reduced either to the work's reception by an audience nor to the intentions of the work's producer.[26] What it 'is' is discussed below.

An equally important difficulty with Kant's transcendental account of aesthetic judgement, Adorno argues, is the historical invariance of the aesthetics thus yielded. Transcendental subjectivity is not subject to temporal or historical specification, any more than to location in space, because it is not a 'being'. Since the account of aesthetic judgement given in the third critique is a transcendental one it represents the conditions of the possibility of aesthetic judgement as timeless invariants. Thus, in Adorno's view, even though it is one of Kant's chief merits as an aesthetician to have 'attained first to a knowledge which has remained valid ever since [*seitdem unverlorene*], that aesthetic conduct is free from immediate desire',[27] and even though this is not a mere idealization, for Adorno, because 'the distinction of the aesthetic sphere from empirical reality is constitutive for art',[28] this is none the less a historical development which is 'transcendentally brought to rest' by Kant, as though it had always been and must always be a condition of the possibility of aesthetic judgement and production.[29] Whole societies and cultures have lacked the very notion of freedom, autonomy and 'disinterestedness', as well as the idea of the 'aesthetic' itself.

Whereas Adorno's earlier objection looked, from a Kantian viewpoint, rationalistic, this objection looks relativistic from such a viewpoint. But, as we shall see in more detail in chapters 6–8, it is central to Adorno's thought to attempt to think non-relativistically, yet without turning aspects of an experience which is temporal and historical into 'invariants'. The conditions of the possibility of aesthetic judgement have their *own* conditions of possibility in the living individuals who judge and in the representations which they judge. Without these individuals there could be no judgement of any kind. The historicality of judgers and of representations means that the conditions of the possibility of their judgement could not be invariant.

Idealist aesthetics and the beauty of nature

Some aspects of Adorno's criticisms of Kantian aesthetics are anticipated by Hegel. Hegel is especially interested in the *Critique of Judgement* because of the way in which, he thinks, it attempts to reconcile some of the governing oppositions of Kant's thought: between freedom and nature, spontaneity and receptivity, the noumenal and the phenomenal. He regards these reconciliations as unsuccessful because they are not fully carried through. He anticipates Adorno's complaint that Kant's account of the work of art considers it only through the contemplating or producing subject. The reconciliation between universal and particular in the work of art is not presented by Kant as an objectively knowable reconciliation – it cannot be demonstrated bindingly for another – but remains 'merely subjective in respect of our appreciation as in respect of our production'.[30] For Hegel, of course, this is a further symptom of Kant's failure effectively to reconcile subject and object.

Hegel's aesthetics attempts to overcome this antithesis. Art has a cognitive content in itself, a content which is not exhausted either by the subjective intentions of its producers or by the subjective responses of its consumers. Accordingly Hegel is no less critical than Kant both of any attempt to lay down a 'science of the beautiful' and of a reduction of aesthetic experience to gratifying stimuli. But for Hegel this criticism must also mean going beyond Kant's own account of the relation between art and cognition. There remains an element of formal prescription in Kant's aesthetics to the extent that the beautiful is taken to be 'that which pleases universally without a concept'. Hegel, accordingly, lays a far greater emphasis on the content of works of art than does Kant. For Kant it could be only an incidental part of a transcendental inquiry into the conditions of the possibility of aesthetic judgement to give detailed accounts of particular works of art. For Hegel, however, no radical separation between the transcendental and the empirical can be sustained. Consequently works of art can no longer be discussed merely as 'examples'.

This idea necessarily introduces a different approach to the historical character of works of art. Historicity can no longer be seen as something irrelevant to a philosophical theory of art. Instead it is inseparable from what works of art are. Hegel attempts to move beyond the bad choice to which we saw Friedrich Schlegel alluding earlier: between a history of art unable to articulate a philosophical account of art and aesthetic experience, on the one hand, and a philosophy of art treating particular works of art as merely accidental examples, on the other. In particular, Hegel lays a great deal of emphasis on a contrast between the 'classical' work of art, the product of a world in which social relations are transparent and unfree, and the 'romantic' work of art, the product of a world in which social relations are opaque and formally free.[31]

Many of the central features of Adorno's aesthetics, then, are already present in Hegel's thought: an insistence on the cognitive element of works of art; a refusal to resign the historicality of works of art to an extra-philosophical realm of contingency; a criticism of subjectivist theories of works of art and aesthetic experience.[32] Yet Adorno believes that Hegel's subject-object is, in aesthetics as elsewhere, a disguised subject; that is, that Hegel's aesthetics remains idealist. Adorno attempts to provide a materialist critique of this idealist aesthetics. Adorno wishes, that is, to articulate a 'priority of the object in art', a phrase whose exact significance will need further discussion later.[33]

In pursuit of a materialist aesthetic, Adorno examines the question of natural beauty. He points out that natural beauty has been strikingly little discussed in philosophical aesthetics after Kant. Hegel's aesthetics marks a decisive stage in this process. For Hegel natural beauty was the lowest and least significant form of aesthetic experience, and his aesthetics moves quickly past it to the beautiful in art.[34] Adorno takes this swift transition as symptomatic of the idealism in Hegel's aesthetics. Natural beauty is of less significance for Hegel than the beautiful in art because it is less thoroughly mediated by spirit. This account of natural beauty is not taken to be a simple mistake on Hegel's part. It registers a historical truth: the intensification of the domination of nature discussed in the *Dialectic of Enlightenment*.

Adorno, indeed, does not think that we could have immediate access to a natural beauty unmediated by history. He is capable of being no less unsentimental than Hegel about naive appeals to such natural beauty. The interest in natural beauty is itself something which has come to be historically, and is dependent on emancipation from immediate need and fear in the face of nature; it is not a universal human sense.[35] The mountains which inspire moderate awe when it is possible to ascend them by cable-car more often provoked horror, disgust or indifference even so recently as the Renaissance. Nor is Adorno wholly hostile even to Hegel's insistence that the beautiful in art is of more significance than the beauty of nature, because this insistence is in part motivated by the element of freely spontaneous activity in art. Birdsong is not *song* but is entangled in the spell of self-preservation.[36] If we choose to ignore its function in self-preservation we delude ourselves.

Yet, for Adorno, crucially, human activity is as yet hardly less fully, although less immediately, entangled in unfree self-preservation; and human song is, consequently, also entangled in this 'spell'. The freely spontaneous element in art is by no means a realized freedom for Adorno, because art remains no less caught up in the spell of self-preservation than any other human activity; rather it is an intimation of a possible future freedom. The beauty of nature which Adorno invokes, then, is by no means a beauty to which we could now have immediate access; not least because nothing like 'nature' yet exists.[37] In a society organized around the production of exchange-value for its own sake, Adorno suggests, it is impossible to say what is 'natural' and what is 'cultural'; it would certainly be naive to think that our sense of the beauty of nature is not culturally mediated. Appeals to an immediate natural beauty merely serve to confer an illusory naturalness on the very history which is overlooked in such appeals.[38] The beautiful in nature is a possible beauty to which we could have access only if nature and culture could be reconciled. This would require culture to abandon its attempt to portray itself as entirely self-sufficient. Idealist aesthetics, with its sense that 'nothing in the world is to be revered except what the autonomous subject owes to itself'[39] is part and parcel of this illusory self-sufficiency of culture.

The idea of the possible beauty of nature, then, acts as a corrective to idealist aesthetics. This idea, in its turn, affects Adorno's conception of the work of art. Instead of being valued primarily as the bearers of the work of human spirit, artworks are valued as a particular kind of work which indicate that the fetishization of work for its own sake could come to an end. Works of art testify to a potential reconciliation between nature and culture. 'Art gives the lie to production for its own sake and opts for a situation of practice beyond the spell of work . . . Happiness would be beyond practice.'[40] Adorno, in effect, is speculatively rewriting the oldest maxim of aesthetics. Art imitates nature: but nothing like 'nature' exists as yet: art imitates what does not yet exist.[41] For Adorno it can be said that all authentic art is a mimesis of utopia – yet this mimesis can be carried out only negatively. Art cannot provide an explicit image of utopia. The possible 'nature' which does not yet exist can only be imitated by the determinate negation of the falsely naturalized culture which does exist.

Materialist aesthetics and the 'language-character' of art

How, though, can Adorno's attempt to provide a materialist aesthetics be reconciled with his insistence on the cognitive character
of the work of art? Adorno is aware of the difficulties faced by such
an attempt. He addresses them in his account of the 'illusory
character' (*Scheincharakter*) of works of art: '[t]he illusory character
of works of art means that knowledge of them contradicts the
concept of cognition in Kant's critique of pure reason. They are
illusion, in that they posit their inside, spirit, outside, and they are
only known in so far as, against the prohibition of the amphiboly
chapter, their inside is known.'[42] Kant insisted that concepts could
not of themselves yield knowledge of objects, without any reference to the non-conceptual (cf. chapter 8 below). This is what
Adorno means by 'the prohibition of the amphiboly chapter'.
Adorno's demand that works of art should be known as cognitive
in themselves, not only through the contemplating or producing
subject, seems to violate this prohibition. It seems to set up works
of art as intelligible entities, and then to ask that they should be
known from the inside. Is this a return to a kind of metaphysical
dogmatism?

Kant, it will be remembered, makes no distinction between the
knowledge that we have of works of art and our knowledge of any
other kind of empirical appearances. This, then, would seem to
rule out the possibility that works of art might have a cognitive
content of their own which is not exhausted either in their production or their reception. Any such idea, from Kant's viewpoint,
would be a metaphysical fantasy. Yet aesthetic *judgement*, for Kant,
can distinguish between the naturally beautiful and the beautiful
in art. Kant argues that in order to judge works of art beautiful, we
need a concept of their purpose, whereas we do not need any such
concept to declare natural appearances beautiful.[43] Our knowledge
of works of art, as objects, depends on exactly the same process as
our knowledge of any other empirical appearances, for Kant; but
our valuation of them must presuppose this qualitative difference
between works of art and natural appearances. In Hegel's *Aesthetics* the objective purposiveness of the work of art is no longer
confined to aesthetic valuation, but is a proper object of philosophical cognition; meanwhile the subjective reception of works of art
can be taken as largely contingent to what works of art are.

Adorno considered that the possibility of materialist thought depended on testifying to a 'priority of the object' (chapter 7). Materialist thought would have to be able to understand its own dependence on the object, to avoid positing the illusion that thinking comes 'first'. Here Adorno is considering the related issue of how the priority of the object can be testified to in aesthetics. Materialist aesthetics insists that works of art add up to 'more' than their production or reception by a human subject. Yet it can hardly present them as objects entirely independent of such subjects. Works of art are appearances which appear to claim to have an essence distinct from merely empirical appearances. This claim is illusory, because works of art would be nothing at all without the empirical elements of which they are made up. Yet it is not a mere illusion, because it results from the fact that these empirical elements are cast into a meaningful configuration. This meaningful configuration is not reducible either to the subjective intentions of the work of art's producer or to the subjective interpretations of its consumers, nor to any result which could be produced by somehow adding up intentionality and reception. Yet the objectivity of this configuration is not like the kind of objectivity that a thing has, but like the kind of objectivity that linguistic meaning has: 'what makes works of art more than mere existence is not in its turn something existent, but their language.'[44]

In order to understand this idea of the 'language-character' (*Sprachcharakter*) of art, we must recall Adorno's account of the 'double character' of language itself, as set out in chapter 1. Modern rationality progressively separates classification from mimesis. The mimetic element of language is progressively extirpated from classificatory cognition. This mimetic element gets surrendered to art, which is in turn regarded by identificatory thinking as a-rational, entirely devoid of any cognitive content.[45] Yet in the event this separation of knowing from mimesis can never be as perfect as its advocates would like. We shall see in more detail later why this is so in the case of identificatory thinking: if such thinking succeeded in liquidating all affinity to the object whatever, it would no longer be a thought of anything; indeed, thinking itself would no longer be possible.

Parallel considerations apply to art. It is a central thesis of Adorno's aesthetic theory that art is itself a kind of rationality: 'art is rationality which criticizes rationality without withdrawing from it.'[46] The extirpation of cognitive moments from art can never be complete without annulling the concept of art altogether and surrendering works of art to the status of empirical stimuli. The work of art cannot be the a-rational sheer object for which it is taken without ceasing to be a work of art. Just as the truest thinking, for Adorno, remains alive to the suppressed mimetic element in cognition, so, conversely, the most authentic art is that which remains alive to the suppressed cognitive element in mimesis.

This still leaves the problem of how it is possible to speak of an artefact as 'cognitive'. Surely only subjects 'know' anything? For Adorno, however, works of art can be spoken of as 'cognitive' in the same sense that we may speak of the organization of a philosophical text as cognitive. The cognitive significance of a philosophical text is not exhausted by the sum of the correct propositions contained in it, because it depends also on the relations between those propositions and the way in which they are organized. Moreover, its cognitive content is not identical with the subjective intentions of its author. In the objective product of any subjective expression 'we mean more than we meant to mean.'[47] Both these features – the excess of meaning over subjective intention and the dependence of meaning on form – are addressed in what Adorno variously calls the 'language-character',[48] the 'affinity to language' (*Sprachähnlichkeit*)[49] of works of art, or their character as 'text' (*Schrift*).[50]

This 'language-character' is shared by all works of art, not only those which have language as their medium. The elements of language, morphemes or phonemes and the lexical items which they constitute, are not atoms of fixed meaning which are then simply added up to produce a sum total of meaning, but are variably meaningful, and meaningful only in their relation to other morphemes or phonemes. In an analogous way, Adorno argues, works of art organize elements which have no fixed or essential meaning in themselves into a meaningful relation. They depend on such relations for their eloquence. Adorno gives the example of a subdominant chord which occurs at a critical moment in Beethoven's 'Kreutzer' sonata. The chord itself is entirely unremarkable, yet is extraordinarily powerful at this point in the sonata.[51] Despite the prominence with which this chord appears to stand out from its surrounding context, its significance is only comprehensible in the light of all the previous developments of the sonata (and ultimately, in the light of all the subsequent developments as well). Any attempt to explain the significance of artistic phenomena from an essential force in the materials themselves – such as

Kandinsky's attempt to assign fixed expressive values to particular colours,[52] or Deryck Cooke's attempt to analyse the units of emotional meaning in music,[53] must fail for this reason.

Truth-content and utopia

Clearly, however, the kind of cognitive character which Adorno claims for works of art is very different from what is usually understood by cognition. Although this cognition is 'language-like', it does not, unlike discursive cognition, produce judgements or propositions. Adorno, indeed, describes the authentic work of art as a 'judgementless judgement'.[54] It is for this reason that Adorno believes that works of art are constitutively in need of a philosophical interpretation of their 'truth-content'.[55] This is an idea which can easily be misunderstood. It might be thought that what is being offered is a way of turning the implicit, 'judgement-less' judgement of works of art into an explicit, propositional judgement. Adorno resists this interpretation. When some such timelessly metaphysical message as 'have the courage to be' is read out of Mahler's ninth symphony its truth-content has been betrayed, not captured. The truth-content of works of art, for Adorno, can no more deliver some such invariant message than can philosophy itself. Instead, the truth-content of works of art, like that of philosophy, inheres in the determinate negation of untruth. It cannot be thought of as a kind of kernel which is inside the shell of the work of art and needs to be got out with philosophical nutcrackers. Philosophy is not to solve the riddle of art's truth-content, but to extrapolate what is insoluble in works of art.[56]

In any non-idealist account of truth, Adorno insists, 'the truth-content cannot be something made.' Yet works of art are products. A central question for philosophical aesthetics, then, is this: in what sense can a product be true?[57] 'Of all the paradoxes of art the most inward is that through making alone, the production of particular works specifically formed in themselves, never through an immediate gaze, art hits upon the not-made, truth.'[58] This 'not-made, truth' would only be fully accessible if production for its own sake, the fetishization of labour, were to come to an end. The truth-content in works of art, that is, points towards the possibility of a nature which 'is not yet'; but it can only do this by determinate negation of what actually is. Although the truth-content of all authentic works of art points towards utopia, for Adorno, it can only do so by a configuration of materials which are historical, not timeless, a configuration which each work of art performs in a singular way.

A philosophical aesthetics which simply extracted assurances of a better world to come out of each and every work of art would be in no way preferable to one extracting elevated motifs like 'the conflict of the finite and the infinite'.[59] Works of art do not *assure* us of anything, and certainly not of utopia; instead, they hold open the possibility of new experience which perfected identificatory thinking would liquidate. It is the task of philosophical interpretation, not to read false assurances out of works of art, but to exhibit the way in which they open the possibility of the new by implying determinate criticisms on what is and has been:

> That by virtue of which truth-content is more than is posited by works of art, is their participation [*Methexis*] in history and the determinate critique which they execute on history through their form. What history is in the works, is not made, and history first frees the work of art from mere positing or production: truth-content is not outside history, but is history's crystallization in the works.[60]

Works of art do not create the materials from which they are made, and, accordingly, these materials are not entirely in the service of artistic production. Instead materials are themselves ineliminably historical. They do not have a timeless meaning or effect but are subject to obsolescence, decay and death like anything else historical. What Adorno means by saying that works of art execute a critique on history, then, is not that they must contain an explicit historical content. Rather, works of art exercise their critique through the way in which they configure materials which already contain history sedimented within them. In this way new works of art exercise a 'judgementless judgement' on what has gone before.[61] How this happens in the case of particular musical and literary works is considered in chapter 5 below.

Technique: domination of aesthetic material

Since works of art, then, are not purely image-like, a-rational in the way that identificatory thinking suggests, but are rather themselves a rational refuge for mimesis, they are by no means exempt from the dialectic of enlightenment which affects rationality in general. For this reason, Adorno's theory of the unavoidable need

for the new in artistic production is very different from a Whig
theory of progress in art. It depends not on the idea that works of
art are getting better and better, but on the *irreversible* character of
cognitive, technical and historical development. Such development
is a matter of what breaks down or decays as much as of what new
invention can be mustered. The diminished seventh chord, which
once sounded shockingly dissonant, has now faded to a melo-
dramatic cliché.[62] This is not to say that contemporary works
without diminished sevenths are better than older works with
them, but only that what has befallen this element of musical
language historically cannot be reversed by an act of will. It does
not imply a retrospective devaluation of Beethoven's last piano
sonata, which opens with a diminished seventh chord.[63] Rather,
Adorno suggests that this problem gives the lie to any idea that
classic works of art are automatically easier to understand than
contemporary works; it is easier to *think* we understand them, but
really to understand them involves fracturing the patina of false
familiarity with which they have been glazed.[64] It requires the
historical imagination to hear the diminished seventh chord as if
for the first time. Such imagination can never be a sheer act of will;
it is only possible through attention to the elements with which
such a chord is in relation and through which alone its historical
specificity is given.

Adorno's concept of the new in art is informed by the *Dialectic of
Enlightenment*. The new only becomes new by a determinate
negation of the old; without a relation to what is not new there can
be nothing new at all. It is no less true in art than in philosophy,
therefore, that whatever aims for an entirely fresh start, far from
presenting us with the really new, will involuntarily recapitulate
the old even whilst claiming to be absolutely new.[65]

Art, then, in no way represents a human activity free from the
domination which persists and is concealed in modern rationality
generally. It strives for advancing mastery over its material just as
does scientific rationality. Yet at the same time Adorno argues that
art's domination does not simply replicate, but also offers a
critique of, domination. It does not do this by providing in its
content an explicit imitation of social domination. Such a model
would imply that the form of works of art would be extraneous to
their social significance, and that such significance is primarily to
be read out of the content of works of art – that is, precisely by
ignoring what makes autonomous works of art *art*.

At first the idea that works of art might offer a 'critique' of domination, but without explicitly picturing or referring to domination in their content, appears paradoxical. Yet it should not be difficult to understand if we consider two of Adorno's theses with which we are already familiar. Firstly, art is not simply image-like, but has a cognitive character. Secondly, cognition is not a collection of positive results, for Adorno, but a work of negation; that is, cognition is critical. The work of art knows the society which it lives off and on which it is irreducibly dependent, not by giving us a picture of that society, but by assembling and organizing materials which are not themselves outside society and history but contain historical experience sedimented within themselves.

What is meant by referring to aesthetic 'materials'? Adorno does not think that works of art can simply be divided into a brute material component, on one side, and the artist's labour, on the other. What makes a work of art art is not reducible to the artist's labour alone. Accordingly aesthetic material is not an inert substrate for the transfiguring hand of the artist.[66] Adorno explains that he does not use 'material' synonymously with 'content': 'material is what artists manipulate: everything from words, colours and sounds through to connections of any kind, and all the ways of proceeding with respect to the whole work so far developed, which are presented to the artist. Forms, then, can also become material; material is everything which confronts artists, everything about which they have to decide.'[67] The aesthetic material, it is made clear, is itself mediated through previous artistic labour. Sonata form in its whole complex history is as much an aesthetic material as a single C major triad; and, equally importantly, no C major triad would sound as it does without the history of sonata form. It is central to Adorno's aesthetics just as it is to his theory of cognition in general that there is no pure sensation, no sensation which is utterly immediate and free from conceptuality. Sensation too is cognitively and hence historically mediated, and this is a further reason why any aesthetic theory which depends on a theory of human nature must fail. It is wrong to claim, for example, that the C major triad is naturally heard as harmonious because of its acoustic properties and their effect on 'the' human ear and brain, because both the terms in such a claim are wrongly converted into invariants outside history: 'the' human ear and brain, 'the' C major triad.

It is in this sense then, that aesthetic materials – not as brute matter alone, but also as form and the whole history of its applications – are themselves already historical. This has significant implications for Adorno's account of technique. Just as the materials with which art works are not brute matter, but are already historically and cognitively mediated, so technique, in its turn can no longer be considered as a question of sheer making, construction. Instead, an understanding of how materials are historical, rather than purely natural, materials, is implicit in artistic technique. Technique, that is, is itself cognitive and critical, not purely instrumental craft in the service of the production of a useful, functional or well-proportioned thing. The falsity of the now ubiquitous 'workshops' for the production or assessment of literary work is not that they take the category of technique to be unavoidably central to artistic production – with this Adorno is in complete agreement – but that they turn such technique into a matter of sheer making, the 'craft' of poetry, and neglect the cognitive aspects which make poetry an art rather than a craft.[68] Technique which is indeed artistic technique, rather than sheer instrumental action in the service of an externally posited end, is not merely mastery over nature. Instead it is domination of historically mediated material, a domination which, by its distance from the empirical world, makes a criticism of the real domination of nature which governs that world.

Aesthetics and the critique of nominalism

A materialist aesthetics organized along such lines faces some obvious further difficulties, however. It needs to be shown how the arguments put forward in favour of it are distinctively applicable to art, rather than to any kind of communicative artefact whatsoever. From this kind of perspective Adorno's theory could be taken to rest on an uncritical desire to retain at all costs concepts of art, beauty and the work of art which are no longer defensible. The objection might be made, for example, that there is 'no such thing' as art and no such thing as a work of art. The attempt to distinguish works of art from any other kind of cultural product could be seen as a subjective evaluation masquerading as an objective distinction; and, in some versions of this criticism, as doing so in the service of social elitism. In this light, the difficulty of constructing a materialist aesthetics would simply be that any theory which privileges certain objects as 'art' is already no longer materialist.

As we should expect from Adorno's critique of ostensive definition in general, this difficulty in saying what art is could not be
solved by supplying some check-list of characteristics.[69] Nor could
he find acceptable an attempt to define art with reference to its
origins, not least because he believes that the earliest art, far from
offering us art in its purest form, is the most determined by
inflexible ritual, magical or political contexts and hence the least,
rather than the best, suited to stand as a type of all art.[70] Instead
Adorno's response to such objections is closely parallel to his
defence of the concept of society against sociological nominalism
(chapter 1 above). Like 'society' and 'history', 'art', 'beauty' and
'the work of art', do indeed not unequivocally refer to 'things'. Yet
this does not suffice to liquidate these concepts:

> To ban the concept of the beautiful, as many currents in psychology ban
> the concept of the psyche, and many sociological currents ban the
> concept of society, would be for aesthetics to give up altogether. The
> reason why it is so unfruitful to define aesthetics as the science of the
> beautiful is that the formal character of the concept of beauty cannot
> capture the full content of the aesthetic. If aesthetics were only a
> systematic comparison of whatever is called beautiful, this would give
> no idea of the life in the concept of the beautiful itself . . . The beautiful
> can as little be defined as the concept of it can be dispensed with, a strict
> antinomy. Without categories aesthetics would be invertebrate, a
> historical-relativistic description of whatever here and there in various
> societies or in various styles had been meant by beauty; a formal unity
> distilled from this would become irresistibly self-parodic and would be
> wrecked on the first concrete particular singled out for attention.[71]

The desire of *Aesthetic Theory* to refuse the bad choice between a
science of the beautiful, on the one hand, and a relativistic report
on whatever has been thought beautiful, on the other, makes the
concept of beauty aporetic – subject, that is, to a contradiction
which is a historically necessary rather than a merely accidental
one. A hasty attempt to get out of this aporia, either by defining
beauty in terms of invariant formal characteristics, or by discarding the concept altogether, would destroy the whole field of
Adorno's interest, which is the non-relativistic evaluation of something which has come to be historically.

How can the refusal to write a science of the beautiful not mean
cancelling the project of aesthetic valuation altogether? Adorno
does not think that works of art are self-evidently a distinct kind of
object, nor that aesthetics has an invariant or unchallengeable right
to exist. Indeed, he concedes that everything today about art and

aesthetics is questionable, including whether they are at all possible any longer.[72] But in Adorno's view the attempt to cancel
aesthetics altogether is questionable because it is not historical
enough. Precisely because the concept of the beautiful is not a mere
intellectual error but is itself closely bound up with the dialectic of
enlightenment, 'emancipation from fear', an attempt to cross it out
and start from scratch will only deliver itself more directly to what
it wishes to resist.

The impossibility of liquidating the concept of beauty, even
though it has become culpably abstract, is essential to Adorno's
parallel, and equally aporetic, defence of the concept of art. A
distinction between works of art and other kinds of communicative artefact is feasible because the distinction is not purely
descriptive, but also already evaluative. Adorno thinks that when
we call an artefact 'art' what we are doing is not first of all
classifying it under a descriptive heading, and only later adding
some valuation such as ugly or beautiful, authentic or inauthentic,
progressive or conservative. Instead the concept of art is simultaneously descriptive and evaluative. The difference between works
of art and non-artistic communicative artefacts contains a judgement on those artefacts which fail to become art, which are content
to remain commodities in the culture industry. The category of
'inauthentic works of art' is an empty set for just this reason.[73]

Theory of art and theory of truth

The series of arguments canvassed in this chapter has been at the
centre of much subsequent discussion of Adorno's aesthetic
thought. It is clear that Adorno's notion of the truth-content of
works of art, in particular, is at odds with most forms of post-
idealist aesthetics, which in general regard 'truth' as not really part
of the province of aesthetics at all, and would insist that aesthetics
should limit itself to beauty, or significant form, or expressiveness,
and let epistemology and ethics address truth and goodness
respectively. Even some critics more sympathetic to Adorno's
aesthetic theory, indeed, have wished to reformulate his way of
understanding the truth-content of works of art.

A useful way of thinking about the plausibility of these arguments is to look at the complex and far-reaching reconfiguration of
the central categories of 'truth, semblance and reconciliation' in
Adorno's aesthetic theory proposed by Albrecht Wellmer. Wellmer

suggests that '[i]f one expands communicatively Adorno's concept of rationality, then his truth aesthetics may also be expanded "pragmatically".'[74] Expanding Adorno's concept of rationality 'communicatively' here means reformulating it along the lines of a theory of communicative action. If we were to drop the utopian hope for a reconciliation of culture and nature in favour of the idea of a reconciliation between subjects, Wellmer suggests, Adorno's notion of the truth-content of art could be interpreted by understanding art as a form of communicative action. For Wellmer, such an expansion would serve some useful purposes in cultural politics. It is a weakness of Adorno's thought, on his account, that Adorno 'denied to modern society that which he ascribed to modern art: the ability of enlightenment to emancipate a potential "expansion of subjective limits" . . . as well as a potential for reification'.[75] Wellmer argues that aesthetic modernism is important primarily because it offers the potential for a form of communicative action 'incorporating diffuse, non-integrated, senseless and excluded material into a space of domination-free communication'.[76] From such a perspective, he suggests, we could also begin to reassess Adorno's pessimistic assessment of mass culture and to take up with Benjamin's more optimistic view of its social and psychological effects.[77]

At the same time, such a language-pragmatic reformulation is philosophically necessary, Wellmer insists, because Adorno's concept of the truth-content of works of art is inoperable in any strict sense. Wellmer argues that there is a slippage in Adorno's account of art between a utopian notion of the truth-content of art as such, art's intimation of a reconciliation between culture and nature, on the one hand, and the truth-content of particular works of art, on the other. This is why Adorno is forced to 'conceive of aesthetic knowledge as philosophical insight and the truth of art as philosophical truth'.[78] The result is that Adorno, who begins, Wellmer suggests, with a complex notion of the truth of art which preserves an interplay between apophantic truth, endeetic truth (truthfulness or authenticity) and moral-practical truth, finally grants supremacy to apophantic truth. A language-pragmatic reformulation of the notion of aesthetic truth, Wellmer suggests, would be able to drop the identification between the truth-content of works of art and their relation to reconciliation; instead it would need to grant a new prominence to the reception of works of art by understanding the truth-content of works of art not as 'truth in the literal sense of the word' but rather as a 'truth *potential*: . . . the epitome of their potential for *disclosing* truth'.[79] It is this disclosive capacity of works of art which misleads us into literally applying the concept of truth to them. Instead, Wellmer concludes,' "truth" can only be ascribed to art metaphorically.'[80] Neither apophantic truth nor endeetic truthfulness may be literally attributed to art. Instead, talk about the truth of art 'may only be explained by appeal to the complex interdependence of the various dimensions of truth in life-historical experience': the three senses of 'a pragmatically differentiated everyday concept of truth' – apophantic, endeetic and moral-practical truth – are literally applicable only to the experience of the work of art, as the experience of 'a symbolic construct with an aesthetic validity claim'.[81]

Wellmer's objections are significant because they must bring into focus not merely Adorno's theory of the truth-content of the work of art, but also his theory of truth in general. It is not difficult to show that his reformulation cannot be implemented without greatly changing the character of the whole project of *Aesthetic Theory*: what most obviously goes missing when Wellmer replaces the idea of a reconciliation of culture and nature with inter-subjective communication is the materialist attempt to articulate a 'priority of the object in art' and the concomitant insistence on artworks as objective spirit, the idea that works of art are not wholly interpretable as a form of communicative action because they are both 'less than praxis, and more' (cf. chapter 5 below); hence Wellmer's emphasis on reception. It will also be suggested later that Wellmer's account of some of the broader difficulties in Adorno's thought is not decisive: in particular, that Adorno's thought cannot adequately be understood as a 'negative theology'[82] and that it does not ignore the emancipatory aspect of the development of modern subjectivity.

But since Wellmer does not set store by orthodoxy, these are hardly decisive responses. The critical issue at this point is the question of the truth-content of works of art itself and whether Wellmer is correct in insisting that ' "truth" can only be ascribed to art metaphorically.' An emphatic opposition between the figural and the literal structures Wellmer's reformulation of the concept of truth in art. Wellmer does not interrogate it, yet it is allowed to decide in advance the issue which is at stake, because it recapit-ulates, in the terms of an analysis of discourse, a perfected separa-tion between concept and intuition which would, on Adorno's account, make truth of any kind impossible. Pure literalness is a chimera, for Adorno, and the force of the objection that works of art cannot literally be understood as true is consequently not clear when applied to his aesthetic theory, since Adorno does not even think that 'A = A' can 'literally' be understood as true. This is not because Adorno somehow thinks in sub-deconstructionist fashion that all concepts can be reduced to metaphors, but because of his account of the constitutive incompleteness of purely analytic judgements, and of an affinity between concept and object as the condition of the possibility of truth (cf. chapter 6 below). These arguments are central to the issue at hand because in Adorno's view it is only with their help that an aesthetic theory can be formulated which can remobilize the radical separations between beauty and truth, art and cognition in post-Kantian aesthetics. Wellmer also wants to avoid any radical separation of this kind – this is why he wishes to make clear how his case differs from Bubner's attempt to set up Kant's concept of the beautiful against any aesthetics of truth[83] – by arguing that the aesthetic validity of works of art is bound up with their disclosive power in a way which structurally, rather than merely accidentally, leads us to attribute truth and falsehood to works of art. Wellmer's reformulation would like, not to sever this connection utterly, but to restrict it to a metaphorical and not a literal application. But once this latter opposition itself is allowed to remain uninterrogated, we are left with a separation between beauty and truth which is to be externally bridged by a figural notion of aesthetic truth or 'truth-potential'.

The argument between Adorno and Wellmer over the truth of art, then, is as much an argument about what truth is as about what art is. Wellmer's theory of truth is less equivocally ex-pounded than Adorno's. Like Habermas, Wellmer wishes to work with an intersubjective theory of truth whose apophantic, endeetic and moral-practical moments are understood as differentiated but necessarily interrelated. Adorno, on the other hand, nowhere gives a summary statement of his theory of truth. Here we need to set aside for a moment the obvious point that Adorno's theory of truth is aporetic and therefore testifies optatively to the truth which we could have under certain conditions rather than to truth of which he is now in secure possession. What 'would' truth be like, if this optative claim is to have any sense? It will be seen later at more length what it would not be like, why Adorno rejects – as not wholly adequate rather than as sheer error – some prevalent theories of truth, such as correspondence theories and coherence theories. He rejects these in part for reasons not dissimilar from

Wellmer's. Instead Adorno wants a theory of a complex truth in which apophantic, endeetic and moral-practical moments would form not a hierarchy but a constellation. Any theory of truth grounded in intersubjective communication, by contrast, produces an internal hierarchy within the concept of truth, in which the notion of truth to the object or the matter itself (*die Sache selbst*) – a truth which Adorno wants to understand endeetically and practically as well as apophantically – would be subordinate to undistorted intersubjective communication. This is not to replace an intersubjective theory of truth with a correspondence theory, but to insist that a theory *grounded* in intersubjectivity cannot sustain the constellated relation between the various 'everyday' senses of truth for which it wishes. For Adorno, indeed, any grounding of truth in an appeal to the 'everyday' would be dogmatic in the same sense as the dictum which he so often repudiates: that the truth cannot run away from us. The truth very well can run away from us, for Adorno, not least because its apophantic, endeetic and practical moments are inextricably entangled with each other. No theory of truth is intelligible for Adorno in which we allow for two or more *radically* separate kinds of truth.[84] Hence the inflexibility of his aporetic insistence that truth is conditional upon a reconciled – which is not necessarily to say a transparent – society; and upon a reconciliation between subject and object – which is by no means to say their undifferentiated unity. Adorno's whole *oeuvre* would testify to, but could not exhaust, nor state with pure literalness, this idea of truth as reconciliation. In the following pages we must turn to consider in more detail how Adorno justifies his claim that works of art themselves testify to the possibility of a reconciled society.

'Illusory character' and 'fetish-character'

It might at times have appeared in the course of this argument as though the central aim of Adorno's aesthetic theory is to defend the categories of traditional aesthetics – in however qualified a form – against those critics who, whether on epistemological or on sociological grounds, would like to eliminate them. Adorno's defence of these categories, however, is not intended to suggest that art has no ideologically questionable moments whatever. His point is that simply discarding these categories will make it more difficult, not easier, to grasp and criticize art's ideological character.

We need to investigate how Adorno understands the relationship between art's ideological character and its truth-content.

Adorno admits that the work of art's implicit claim to be more than a mere thing is an illusion. Yet this illusion has both false and potentially true aspects. It is false because works of art clearly are, at least, things and would be nothing at all without this thing-like character above which they set themselves. Yet '[a]rt has truth as the illusion of the illusionless.'[85] What makes a work of art more than the empirical world from which it distinguishes itself is something non-existent: 'that works of art are there, however, points to the possibility that the non-existent could exist.'[86]

These rather paradoxical formulations indicate why aesthetics is of such central importance to Adorno's particular kind of materialism. The connection may become clearer if we consider it in the light of Adorno's theory of essence and appearance. The work of art claims to be not a mere thing but something in-itself, an essence. This claim is an illusion because 'essence must appear.'[87] Yet, unlike Nietzsche and unlike the positivists, Adorno does not think that the category of essence can therefore be liquidated. Indeed, materialist thought cannot do without it. If we were to collapse everything there is into mere appearance, if it is in principle impossible to know the object as it really is in itself, materialist thinking would be impossible. For Adorno, therefore, the thing as it is in itself is not merely a metaphysical chimera, but something to which there cannot yet be any immediate access; it would be knowable only if our experience were to change (the detailed justifications for this argument are explained in chapter 8).

This is what Adorno means by saying that art is the illusion of the illusionless. The work of art is the illusion of a thing in itself which would not merely be for consciousness – the illusion of what is beyond the subject, the illusion of what he elsewhere calls 'the non-identical' (chapter 6). The work of art's claim to be a realized in-itself is illusory, but no state beyond illusion has yet been reached: 'no correct consciousness' has ever yet existed.[88] Because of this, the illusion cannot simply be dispelled. The standpoint of a sober materialism from which art's illusion could be dispelled right now is not available, because thinking itself as yet remains ineliminably entangled with idealism. Instead, Adorno suggests that art's illusory character is to be 'redeemed' or rescued. Adorno's own philosophical interpretations of works of art aim at such a redemption of art's illusion, through an interpretation of art's historical truth-content. It is only on the basis of a redemption, rather than a liquidation, of such illusion that it becomes possible to imagine freedom from illusion – to think as a materialist, at all.

The links to Adorno's revised theory of ideology (chapter 2) should be clear. Under high capitalism, the characteristic form of ideology was a faith in illusory universals. But in late capitalism the most worrying prospect is that the very idea that our social experience could change will be lost altogether. In these circumstances the attempt to dispel all illusion may merely serve the idea that the real is absolute: that what is cannot, and therefore should not, change. Accordingly, for Adorno, the most pressing task is not so much the dissolution of illusion as a redemptive critique of art's entanglement with social experience.[89] It is important to recognize that this entanglement cannot be regarded as necessarily ideological. It may be an index of art's truth-content as much as of its ideological status, because works of art are not only precipitates of natural-historical experience but are also cognitive, attempts to know and to criticize that experience.

Accordingly, the claim on the part of the artwork to be more than a mere thing, what Adorno calls its illusory character or its 'fetish-character',[90] is not merely an idol in need of shattering. From the perspective of the *Dialectic of Enlightenment*, to take this view would be to perpetuate the process whereby enlightenment against its own best intentions turns into mythology. Instead Adorno emphasizes the distinction between this fetish-character of art and the literal fetishism of a cultic object.[91] Works of art are themselves made possible, for Adorno, by the dialectic of enlightenment. They are a rational refuge for mimesis in a world in which the mimetic impulse of thinking is progressively suppressed in classificatory thinking. Whereas the cultic value of a real fetish is dependent on its heteronomy, its inflexible insertion in a context of magical or ritual function, the fetish-character of art lies in its claim to autonomy – its illusory claim to be a being in and for itself, governed by its own law rather than by a law outside it. Talk about 'the magic of art' sounds crass precisely because it misses this fundamental distinction between literal magical fetishism and the 'fetishism' of the autonomous work of art. 'Ihr Zauber ist Entzauberung': 'the magic of works of art is a disenchantment.'[92]

The progressive deepening of art's claim to autonomy, then, is not to be considered in isolation and then unequivocally celebrated or lamented, because it brings both losses and gains to art. On the one hand, it heightens the illusion of art's independence; yet on the other, it is this illusory being-in-itself which makes possible the thought of real freedom from naked coercion, total dependence. The problem follows from the more general problem of the way in which rationality is entangled with domination (chapter 1). The entanglement is not to be dissolved, say on the grounds that domination would then 'at least be honest'. Rather, only at the price of rationality's partial concealment of domination can freedom from domination be imagined at all. In a similar way, art's claim to autonomy is to be made good rather than got rid of.

The absolute commodity

This is the context for Adorno's account of the work of art as a 'fetish against commodity fetishism'.[93] The work of art is an object which makes an illusory claim not merely to be valuable as a for-another but also as something in itself. In the language of Kantian ethics, it claims a dignity rather than merely a price.[94] It is the fact that this claim is illusory which allows Adorno to describe it as art's 'fetish-character'. But this illusory in-itself makes a true criticism of the advancing conversion of everything to a for-another, that is, the advance towards a situation in which things only have substance and value in so far as they can be exchanged with something else. In late capitalism everything, living human activity included, is increasingly so determined by valuation for-another (exchange-value) that its value in and for itself tends to disappear. By persisting with its illusory claim to a non-exchangeable dignity, art resists the notion that the qualitatively incommensurable can be made quantitatively commensurable.

For Adorno this fact is of determining importance in understanding the shift in modern aesthetic practice away from direct reference, representation or communication, whether in the rise of anti-figurative practices in the visual arts, of hermeneutic difficulty in literary texts, or the emancipation of dissonance in twentieth-century music.[95] The more it is insisted that nothing is worth anything in itself but only as it can be valued against something else, the more works of art, in desperate defence of their illusory non-exchangeable character, refuse immediate access to their consumers. They obstruct communication, that is, precisely as a way of communicating a criticism of the idea that all value must be communicable.[96]

Yet the idea of art as a 'fetish against commodity fetishism' is still more paradoxical even than it appears at first sight, because art is only able to claim autonomy as a result of its own commodity character.[97] It is the commodification of culture which frees works of art from serving some immediate function. A work of art which must serve some particular and inflexible political or ritual context has its law given to it from outside; that is, it is 'heteronomous'. Only when artistic labour and artworks themselves become freely alienable does the possibility even arise that the work of art might be autotelic, an end in itself.

The 'fetish against commodity fetishism', then, does not criticize commodity fetishism by being *less* fetishized and accordingly less illusory than the fetishized commodity, but by being *more* fetishized. This is the sense in which Adorno speaks, hyperbolically, of the work of art as 'the absolute commodity'.[98] In commodity fetishism, it will be remembered, relations between people appear as though they were the property of a thing, the commodity (cf. chapter 2). Production which takes place within this relation of production – the commodity form – tends to become, in Adorno's view, the production of exchange value for its own sake. Yet despite this tendency commodities perpetuate the illusion that they exist only to satisfy need, that they are use-values. The 'absolute commodity', on the other hand, would be 'that social product which has utterly thrown off that illusion of being-for-society which commodities otherwise desperately keep alive'.[99] The work of art, as the 'absolute commodity', openly exposes, rather than desperately concealing, its own character as surplus labour, production for no need at all, for its own sake. In consequence it 'would be free of the ideology which inhabits the commodity form, which claims to be a "for-other" whilst it is ironically a mere "for-itself".'[100]

Yet if the autonomous work of art is free of this particular kind of ideology, it is by no means free of ideology as such. As the 'absolute commodity' the work of art cannot escape the antagonism between the forces and relations of production which governs capitalist production.[101] Accordingly artisanal models of artistic production, in which the work of art is taken to represent a free or unalienated unfolding of productive forces which are alienated in capitalist production, cannot provide a theory of the production of modern art.[102] The artisanal model presents artistic production as production for true need in a world of false needs; but no theory of true needs is yet possible (chapter 2).

Authentic art questions any dogmatic distinction between true and false needs. Instead it implicitly indicts the production of exchange-value for its own sake, by deliberately exposing its own fetish-character. Even the 'absolute commodity', the image of that which would be fetishized to the point of non-exchangeability, has remained saleable in practice. The sale and purchase of works of art is not an external violation of something which should be untouchable but is 'a simple concomitant of their part in the relations of production', of their fetishism. 'It is absolutely impossible for art to be non-ideological through and through',[103] as a consequence, because this fetish-character is constitutive of what art is. Accordingly, this fetish-character itself cannot simply be deleted to provide aesthetics with a remnant which would be its truth-content: 'ideology and truth in art are not like sheep and goats. Art cannot have the one without the other . . .'[104] Art's truth-content is accessible only by interpreting art's illusory character, not by abruptly deleting or 'demystifying' that illusory character.

Autonomy and heteronomy in art

From any perspective informed by a dialectic of enlightenment, of course, the claim of modern art to be autonomous cannot represent unambiguous progress. It is instructive to consider the distinction between autonomous and heteronomous art in the light of the closely related distinction made by Hegel between Greek ('classical') art and post-Greek ('romantic') art. For Hegel the transition from the first to the second can be seen both as an emancipation and as an impoverishment of art. It is an emancipation in the sense that the subject matter and its manner may be autonomously chosen: art acquires an 'infinitely subjective'[105] aspect by this, both in the range of matters it can address and in the reflexive self-consciousness of its treatment of them.[106] Yet Hegel can also refer to this transition as 'the decay and dissolution of art itself'.[107] Just what makes the romantic work of art autonomous – the free alienability of artistic labour and of the work of art – is also what deprives it, in Hegel's view, of the classical artwork's formative cultural and political significance.[108]

Many of the features of Hegel's contrast between the 'classical' and the 'romantic' work of art reappear in Adorno's account of the distinction between heteronomy and autonomy in the work of art. For Adorno the critical transition is less that from classical Greek to

Christian and modern art than that from feudalism to capitalism.
Adorno too sees losses rather than merely gains in the rise of
autonomous art: it is a 'Pyrrhic victory'.[109] The idea of autonomy is
not simple, but necessarily internally contradictory. The work of
art's claim to autonomy depends upon a heteronomous element:
'the autonomy of the work of art originates in heteronomy, just as
the freedom of the subject originates in the sovereignty of the
master.'[110] This means that the concepts of heteronomy and autonomy in art cannot be applied as a kind of classificatory schema,
with a date setting the border between the two categories. Rather
Adorno's focus is on a process of autonomization of the work of
art. If this process were completed, it would in fact be the death of
art. As Adorno remarks in his essay on Zemlinsky, 'Art which had
removed every trace of what is not art, would scarcely continue to
be art.'[111]

Art and political practice

Much of the reception of Adorno's aesthetic theory has focused on
his view of the relationship between works of art and political
practice. Unlike some Marxist aestheticians and artists, Adorno
does not take an optimistic view of the possibility of deploying
artworks as an instrument in the service of social justice. The aim
of critical theory is to bring to an end the primacy of instrumental
reason – reason used as a tool without regard for the specific
qualities of the object. If we regard practice as the first or founda-
tional consideration, then that instrumentality which critical theory
wants to bring to an end is actually installed as a transhistorical
invariant.

Adorno suggests, instead, that works of art, rather than being
instrumental 'interventions', offer a criticism of instrumental reason and action as such. In so far as art is autonomous, it does not
criticize some particular good or bad action, as though actions
could be weighed outside their increasingly total context, but the
whole framework within which practice takes place. Accordingly,
works of art cannot simply be pressed into the service of a just
practice, because what they criticize is the depracticalization of
practice itself. Once works of art are pressed into the service of
some higher end, they immediately lose their autonomous character. As sheer instruments they could no longer offer a critique of
instrumental reason. Modern works of art are products without an

obvious purpose, in a world where everything is presented as existing not for its own sake but for the sake of something else. They thus point to the fact that production is becoming the production of exchange-value for its own sake.

Adorno does not pretend, however, that the work of art can actually stand in some politically disinterested realm outside society. Instead Adorno understands art as 'the social antithesis to society'.[112] All art has a political significance, whether it explicitly thematizes such significance or not. Adorno's critique of the idea of political commitment in art does not attempt to specify art's job description, to insist that art should not dirty its hands with politics. Instead, Adorno's critique of politically committed art is, in part, a political one. The danger for politically committed art is that it will end up as bad art without becoming good politics either.

Adorno illustrates this through a discussion of Brecht's play *The Resistible Rise of Arturo Ui*.[113] In the play Chicago gangsterism is used as an allegory of the rise of the Third Reich. Adorno points out that both terms of the comparison are diminished by this procedure. On the one hand, the world of gangland Chicago becomes an empty cipher for the real political content, an attack on the Third Reich. Still more seriously, however, the use of Chicago gangsterism as a metaphor for Nazism is quite inadequate because it grotesquely underestimates the systematic power and qualitative novelty of Nazism. The work is as useless towards any just practice as any other piece of weak theory would be. It represents the literary equivalent of arguments that fascism is doomed to collapse because it is against the real interests of the workers.

It is no part of Adorno's argument to insist that work produced with the intention of influencing political practice can never be good art; here as elsewhere, the producer's intention is by no means the decisive criterion. (Adorno, indeed, on several occasions pays tribute to what he takes to be the aesthetic and critical merits of aspects of Brecht's work.)[114] The decisive fact is not what the author, painter or composer wishes to use the work for, but what happens in the work itself. Adorno is not, then, opposing a purely contemplative notion of the work of art to the instrumental use of art which he wishes to criticize. Indeed, he argues that 'the more thoroughly works of art are deciphered, the less absolute can their opposition to praxis remain.'[115] Works of art, Adorno suggests, 'are less than practice, and more'.[116] They are 'less' than practice because, like theory, they put off a practice which 'cannot wait', and are no less compromised by this than is theory itself (chapter 7). But they are 'more' than practice because they criticize the whole framework within which practice takes place, the absolutization of production for its own sake: 'the critique carried out by works of art is a critique of activity as the cryptogram of domination.'[117]

Adorno argues that only works of art which do not cancel out their own autonomous character in the service of some political end can in fact be authentically critical. He gives the example of how works of art relate to the experience of monopoly capitalism. The decisive experience of monopoly capitalism is a *loss* of individual experience; the experience of one's own life as utterly contingent, dispensable, and having significance not in itself, but only as it is a means to something else (chapter 2). Naturalist art, Adorno believes, has become inauthentic in late capitalism, because it treats as straightforwardly and unambiguously concrete a social experience which is itself deeply ideologically pre-formed and increasingly abstract, emptied of content. The 'reality' which naturalism would imitate is not reality *tout court*, but is entangled in a social context which is a real illusion.

Modern art, by contrast, has become abstract because it senses the need to imitate this loss of experience. 'In Kafka's work monopoly capitalism appears only in the background; yet it codifies in the flotsam of the administered world what human beings have experienced under the total social spell, more faithfully and more powerfully than novels about corrupt industrial trusts.'[118] Authentic modernist art does more justice to the 'loss of experience' under late capitalism by renouncing an attempt to replicate experience. It is still a kind of mimesis, Adorno argues; but it is mimesis of the systematic framework which impoverishes experience, not a mimesis of individual impoverished experience which misrepresents such experience as though it were immediate and untouched after all.

> Modern art is as abstract as the relations between people have in truth become . . . Since the spell of external reality over the subjects and their mode of behaviour has become absolute, the work of art can only oppose it by making itself like that spell. At the point of absolute zero, however, at which Beckett's prose exists, a second world of images is produced, as sad as it is rich, the precipitate of historical experiences which in their immediate form would be unable to impinge on what is decisive, the hollowing out of the subject and of reality. The poverty and damagedness of this world of images is an imprint, a photographic negative of the administered world. To this extent Beckett is a realist.[119]

For Adorno, then, the reproach that modernists are 'formalists', excessively preoccupied with style and technique and uninterested in human experience, misses the point, because it simply posits the richness of 'experience' as a given without considering what has become of such experience. Equally, Adorno argues that 'Kafka's epic style is, in its archaism, mimesis of reification.'[120] Authentic modernist art is not formalism, but a realism of the loss of experience.

This kind of defence of autonomous art as socially critical, then, distinguishes Adorno's approach from any aestheticist appeal to art as inviolably or absolutely autotelic – *l'art pour l'art* (art for art's sake). Adorno does not recommend to works of art that they 'ought' to become autonomous, but interprets the autonomization of the work of art as a historical process which cannot be wished out of existence. Autonomy depends on a heteronomous moment for its very possibility. As soon as art attempts to cut out this heteronomous moment entirely, it also liquidates the conditions for its own autonomous, critical relation to the empirical world. It loses its character as art altogether and shrinks to ornament, to a mere thing. The paradox of the work of art's autonomy is that it can be preserved only in so far as it is not made absolute.[121] In the following chapter we shall see how Adorno understands the socially critical character of modern music and literature as depending upon art's precarious autonomy.

5

Truth-Content in Music and Literature

Introduction

One obvious objection to the theory of art so far put forward is that it is just that: a theory of 'art' in general which operates at too general a level to furnish a theory of any particular art. Adorno resists any attempt to provide summary definitions for, say, music, visual art or literature, whether based on some functionalist attempt to specify their limits or the nature of their materials, or, still more questionably, on the historical 'origins' of the various arts, and regards this kind of attempt at instant definition as both doomed and tedious.

Yet although Adorno is deeply concerned to defend the concept of art against nominalist attacks on it, he is not blind to the qualitative differences between the different arts. Adorno does not think, however, that the relation between the concept of art and those of the individual arts can be discussed in isolation from what has happened to art itself and to works of art themselves. In an essay on 'Art and the Arts' he discusses this question from the standpoint of the collapsing of generic boundaries in contemporary art: in Bussotti's 'graphic scores' which are visual as well as musical artworks, or in the influence of the techniques of serial music on the literary works of Hans G. Helms.[1]

Adorno argues that a 'dialectic of spiritualization [or 'intellectualization': *Vergeistigung*]' is at work in autonomous art.[2] The more art strives for autonomy from sheer heteronomous function, the more it insists on mastery over the material of which it makes use. Accordingly such material – in which the difference between the various arts is often located by naturalist or functionalist theories of their radical mutual incompatibility – comes increasingly to be regarded as a vehicle for the artist's purpose. In Wagner's idea of a 'total work of art', for example, the various arts are to be placed in the service of the artist's unified conception. Any idea that there might be separate procedures appropriate to the individual arts, and which the artist is not at liberty to coerce into unity, is set aside, in favour of the immanent demands of the unified work itself.[3] Yet when such 'spiritualization' is followed through to its conclusion, 'that which wanted to spiritualize [*vergeistigen*] the material, terminates in naked material as something merely existent . . .'[4] Total spiritualization of the work of art is not possible, because once it dispenses with all objectification, the work of art can no longer distinguish itself from any other empirical stimulus, is no longer a 'work'.[5]

It is in the context of this 'dialectic of spiritualization' that the relationship between 'art' and the individual arts needs to be understood. The weight given to the concept of 'art' is not merely a professional mystification of aestheticians, because it is entangled with this real historical process. The more autonomous works of art insist on free mastery over material, the less absolutely can boundaries between arts which are primarily defined with reference to such material means be insisted upon. 'Art' cannot simply be taken as a classificatory cover-concept for the individual arts, both because its force is evaluative as well as descriptive (chapter 4), and because it is indissociable from the historical dialectic of spiritualization in art. It is a condition of the possibility of interpreting art philosophically today that 'art' cannot simply be collapsed into the sum total of the various arts.

Yet, as we saw, Adorno also believes that art which seeks to present its autonomy as absolute will in the event lose its autonomy, its character as art, altogether. Authentic modern art, Adorno believes, has sensed the impossibility of Wagner's project of the *Gesamtkunstwerk*: with the total work of art, art hopes to lift itself by an act of will out of a division of labour which governs artistic no less than intellectual or any other kind of production. It may thereby fall victim to just the same charges of dilettantism as scientific work which arbitrarily forces divided intellectual labour togther (chapter 6).[6] Adorno emphasizes the difference between the 'fraying' (*Verfransung*) of generic boundaries in contemporary art and Wagner's 'total work of art': in authentic instances of the former this process 'emerges immanently, from the genre itself'.[7]

Consequently it would be no more satisfactory simply to submerge the concepts of the individual arts in 'art' than it would be to liquidate the concept of art altogether. Although in *Aesthetic Theory* Adorno is chiefly preoccupied with what the arts share, in much of his other work he pays as much attention to the categories of 'music' or 'literature' as to 'art'.

Music and the concept

Adorno's engagement with music is of particular importance to his work. By the time of his early philosophical manifestoes Adorno was already the author of a substantial body of music criticism, not only of the new music produced by the composers of the so-called second Viennese school, Schoenberg, Berg and Webern, but also a range of other contemporary composers, such as Bartok, Krenek and Hindemith.[8] This early work already indicates much of Adorno's later trajectory as a music critic and philosopher of music. The primary difficulty faced by aesthetics could be seen with especial clarity in the case of criticism of contemporary music. The legitimation of avant-garde music through detailed musical analysis often relied on unelaborated or formalistic aesthetic presuppositions, so that the genuine newness of the work had not been matched by a comparably advanced aesthetics.

It is impossible in an account of this size to do justice to the breadth and complexity of Adorno's music criticism.[9] What this section of the book will attempt to do instead is to give an account of its basic premises and to examine in more detail several of Adorno's most important engagements with music. The premises of Adorno's music criticism are unfamiliar in musicology and often discourage those who might otherwise be attracted to Adorno's musicological thought. Although it is possible to give an account of the philosophical premises of Adorno's music criticism, it is not possible to use such an account to yield a universally applicable method for musicology. A method which did not alter with its subject matter would, for Adorno, already have made itself dogmatic.[10] Adorno is a philosophical critic of music rather than a methodologist of musicology.

One consequence of Adorno's insistence that works of art have a cognitive content is that he can use the entire spectrum of philosophical terminology usually reserved to discursive cognition as a way of describing elements of works of art themselves. For many kinds of philosophical aesthetics 'subject', 'object', 'dialectic' or 'antinomy' would be terms which could only be appropriate as a way of formulating the categories and criteria of aesthetics itself, not as a way of describing works of art. For Adorno, any such radical separation between the method of cognition or judgement and what is to be known or judged is already dogmatic. Because works of art are not just the objects of our knowledge but are themselves attempts to know, philosophical terminology cannot be restricted to the sphere of discursive cognition. The separation of art from discursive cognition is a real but not perfected historical process. Because it is not perfected, the cognitive moment in works of art is still open to philosophical interpretation. Yet because it is real, such interpretation must first of all recognize the gulf between what its categories might mean in discursive cognition and what they might mean when applied to works of art themselves.

Music – constitutively distanced from explicit discourse and direct representation alike, to an extent which is true neither of literature nor of visual art – raises the most testing questions for an account of art preoccupied with its cognitive moment. Adorno's music criticism perplexes many musicologists because of the frequency with which epistemological, logical and metaphysical terms are applied directly to particular musical works or to individual aspects of them. More provocatively still, whole musical *oeuvres* are compared to whole philosophical authorships. In the notes left for his unfinished study of *Beethoven* Adorno again and again discusses Beethoven as a musical Hegel;[11] formulations in his monograph on *Mahler*, meanwhile, often anticipate *verbatim* Adorno's own philosophical positions in *Negative Dialectics*.[12] This practice can offend professional philosophers and musicologists alike because it looks like a category-mistake: to philosophers like an aestheticization of reason and to musicologists like a violation of the autonomy of music.[13] However, it should be less surprising in view of Adorno's theory about the language-character of works of art.

In a short but important fragment, 'Music and Language', Adorno attempted to specify the language-character of music:

> Music resembles language in that it is a temporal sequence of articulated sounds which are more than just sounds. They say something, often something human. The better the music, the more forcefully they say it. The succession of sounds is like logic: it can be right or wrong. But what

has been said cannot be detached from the music. Music creates no semiotic system.[14]

Talk of musical 'idiom' or 'vocabulary' is more than simply metaphorical, in Adorno's view. Atonal music problematizes this affinity between music and language because it rejects the 'recurring ciphers' of tonality. This is one reason why complaints about atonal music are often couched as complaints about its language – that 'I don't understand it' or 'it doesn't mean anything to me'. Yet despite the resemblance of music and language, no semantic 'content' can be paraphrased from a musical work.

If Adorno agrees that 'music creates no semiotic system', however, he nevertheless has reservations about any insistence that 'concepts are foreign to music.' Indeed, he believes that 'the succession of sounds is like logic: it can be right or wrong.'[15] In what way are musical compositions 'like logic'? Adorno argues that the 'recurring ciphers' established by tonality – 'chords which constantly reappear with an identical function, well-established sequences such as cadential progressions, and in many cases even stock melodic figures which are associated with the harmony', for example – have an affinity with the basic concepts of epistemology.[16] The affinity of such recurring ciphers to concepts lies above all in the way in which they relate to what does not recur. They organize and shape less familiar material, yet their own force and significance is not identical wherever they appear, but rather itself determined by the particular context. Adorno believes that a closely related pattern is at work in philosophical compositions. The basic concepts of epistemology are supposed to ground and organize a philosophical argument, yet, similarly, the significance of any fundamental concept is never unitary but dependent on its context, on its place in a philosophical text.

In *Negative Dialectics*, a work which in general renounces discussion of aesthetic topics, Adorno indicates how seriously he takes this affinity between philosophy and music:

> In philosophy, an experience which Schönberg noted in traditional music theory is confirmed: one really learns from it only how a movement begins and ends, nothing about the movement itself, its course. Analogously philosophy would need first, not to arrive at a series of categories, but, in a certain sense, to compose itself. It must tirelessly renew itself as it proceeds, out of its own strength as well as through its friction with what it measures itself against; it is what happens in philosophy that is decisive, not a thesis or a position; its fabric, not the single-track train of thought, whether deductive or inductive. For this reason it is essential to

philosophy that it is not summarizable. If it were, it would be super-
fluous.[17]

Adorno does not identify philosophy with music. He was given to
reminding himself of Horkheimer's warning: 'But philosophy
shouldn't be a symphony.'[18] Yet the connection is more than a stray
metaphor. This passage makes it clear that Adorno believes there is
a very important affinity between the two. The affinity can be
approached through the fact that both are non-summarizable.
Criticism of philosophical texts often proceeds by extracting for
discussion what are taken to be the founding arguments in them,
in the belief that everything else follows from these. Adorno argues
that such a procedure is no more adequate to understanding a
philosophical text than an attempt to interpret a musical composition by summarizing the key-changes in it. Both philosophy and
music have a constitutive internal organization, whose articulation
is as essential to the meaning of a philosophical text or musical
composition as the individual propositions or thematic elements
without which there would be no composition at all. Adorno's
philosophical terms are never given their meaning by ostensive
definition alone, but more emphatically through their places and
relations within philosophical compositions.[19]
    Accordingly, individual musical elements cannot simply be
mapped on to individual philosophical motifs or arguments in
advance. Instead the philosophical interpretation of musical works
must be conducted on the level of whole philosophical compositions and authorships, and of whole musical works and *oeuvres*. It
is a minimal condition of understanding individual passages that
this compositional dimension is continually borne in mind, no less
than it is true that without the individual elements there could be
no composition whatever.

Musical and philosophical composition

A closer idea of the implications of these arguments for Adorno's
music criticism can be arrived at by looking at one quite detailed
instance of Adorno's account of the philosophy in music: his
confrontation of Beethoven's use of sonata form with Hegelian
dialectic, a confrontation which Adorno insisted would need to be
'no analogy, but the matter itself',[20] or, as he put it in the last of his
Three Studies on Hegel, 'an analogue which goes beyond mere

analogy'.[21] For Adorno 'the history of music at least since Haydn is the history of fungibility: that nothing individual is "in itself" and that everything only is in relation to the whole.'[22] Increasingly, all motivic-thematic material must not be merely recapitulated, but worked on and developed, a demand which is strikingly exemplified in Beethoven's relentless breaking-down and reworking of thematic material. This demand places its own strain on the recapitulation section of sonata form, however: that is, on that section of the sonata form which is to bring such development back into a unity. The more extensive the reworking of motivic material in development, the less convincing is a straightforward reprise of such material in its first, undeveloped, state. Accordingly, Beethoven increasingly begins to carry out development in recapitulation sections too, and greatly to expand his codas both in extent and significance.[23]

Adorno takes the aim of such manoeuvres to be a coercionless relationship between individual motifs and the form of the whole: the hope, in Adorno's view, is that the whole form could be developed out of the impulses inherent in the individual motifs themselves, rather than externally imposed on them.[24] The recapitulation section of sonata form is a point of such difficulty because at such moments it tends to become clear that the unity of the whole form can never be entirely without a moment of coercion, that sonata form remains to some extent externally imposed on the motivic-thematic material.

Adorno believes that there is a deep affinity between Beethoven's approach to sonata form and Hegel's to dialectic.[25] The fungibility of all individual thematic elements in autonomous music is compared to Hegel's refusal to allow an external limit to be set to thought, his refusal to allow a being which cannot be thought. Just as all themes must be developed in Beethoven, so all supposedly brute individual facts must be shown to be entangled in thinking for Hegel. The insistence that all thematic material must be worked on and developed is compared to Hegel's emphasis on 'the labour of the concept': the more so because, as with the labour of the concept, such musical development aims not externally to impose 'form' upon 'material' but to grow out of the way in which development and the material itself are already interrelated. Finally, and most importantly, the hope for a coercionless identity of form and material is compared to Hegel's hope for a coercionless identity of identity and non-identity. Adorno believes that the strains placed on the recapitulation section in

Beethovenian sonata form are closely parallel to the strains placed on Hegelian dialectic by what he takes to be its final turn to identity (chapter 6). The recapitulations in sonata form tend to indicate that the whole form still does after all externally coerce the particular thematic material: the moments at which Hegel's turn to identity allows itself in practice to forget or castigate non-identity show that Hegel's reconciliation of identity and non-identity is a coerced rather than a full reconciliation.[26]

At this point, however, Adorno begins to develop this confrontation between Hegel and Beethoven so as to indicate differences as well as affinities. Adorno regards Beethoven's late style as having developed a criticism of the identity of identity and non-identity: 'in his last works Beethoven did not get rid of the reprise but rather let the ideological moment in it appear openly.'[27] Rather than attempting to integrate recapitulations by conducting further development in them, the later works generally allow the conflict between development and recapitulation to appear quite openly. We might see the recapitulation in the first movement of Beethoven's Sonata in C minor op. 111 as an instance of this. The exultant material appearing in a major key at the close of the exposition is followed by a brief but complex and troubling quasi-fugal development section. When the material stated at the close of the exposition reappears, it does so *verbatim*, but now in the home key of C minor. The effect is of an acknowledged impossibility of synthesis; finally, the short and quiet coda is strikingly at odds with the powerful gesture with which the movement has opened and which has been developed throughout its course. At such moments, Adorno will argue, music 'becomes aware of the *limits* of its movement – of the impossibility of sublating its premises by force of its own logic. The late style is the μετάβασις εἰς ἄλλο γένος [leap into another domain]'.[28] Here we can clearly see affinities between Adorno's account of Beethoven's late style and his own critique of Hegel. The late Beethoven, in fact, is a model for Adorno's own negative dialectic, which sees risking the imputation of a 'leap into another domain', as a risk necessarily run by any would-be materialist thinking (chapter 8).

Immanence and musical analysis

This 'analogue which is more than an analogy' between philosophy and music, then, does not rest on a series of allegorical decodings – in the way that, say, Wagner's operas are sometimes crudely decoded by a process of motif-identification so as to extract a kind of prose précis of their supposed emotional content. Adorno does not think that the truth-content of musical works can be extracted by adding up supposedly individual atoms of musical meaning, any more than philosophical truth is just the sum total of correct propositions.

This helps to explain Adorno's distance from musical analysis. From the standpoint of professional musicology Adorno's account of the affinity between philosophy and music might appear insufficiently demonstrated with respect to musical detail. Although Adorno can scarcely be reproached with insufficiently concrete musical reference – his music criticism continually gives chapter and verse – he rarely proceeds by concentrating upon a single work and providing a consecutive account of it. Adorno is by no means dismissive of this requirement and indeed provided detailed accounts of individual works on a number of occasions.[29] He regards the demand that works of art should be analysed immanently, on their own terms, as an advance over forms of criticism which attempt to judge the work with some quite external normative criteria – that sonata forms, say, must have an exposition, development and recapitulation, or that tragedies must include a moment of recognition and a moment of reversal of fortune.[30]

But it should be clear from what has been said so far that he could not regard this demand as an absolute requirement of method. It is part of the necessary illusion of works of art to present themselves as closed monads, obeying their own law, but this is not an illusion to which philosophical interpretation should submit.[31] The self-sufficiency of the analysis of a single musical work or movement is itself illusory. Because of art's language-character, the works do not generate their significance, nor even at a minimally descriptive level their qualities, purely from within themselves. The criticism of a single song by Schoenberg may require not only an understanding of Schoenberg's whole *oeuvre*, but also a theory of the relationship of free atonality to diatonic harmony, of the *Lieder* tradition, of the relationship between music and text in song settings. That no individual essay will be able to exhaust these requirements does not justify pretending that music criticism can confine itself to the supposedly 'complete' analysis of a closed monad. Indeed it is in Adorno's view one of the primary virtues of the essay form that it frees the critic from the delusory and impoverishing goal of 'coverage'.[32]

The dialectic of musical enlightenment

Autonomous and heteronomous music are not discrete classificatory zones. The autonomization of music is a process, subject to the same dialectic of enlightenment which attends the autonomization of the subject itself. This is well illustrated by Adorno's account of Bach. In his essay 'Bach Defended against his Admirers' Adorno attacks the way in which Bach's music has been reinterpreted as though it were pre-autonomous art. Such interpretations have presented Bach's work as a monumental and internally static edifice constructed according to 'objective' contrapuntal and harmonic requirements.[33] Bach himself has been taken as an artisanal figure, a 'master craftsman' of music who stands as an implicit reproach to a supposedly inflated and subjectivist conception of genius.[34] These musicological emphases have been accompanied by an insistence upon historically authentic performance which seeks to correct the romantic and subjectivist performance tradition inherited from the nineteenth century.[35] Bach's work is invoked as a corrective to the shallow subjectivism of modern autonomous art, as though his music were wholly heteronomous, in the service of a static ritual context. Yet such invocations are themselves romantic, because they refer only to the *feeling* of an objective ritual order free of all doubt; such an order has been irrevocably lost and appeals to it are in the event no less romantic than the romanticism which they eagerly reproach.[36]

This indicates an important aspect of Adorno's approach to the problem of autonomy and heteronomy in music, and its consequences for interpretation in performance as well as for music criticism. His argument is not that autonomous art is better than heteronomous art. Rather, the autonomization of art is an inescapable historical process which can be seen powerfully at work just where the most zealous protests are made in favour of supposedly heteronomous, 'objective' art. Adorno draws attention to the presence of a dialectic of musical enlightenment in Bach's work. Just those apparently archaic pieces most appealed to by those who would turn Bach into a composer of static music in fact bear witness to Bach's dynamic 'developing variation' (Schoenberg).[37] Adorno analyses Bach's free and flexible use of polyphony so as to emphasize its difference from medieval polyphony. That Bach's music is sometimes archaizing, rather than literally archaic, already testifies to its autonomous character. Adorno gives the example of how

> The C-sharp minor fugue, which begins as though it were a dense network of equally relevant lines, the theme of which seems at first to be nothing more than the unobtrusive glue which holds the voice together, progressively reveals itself, starting with the entrance of the figured second theme, to be an irresistible crescendo . . .[38]

The keyboard instruments for which Bach wrote, of course, were unable to produce a crescendo. Adorno is arguing that advanced music can point beyond the currently available possibilities of realization in performance. Performance is interpretation, not historicist recreation, and cannot ignore what has happened to music since its composition.[39]

The extent to which Adorno's approach to the idea of progress in art is informed by the ideas developed in the *Dialectic of Enlightenment* can be seen in more detail if we consider the account of Schoenberg's twelve-tone composition in *The Philosophy of Modern Music*. The work was completed shortly after *Dialectic of Enlightenment* and was seen by Horkheimer as 'the basis for our common efforts' and by Adorno as 'an extended excursus' to that book.[40] The basis of twelve-tone composition is a note-row using each of the twelve tones of the octave, in which no tone may recur before each of the others has been heard. Further rows are yielded by inverting it, by playing it back to front (retrograde) or both (retrograde inversion); the possible rows can be further added to by beginning each of these four rows at any of the twelves tones of the octave, thus yielding a total set of 48 rows.

The mathematical neatness of this procedure delighted some supporters of Schoenberg. Twelve-tone composition was seen as an entirely fresh start in music. By rejecting the merely traditional and hence heteronomous formal dictates of diatonic music, it could be claimed, a wholly 'rational' or 'logical' schema of musical construction had been arrived at which was as systematic as diatonic tonality, yet more rational. It could thus be held to make possible the construction of large-scale musical forms as, it was claimed, 'free atonality' had not. The problem of a post-diatonic musical language had been solved and composers could confidently get on with production within this framework.[41]

As early as his correspondence with Krenek in the late 1920s and 1930s Adorno rejected this view of twelve-tone composition.[42] The justification for twelve-tone composition was not formal or mathematical, still less grounded in a theory of human nature, but historical. Accordingly twelve-tone composition could not be turned to with relief as a kind of substitute for tonality, an escape from the anxiety of musical lawlessness. The refusal to submit to diatonic harmonic restrictions or the traditional forms dependent on them, a refusal which was made systematic in twelve-tone technique, could not be understood in isolation from a wider dialectic of enlightenment. Twelve-tone technique announces that no musical dictates which are purely heteronomous, given by an externally authoritative tradition, are to be tolerated. It is closely bound up with the distinct but related refusals of autonomous reason and of exchange-value to tolerate anything heteronomous to themselves.[43]

In itself, therefore, twelve-tone technique is neither good nor bad; 'the great moments of late Schoenberg are won as much against as by virtue of twelve-tone technique.'[44] It is a 'musical domination of nature',[45] not a natural language of music, and Adorno emphasizes the extent to which its 'progress' is always also bought at the price of necessary impoverishments. Indeed, twelve-tone compositions are not somehow guaranteed to be authentically new simply by the application of an up-to-date method. As Adorno points out, the twelve-tone 'system' is not a method of composition but a preparation for composition. 'It is better compared to the arrangement of colours on the palette than to the painting of a picture.'[46] Instead, successful twelve-tone composition is new by determinately negating tradition rather than by simply jettisoning it.

This difference can be further explained by considering a contrast between a good twelve-tone composition and a bad one. In the work of Joseph Hauer a 'particular row runs its course unaltered except for placing and rhythm throughout the composition . . . the results are of the most barren poverty.'[47] In Schoenberg's work, however 'classical and, to an even greater extent, archaic techniques of variation are radically absorbed into the twelve-tone material';[48] the device of retrograde rows is developed from prediatonic music, for example. In Hauer's music heteronomous tradition is abstractly negated, by being abandoned; in Schoenberg's, it is determinately negated. Consequently, just as twelve-tone technique has its justification in historical experience, rather than in invariant laws of music, it can pass away rather than furnishing the immutable rules for subsequent composition.[49]

There is thus a dialectical, rather than a unilinear, relationship between tradition and the new, convention and the breaking of convention. What crucially distinguishes the really new from the abstract novelty – and hence eternal self-sameness – of commodity production in the culture industry is that the really new work is made in undiminished awareness of the possibilities afforded by tradition rather than by a simple forgetting of tradition. So that, for example, a central feature of the radical newness of Beethoven's last piano sonatas is precisely their recourse, within sonata form, to apparently obsolete and incompatible contrapuntal techniques.[50]

It is in the context of this dialectic of enlightenment that Adorno's celebrated contrast between 'Schoenberg and progress' and 'Stravinsky and restoration' in the *Philosophy of Modern Music* needs to be understood. The contrast is not one between a zealot for progress and a zealot for reaction, but between two composers who have both recognized the way in which tradition and the new are entangled. Schoenberg's music, no less than enlightenment in general, represents a process of relentless subjectification in which 'nothing may remain outside' the will of the composer. Schoenberg's relentless extension of this musical domination becomes a critique of the real advance of the domination of nature.[51]

What Adorno describes as Stravinsky's 'objectivism', on the other hand, uses a critique of the advancing subjectification and domination of musical material to place subjective expression under a ban. Adorno explicates a whole series of central features in Stravinsky's music after the early 1920s from this perspective. The emphasis on dynamic formal and development characteristic both of late diatonic works and of Schoenberg's school is replaced by a new interest in dance forms where blocks of material are placed in static contrast, side by side with each other;[52] there is an interest in ritual repetition of musical material or static figuration in place of the perpetual thematic variation of Schoenberg;[53] conventional forms whose significance is bound up with tonality return to be imposed on a musical content which is only partially diatonic.[54]

Adorno continually emphasizes Stravinsky's musical mastery and technical brilliance. It is precisely because of Stravinsky's justified status as a central figure in twentieth-century musical life that he is worth criticizing.[55] The counterpart of Adorno's emphasis on the historical truth-content of works of art, however, is an insistence on their historical ideology-content. Adorno's target in his critique of Stravinsky is the misuse of a critique of sub-jectification to the goal of liquidating the category of the subject altogether. Apparently objective elements – archaic forms, static figuration, ritual and liturgical texts – are restored to the musical work, whilst the 'subjectivism' of free atonality is deplored. But the point is that these objective elements are restored *by the subject*. This appeal to objective and collective conventions is in fact no less thoroughly subjective and arbitrary than the subjectivism it de-plores.[56] In a work such as the *Symphony of Psalms* Stravinsky provides us, not with literal ritual, but with the taste of ritual – inviting us, in Adorno's view, to chastise ourselves for the shallow-ness of our secular culture with a taste of something more archaic and primordial.[57] Such works offer, not actual ritual and collective solidarity, but an arbitrary and fantasized invocation of it. They are a subjective degradation of the subject.[58]

The essay as form

Like other European philosophers with a strong interest in lit-erature, Adorno has recently found perhaps his most pervasive impact in Britain and America as a 'literary theorist' or simply as a 'theorist'. Yet where it has been hoped to extract a critical method from Adorno's work, the results have in general been disappoint-ing. Unlike some other Marxist thinkers, Adorno does not lend himself to this kind of application. In the work of Althusser, for example, there is a more decided bifurcation between 'science', on the one hand, and 'ideology', on the other, than Adorno's negative dialectic could ever accept. This has made Althusser's work more readily exploitable as a source of a methodology for literary criticism; and much Marxist-structuralist literary criticism from the mid-1970s to the mid-1980s found it more helpful than Adorno's thought for just this reason.

Yet such approaches often suffered from presenting a largely static antithesis between theory and the texts which were to be processed by it. Such theory came to resemble a series of increas-ingly elaborate grids through which the hapless text could be fed as though it were so much raw material; objections to such procedure were ruled out of court as commonsensical or anti-theoretical.[59] The influence of deconstructive and postmodern thought, although it has been largely unfavourable to any idea of dialectic, even a 'negative' dialectic, has nevertheless created a climate in which it is understood that theoretical and philosophical reflection on literature need not mean the prior completion of a fully armoured method and its subsequent application to literary works. In such a climate it has once again been possible to turn to Adorno's literary criticism without demanding that a methodology should be extorted from it.

For Adorno, the idea of a prior method is no more acceptable in literary criticism than in any other of the human sciences. Methodologism is necessarily dogmatic because it presupposes in advance method's adequacy to its own subject matter, that 'the order of things is the same as the order of ideas.'[60] It is thus condemned to misrecognize what it would process. Adorno is more aptly described as a philosophical literary critic than as a literary theorist. This is one reason why he places such emphasis on the significance of the essay form for literary criticism. A central virtue of the essay form is that it 'has successfully raised doubts about the absolute privilege of method'.[61]

Adorno regarded his essay on 'The Essay as Form' as one of the most important statements of his thought. The tradition of the essay which Adorno wishes both to defend and to criticize is exemplified by certain German critics of the turn of the century – the young Lukács, Simmel, and Benjamin – but some of its features can also be seen in the work of a philosophically informed English critic such as Coleridge. The philosophically informed critical essay has become suspect wherever the advancing division and professionalization of intellectual labour has been most powerfully enforced. It offends both against pseudo-scientific demands for a prior consistent methodology and against related demands for a clean separation between philosophy and the human sciences. It has a belletristic or dilettantistic element to it which has incurred the intense suspicion of professional specialists, a suspicion which Adorno regards as only partially justified.

The attraction of the philosophical essay for Adorno lies in the way in which so many of the central aims of his thought are not merely practicable within the essay form, but actually demanded by it. The essay addresses artefacts rather than attempting to create a system *ex nihilo*; its objects are consequently already historical rather than invariant.[62] Its form is given by an attempt to understand the multi-faceted qualities of its particular object rather than by prior methodological imperatives; yet it is liberated in advance by its limited scope from the positivist requirement for total replication of its object.[63] The philosophical essay as Adorno

conceives it, that is, already presents the tension between systematic and anti-systematic thinking which is so central to Adorno's
broader epistemological and methodological projects.

All Adorno's literary-critical work takes the form of essays.
Their freedom from methodologism also means that they are free
from many of the more familiar taboos of literary criticism, because they do not start from a specified 'function of criticism' but
rather from constellations of concepts and objects and the determinate negation of all such professional or methodological function specified from outside which attention to such constellations
implies. There is accordingly no prohibition in Adorno's work on
biographical, anecdotal or kindred material, any more than there
is, conversely, a reduction of meaning to a prior authorial intention.

The aim of Adorno's literary criticism, then, as of his aesthetics
generally, is to proceed as a non-dogmatic materialist. An instance
of this can be seen in Adorno's treatment of hermeneutic canons
for reading. They show how Adorno's idea of a 'priority of the
object in aesthetics' – an idea which, as we have seen, is not to be
confused with any objectiv*ism* – is at work in his literary criticism.
Adorno criticizes both a subjectivism in thrall to the work's
production and a subjectivism in thrall to the work's reception.
Like many other mid-twentieth-century literary critics, he attacks
the presupposition that it is the critic's task dutifully to extract
from a literary work what the author put into it, that is, that a
reconstruction of the author's intention is decisive for the meaning
of a work or of a passage in a work. Indeed, since the truth-content
of an artwork, in any non-idealist account of truth, cannot be
something made (chapter 4), 'the content of a work of art begins
precisely where the author's intention stops; the intention is extinguished in the content.'[64] Yet Adorno is equally critical of any idea
that the meaning of the work can be specified as the sum total of
subjective empirical responses to it. All readers may be in agreement and nevertheless be wrong.

This simultaneous attack on two kinds of subjectivism would
appear to leave us with a straightforwardly objectivist literary
criticism, committed to describing the qualities of 'the work itself'.
Yet a priority of the object in aesthetics cannot, any more than in
negative dialectic, be reached simply by deleting everything subjective (chapter 7), or by deleting valuation altogether: 'objectivity
is not what is left over after the subject has been subtracted.'[65]
Accordingly, Adorno's essays do not scruple to make use of

material which positivistic philology and theoretical methodologism alike – including Marxist varieties – may find hopelessly subjective or belletristic. His essay on Bloch and his *Spirit of Utopia* begins by recounting how 'the dark brown volume of over 400 pages, printed on thick paper, promised something of what one hopes for from medieval books, something I had sensed, as a child, at home, in the calf's leather *Heldenschatz*, a belated book of magic from the eighteenth century, full of abstruse instructions many of which I still ponder even today.'[66]

If Adorno's work were content to rest at this level of anecdote it would indeed be feuilletonistic; such elements would not by themselves suffice to distinguish Adorno's literary essays from the work of many other critics unintimidated by professionalized positivist or methodologist prescription. Adorno's literary criticism is further distinguished by its insistence on the need for the philosophical interpretation of literature. His childhood reminiscence of Bloch's book is the starting point for a consideration of the relationship between the apparent contingency of individual experience and utopian thought, a relationship which is itself a central theme of Bloch's book. Adorno is no more willing to write off subjective experience of such material details as mere contingency than he is to reduce the meaning of works of art to subjective experience of them. Rather than discounting such considerations as purely personal, unprofessional, his essays move from such subjective experience to show how it is never utterly subjective but is entangled in the object itself. There can be no 'objectivist' literary criticism which just offers to describe the literary object 'as it is in itself' by deleting every trace of the subject; the path to the priority of the object, instead, leads through the determinate criticism of subjective misrecognition, not through its immediate liquidation.

Poetry and the domination of language

A model of what this means in a particular case is provided by Adorno's interpretation of Hölderlin's late hymns.[67] Wherever philology takes a recovery of the author's intention as its primary goal, Adorno argues, it provides an insufficient basis for the interpretation of Hölderlin's late work. Adorno's essay, instead, aims to recover the 'truth-content' of Hölderlin's late hymns: 'the truth manifested objectively in them, the truth that consumes the subjective intention and leaves it behind as irrelevant'. Yet, as we should expect, an Adornian account of such an 'objective' truth-content proceeds not from the fixed standpoint of first philosophy, but by way of a determinate negation of subjective misrecognition.

Such a path needs to go beyond immanent critique, an attempt to judge the works on 'their own' terms alone. Although Adorno regards an insistence on such immanence as a necessary corrective to an older philology which mistakenly imagined that it had fully interpreted a work when it had exhaustively catalogued its sources, 'influences', and circumstances of production, he does not believe that immanence can be turned into a self-sufficient canon of critical procedure. As in the critique of metaphysics and epistemology, critique cannot be sealed in a sphere of immanence, but instead is to point beyond such immanence:

> The aim of immanent analysis is the same as the aim of philosophy: the truth-content. The contradiction according to which every work wants to be understood on its own terms, but none can in fact be so understood is what leads to the truth-content . . . The path followed by the determinate negation of [subjectively intended] meaning is the path to the truth-content.[68]

These limits to 'immanent' criticism do not, however, justify 'recourse to a philosophy that in any way seizes possession of the poetry' and reads its own motifs without hesitation out of its semantic content.[69]

Adorno develops this point through a criticism of Heidegger's philosophical essays on Hölderlin. He applauds Heidegger's recognition that the hymns demand philosophical rather than purely philological interpretation, but has two objections to the way in which Heidegger carries out this task. Firstly, he contests the content of Heidegger's interpretation. Hölderlin is taken as a kind of verse Heidegger, centrally preoccupied with rootedness in a homeland and with a questioning of the rootless modern world.[70] Heidegger thus reads Hölderlin's work in implicit contrast to the German idealist tradition, of which Heidegger's own thought is very critical.[71] Adorno concedes that there is a moment of truth in this interpretation. The philhellenic moment in Hölderlin's poetry is closely bound up with this kind of critique of modernity and is a genuine link between Heidegger and Hölderlin.[72] But he argues that Heidegger's true perception of a mythic element in Hölderlin's poetry miscarries because he seeks to isolate and fix it, rather than considering its relation with other elements in Hölderlin's work.[73] Instead, Adorno demonstrates that Hölderlin's close links with the German idealists Hegel and Schelling can be seen at work within the minutest semantic details of his texts.

Just how condensed and complex Adorno's account of the relationship between philosophical motifs and aspects of poetic form and content can be is indicated by his analysis of Hölderlin's use of 'abstractions, or more precisely, very general words for existing entities which waver between entities and abstraction, like Hölderlin's pet word "Äther" [ether]'.[74] Adorno considers these through a comparison and contrast between Hölderlin and Hegel. Both, he argues, are 'antinominalists', opposed to the notion that universal concepts are mere false subsumptions of what alone are real, particulars. Yet both are equally committed to a belief that all knowledge is mediated through experience.[75] For both, the ideal, then, is a reconciliation between universal and particular. But whereas, Adorno believes, Hegel's thought ultimately declares such a reconciliation already to have arrived, Hölderlin's very general substantives testify to the real lack of reconciliation. They refuse to supply us either with clear-cut concepts, as a 'poetry of ideas' might do, or, on the other hand, with the impression of concrete lived experience, as subjective lyric might do.[76] Instead, words like 'Äther' and 'Ozean', as Hölderlin uses them, 'waver' irresolutely between the two. This is just the aspect of Hölderlin's work which prompted Weimar classicism to regard it as 'formless, vague and remote';[77] and Adorno concedes that it is just this feature of Hölderlin's diction which makes him ripe for Heideggerian interpretation. Adorno himself, of course, complains forcefully about just such a wavering in Heidegger's philosophy as a form of 'pseudo-concretion'. But he insists that Hölderlin's equivocal general substantives cannot be assimilated, as Heidegger tends to assimilate them, to what Adorno calls the anti-conceptual concept. Instead – and the anticipatory echo of *Negative Dialectics* is no accident – 'they are animated, because they have been immersed in the medium of the living, which they are to lead out of; their death-like aspect, over which the bourgeois spirit habitually makes sentimental lament, is transfigured into a saving quality . . . concepts are emancipated from individual experience instead of merely subsuming it. They become eloquent; hence the primacy of language in Hölderlin.'[78]

By this point it may be suspected that Adorno has simply replaced the extraction of Heideggerian themes from the content of

Hölderlin's poetry with the extraction of his own – Hölderlin as a verse Adorno instead of as a verse Heidegger. It is here that Adorno turns against his own reading and concedes that if Heidegger's method is simply replaced by another method nothing will have been gained. Instead '[t]he corrective to Heidegger's method should be looked for at the point where Heidegger breaks off for the sake of his *thema probandum*: in the relationship of the content, including the intellectual content, to the form.'[79] Accordingly the second part of the essay turns to consider formal aspects of Hölderlin's work. Although Adorno concedes that no invariant distinction can be made between form and content – whatever is called form 'is' nothing more than the content, and, conversely, a content without any form is not thinkable – he does not think that these terms can simply be done away with. Accordingly the second part of the essay attempts to consider Hölderlin's syntax, diction and metre – aspects which scarcely figure in Heidegger's interpretation, which is largely given over to the semantic content of Hölderlin's work – yet without quarantining these aspects in some realm of pure form, away from semantic content.

Adorno's treatment of Hölderlin's syntax offers an especially interesting instance of this. As we have seen, Adorno takes the intellectual content of Hölderlin's poetry to be especially concerned, like Hegel, with the possibility of a reconciliation between universal and particular, and also between culture and nature. If such a reconciliation were simply to be made into the subject matter of a didactic 'poem of ideas', however, the intellectual content would already have been betrayed by the form: '[t]he logic of tightly bounded periods, each moving rigorously on to the next, is characterized by precisely that compulsive and violent quality for which poetry is to provide healing and which Hölderlin's poetry unambiguously negates.'[80] Instead, Hölderlin's poetry pursues the implications of an idea of a reconciliation of universal and particular for poetic syntax itself: hypotactic syntax is disrupted by paratactic syntax, in which clauses are connected by juxtaposition rather than by syntactical subordination.

If Adorno's account of Hölderlin's syntax stopped here, of course, it would perpetuate some very un-Adornian misunderstandings indeed. It would imply that freedom from identity thinking can be attained in a privileged realm of poetry despite the persistence of systematic social domination and misidentification. It would further imply that poetic syntax stands outside a dialectic of enlightenment; that it can set itself free with an act of will from its tradition. Adorno's account, however, is more dialectical than this:

> He began by attacking syntax syntactically, in the spirit of the dialectic, with a venerable artistic technique, the inversion of the period. In the same way, Hegel used logic to protest against logic. The paratactic revolt against synthesis attains its limit in the synthetic function of language as such. What is envisioned is a synthesis of a different kind, language's critical self-reflection, while language retains synthesis. To destroy the unity of language would constitute an act of violence equivalent to the one that unity perpetrates; but Hölderlin so transmutes the form of unity that not only is multiplicity reflected within it – that is possible within traditional synthetic language as well – but in addition the unity indicates that it knows itself to be inconclusive.[81]

Hölderlin's syntax could not be a completely new self-sufficient procedure, any more than twelve-tone musical composition; it must proceed through the determinate negation of tradition. If poetry were to 'destroy the unity of language' – certain forms of 'concrete poetry' in which the semantic dimension of language has been almost entirely liquidated come to mind – this would not at all be a 'liberation' from syntax but would only confirm all the more grimly the power of what it intends to resist. The end of Hölderlin's new syntax is held to be, not the liquidation of semantic meaning, but an intimation of the possibility of meaning which would not be the relentless subsumption of particulars by universals.

Hölderlin's syntax, that is, points to the possibility of a non-coercive affinity between concepts and objects. As we shall see in chapter 7, Adorno takes language itself to be a model for this possibility. This is what Adorno has in mind when he talks of the 'emancipation' of language in Hölderlin's work,[82] and of the sense that 'at times, language itself is speaking' in the work of Stefan George[83] or Rudolf Borchardt.[84] But this is possible as yet only as an illusion, because in a systematically coercive world the idea of an already established wholly non-coercive sphere of 'language' is a dangerous delusion which would merely conceal real coercion. It is just this illusory freedom from domination in art which, as we have seen, Adorno's aesthetics aims, not to liquidate, but to save. Hölderlin's poetry is domination of language in the service of the end of domination, not a region of already achieved freedom from such domination.

Autonomy and heteronomy in literature

Adorno has much to say about the special status of works of art whose medium is language; and, in particular, about how this changes their relation to the idea of the autonomy of works of art. It will be remembered that Adorno takes the autonomy of works of art to follow upon the separation of mimesis from discursive cognition. The more profound this alienation becomes, the more discursive cognition must renounce its affinity with what it refers to, any attempt to be like it; the more aesthetic mimesis must renounce any discursive element, any formulation of explicit judgements, and confine itself to mimesis. This goes even for works of art which have discursive judgements as their medium; hence Adorno's insistence that 'what works of art say is not what their words say.'[85] The cognitive import of a poem could never adequately be settled simply by paraphrasing it, since the constellation of individual elements in the work of art is essential to the distinguishing of those elements from merely empirical material, to their having a cognitive import at all.

Nor is it possible to separate out a liter*al* semantic 'content' from a liter*ary* 'form', because, in Adorno's view, the alienation of art from cognition affects the supposedly literal meaning of the most elementary judgements within linguistic works of art. 'Even the copula "is", omnipresent in Trakl's work, is alienated in the work of art from its conceptual meaning: it expresses, not any judgement that something exists, but the faded echo of such a judgement, qualitatively altered to the point of becoming its own negation.'[86] The price of the autonomization of the literary work of art is that its semantic content can less and less be taken literally, even where the poetic programme is a literalistic one. Adorno gives the example of poems by William Carlos Williams which appear to approximate to 'reports on experience': 'empirical judgements, once translated to the aesthetic monad, take on a different quality through their contrast to that monad.'[87] The work of art is a sphere in which 'nothing can remain unchanged'; nothing signifies the same as it does in discursive cognition, outside the work of art.[88]

It is in this context that Adorno makes what is perhaps the central claim of his poetics, that 'the barbaric is the literal.'[89] It represents an oblique comment upon Benjamin's more famous aphorism that 'there is no document of civilization which is not at the same time a document of barbarism.'[90] Adorno is in complete agreement with this claim. But he wants to prevent false conclusions from being drawn from it. In particular, any idea that culture should be liquidated so that we could then at least have honest barbarism is strongly to be resisted. Only culture's concealment and mediation of barbarism, whilst themselves still dependent on barbaric domination, make it at all possible to imagine the possibility of life without barbarism. To liquidate this mediation on the grounds of its deceptiveness, in favour of a domination which is 'at least honest', is barbaric. The consequences run right through to the artifice of thought and of artistic production, since there is as yet no artifice of any kind which does not live off and conceal some form of domination. The claim that 'the barbaric is the literal' holds, indeed, not only for art but also for discursive cognition. If the demand that the concept's mimetic moment, its affinity with its objects, should be extirpated in favour of its purely literal moment, its referential function were fulfilled, Adorno insists, thought itself would capitulate.

The consequences of this thought for the question of the truth-content and ideological content of literary works of art are extensive. They can be illustrated by considering Adorno's altercation with Lukács over the political import of a poem by Gottfried Benn:

> O that we were our most primordial ancestors. / A little bit of slime in a warm bog. / Life and death, fertilization and giving birth / would slide forth from our silent juices. / A piece of seaweed or a dune, / formed by the wind and bottom-heavy. / Even the head of a dragonfly or the wing of a gull / would be too far and would already feel too much.[91]

Lukács takes Benn's poem to be expressing a regressive anti-humanism, 'the opposition of man as animal, as a primeval reality, to man as a social being'.[92] For Adorno, the mistake of Lukács's reading is that he takes the poem literally:

> The line 'O daß wir unser Ururahnen wären', has a completely different value in the poem than it would if it expressed a literal wish. There is a grin written into the word 'Ururahnen'. Through the stylization, the impulse of the poetic subject – which in any case is old-fashioned rather than modern – is presented as comically inauthentic, as a melancholy game. It is precisely the repulsive quality of what the poet pretends to wish himself back to and what one cannot in fact wish oneself back to that emphasizes his protest against historically produced suffering . . . Through exaggeration, Benn suspends the regression that Lukács immediately ascribes to him . . . Simplifications like the one Lukács makes in his excursion on Benn not only misrecognize the nuances; along with

the nuances they misrecognize the work of art itself, which becomes a work of art only by virtue of the nuances.[93]

The closing lines of the passage make it clear that what is at stake here is the autonomy of the work of art. Lukács's failure to take Benn's wish as a gesture rather than a real wish does not only miss the subtleties of the work of art's expression, but fails to recognize Benn's poem as an autonomous work of art at all. What Lukács reads literally as a desire for regression to the pre-social, Adorno reads as an implicit protest against socially produced suffering.

Yet art's alienation from cognition is not complete; and, in particular, literary works of art have an ineliminably discursive moment: 'literary compositions . . . are both works of art and, because of their relatively autonomous discursive component, are not only works of art and not works of art throughout.'[94] Literary works can therefore no more be read with cavalier disregard for their literal meaning than they can successfully be read with sheer literal-mindedness. Confronted with this later thought, Adorno's own reading of Benn's poem looks one-sidedly anti-literal – almost as though any wish or hope, no matter how unpromising in itself, can through the transformative autonomy of the work of art become a utopian protest. In *Aesthetic Theory* Adorno develops the thought that there might today be a particular timeliness in the hybrid character of literary works of art. As we have seen, Adorno argues that autonomous works of art are increasingly driven to expose their dependence on a heteronomous moment: 'At present art is at its most vital when it corrodes its cover-concept. In such corrosion it is true to itself, an infringement of the mimetic taboo on the impure or the hybrid.'[95] Poetry which fulfils this demand holds literal reference and artifice in tension, without capitulating to the demand to liquidate one in favour of the other.[96]

It will have become clear by now that both Adorno's social theory and his aesthetic theory are intimately connected to his broader philosophical thought, especially as that thought is related to classical German philosophy (above all, Kant and Hegel). We must now move, in the final three chapters of this book, to a full consideration of Adorno's relation to classical German philosophy and of how far his criticisms of that tradition can be justified.

6
Negative Dialectic as Metacritique

Introduction

The accounts of Adorno's social and aesthetic theories given so far in this book necessarily raise a series of difficult philosophical questions. Although Adorno's reception in the English- and French-speaking worlds has concentrated on his social and aesthetic theory, his arguments address questions of the broadest possible contemporary philosophical interest. From the time when Adorno first became involved in discussion with Horkheimer's circle in Frankfurt in the later 1920s until his death, the problem of formulating a philosophical materialism remained at the centre of his thought. The remaining three chapters of the book offer an account and a defence of this materialism, drawing both on the most important sources published in Adorno's lifetime – the studies of Hegel, the 'metacritique of epistemology', and above all, *Negative Dialectics* – but also on those lecture courses so far made available – in particular those on philosophical terminology, on moral philosophy and on epistemology. These chapters aim to show, above all through continual reference to Adorno's complex and lifelong engagement with the thought of Kant, how seriously Adorno recognizes that he cannot be excused from epistemological argument by appeal to a prior theory of society or philosophy of history. The central point of this part of the book will be to show how Adorno formulated his thinking as a *critical thinking without transcendental method*.

The next three chapters, then, explore three fundamental aspects of Adorno's materialism, and consider some of the most powerful actual and possible objections to it. In the present chapter, it will be shown how Adorno attempts to free critical thought from transcendental method, by reformulating the transcendental idealist concept of experience and its supposed components. This reformulation yields a materialist or 'negative' dialectic. Chapter 7 looks at how Adorno understands the relation of such a materialism to central issues of praxis. Chapter 8 considers its relation to metaphysical speculation.

Why should it be so difficult to say what materialism is? Surely materialism is the most straightforward of philosophical creeds, not one requiring any especially complex negotiation with other schools of thought? So at least the confidence with which the word 'materialism' is sometimes used in the human sciences would suggest. But Adorno's materialism starts from a painful awareness that it is much more difficult really to think as a materialist than it is to lay claim to that label; through an awareness, indeed, that it is often just where this label is most vehemently and immediately claimed that a particularly unreflective kind of metaphysics is all the more powerfully at work. Adorno's attempt to rethink materialism without dogmatism addresses nothing other than the problem of 'givenness, or, to use the Hegelian term, immediacy',[1] which has proved of such continuing importance, in radically divergent ways, not only for phenomenology, fundamental ontology and deconstruction, but also for much recent work in analytical philosophy.[2]

The problem may be put like this. All attempts to get beyond idealism – claims of the type that thought constitutes, shapes, or is identical with, its objects appear to run the opposite risk of claiming access to immediacy, to a transcendence which is just 'given'. In such invocations, as Hegel himself forcefully pointed out, we are effectively invited to *have faith* in some datum or framework for data which cannot be interrogated further. Our knowledge of such 'givens' is mistakenly thought of as being purely passive.[3] Inquiry must simply halt before them. The difficulty is that dogmatic materialism of this kind is not at all free from metaphysics in the way it supposes. When thinking comes to a halt with an *abstract* appeal to history, or society, or 'sociohistorical material specificity', or any other form of givenness, it might as well stop with God. The lesson which Adorno draws is that whether thinking is really materialist is not decided by how often the word 'materialism' is repeated, but by what actually happens in that thinking. Materialist thinking would need to ask how it would be possible to think about that which appears to escape conceptuality.

Adorno, then, wishes to ask whether, and if so, how, idealism can be contested without lapsing into a straightforwardly metaphysical invocation of an immediate access to transcendence. He suggests that these difficulties cannot be avoided simply by inventing a new philosophical language. Instead, we will need to continue to use, even whilst criticizing, the language of concept and intuition, subject and object.

The immanent critique of idealism

Adorno's early manifestos, 'The actuality of philosophy' and 'The idea of natural history', describe a crisis in philosophy and the human sciences.[4] One kind of response to this crisis might be to clear the decks: to insist on an entirely fresh start which would lay the foundations for a new certainty. Adorno, however, believed that really new work in philosophy could only be undertaken by engaging with the philosophical tradition. In an important passage from his Introduction to *Negative Dialectics*, 'Tradition and Cognition', Adorno referred to 'the traditional' as 'quasi-transcendental'.[5] Even thinking which regards itself as wholly new, that is, at least partly depends upon a tradition which comes before it.[6] Trying to wipe the slate clean, therefore, only prevents thinking from inquiring properly into one of its own conditions of possibility, the tradition which comes before it.[7] Once enlightened thought treats the tradition which it has overcome as sheer error, myth, it becomes unable to understand its relation to its own history.[8] It endlessly repeats a 'dialectic of enlightenment'.To this extent, enlightenment becomes constitutively *un*enlightened.

The idea that we could make a completely fresh start in philosophy, then, perpetuates, whether intentionally or not, the primal illusion of idealism: the illusion that the autonomous thinking subject produces or founds what it thinks of. However, Adorno argues that this illusion is not simply a mistake on the part of philosophers, but is indissociable from certain structural features of all natural-historical experience to date. As a result, the illusion that the thinking subject is self-sufficient returns all the more powerfully wherever philosophy tries simply to dismiss it by an

act of will. For this reason, Adorno argues, 'the fallacy of constitutive subjectivity' cannot just be set aside. Instead, Adorno
suggests that it must be 'broken through using the strength of the
subject itself'.[9]

What does this paradoxical phrase mean? Initially, it indicates
that we cannot start from a first principle. The relation to tradition
has to be part and parcel of any new thinking. Adorno attempts to
think anew not by producing a supposedly self-sufficient new
method or new system, but through the criticism of the tradition
from which it emerges. This is why Adorno described his own
philosophical work as undertaking a 'transition to interpretation'.[10]
Such a transition aims to rescue thinking from an endless repetition of its dialectic of enlightenment.

This attempt sometimes makes Adorno's philosophical work
appear rebarbatively abstract. At the beginning of *Negative Dialectics* Adorno quoted, approvingly, Walter Benjamin's remark on
Adorno's study of Husserl, that 'it was necessary to pass through
the frozen wastes of abstraction in order to philosophize concretely
without sacrificing rigour.'[11] Adorno argued that the 'frozen
wastes' referred to by Benjamin were not the result of a wilful
abstractness in his own style, but were a necessary consequence of
a series of real abstractions structuring social experience (chapter
2).[12] Because conceptual abstraction is connected with these real
abstractions, any thought which hoped simply to by-pass abstraction altogether would fail. It would present only an undemon-
strated fantasy. Hence his suggestion that 'Cognition, which wants
content, wants a utopia.'[13] Only if these real processes of abstraction were to come to an end could cognition really become
'concrete philosophizing'. Because Adorno's thought approaches
such a goal negatively, through the criticism of the philosophical
tradition, the expressions which he uses to refer to his own
theoretical practice – for example, where he refers to 'constellations
of concepts' or to 'naming' and thus 'breaking' the 'spell' of the
subject – need to be understood in context. Readers of his work
need to be aware that these motifs are not detachable positive
results, nor a portable method for achieving such results.

Adorno's pervasive engagement with the German philosophical
tradition in particular, and above all with Kant and Hegel, is a
serious difficulty for the Anglophone reader of his work. Adorno's
social criticism and aesthetic theory are conceived in terms of this
tradition, and cannot be understood if it is set aside. Why are Kant
and Hegel so important to Adorno? Adorno believes that thinkers

who take themselves to have gone beyond German idealism have often, in the event, only fallen back behind it to some position which German idealism has already anticipated and criticized. Adorno's own thought, by contrast, explicitly acknowledges its own entanglement with idealism. It aims at materialism, but does so with the proviso that materialist thinking is not the easiest in the world, a thinking, say, which would demand only that we should be sufficiently literal-minded in defence of a 'natural attitude', but rather the hardest and the most demanding of philosophical artifice.

The main features of Adorno's relationship to German idealism can be sketched at the outset. Firstly, he criticizes a series of systematic separations which governs Kant's thought – between, for example, concept and intuition, form and content, spontaneity and receptivity, reason and intellect. Adorno argues in each case that neither pole of the separation can properly be thought without the other, and so that the terms cannot be separated for the purpose of analysing them in isolation from each other. This account of Kant owes much to Hegel's earlier and more systematic reading of the aporias of the critical philosophy. But, secondly, Adorno also criticizes Hegel's speculative identifications of the terms separated by Kant. It is partly true, then, to say that Adorno uses Kant to criticize Hegel and Hegel to criticize Kant. This is done in order to display what Kant and Hegel share. Idealism is subjected to a further criticism, a 'metacritique', in which its own conditions of possibility are examined.

Adorno suggests that those contradictions which classical German philosophy cannot eliminate bear witness to real social antagonisms. Because these contradictions are necessitated by certain features of what is being thought about, they cannot be understood properly if they are regarded simply as mistakes. They do not simply disqualify classical German thought. Indeed they are, for Adorno, an index of German idealism's truth, because they make social antagonism visible right at the centre of German idealism, rather than handing it over, as though it were of no concern to philosophy, to historiography or sociology. But the idealist tradition can be false in two ways: either in so far as it represents these real antagonisms as something unchangeable, as a kind of fate to which we should simply reconcile ourselves; or in so far as it attempts to conceal these antagonisms in logical non-contradictoriness.

The status of the social and political import of this account has sometimes been misunderstood. It is not a sociology of knowledge; it does not, that is, view Kant's or Hegel's thought simply as secondary results of a prior social process.[14] Nor does it focus exclusively or even primarily upon the explicit political positions taken by classical German thought. Instead Adorno insists that 'the only way to reach social categories philosophically is to decipher the truth-content of philosophical categories.'[15] This process of 'deciphering' is sometimes thought of as an 'analogy' between idealist concepts and aspects of modern society, but the notion of an 'analogy' is somewhat misleading, since it implies that two elements which do not have any particular connection with each other to begin with are being arbitrarily brought together for comparison.

Adorno argues, instead, that reference to social experience is part and parcel even of apparently 'purely' logical or epistemological concepts themselves. Adorno calls such reference 'metalogical'.[16] Metalogical reference is not brought to concepts from somewhere else. All concepts already contain an element of reference to experience and are unthinkable without such reference. Immanent critique seeks to make explicit the reference to social experience which is already sedimented in philosophical concepts. Such criticism must often be presented in the *form* of an analogy, not because philosophy and social experience are really in some way entirely unconnected matters, but rather because the division of intellectual labour which has increasingly led them to be separately considered, under the professional headings of 'philosophy' and 'sociology', is a real division, and cannot be wished away. This raises a more general question: is philosophy possible at all in a context of divided intellectual labour?

The metacritique of transcendental inquiry

Adorno does not think that philosophy can be reduced to 'epistemology', that is, to a theory of what could count as knowledge in general, considered in abstraction from any particular knowledge. He thinks that the idea of restricting philosophy to such a function is closely linked to a progressive division of intellectual labour in modern society.[17] Academic disciplines increasingly legitimate themselves by protecting their special 'field' of knowledge which they alone are competent to address. Academic philosophy is accordingly left with no field not already occupied by one or another of the special sciences. The response of epistemology is to turn philosophy into the department of grounding the other departments: to provide a theory of the rules and instruments for knowledge as such irrespective of any particular knowledge.

If Adorno is dissatisfied with this idea of philosophy as a kind of department of grounding the other departments, he is well aware of the dangers which lie in a hasty reaction to this restriction.[18] Like Max Weber, Adorno believes that attempts directly to seize for philosophy the subject matter of individual disciplines will end in dilettantism.[19] In such cases philosophy will turn into pseudoscience. Instead, it is the aim of Adorno's work 'stringently to transcend the official separation of pure philosophy and the substantive subject matter'.[20] If this aim is indeed to be served stringently, we cannot 'skip epistemology by *fiat*'.[21] This is why Adorno does not write so much *against* epistemology – and it is unfortunate that his *Zur Metakritik der Erkenntnistheorie* has been translated into English under this title – but rather conducts a 'metacritique of epistemology'.[22]

What does Adorno mean by this phrase? Although the word 'metacritique' was first used by J. G. Hamann to name his simultaneously sceptical and mystical response to Kant's 'critical' philosophy,[23] Adorno's own metacritique owes little to Hamann. The Greek word *meta* means both 'beyond' and 'after'. According to its etymology 'metacritique' would mean a further inquiry beyond or after 'critique'. To understand Adorno's use of the term we need to remind ourselves of the special sense in which Kant used the word 'critique'. Kant understood critique as a mode of philosophical inquiry beyond the alternatives of empiricism (Locke and Hume) and rationalism (Leibniz and Wolff). Each of these alternatives was in Kant's view equally 'dogmatic', whether voluntarily or not. For Kant, 'Leibniz *intellectualised* appearances, just as Locke . . . *sensualised* all concepts of the understanding, *i.e.* interpreted them as nothing more than empirical or abstracted concepts of reflection.'[24] Leibniz and Locke had each taken understanding and sensibility, respectively, as primary, rather than recognizing that each 'can supply objectively valid judgements of things only in *conjunction* with each other'.[25] Kant's own 'criticism', by contrast, was to present a 'transcendental' inquiry, an inquiry into the conditions of the possibility of experience. Such an inquiry would separate out for the purposes of critical investigation those elements – 'concepts' and 'intuitions' – which could only provide knowledge of objects in conjunction with each other.

Kant thought that this inquiry had the result of showing that there were certain structural features of all experience – the fact that it was impossible to understand events without having a concept of causation, for example – were not 'out there' like things, but were brought to experience by the knowing subject. This did not mean that these conditions of the possibility of experience were fabrications (as Nietzsche, for example, later suggested): on the contrary, no experience of any kind would be possible without them.[26] Kant emphasized, however, that transcendental inquiry could not by itself provide any new knowledge of objects. Its achievement was rather to show what were the invariant conditions for any knowledge of objects whatsoever to be possible. Kant warned that if these invariant conditions were mistakenly taken to provide knowledge of invariant objects – such as God, a free will, or an immortal soul – then transcendental inquiry would relapse into a dogmatic variety of metaphysics. These conditions of the possibility of experience, that is, are not themselves beings of any kind, for Kant, but rather pure forms, conceptual conditions of the possibility of knowing beings. All knowledge of objects demands experience.

This point is of central importance to Kant, who wants to draw a sharp distinction between those objects which we can claim knowledge of, and those which we can only think of. The pure concepts of the understanding do not by themselves afford any knowledge of objects. But we must be able to *think* of an object as it is in itself irrespective of all experience of it. If we could not think of things in this way, Kant argues, we would be left in the absurd position of referring to an appearance without anything that does the appearing.[27] Yet although we must be able to think the idea of a thing 'considered as it is in itself', it is nevertheless beyond our experience. We can only *know* things considered as they 'appear' to consciousness, only as 'phenomena'.

Adorno's approach to epistemology is a *metacritique* in the sense that it performs a further critique on critical inquiry itself. It asks not only 'what are the conditions of the possibility of experience?', but 'what are such a transcendental inquiry's *own* conditions of possibility?'

The centrepiece of this metacritique is an account of Kant's transcendental subject. Adorno proceeds by radicalizing Kant's own insistence that all knowledge of objects must be mediated through experience. He points out that there are problems with Kant's distinction between 'thinking' and 'knowing'. A pure form without any content is not merely unknowable, but also unthinkable. A thought which is not a thought *of* anything will be not merely 'empty', as Kant concedes, but also 'blind', not a thought at all.[28] If the categorial forms specified by Kant are the conditions of the possibility of experience, the reverse is equally true: the categorial forms themselves are only made possible by the experience whose conditions of possibility they are supposed to provide.[29] Accordingly those forms could not be invariant, but would necessarily change as experience changes.

Adorno's account is motivated by a wish to arrive at a different kind of concept of experience from Kant's.[30] Kant insisted that all experience requires a concept, or form of understanding, to be joined with a (sensible) intuition. Without intuitions, my experience would simply be empty, nothing, because concepts have no content of themselves. Nor is it any easier to imagine the possibility of experience without conceptual forms, in Kant's view, since not only would there be no sense in which I could be said to 'have' my experiences, but it is impossible to imagine what a substance devoid of all form could actually be like. But this did not mean that concepts and intuitions could not be separated out by philosophers. On the contrary, it was 'a strong reason for carefully separating and distinguishing the one from the other' for epistemological purposes. Adorno is less convinced that this kind of methodological separation is possible. The result of any such separation, for Adorno, is that experience comes to look as though it were something which is somehow added up by joining concept with intuition, or as though it were manufactured by the pure activity of concepts upon the raw material of intuition.[31]

These considerations throw a rather different light on Kant's 'block' – his insistence that pure concepts of the understanding cannot by themselves provide knowledge of objects. This prohibition on metaphysics, Adorno suggests, is itself dogmatically formulated, because of the claim that the conditions of the possibility of experience are timeless. This invariance has the result of converting certain features of variable experience itself into invariants. In particular it implies that it is impossible for us to *experience* (rather than just to 'think' or to 'postulate') freedom, or our own subjectivity in general. It also suggests that it is impossible to know things as they are in themselves rather than as they appear to consciousness.[32]

Adorno does not think that all this is simply the result of a mistake on Kant's part. He argues that Kant's inquiry into the conditions of the possibility of experience truthfully bears witness to certain structural features of modern natural-historical experience. The Kantian object (*Gegenstand*) produced by 'pure' conceptual activity upon the material of intuition closely resembles the commodity as a supposed product of 'pure' or abstract labour.[33] The insistence that for experience to be possible, a concept must work upon an intuition, is conditional upon what experience itself is increasingly becoming: a production of exchange-value for its own sake (chapter 2). For Adorno, this is both the truth and the untruth of Kant's 'experience'. It is a true index of the real historical emptying-out of our experience.[34] Any attempt simply to wish away that prohibition in advance of a real change in our experience would amount to a merely hopeful or dishonest declaration that an unfree society is in fact free. To this extent Kant's prohibition remains in force.

Yet at the same time, because Kant's is a transcendental account, it implies that this emptied experience, bereft of real content, is the model of what experience itself has been and must be like. Adorno's interest here is in suggesting that this transcendental account of experience need not be taken as legislative for all future experience. If our experience were different, both these transcendental blocks – on experiencing freedom and on knowing the thing as it is in itself – might no longer apply.

The concept of experience

Like all attempts to criticize transcendental inquiry by 'radicalizing' it, Adorno's attempt to think with and against Kant has remained liable to the suspicion that, far from really radicalizing transcendental inquiry, it instead falls back from it, into one or other of the bad alternatives – scepticism or dogmatism – which Kant was attempting to get beyond. Its appeal to experience can be seen as a relapse into a historicizing or sociologizing scepticism, which thinks about Kant from a perspective already set up by some dogmatically posited opinions about social history. Its attack on the prohibition on the experience of transcendence, conversely, can be seen as a relapse into pre-critical metaphysics. The charge of a relapse into pre-critical metaphysics is discussed in chapter 8. Here we need to focus in more detail on Adorno's arguments about experience and its conditions of possibility.

As Hans-Georg Gadamer has remarked, the concept of experience is one of the least clarified concepts used by philosophers and yet one of those to which appeal is most often made.³⁵ Adorno's use of the concept appears to struggle beneath this difficulty more than most others. The concept of experience is a constant point of reference in his criticisms of the continental philosophical tradition since Kant, yet he refuses to provide an unambiguous definition for it. What is more, it is not hard to think of plausible defences against Adorno's criticisms of the transcendental concept of experience. A Kantian might point out that for Kant, the conditions of the possibility of experience yielded by transcendental inquiry are not simply the conditions of the possibility of 'our' experience at present or to date, but, rather, the conditions of the possibility of any thinkable experience whatever. The point is not that historical and/or current experience is made possible by these conditions, but that we cannot in principle even imagine any experience which would be intelligible without these conditions. They make possible *all possible*, not merely actual or historical, experience.

If Adorno's reformulation of the concept of experience rested only on the argument that because experience itself changes, the conditions of its possibility must change, it would clearly have failed to take this objection into account. But this is the conclusion, not the presupposition of Adorno's argument. The argument rests instead on a thoroughgoing re-examination of what Kant splits up for epistemological analysis as the two indispensable components of human experience, understanding and sensibility. To understand this re-examination, it is useful to draw on a course of lectures which Adorno gave in 1957–8, the second half of which comments in more consecutive fashion than was Adorno's habit on some central issues in the *Critique of Pure Reason*.³⁶

If we look in more detail at Adorno's criticism of Kant's concept of experience, we will see that it marshals three primary sets of arguments, the first addressing Kant's account of the intellectual conditions of knowledge, the second addressing his account of the sensible conditions of knowledge, and the third addressing Kant's account of the connections between these. All three groups of argument are contentious and are open to many objections. The first set is intended to show why concepts devoid of all reference whatever to a 'something' are not only 'empty', as Kant would have it, restricted to a logical rather than a synthetic use, but 'blind', unthinkable, and consequently devoid of a logical as well as of a synthetic use. Here Adorno is clearly in disagreement not only with Kant but also with his twentieth-century semanticist critics.[37] The second set of arguments is intended to show that an experience supposedly free from all conceptual mediation would not only be 'blind', as Kant suggests, but also empty, not experience at all. This second set of arguments addresses both Kant's theory that time and space needed to be considered 'pure forms of intuition' which were necessary to all synthetic a priori knowledge, and his characterization of phenomenal reality as a 'sensuous manifold' devoid of qualities prior to conceptual determination. Here Adorno's arguments, perhaps surprisingly, have something in common with those of Kant's semanticist and empiricist critics. These two sets of arguments lead on to a more general case about the project of transcendental inquiry itself. Adorno argues that such inquiry dogmatically answers its own questions in advance by asking *how* synthetic a priori judgements – judgements which have content, yet whose truth we can know without any reference to experience – are possible rather than *whether* they are possible.[38] What links the arguments as a whole may be understood by saying that for Adorno, Kant indeed provided a critique of pure *reason*, but one which rested on a failure to criticize the notions of pure *understanding* and pure *sensibility*. Adorno's critical thinking understands itself as a radicalization rather than a relapse from critical thinking, in that it criticizes not only pure reason but the very idea of 'pure concepts' and 'pure intuitions'. 'Thinking without purity' is the model for Adorno's attempt to free critical thinking from the armour of its transcendental method.[39]

Let us examine the first limb of Adorno's account of the concept of experience. He attempts to argue that *pure* concepts of the understanding are not only empty but blind: that they are by themselves unthinkable, not just lacking in content. It might initially be thought that this is a psychologistic argument. It might be thought, that is, that Adorno is making the mistake of trying to use empirical means, to argue from the way human beings happen to be able or unable to think, to settle a non-empirical point about the *validity* of logical concepts. Kant himself had already argued that this kind of argument could be of no help in transcendental thought. Pure concepts of the understanding could not be simply inductive abstractions from experience, because otherwise we

would not be able to account for the 'fact' of that scientific
knowledge which we can possess a priori: 'namely, *pure mathematics* and *general science of nature*'.[40] Adorno's argument, however, rests on an account of what makes a thought thinkable. This
is why it is a metacritical rather than a psychologistic argument.
For Kant non-contradictoriness is a sufficient condition of intelligibility. In his discussion of the possibility of thinking freedom,
intelligibility is taken as synonymous with non-contradictoriness:
'I can none the less *think* freedom (that is to say, the representation
of it is at least not self-contradictory)';[41] 'I can think whatever I
please, provided only that I do not contradict myself, that is,
provided my concept is a possible thought.'[42] The subjective
intelligibility of the pure concepts of the understanding is taken as
read; the question of their referential content – what Kant calls
their objective validity and reality – is addressed later in the
transcendental deduction and is not regarded as essential to their
intelligibility. For Adorno, though, the referential content of concepts is a necessary condition of their intelligibility. Without reference to a 'something', no formal logic *could* be thinkable.[43] A
thought which is not a thought of anything is not only empty but
unintelligible: 'the meaning of logic itself demands facticity.'[44]

Here not only Kantians but their positivist or semanticist opponents may have a strong objection. It can be protested that Adorno is
confusing the question of how logical propositions are arrived at –
their 'genesis' – with whether they are true – their validity. Another
way of putting this would be to say that he confuses the *quid juris*
of a transcendental deduction – what right do we have to these
concepts? – with the *quid facti* of an empirical deduction – how do
we come by these concepts?[45] As we shall see later, Adorno does
not think that the genesis and validity of logical propositions can
be quite so easily separated. More importantly here, for Adorno
intelligibility is not a merely psychological criterion. It is inseparable from the very notion of validity. Validity can never be
meaningfully ascribed to a proposition which is in principle unthinkable, even an analytic one: 'Every judgement, even, as Hegel
showed, an analytical one, carries within itself, whether it will or
no, the claim to predicate something which is not merely identical
with the bare subject-concept.'[46] Adorno's critique is thus directed
from the start against the notion that pure concepts of the understanding really are 'pure'. The condition of their even being
thinkable, not only of their having any content, lies for Adorno
precisely in their not being pure, but rather already contaminated

with some reference, however minimal. (The charge that this view necessarily obliges Adorno himself to develop a positive ontology is discussed in chapter 8).

If we move now to look at the second limb of Adorno's account of Kant's concept of experience, we can see that it rests on some complementary arguments. Kant's account of the sensible conditions of human knowledge in the transcendental aesthetic is notoriously complex. Adorno at some point or other discussed most of its arguments, and it would be impossible to give a complete catalogue here. Instead an especially critical instance, Kant's account of time and space as pure forms of intuition, will be discussed. What does it mean to describe space and time as 'pure forms of intuition'? Adorno is sympathetic to the impulse which lies behind such a description. Any attempt simply to define space and time will inevitably appeal to spatial and temporal concepts. But our right to use such concepts is precisely what an account of space and time is supposed to ground. This, of course, is itself an argument in favour of the need for a transcendental account of spatial and temporal concepts. They are concepts which we cannot *not* use.[47] Space and time, such an argument runs, cannot be inductive abstractions from experience because they are already presupposed in any attempt to describe experience. Yet they cannot be pure concepts of the understanding, according to Kant's view of such concepts, otherwise they would be empty, whereas Kant's account of them is supposed to show how *synthetic* a priori knowledge is possible. Accordingly Kant regards space and time as 'pure forms of intuition', or, as he elsewhere puts it, 'pure intuitions'[48] – that is, as a kind of a priori form of sensibility.

Adorno argues that the vacillation between these two formulations is not accidental but symptomatic.[49] Kant must place the emphasis he does on the argument that space and time are not categories because otherwise the immediate givenness of sensibility would be endangered. Kant would have to concede that the 'material' which the activity of the categorial forms is supposed to shape is already pre-formed, a subjectified object. Hence the description of space and time as 'pure intuitions'. Yet at the same time space and time must not be empirical intuitions, otherwise synthetic a priori knowledge itself would be impossible. Hence the description of space and time as 'pure *forms* of intuition'. Adorno, by contrast, argues that 'space and time as developed by the transcendental aesthetic are, despite all assurances to the contrary, concepts: in Kantian parlance, representations [*Vorstellungen*] of a representation.'[50] For Adorno, this testifies to the impossibility of freeing space and time from all conceptual mediation whatever. 'Pure intuition would be wooden iron, experience without experience.'[51]

Kant insisted, of course, that the separation of concept and intuition, of understanding and sensibility in his work, had an epistemological rather than an ontological status. These were not opposed kinds of being for Kant, but an opposition between form and content. It is important to recognize that the above arguments do not misattribute an ontological separation between concept and intuition to Kant.[52] They are not complaining that the pure concepts and pure intuitions discussed by Kant are non-entities, that there are 'no such things', but rather that their very epistemological 'purity' renders them unintelligible. Adorno expresses this by a joke. In Kant's epistemology, Adorno suggests, adding nothing to nothing produces something.[53] What Adorno is pointing to is that the very rigour of Kant's exclusion of any ontological moment from his epistemological separation makes it unworkable, because unintelligible, as epistemology. *Pure* understanding and *pure* sensibility have not been subjected to the same critique as pure reason. Or rather: how they may legitimately *be used* has been intensively discussed. But what these expressions *signify*, what pure concepts and pure intuitions 'are', cannot be made intelligible without already destroying the methodological separation in which they are supposedly held apart for epistemological analysis.

It is here that we come to the third limb of Adorno's account, his examination of the connection between Kant's accounts of pure understanding and pure sensibility. The aim of the transcendental deduction (most clearly in the version provided in the second edition of the *Critique of Pure Reason*) is to establish a connection between the conditions of the possibility of human knowledge provided by the understanding and those provided by sensibility: to show, crudely summarized, that the categories have a synthetic rather than a merely analytic use. In one sense, of course, the transcendental deduction does not have the decisive status for Adorno which it so often takes on in assessments of the success or failure of transcendental idealism, since he has already argued that the notions of 'pure' concepts and of the sensible manifolds which they are to determine in order to make experience possible are not merely empty but unintelligible. Nevertheless, the transcendental deduction is of special interest to Adorno because it offers to show in just what way the two sets of conditions of human knowledge which Kant has been investigating in isolation are connected to each other. It provides further confirmation in Adorno's view of the internal difficulties produced by an epistemological separation of understanding and sensibility. It shows how hard it is subsequently to put back together what has first been analysed in radical separation.

The transcendental deduction is littered with the bones of the many attempts to provide an exhaustive interpretative account of it – not least because of the many important differences between the forms it takes in the first and second editions of the *Critique* – and such an account certainly cannot be attempted here. Instead discussion will have to be limited to one crucial aspect to which Adorno points – the facticity of the categories. In one passage of the second edition of the transcendental deduction Kant answers the question of why it is that 'our understanding . . . can produce *a priori* unity of apperception solely by means of the categories, and only by such and so many' by ruling it out of court: it is 'as little capable of further explanation as why we have just these and no other functions of judgement, or why space and time are the only forms of possible intuition'.[54] The categories and the logical functions of judgement are at this point regarded as raw givens no less than the forms of sensibility. For Adorno this, if true, means that the deduction has in fact not taken place. In the transcendental deduction itself we come to a halt before 'something given, something simply to be accepted [*etwas Hinzunehmendes*], something which can no longer properly be deduced at all'.[55] In this sense the question *quid juris* – with what right do I use these concepts? – has become, with this appeal to brute givenness, a question *quid facti* – how did I get hold of them? Adorno is dissatisfied with the way in which the question of right is itself thus modelled on facticity in the heart of the deduction – with what he thinks is the dogmatic aspect of transcendental method itself.

One interesting question to ask at this point, however, is whether Adorno really needs to object to the givenness of the categories. Some commentators on Kant have recently wanted to insist that appeals to conceptual or rational facticity need not be regarded as dogmatic. Dieter Henrich, in particular, has offered a rethinking of Kant which is the more relevant here for those features which it shares with Adorno's: particularly, a demonstration of the difficulty of doing without a concept of subjectivity, a refusal to liquidate metaphysical speculation, and an insistence on the internal opacity of the concept of freedom.[56] For Henrich, to speak of facts of reason which are not further interrogable is not dogmatic, as long as such data *really are* not further interrogable and instead represent genuinely ineliminable obscurities within finite experience itself. Such facts of reason do not prohibit metaphysical speculation, but, much rather, explain why speculation can neither be settled nor done away with.

Here it becomes clearer why Adorno's idea of release of critical thinking from the armour of transcendental method could not be understood through Henrich's kind of Kantianism. Metaphysical speculation, for Henrich, is an endless task; as one recent commentator has put it, 'the attempt to reach a definite and comprehensive self-description, with the added proviso that the attempt is never successful'.[57] For Adorno, on the other hand, these ineliminable obscurities are those of our finite experience, but not of any possible finite experience whatever (cf. chapter 8). They cannot be regarded as transcendent invariants, as they must be once they are taken as 'facts' of reason. Any conception of metaphysical speculation as a transcendentally endless task must commit itself again to a Kantian separation of thinking from knowing.

How, then, has the concept of experience been reformulated? Firstly, Adorno has argued that experience is both somatic and conceptual. It is so, not only in the sense that two elements must come together for experience to be possible, but also in the sense that these cannot be separated out as 'elements' for analysis in isolation from each other. There can be no account of Experience without an account of experiences. Secondly, it has been suggested that the future of experience cannot be legislated for in the image of its past. This dual reformulation has consequences for every aspect of the project of transcendental inquiry. It remobilizes the whole series of methodical separations – of form from content, of spontaneity from receptivity, of thinking from knowing – upon which Kant's account of transcendental subjectivity depends.

We have already seen why Adorno thinks his argument can be sustained against Kantian objections to it. But two different kinds of objection may already have become clear. Firstly, his reformulation of the concept of experience is deeply indebted (although, as we shall see, by no means identical) to Hegel's earlier and more systematic criticism of all Kant's radical separations. This debt is a clear difficulty for Adorno's own account of Kant. How far does Adorno's critique of Kant commit him to just that idealist identification of thought and being which a negative dialectic is supposed to help us out of? The rest of this chapter examines this question. Secondly, do Adorno's criticisms of Kant's transcendental account of experience obligate Adorno himself to provide a fully-fledged ontology, an examination of what is meant by 'being'? This question is examined in chapters 7 and 8.

Identity thinking, dialectic and social exchange

At this point, the notion of dialectic itself demands a preliminary explanation. What does it mean to say that 'dialectic' is 'negative'? Adorno contrasts dialectical thinking with what he calls 'identity thinking' or 'classificatory' thinking in the following way: 'Dialectical thinking wants to say what something is, whilst identity thinking says what something falls under, of what it is an example or a representative – and what it therefore is not itself.'[58] What Adorno has in mind can be seen if we consider Hegel's account of the immediate judgement from the *Encyclopaedia Logic*:

> The untruth of the immediate judgement lies in the incongruity between its form and its content. To say 'This rose is red' involves (in virtue of the copula 'is') the coincidence of subject and predicate. The rose however is a concrete thing, and so not red only: it also has an odour, a specific form, and many other features not implied in the predicate red. There are other flowers and objects which are red too. The subject and predicate in the immediate judgement touch, as it were, only in a single point, but do not cover each other.[59]

Hegel's point is that the copula, 'is', in 'this rose is red' is habitually taken merely as being the 'is' of predication, where 'is' can be replaced with 'comes under the class': thus, 'this rose comes under the class "red".' But the word 'is' also carries an implicit claim not merely to classify the subject under the predicate, but also to identify the subject with the predicate. In this sense, Hegel explains, the immediate judgement may be 'correct', but it cannot be fully 'true' because its correctness depends upon an interpretation of the copula 'is' which arbitrarily excludes one of its senses.

Identity thinking seeks to know its object by the sum total of correct classifications of it. For this kind of thinking we would know an object once all possible correct classifications of it have been completed. But for Adorno, there is an element of untruth in the very form of the classificatory judgement itself. When truth is conceived according to the model of such judgements the concepts become purely classificatory, merely the common denominator of what is gathered under them. The objects become merely illustrative, of interest only as examples of the concept. No amount of simply aggregating such judgements will allow thought to say what something is, but only to say 'what it comes under, of what it is a representative or an example, and what therefore it is not itself'. Adorno's preliminary characterization of dialectic is that it marks the insufficiency of correspondence models of truth: 'The name of dialectic says no more to begin with than that objects do not go into concepts without leaving a remainder, that objects turn out to contradict the traditional norm of adequation.'[60]

Thus whatever seems wholly 'immediate' or independent turns out in the event to be 'mediated', to be related to and hence dependent for its identity on some element differing from it. In the Introduction to the *Phenomenology of Spirit*, for example, Hegel shows that no attempt to point to a sensuous particular can wholly free itself from universal categories.[61] For Hegel, dialectic is the repeated experience of this implicatedness or 'mediatedness' of whatever is offered up as something pure, 'immediate' or self-sufficient.

This indicates why one prevalent conception of Hegel's *Phenomenology of Spirit* – that it presents a triumphal progress from sense-certainty to absolute knowing – needs qualification. Dialectic, for Hegel, is not simply a progress, but at the same time a working-back, an uncovering of the ways in which what is apparently certain and immediate already contains presuppositions. Hegel took this kind of working-back to demonstrate, in particular, that apparently purely logical or perceptual identifications were already tied up with political, social and cultural patterns of recognition. This is why Hegel feels obliged to offer in the *Phenomenology of Spirit* what has often seemed to philosophers with a more strictly limited conception of philosophy's task a bewildering combination of philosophical, historical, aesthetic and scientific reflection. For Hegel, these questions are not arbitrarily added together in the *Phenomenology*; rather, a consideration of the most elementary judgement necessarily demands a consideration of its conditions of possibility, conditions which are not only transcendental but also empirical-historical. In giving such an account the *Phenomenology* comes to question the finality of the very distinction between the transcendental and the empirical itself.

It is only in the experience of the insufficiency of the identificatory judgement itself, however, that this implicatedness comes to light. For this reason, dialectical thinking cannot simply be separated out from identity thinking, as though it were a superior technique which could be applied to the same material with improved results, or as though it could avoid ever using the copula, 'is', predicatively. Adorno insists that 'thinking means identifying';[62] 'consciousness is still capable of seeing through the identity-principle, but cannot think without identifying.'[63]

Identificatory thinking is, then, not merely an intellectual error, nor, indeed, is it purely a logical or linguistic problem.[64] No less important to Adorno's account of identity thinking than Hegel's analysis of the predicative judgement is Marx's theory of commodity fetishism (cf. chapter 2) – a theory which is itself deeply indebted to Hegel's dialectical logic. In the exchange of commodities Adorno finds the epitome of an identificatory judgement. That which is not merely quantitatively unequal but qualitatively incommensurable is misidentified as though it were equal and commensurable. The moment of qualitatively incommensurable use-value in exchange is accordingly increasingly misidentified.[65]

However, Adorno does not want merely to *protect* use-values against commodification, any more than he thinks it meaningful to *protect* particulars against identification. The consequences of Adorno's insistence that 'consciousness . . . cannot think without identifying' run right through to his account of social exchange. The point is not to put a stop to exchange, but to show up the misidentification, the inequality, in apparently fair exchange. Even the idea of equality would be void without the possibility of identification. Adorno insists that any arbitrary abrogation of the illusory fair exchange of commodities would simply fall back into still more directly coercive exchanges.[66] Identity thinking, then, is by no means peculiar to capitalism. Identification has been a condition of the possibility of natural-historical life and human self-preservation.[67] It is not just that identity-thinking is not 'avoidable'; it is not *only* deplorable. Dialectical thinking lies not in an attempt to purge thinking of all misidentification, but in the recognition of the insufficiency of any given identification. It is thus not a new and non-identificatory kind of thinking, but a demonstration of the insufficiency of identification.

This is the first sense in which dialectic is 'negative' for Adorno. It indicates why he thinks that dialectic cannot be regarded either as a method or as a world-picture.[68] Dialectic shows up the mutual implicatedness of concepts and objects, thought and being. As soon as it is wholly given up to thought (method) or to being (world-picture), it is no longer dialectic at all, but only a new kind of classifying schema, and a wholly arbitrary one at that. The title *Negative Dialectics*, then, does not promise a portable method which could then be taken away and applied at will to an inert 'material'; nor does it offer a dogmatic world-picture; instead it intends to name what happens in Adorno's thought itself.

Nevertheless, the idea of a 'negative' dialectic still sounds paradoxical. This is partly a consequence of the currency in some quarters (rarely amongst interpreters of Hegel) of a misleading notion of Hegelian dialectic as a method subjecting all subject matters to an inflexible tripartite schema – 'thesis, antithesis, synthesis'.[69] 'Negative dialectic', however, does not mean that dialectic is now positive and ought to become negative, but that genuinely dialectical thought already is negative.[70] Adorno's idea of negative dialectic is not a simple reversal of Hegel, another attempt brusquely to 'stand the dialectic on its feet'.[71] Adorno prefers another of Marx's metaphors: he suggests that German idealism can be made to 'dance to its own tune'.[72] Adorno attempts to prevent a dialectical thinking of which he takes Hegel to be the outstanding exponent from freezing into a method or a world-view and thereby becoming, precisely, undialectical.

Contradiction and speculative thinking

The chief difficulty for this idea of negative dialectic is obvious. How can a dialectic which is neither a method nor a world-picture work without being idealist, without claiming that thought and being are finally identical? This is the second sense in which dialectic is 'negative' for Adorno, and it is in this sense that negative dialectic is to differ from Hegel's. The answer to this difficulty is provided in the immanent critique, firstly, of the German idealist tradition, and, secondly, of major subsequent attempts to attack, go beyond, or dismantle that tradition.

Adorno's deeply and consciously self-divided engagement with Hegel is as important to his thought as a whole as his engagement with Kant. If it is read only through the account in the section of *Negative Dialectics* explicitly devoted to Hegel, 'World-Spirit and Natural History', the persisting centrality of Hegel to Adorno's work cannot be fully understood.[73] The *Three Studies on Hegel* which were explicitly conceived of as preparatory studies for Adorno's own 'changed concept of dialectic',[74] accurately indicate a difficulty which still faces contemporary interpreters of Hegel who wish to regard his work as more than a museum-piece. If dialectic is separated out as a 'method' or as a series of 'laws'[75] it at once ceases to be dialectical; but when Hegel is treated as a source to be quarried for social or historical or aesthetic 'insights' which could supposedly be shorn of their philosophical context, we are simply left with unintelligible fragments. Where much other left-Hegelianism has focused on Hegel's explicitly political thought, Adorno concentrates his reflection above all on Hegel's critical expositions of logic and epistemology.[76] For Adorno it is just those elements of Hegel's thought which are often derided as obsolete forms of 'speculative identity' which make possible its unprecedented depth and range of social, political and historical reflection.[77]

What is meant in this context by a 'speculative identity'? The most celebrated instance of a speculative identification in Hegel's work is the assertion of the Preface to the *Philosophy of Right* that 'what is rational is actual; and what is actual is rational.'[78] This has often been read as an abstract identification stating to politically conservative effect that whatever is, is right. Hegel insists, however, that the proposition is a speculative, not an abstract identification.[79] Speculative identification proceeds out of the collapse of attempts at radical separation. In the example given above, Hegel argues, especially through a rereading of Kant and Fichte, that any attempt radically to separate a purely rational 'ought' from an a-rational 'is' leaves an 'ought' which is contentless and an 'is' which is unintelligible.[80]

But this does not mean that such attempts at radical separation are mere blunders. Because the speculative identification of 'ought' and 'is' proceeds only out of the collapse of attempts absolutely to separate them, it also depends on this attempt at separation, and includes the experience of that attempt within itself. Whereas abstract identity tries to get rid of difference and contradiction as mere error, speculative identity is to contain the experience of difference and contradiction within itself.[81] Difference and contradiction are thus recognized as *real, but not absolute*. To return to our example, Hegel's speculative identification of the actual and the rational pushes him to a highly detailed exposition of the real but not absolute experience of their difference. An instance to which Adorno refers is Hegel's account of poverty, which Hegel understands as testifying to structural conflict in modern societies rather than to merely accidental or technical difficulties.[82]

Adorno is deeply aware of this dependence of speculative identity on the experience of differentiation. For this reason, unlike some other critics of Hegel, left and right,[83] he does not regard Hegelian speculation as a simple attempt to coerce what is other to thought into identity with thought. His criticism of the identity of thought and being cannot be assimilated to criticisms proceeding from a radically anti-speculative perspective. He emphasizes that what makes speculative identity speculative, rather than merely abstract, is its continued reliance on the experience of difference. He repeatedly stresses Hegel's insistence that absolute knowing is nothing without the process which leads up to it.[84]

For Adorno Hegel is thus the first philosopher who makes it possible to present contradiction in philosophical thought as something more than an accidental error on the part of the thinker. Hegel makes this point explicitly in his *Science of Logic*. If we insist that contradiction is 'unthinkable', he argues, we have presupposed that the contradictoriness cannot lie in the object of thought itself. We rule in advance that 'there is nothing that is contradictory'.[85] To insist that there can be nothing contradictory is to relapse into dogmatic rationalism. Speculative thinking, by contrast, does not treat contradiction as an accidental error, but as something real.[86] Hegel's thought, Adorno emphasizes, is thus also unprecedentedly able to do justice to what is not reducible to formal identity – to the dependence of all identifications on some non-identical element.

Hegel is thus the primary source for Adorno's unusual attitude to contradiction. Contradiction testifies that thought and being are not identical.[87] Negative dialectic, accordingly, does not aim to resolve all contradictions in a final non-contradictory position. It is easy to misunderstand Adorno's 'immanent critique' as a generalized application of the law of non-contradiction as a means of discovering contradictions in criticized texts. This, though, would be the epitome of that formal identification which Adorno takes as the 'Ur-form of ideology'.[88] Rather, negative dialectic seeks to make *visible*, as contradiction, the real antagonisms which are masked by philosophy's striving for logical identity. The aim of negative dialectic is not the liquidation of contradictions in logic, but the reconciliation of antagonisms in reality. This end cannot be served by imposing an illusory and formal non-contradictoriness, but only by showing how logical contradiction is embedded in, and dependent upon, the experience of antagonism. It is in this context that the contradictions of negative dialectic itself, contradictions which are so often used in an attempt to dispatch it, must be understood.[89] The deployment of Hegel against Kant and Kant against Hegel is not sceptical. The set of contradictions which are thus displayed testify to natural-historical antagonisms. Any attempt to overcome the appearance of scepticism by adopting an invariant standpoint would be ideological in the sense that it would conceal, not display, these real antagonisms.

For many of Adorno's critics, of course, to call such an attitude towards contradiction 'unusual' is unnecessarily polite. Vittorio Hösle, in the course of a systematic commentary on Hegel, has ranked critical theorists with vulgar Marxists for their alleged willingness to believe that self-contradictions constitute no valid objection to their argument.[90] Hösle argues that two primary senses of Hegel's argument about the principle of non-contradiction need to be distinguished. Hegel does not wish to claim that self-contradiction is no objection to a theory. This is clear from the central place of demonstrations of self-contradiction in, for example, Hegel's critique of Kant. But Hösle insists that this discursive [*argumentationslogisch*] sense of the principle of non-contradiction is to be distinguished from an ontological principle of non-contradiction which declares that 'there cannot be anything which is contradictory.' It is this ontological application of the principle of non-contradiction which Hegel wishes to resist.

For Hösle, then, critical theorists have mistakenly conflated Hegel's objections to ontological misemployments of the principle of non-contradiction with their own dogmatic objections to the discursive version of the principle. It may be clear from what has already been said why it is difficult to apply this criticism to Adorno, however. As with Hegel, the making-explicit of concealed or insufficiently thematized contradiction is an indispensable means of Adorno's immanent critique. Clearly, if any contradiction whatever could be excused by saying that the principle of contradiction itself is a piece of dogmatic rationalism, Adorno's own critique would be impossible. Instead negative dialectic aims to exhibit those contradictions which *ineliminably* arise in the course of consequential attempts to eliminate them. Only ineliminably arising contradictions testify to natural-historical antagonism. The decisive issue is whether the aporias of critical theory really do testify to such antagonism or whether they are contingent upon a mistakenly totalizing critique. Any radical separation of a discursive and an ontological sense of Hegel's theory of contradiction would in any case simply recapitulate an abstract separation between thought and being, a separation which would liquidate the possibility of dialectical, as well as of speculative thinking.

Totality

Adorno's appeal to the 'non-identical', it has become clear, cannot be understood in simple opposition to Hegel. Instead Adorno's thought aims from within Hegelian speculation itself, from within the restless return to contradiction in Hegel's compositions, against those moments in Hegel's thought where Adorno regards him as having come to rest in identity after all. Adorno's view of the place of 'totality' in Hegel's thinking is thus more complex than has sometimes been recognized. Where Hegel's Preface to his *Phenomenology of Spirit* suggests that 'The true is the whole', *Minima Moralia* responds with the counter-aphorism that 'The whole is the false.'[91] Taken in isolation, the aphorism gives a misleading impression. The whole is the false for Adorno not in the sense that a philosophical emphasis on totality is a mistake, but in the sense that this emphasis is inseparable from an increasingly self-totalizing society. In this sense, the whole may be false, but it is none the less real. Because it is inseparable from this natural-historical whole, the meaning of Hegel's own emphasis on totality can only be understood historically. Adorno argues that the emphasis of German idealism on 'the whole' was a necessary corollary of an enlightened criticism of merely particular social interests and their intellectual counterpart, a division of intellectual labour misrepresented as an immutably given framework for cognition.[92] But the truth-moment of Hegel's emphasis on totality has since been falsified by the self-absolutizing production for which this category has since come to apologize. That is, Adorno holds it against history as much as against Hegel that the whole has become the false.[93]

But is dialectic at all possible without finally positing such a totality, without finally positing the identity of thought and being? Adorno's answer to this difficulty lies in his account of 'determinate negation'. Hegel had pointed out that to negate implied negating something. For this reason, any given negation would not simply leave thought with nothingness ('abstract negation'), but would itself be a determinate or specific negation, a negation of something. For Hegel what this shows is that such 'determinate negation' must in its turn yield a new result with a particular content.[94] Speculative thinking itself, for Hegel, consists in an ability to understand how positing and negation are related in this way, or, as he puts it elsewhere, to think the 'unity of identity with difference'.[95]

Adorno agrees that negation must always be determinate, but not that this means that it is therefore in its turn positive. He calls Hegel's approach a 'positive negation'. What happens for Adorno in Hegel's 'positive negation' is that 'the anti-dialectical principle, that logic which, *more arithmetico* [in mathematical fashion] chalks up minus times minus as a plus, wins out in the inmost core of dialectic itself.' Adorno argues instead that 'the only positive element in the negation of particularities would be determinate negation, critique, not a circumventing result emerging happily with affirmation in its hands.' What is once negated stays negative.[96]

Hegel's systematic thought, of course, would be impossible without what Hegel calls 'speculative thinking' and what Adorno calls 'positive negation'. Yet Adorno insists that dialectical thought need not be a closed system and that it is not exclusively dependent on the identificatory moment in speculation:

> Were it to be objected that such criticism of the positive negation of negation would sever the vital nerve of Hegel's logic and would make dialectical movement itself impossible, this objection would, trusting in Hegel's authority, restrict such movement to his self-understanding. Although the structure of his system would certainly collapse without this principle, dialectic's experiential content does not come from the principle but from the resistance of the other to identity; this is the source of its power.[97]

For Adorno dialectic is thought's repeated experience of its inability finally to identify what is non-identical to it. So far from being an experience which is only made possible by 'the identity of identity and non-identity', as Adorno's imaginary objector protests, this is an experience which is only made possible by the *non-identity* of identity and non-identity, by the fact that identity and non-identity are not the same. Non-identity, more radically than identity, makes dialectical experience possible. Hence Adorno's insistence that dialectical thinking relies on an undialectical element precisely in order to remain dialectical. Adorno, then, asks how the dialectical experience of thought is possible. It is made possible by that which it cannot yet exhaustively think, the non-identical.[98]

The Hegelian objector is unlikely to be satisfied by such a defence. It will need to be shown how this argument can avoid lapsing into dogmatism. Must Adorno claim immediate access to a given element transcending thought – that is, must his materialism be metaphysical? This question is addressed in the following chapters.

7

Constellations: Thinking the Non-identical

'Constellation': language and mimesis

So far we have been considering the way in which Adorno's thought emerges from a critique of classical German philosophy. This has raised questions which cannot be settled simply by remaining within that tradition. We need to look at those motifs in Adorno's thought whose sources lie beyond the immanent critique of German idealism, in particular the idea of a 'constellation' of concepts, of language as a model for thinking, of the role of mimesis in cognition, as well as at his idea that materialist thinking demands a 'priority of the object'. This will help us to begin to see why an account of the problems faced by the philosophy of practice becomes so important to Adorno's way of understanding materialism.

The initial source for Adorno's notion that negative dialectics brings together a 'constellation' of concepts is Walter Benjamin's *The Origin of the German Play of Lamentation*. In the 'epistemo-critical prologue' to that work Benjamin announced that 'ideas are related to objects as constellations are to stars. This means, in the first place, that ideas are neither the concepts of objects nor their laws. They do not contribute to the knowledge of phenomena, and in no way can the latter be criteria with which to judge the existence of ideas.' Benjamin followed this with a declaration that 'Ideas are timeless constellations . . .'[1] There are two important differences between Benjamin's notion of the constellation and Adorno's. Firstly, Benjamin makes a radical distinction between concepts, which are a way of classifying or subsuming particular phenomena under a universal, and ideas, which are above merely positive knowledge. When Benjamin talks about 'concepts' he is addressing what Adorno means by subsumptive or classificatory thinking, thinking which is primarily concerned with what the object comes under, not what it is in itself (cf. chapter 6). But Adorno is less confident than the early Benjamin that it would ever be possible to separate out such 'ideas', indifferent to particular experience, from concepts. This is why he suggests, in one of his rare critical remarks about Benjamin, that 'in Benjamin's work the concepts have an authoritarian tendency to conceal their own conceptuality.'[2] The risk run by any such radical separation of 'ideas' from concepts is that what are actually concepts will be wrongly promoted to the rank of ideas. This would be 'authoritarian' because it implies that 'ideas' are in principle not susceptible to falsification by experience.

Secondly, Adorno's constellations could no more be 'timeless' than the elements which constitute them. Just as a constellation is nothing without the stars, Adorno's constellations *are* nothing in themselves but a relation between (necessarily time-bound) particulars. Adorno makes the difference between his position and Benjamin's explicit in the 'Constellation in Science [*Wissenschaft*]' section of *Negative Dialectics*, where Benjamin's early account of the constellation is described as 'metaphysical'.[3] Instead Adorno appeals, provocatively, to Max Weber – not to the positive content of his work, but to his refusal to provide summary definitions for concepts which were historical, and his insistence in his essay on *The Protestant Ethic and the Spirit of Capitalism* that such concepts must be 'gradually *composed* out of component parts which are only to be taken from the historically actual. Definitive conceptual comprehension cannot for this reason appear at the beginning, but only at the *end* of the inquiry.'[4]

How is the idea of a constellation of concepts related to Adorno's account of identity thinking? The use of concepts as though they were mere mechanisms for classification or 'sets' is to be criticized in detail. Yet individual particulars are not ineffable or non-conceptualizable:

> The unifying moment survives, without any negation of the negation, but also without delivering itself to abstraction as the highest principle, because the concepts do not progress step by step to a more universal cover-concept, but enter into a constellation. The latter illuminates what is specific in the object, that which is burdensome or a matter of

indifference to a classificatory procedure. The model for this is the procedure of language. Language does not merely offer a system of signs for cognitive functions. Where language appears essentially as language, where it becomes an exposition [*Darstellung*], it does not define its concepts. It lends objectivity to the concepts through the relation into which it places them, centred around a subject-matter. Language thereby serves the intention of the concept, wholly to express what is meant. Only constellations can represent from outside that which the concept has cut out inside . . .[5]

This difficult passage is quoted at length because of its importance. Classificatory thinking, as we have seen in the previous chapter, does not say what something is, but 'only what it comes under, of what it is an illustration or an example, and what therefore it is not itself'. Adorno is arguing that this specificity of the individual, the 'inside' which has as it were been 'cut out' by the concept, disregarded by classificatory thinking, can be illuminated by the relations between concepts. The idea of a constellation of concepts is thus not a new *technique*, separate from what has earlier been regarded as negative dialectic. Instead, it is another way of explaining what is meant by a dialectic that does without the negation of the negation (cf. chapter 6).[6]

'Language' is a model for this kind of dialectic because of what Adorno calls its 'double character'. Adorno and Horkheimer argue in *Dialectic of Enlightenment* that the separation of art from science in modern rationality has confined language to two equally false functions: 'As a system of signs, language is required to resign itself to calculation in order to know nature, and must discard the claim to be like nature. As image, it is required to resign itself to copying in order to be nature entire, and must discard the claim to know nature.'[7] The 'language' invoked in Adorno's account of 'constellation' is a language which still retains its double character, a language which has not yet wholly surrendered itself to sign or image, concept or intuition. In this it is distinguished, for example, from mathematics. 'Language' is distinct from the most formal possible concepts, mathematical symbols, on the one hand, and from pictorial representation, on the other. In contrast to either of these extremes, language still retains both a classificatory and a mimetic element.

The division referred to in the *Dialectic of Enlightenment*, that is, is not yet complete. A dialectic of enlightenment seeks affinity with its object rather than classification of it. It refuses the scientistic requirement that language should cut out its mimetic element. Adorno regards this, once more, as another way of putting what is meant by dialectic itself.[8] This idea can be explained by comparing Adorno with a thinker such as Hobbes. For Hobbes it was an obvious first requirement of rigorous thought that it should define its terms unambiguously, as a geometrician might do.[9] These terms would then be employed with a fixed sense throughout a given inquiry. For Adorno, by contrast, it is not possible to keep the sense of concepts inertly fixed in this way unless they really are empty – unless language really is reduced to an entirely formal logic, something which Adorno has already argued would in fact be unintelligible.

Adorno's appeal to the mimetic component of language, to the aim of *affinity* between concept and object, clearly carries certain risks. It has sometimes been taken to appeal nostalgically to an original unity of the mimetic and classificatory aspects of language, a unity which has supposedly been disastrously lost through a fall into enlightenment. Yet the point of the appeal to mimesis is not to get rid of predicative judgement, or to turn philosophy into a kind of 'conceptual poetry', a phrase which Adorno always used pejoratively.[10] *Negative Dialectics*, that is, does not recommend an 'aestheticized reason', but is giving an account of what reason *is like*. Reason cannot avoid being aesthetic, in the minimal sense that its concepts are all entangled with experience, rather than being rigid atoms of designation. Mimesis is itself a kind of rationality for Adorno, and not one which is less coercive than classification.[11]

The ideas of 'mimesis' and 'affinity' are not, then, a way of clinging protectively to an 'archaic remnant' which is increasingly under threat. Instead they are developed in the context of Adorno's account (chapter 6) of the way in which thinking *needs* to be contaminated with experience in order even to be possible.[12] This is why Adorno explains affinity in terms of the idea of 'determinate negation' which we have already seen to be so central to his negative dialectic:

> But even affinity is no positive ontological individual determination. Once affinity is turned into an intuition, into an immediately, empathetically known truth, it will be ground to pieces by the dialectic of enlightenment, as a warmed-over myth; as something in accord with a mythology which reproduces itself out of pure reason, with domination. Affinity is not a remnant, which cognition could have securely in its hands once the identificatory schemas have been excluded; rather it is the determinate negation of those schemas.[13]

Enlightened rationality would be right, in Adorno's view, to critic-ize any appeal to immediate mimesis. But a mimetic moment is at work even in identification: 'cognition cannot be conceived with-out a mimetic element, however sublimated.'[14] Classificatory thinking is to be reminded of its own mimetic element, an element which it can never entirely get rid of. The mimetic moment of philosophical language, however, cannot be filtered out from con-ceptual identification and presented as something independent. It can only be illuminated by showing how identification *mis*-identifies.

There is an important caveat to be offered here, then. Adorno's account of the idea of a 'constellation' of concepts, of language as a model for thinking should not be thought of as a kind of positive result – as, say, what would be left over after the purely negative critique of idealism. These motifs make sense only in the context of Adorno's account of identity thinking and the associated account of a negative dialectic. Taking such ideas as that of a 'constellation' of concepts out of this context, whether in order to obtain a portable methodology or a world-picture, distorts them, by mak-ing them into a kind of new mythology.

Affinity and schematism

The idea of an 'affinity' between concept and object remains in need of further clarification. Is it simply an attempt to bridge the gulf between concept and object by positing some third term between them? We can see more clearly what philosophical issues are at stake in Adorno's account of 'affinity' if we consider it in the context of Kant's chapter on the 'Schematism of the Pure Concepts of the Understanding' in the *Critique of Pure Reason*.[15] Although the term 'affinity' itself occurs in the first edition transcendental de-duction, rather than in the schematism chapter, the latter is of central importance to an understanding of Adorno's account of affinity. Kant is addressing a version of the problem which so preoccupies Adorno, namely the connection between pure con-cepts of the understanding and sensible appearances. Kant asks 'how is the application of categories to appearances possible'? He answers this question by saying that there must be a third element (*ein Drittes*), which he entitles a 'transcendental schema'.[16] Tran-scendental schemas are universal and necessary characteristics of things in time which allow time relations to be expressed. The schema of the category of substance, for example, is 'permanence of the real in time, that is, the representation of the real as a substrate of empirical determination of time in general, and so as abiding while all else changes'.[17] These schemas are the products of the transcendental imagination, 'an art concealed in the depths of the human soul', as Kant famously characterized it.[18] The transcendental imagination is not to be confused with the empirical imagination. It is a source, not of empirical intuitions, but of transcendental schemata, determinate *pure* intuitions which make possible the application of categories to appearances.

It is clear that Kant is by now making claims that can no longer be understood as purely epistemological. These claims must in part be metaphysical. To say how it is possible for pure concepts of the understanding to apply to appearances is to specify just what is being claimed about the phenomenal world when it is claimed that pure concepts of the understanding can apply to it.[19] This metaphysical element in the schematism attracts Adorno's interest. It is occasioned by Kant's awareness of the limits to an epistemological separation of concept and intuition, an awareness which had already been emphatically signalled at the beginning of the *Critique*.

It can be seen at once, then, what Adorno finds interesting in the schematism: Kant discovers from the internal needs of his own thought that some explicit account needs to be provided of how concepts and intuitions relate to each other. As Adorno put it in a course of lectures which focused primarily on the first critique, the 'immediate antithesis of receptivity and spontaneity, of sensibility and understanding is actually already sublated in the course of the Kantian analysis itself, and thereby, if I may say this without being too presumptuous, Kant granted a certain *placet* to the speculative deliberations with which I have been engaged here.'[20] For Adorno the schematism is a place where Kant's epistemology begins to indicate its own metaphysical presuppositions. Adorno takes it as testifying to his own view that any logic or epistemology which today attempted absolutely to divest itself of any metaphysical moment whatever would end by liquidating the very possibility of thinking, and with it, logic and epistemology themselves. Although the implications of the schematism were understood somewhat differently by Kant himself – the absence of a transcendental schematism would not mean that thinking itself would be impossible, but only that the pure concepts of the understanding would not have a real, as well as a logical, use – Adorno wishes to criticize the separation between thinking and knowing itself in this and its other forms.

This already begins to indicate some of the differences between Kant's notion of a transcendental schema which makes all knowledge of objects possible, and Adorno's idea of an affinity between concept and object. For Adorno, Kant's schema becomes a positive mediating 'third' element. This 'third' element is needed only because the terms which it is to connect have been conceived as too radically separate. This difficulty can be seen in the structure of the transcendental schema itself. It is already, internally, made up of a combination of those elements which it is supposed to connect. Because the schema is a *determinate* pure intuition, it must already, in fact, surreptitiously incorporate a conceptual element. Adorno's ultimate dissatisfaction with the schematism reflects his thesis that 'pure' concepts, 'pure' intuitions, and an undetermined sensuous manifold, are alike unintelligible. The difference between Adorno's account of affinity and Kant's schematism chapter is not that Adorno tries a different method for bridging the same fixed separation as Kant, but that the separation itself has already been remobilized in Adorno's account of concepts and objects. The difference can be summarized like this. The schematism accounts for how *pure* concepts of the understanding may be successfully *applied* to *pure* appearances. Affinity, by contrast, is the name for how *impure* concepts can interpret *impure* objects with which they are not identical. In order to show how this position is grounded, a look at Adorno's paradoxical attempt to articulate a 'priority of the object' by means of the concept becomes necessary.

The 'transition to the priority of the object'

For Kant 'objects' [*Gegenstände*] were formed by the activity of conceptual forms upon a sensuous manifold of intuition. As such they represented a logicized object, an 'object', that is, which had already been shaped by conceptual determination. For Kant, we could only know things as they appeared to consciousness. In this sense Kant's objects were phenomena, rather than things known as they were in themselves. Yet he insisted that we must be at least able to *think* of a thing 'considered as it is in itself'. If this were not the case we should be left in the absurd position of postulating appearances without anything that does the appearing.

This complex theory of the object has given rise to many conflicting interpretations. Some readers have thought that an ontology, a doctrine or science of being, could be developed from Kant's idea of the thing considered as it is in itself. Others have insisted that the thing-in-itself is a merely regulative limiting concept with no ontological content whatever.[21] Adorno did not believe that either reading was fully satisfactory, because Kant's own thought was tellingly ambiguous on this point. Adorno recalled that his early studies of Kant with Siegfried Kracauer had shown him 'how objective-ontological and subjective-idealistic moments are in conflict in Kant; how the most eloquent passages are the wounds which this conflict left behind it in Kant's doctrine'.[22] The idea of a thing considered as it is in itself marks a problem for philosophy, a problem which it has still not solved.

Adorno's theory of the 'priority of the object' is an attempt to ask on what conditions it would be possible to have *substantive* knowledge, knowledge of the object as it is in itself, not merely knowledge of appearances. The attempt is necessarily paradoxical because it seems to ask for knowledge of an essence beyond appearances. Yet if we were to have knowledge of such an essence it would necessarily have appeared to us. This argument is expressed in Hegel's dictum, often quoted by Adorno, that 'essence must appear', or that the essence of essence is to appear.[23]

Adorno agrees with the post-Kantian idealists that it is more consistent not to separate the thing in itself from the thing as it appears to consciousness. But he suggests that Kant's inconsistency may have its virtues here.[24] The idea of a thing as it is in itself bears witness to what Adorno himself has earlier called 'the non-identical' – although since the thing as considered in itself is necessarily devoid of all qualities it does not fully correspond to Adorno's own notion of the non-identical.[25] But if we do not admit the *possibility* of knowing things as they are in themselves, Adorno thinks, we are in fact committed to a kind of scepticism, in which the object is always pre-formed by conceptuality – in which the object must always remain a logicized object.

Adorno's own attempt to address this problem takes place under the heading of the 'priority of the object'. The impulse behind this phrase is clear: it is a materialist rejoinder to those idealist thought-forms which grant priority, whether against their will or not, to the subject. There is a moment of blunt materialism in this motif, well captured by Adorno's almost commonsensical insistence that whilst it is impossible for us even to conceive of a subject which is not an object, we can very easily conceive of an object which is not a subject.[26] Adorno believes both that what is apparently immediate, independent or self-sufficient, shows itself to be 'mediated', dependent and not sufficient unto itself, and, conversely, that there can be no mediation without something to mediate. But he insists that the relation between immediacy and mediation is asymmetrical.[27] Mediation is nothing at all, by itself, without immediacy; whereas immediacy is not nothing without mediation. This is another way of putting the asymmetrical relation between subject and object.

Adorno is not suggesting that we could have access to some kind of immediate objectivity wholly free of subjective mediation. Any such promise would be delusive because cognitive 'access' to immediacy is already a mediation of it. Adorno does not think, for example, that the object can simply be promoted to the same kind of position of priority which he takes to be occupied by the subject in German idealism. 'On that throne the object would be nothing but an idol', because the decision that the object has priority would be the subject's decision: we would effectively be subjecting ourselves not to the object itself, but to a placeholder for it which we ourselves had installed in its place, deludedly believing it to be transcendent and independent of our thinking.[28] Nor does Adorno think it possible to guarantee objective knowledge simply by stripping away those elements of cognition considered to be subjective, as though they were an accidental extra. Hence Adorno's apparently paradoxical suggestion that 'Only for subjective reflection, and for subjective reflection on the subject, is the priority of the object attainable.'[29]

Do such reflections, though, leave us back with the very subject-object against which the notion of the 'priority of the object' was devised? This latter formulation, after all, sounds very much like the way in which Adorno himself characterizes Kant's 'Copernican turn' and its consequences in post-Kantian idealism: 'to propound the objectivity of truth and of any given content which has been nominalistically eroded by subjectivity, by means of the same subjectivity which has liquidated them'.[30] The consequences of Kant's Copernican turn for his theory of the object can be seen not only in his insistence that nothing can be predicated of things as they are in themselves, but also in his appeal to a logicized notion of the object in the transcendental deduction of the second edition of the *Critique of Pure Reason*. In one of his many formulations of the aim of *Negative Dialectics*, Adorno referred to its wish to give the Copernican turn an 'axial twist'. It is this twist which is reflected in Adorno's reformulation of the concept of experience towards a priority of the object: towards experience which really would be experience of the object itself, in all its qualitative complexity, rather than of a subjectified or logicized placeholder – intuition, appearance of the object 'in a logical sense' – for the object itself.

Adorno admits that the thesis that the object has priority is self-collapsing when abstractly stated.[31] Negative dialectic, however, is not merely to state but to bear witness to the priority of the object by its philosophical process. For this reason Adorno insists that the only way to do justice to the priority of the object is by pushing subjectively mediated identifications to the point where they collapse. This is what Adorno means by describing negative dialectic as an attempt 'to use the strength of the subject to break out of the delusion of constitutive subjectivity'.[32] But the delusion referred to here is not simply theoretical, but also practical. The attempt could only be realized if the whole nexus of acts of identification and classification, acts which are both theoretical and practical, could change. This is why the 'models' offered in *Negative Dialectics* – a metacritique of practical reason in Kant and an excursus on Hegel's account of world history – turn to central questions in practical philosophy. Reflection on the possibility of practice is essential to Adorno's idea of a materialism without dogmatism.

Hence, too, the way in which these 'models' differ from a sociology of knowledge or from any straightforward ideology criticism. Neither society nor history can be installed as a first being, of which thought would be a merely superstructural result. To this extent even a dictum such as Marx and Engels's that '[l]ife is not determined by consciousness, but consciousness by life' becomes inadmissible dogmatism once universalized.[33] The Marxian idea of natural history itself is used by Adorno against just such an effect, whereby whatever is introduced to eliminate all illegitimate transcendence – history or materiality or finitude, for example – ends up, *de facto*, as itself inexplicably transcendent. Access to natural-historical experience is not immediate; instead it is to be deciphered from the metalogical reference in which transcendental subject and subject-object are already entangled.

Freedom and compulsion

The link between the theoretical and practical aspects of Adorno's materialism can best be understood in the context of what he describes as the 'metacritique of practical reason' carried out in the third part of *Negative Dialectics*. The 'metacritique' is carried out on Kant's theory of the moral law and those features of his epistemology associated with it. Adorno's metacritique thinks with Kant as much as against him.

In the third antinomy of the *Critique of Pure Reason* Kant tried to show that although we could not have knowledge of a special kind of causality differing from causality under laws of nature and described as a 'causality of freedom', neither could we have knowledge that such a causality was impossible.[34] Radical spontaneism and radical determinism were shown to be equally dogmatic. In his account of the moral law in the *Critique of Practical Reason* Kant was then able to argue, further, that the first critique had already shown that even though 'speculative reason could not assure any objective reality to [freedom]' it nevertheless 'could think of freedom without contradiction'.[35] Kant then argued that even though we could not have theoretical knowledge of freedom, the concept of freedom was 'given objective reality' by the validity of the moral law, 'So act that the maxim of your will could always hold at the same time as a principle establishing universal law.'[36] The objective reality of the moral law is not established by freedom; rather the objective reality of freedom is established by the moral law.[37] 'Freedom' is thus in a certain sense *commanded* for Kant. Kant then took the further step of suggesting that this practical objectivity 'sufficiently proves [freedom's] reality even for the critique of speculative reason' because theoretical reason was already compelled to assume the possibility, at least, of freedom.[38]

The attempt to prove freedom's reality even for speculative reason appears to differ in emphasis from the third antinomy, whose result was less that speculative reason is compelled to assume the possibility of freedom than that it could neither legitimately assume its reality nor legitimately assume its unreality.[39] This is a local form of a much wider difficulty in Kant's moral theory concerning the contradiction between the practical objectivity of freedom and the fact that experience is understood under laws of causal determination. Crudely put, Kant risks insisting that we must *think* of our actions 'as if' they were free whilst *experiencing* our actions as determined. Transcendental freedom is necessarily beyond the determinations of time (since only experience can be determined in time) and therefore also beyond history. For Adorno this amounts to a resigned admission that freedom will never be realized in history, despite the hopes of Kant's own political and historical writings.[40]

That Kant's 'freedom' is never to be historically experienced, only postulated, converts it in Adorno's view into a philosophical legitimation of the merely formal freedom offered in the modern state. The political freedom enjoyed by citizens of the modern liberal state is freedom 'as if', concealing the subjects' unfreedom in social and economic relations. The experience of legal persons, including their social experience of unfreedom, is taken as a private matter quite contingent to their legal personality.

Adorno's case here is heavily indebted to Hegel and Marx. Hegel argued that Kant's moral theory proposed an 'ought' which was necessarily contentless, and, finally, unintelligible, despite Kant's attempts to provide a content for it. For Hegel, the unsatisfactoriness of all Kant's bridging devices was an inevitable result of the way in which Kant had radically separated the empirical from the intelligible aspect of knowledge. Consequently Kant's autonomous moral agent, the subject giving itself its own universalizable law, was not only its own master, Hegel insisted, but also necessarily its own slave, because the actions of the Kantian empirical subject were necessarily conditioned, non-universalizable, and would hence inevitably not merely fall short of, but appear utterly incommensurable with, the categorical imperative, incapable even of approximating to it by the 'asymptotic convergence' imagined by Kant.[41] Marx developed Hegel's critique of Kantian ethics into a critique of the formal legal idea of freedom presupposed by classical political economy.

Yet Adorno's charge is not simply that Kant's moral theory is 'merely formal'.[42] The charge that Kant's freedom and moral theory are 'merely formal' can stand in, as Adorno is well aware, for a falling-back behind the standpoint of universalizable morality to an arbitrary legitimation of heteronomous and traditionally given custom. This worry has been central to the modified Kantianism behind Jürgen Habermas's discourse ethics; Adorno has much sympathy with this concern, and is highly critical of an attempt like Max Scheler's to revoke Kant's ethics by pointing to its formalism.[43] But Adorno did not believe that this apparent fall into heteronomy could best be protected against by a vigilant insistence on Kantian universalism as the most advanced possible ethical framework. The strengths of Kantian universalism could not be filtered out from its limitations to provide a model for a pragmatics, whether 'universal' or 'transcendental'.[44] Rather, Adorno wanted to show that it was just Kant's radical insistence on moral autonomy, his suppression of a necessarily heteronomous moment in freedom, which already contained within itself the seeds of a capitulation to heteronomy. The Kantian subject is to be both free (as transcendental subject) and unfree (as empirical subject).[45] Even transcendental freedom, however, is not free from compulsion. Kant's concern to provide an a priori deduction for freedom leads him to ground it in the moral law. Freedom is thus dependent upon a prior obligation. Something of this surfaces in the *Critique of Judgement* when Kant argues that our liking for the good – a liking supposedly based upon a causality of freedom – is no more free than phenomenal inclination. This is why Adorno argues that 'Kant, like the idealists after him, cannot bear freedom without compulsion.'[46]

But can Adorno bear freedom without compulsion? Had either Kant or Hegel attempted to present freedom without compulsion, Adorno would undoubtedly have censured the presentation as ideological. Indeed, it was precisely in considering Fichte's attempt to deduce an entire (and in the event highly coercive) a priori politics from absolute freedom that Hegel noted how promises to start out from pure freedom terminated all the more surely in absolute compulsion.[47] Adorno is aware of this series of difficulties. He argues that the attempt to erase all heteronomy in the name of free moral action is just what turns that freedom into compulsion. Instead '[f]reedom would require what in Kant is something heteronomous.'[48] Only once the subject can come to accept what is other to it as other, rather than seeking to master it, could it be released from its own slavery.[49]

Adorno's own account of freedom, then, remains a negative one. He can no more successfully *posit* freedom without compulsion than can Fichte. Yet that we cannot now *posit* the meaning of freedom does not mean that the concept has no meaning, or can never have one. Positivistic attempts to liquidate the question as a pseudo-problem are mistaken.[50] The entanglement of freedom with compulsion in philosophical reflection is true to our natural-historical experience, but false in so far as it would render that experience invariant. The experience of unfreedom is particular and mutable; it is the aim of negative dialectic not to allow the conversion of such experience into a mythically invariant destiny.

Theory, practice and production

We could have experience of freedom, then, only on condition that the subject could accept what is other to it as other. The conditions of the possibility of freedom would be twofold: an end to philosophical attempts to present the subject as constituting its own objects, and a change in the social experience in which such attempts are embedded, namely the conversion of production into an end in itself.[51] It might seem as though philosophy were thereby condemned silently to await a structural change in social experience; and that, accordingly, Adorno installs social practice as having primacy over theory. But this is misleading. Adorno is not criticizing some merely negative restriction on a posited free activity, but rather an energetic activity: the ever-advancing production of exchange-value for its own sake. When production is conceived of as an end in itself, human action becomes a mere parody of itself. It becomes, as Lukács put it, not genuinely practical but rather contemplative.[52] Hence Adorno's dictum that '[f]alse practice is not practice at all.'[53] Any attempt to give primacy to practice over theory only reinforces this self-absolutizing production.

It is in this context that Adorno's account of the relation between theory and practice in German idealism and in its Marxist inheritance needs to be understood. Lukács protested that Adorno had taken up residence in a 'Grand Hotel of the Abyss' whence the disaster of the modern world would only ever be contemplated, not changed.[54] But the truth is more complicated than this. Adorno resists any idea of the 'primacy' of practice, or any attempt to identify theory and practice. But he does not criticize the notion of a primacy of practice in favour of a merely contemplative theory. Instead, the separation of theory and practice is taken as a historical separation which cannot simply be wished back together.[55]

The idea of a primacy of practice, or of an identification of theory and practice, is for Adorno the very image of production for its own sake. The notion of primacy is itself, unavoidably, theoretical, even when it is a primacy of practice which is in question. The attempt to give *primacy* to practice would complete that 'depracticalization [*Entpraktizierung*] of practice' which is the characteristic of the 'bad infinity' of absolute production. It is just because the idea of a primacy of practice leads to the depracticalization of practice, converts it into a *theoretical* 'first', that Adorno resists it.[56] Adorno regards Marx's emphasis on practice not as an anti-philosophical reversal of classical German thought, but as a direct legacy of Kant's thesis that pure reason is practical or that the practical use of reason has primacy over its theoretical use.[57] His criticism of this thesis in Kant and of its consequences for his German idealist successors is thus the necessary context for understanding this aspect of his relation to the Marxist tradition. By allowing only reason as a valid mover of practice, Kant remakes practice in the image of theory. It is this that allows Kant to talk, misleadingly in Adorno's view, of practical and theoretical reason as only 'differences of application' of one and the same reason. Adorno thus believes that the speculative identification of theory and practice in later German idealism is, like other such identifications, already embryonically present in Kant.[58]

Adorno does not argue for a radical separation between theory and practice: 'Practice is put off, yet it cannot wait: this ails theory too.'[59] Rather, because all our current practice is already entangled in the false practice of production for its own sake, only if theory retains an element of independence from practice can a different practice become possible:

> The dialectic of practice also demanded that practice as production for production's sake, as the universal cover for false practice, should be done away with. That is the materialist ground for those traits in negative dialectic which rebel against official materialist doctrine. The moment of independence and irreducibility in spirit might indeed sit well with the priority of the object. Wherever spirit here and now becomes independent, as soon as it names the bondage into which it falls in so far as it binds others, it, and not an entangled practice, anticipates freedom.[60]

Adorno resists the primacy of practice, but in favour of a theory which would change the existing framework for practice, rather than just acting, contemplatively, within that framework. Only if practice is not absolutized, only if it does *not* have 'primacy', is it genuinely practical, Adorno suggests. The condition of this possibility is a theory not immediately subservient to falsely theorized practical ends or uses.[61] This is why Adorno emphasizes the significance to his account of theory and practice of 'those traits in negative dialectic which rebel against official materialist doctrine'.

For most materialisms the idea of a 'moment of independence . . . in spirit' is simply metaphysical. Adorno, however, does not mean to designate an intelligible entity or a 'thinking thing' by referring to this moment.[62] Rather, thinking's *only* moment of independence is to recognize its dependence, 'the bondage into which it falls in so far as it binds others'.

A non-identical moment in the subject, that is, is necessary for justice to the priority of the object to be conceivable. Any materialism which directly decreed the priority of the object and treated thought as a mere result would be involuntarily metaphysical, because it would set up some mutable element as an unconditioned ground. Those elements of negative dialectic which appear anti-materialist are, then, a way of articulating a materialism in which the 'material' is *changing*, not involuntarily converted into an invariant ground. The thesis of the primacy of practice, by contrast, prevents just the change it demands because it installs practice as a *de facto* invariant first.

The consequences of this aspect of Adorno's immanent critique of German idealism run right through to his Marxism. One motif in particular in Adorno's engagement with the tradition is of special importance here. Kant's idea of a thing as considered 'in itself' is a moment in Kant's thought which testifies to the inability of the subject to produce its objects. As we have seen (chapter 6), Adorno strongly resists Kant's way of discussing all objects considered as they appear to consciousness as worked over by conceptual forms which are pure activity. This kind of account of objects (*Gegenstände*), we saw, testifies in Adorno's view to an increasingly powerful idea of production as the source of all value. Kant's appeal to a thing considered as it is in itself, conversely, testifies to the fact that labour must be labour *on something*. Although Adorno agrees that the post-Kantian idealists are more consistent in criticizing the separation between a thing in itself and as it appears to consciousness, it is just this consistency that leads to the self-producing Absolute, the philosophical image of absolute production.

The 'failure' to follow Marx's theory of exchange through to a full account of production, for which Adorno has sometimes been taken to task, represents, then, a deliberate shift of emphasis. Adorno does not believe in a self-sufficient labour theory of value. He is critical of those aspects of Marx's work which he considers to underwrite the absolutization of production.[63] Instead he emphasizes those moments in Marx's work which are sceptical of it, especially the *Critique of the Gotha Programme* in which Marx insisted that '[l]abour is *not the source* of all wealth'.[64]

For analogous reasons Adorno wishes to qualify 'the lament over reification [*Verdinglichung*]'.[65] Adorno does not use this term in any ostentatiously technical sense, but with an emphasis on its root sense of the conversion of a process into a thing; particularly, the presentation of social process as the property of a thing. In this sense Adorno insists that, far from reification being a result of capitalism alone, there has never been a non-reified or purely transparent society.[66] Society is not only a human product. This was already part of Adorno's point in describing society as natural-historical rather than simply as historical. Intersubjective activity is always objectively mediated. The insistence that human relations should never appear as the property of a thing, that they should be pure activity, only testifies further to an idealist determination that the subject should be self-constituting and self-sufficient, that the subject should not in any way be conditioned or dependent. Adorno identifies Lukács's *History and Class Consciousness* as to this extent still idealist – even though Adorno himself draws heavily on Lukács's account of the false naturalization of social process.[67] Because, as we have seen, freedom would for Adorno require what appears a heteronomous element, it would mean that persons would be reconciled to their own mediatedness by things, not that they would be determined to abolish that mediatedness, as though such an abolition were the necessary condition of their own freedom. For this reason the end of reification would by no means be the end of domination. The hope of Adorno's thought is not only life without reification, that is, but life without domination.

The difficulties incident to any attempt even to articulate the bare idea of 'life without domination', let alone 'life without self-preservation' are obvious. They make it clear that Adorno's materialism is deeply aporetic. The critical question is whether these aporias really testify to an antagonism in the matter under consideration itself, as Adorno insisted, or whether they are not rather, as an analysis informed by other post-idealist traditions might wish to suggest, the inevitable result of any attempt to articulate a materialism through negativity. The centrality of this question explains the importance of Adorno's work on other post-idealist philosophical traditions. This work retrieves the way in which disguised and misrecognized features of idealist thought are still aporetically at work even where a method or a mode of composition appears to have been found which goes radically beyond or behind them, and thus provides support for Adorno's own belief that philosophical thinking at present must needs have an aporetic, rather than a seamlessly non-contradictory character. These studies, above all of Kierkegaard, Husserl and Heidegger, prepare the way for Adorno's own encounter with the problem of metaphysics, and it is to these that we must now turn.

8

Materialism and Metaphysics

Introduction

The problem around which all the difficulties discussed in the previous two chapters circle is that which has dominated the history of philosophy in the twentieth century: the problem of whether thinking may at all free itself from metaphysics, how this might happen, and whether such an escape, if feasible, is even desirable. One very powerful tradition in twentieth-century thought, that of logical positivism, has, of course, regarded this as not really a problem at all. For Rudolf Carnap, for example, so-called metaphysical problems were 'pseudo-problems' which were the result of incautiously allowing words with no meaningful referent into philosophical talk.[1] But most other European philosophical traditions have regarded metaphysics as not so easily liquidable. Adorno, indeed, does not regard the *liquidation* of metaphysics as of itself desirable, despite – indeed, as will be seen, precisely on account of – his materialism. Instead, he regards a moment of metaphysical speculation as currently ineliminable from thinking which is to be thinking at all, including materialist thinking.

The miscarried attack on idealism

Given the complexity, even the contradictoriness, of Adorno's relation to the German idealist tradition and its Marxist inheritance, perhaps the very terms of the conceptual oppositions reworked by German idealism – subject and object, immanence and transcendence, theory and practice – are at fault? Perhaps these terms need not simply to be subjected to this complicit, immanent critique, but to a more radical attack or dismantling which would prepare the way for the possibility of leaving behind these concepts altogether? Adorno's studies of Kierkegaard, Husserl and Heidegger are not only polemical 'interventions'. Their significance lies in their relevance for Adorno's own attempt to go beyond transcendental idealism and absolute idealism without relapsing into dogmatism.

This can already be seen in Adorno's first mature monograph, *Kierkegaard: Construction of the Aesthetic.* Although the vogue for Kierkegaard in 1920s Germany is an important context for the book, Adorno takes care to distinguish Kierkegaard's thought from Heidegger's.[2] Instead Adorno's central interest in Kierkegaard lies in his miscarried anticipation of Adorno's own attempt to criticize idealism. Like Adorno, Kierkegaard wishes to contest the idealist notion of an identity of thought and being.[3] Kierkegaard does not propose any simple restoration of an ontology forbidden by Kant.[4] Kierkegaard does not dogmatically posit a being or a truth transcendent to thought; rather, Adorno argues, in Kierkegaard's work, '[t]ruth's transcendence is produced instead through the negation of immanent subjectivity.'[5] Kierkegaard, Adorno suggests, wishes to break out of the subject–object relation, yet without lapsing into a theory of truth which is either objectivistic or *simply* subjectivistic.[6]

Thus far Adorno formulates Kierkegaard's approach to the problem of a non-dogmatic criticism of the idealist identity of thought and being in not un-Adornian terms. Yet despite these affinities Adorno takes Kierkegaard to have failed in his attempt.[7] Adorno's account of this failure is instructive not only for his reading of Kierkegaard but for his understanding of the whole problem of a criticism of idealism, including a Marxist criticism:

> Of those modern philosophies in which the self-imprisoned consciousness of idealism is aware of its own imprisonment and attempts to escape from its immanence, each develops an exclusive category, an undeviating intention, a distinguishing trait, that, under the rule of the idea of totality acknowledged by all these philosophies, is intended to mollify the rigidity of this imprisonment. Ultimately, however, this category dissolves the idealist construction itself, which then disintegrates into its antinomies.[8]

Overcoming idealism, whether as a materialist or as an existential-ist thinker, is much more difficult than wanting to overcome it. Each of the attempts discussed by Adorno – he goes on to make analogous points about Feuerbach and Marx – is aware of this difficulty, yet each focuses on some primary motif which is to be irreducible to thought and is thus to break open the identity of thought and being. The result is dogmatically posited transcen-dence: a being which is supposed to be prior to or beyond thought, yet which is nevertheless invoked in some way by the thinker.

In Kierkegaard's case it is the self-relating self itself which brings about this result. The insistence on the subject's irreducible indi-viduality is intended to replace what Kierkegaard regards as the abstract subject of idealism, which nowhere exists, with a concrete and irreducible individual. But Adorno argues that its real effect in Kierkegaard's own work is to reduce the subject to an 'empty and blind x' which is in the event *more* abstract even than the transcen-dental subject itself: 'abstractness returns in the narrowing of concretion to the pure this-there.'[9] It becomes impossible to think the relationship between such an utterly individual subject and the history by which it is mediated: 'Only at particular instants do person and history come into contact. At these moments of contact, however, the historical dimension shrivels.'[10] Kierkegaard's ind-ividual, as an empty and blind x, becomes just what it was supposed not to be: a universal and invariant refuge from his-tory.

Although Kierkegaard repudiates Hegel's subject as too abstract, Hegel's presentation, Adorno argues, in fact allows a far more developed exposition of subjectivity.[11] This pattern – whereby a protest against the 'formalism' or 'abstraction' of idealism pro-duces still more abstract formulations, whether in the name of 'existence', materialism, phenomenology, or ontology – is the model for Adorno's understanding of how critiques of idealism can miscarry. An appeal, voluntary or involuntary, to some moment of timelessness is a central target of Adorno's in his account of miscarried critiques of idealism.

The phenomenological antinomies

If Adorno's criticism of Kierkegaard had its origins in a certain proximity to aspects of Kierkegaard's thought, the same is no less true, although in a very different way, of Adorno's work on

Husserl. The decisive factor prompting Adorno to devote prolonged attention to Husserl's work was his belief that Husserl's
work not only represented the most advanced reflection upon logic
and epistemology available, but also shared certain central motifs
with Adorno's own thought. In an article which was first published in English, 'Husserl and the Problem of Idealism', Adorno
described Husserl's phenomenology as 'an attempt to destroy
idealism from within, an attempt with the means of consciousness
to break through the wall of transcendental analysis, while at the
same time trying to carry on such an analysis as far as is possible'.[12] What especially interested Adorno was Husserl's awareness of the danger of falling back into various kinds of dogmatism
in carrying out such an attempt. Husserl is a critic of positivism,
yet is not a dogmatic rationalist either: 'His struggle against
psychologism does not mean the reintroduction of dogmatic prejudices, but the freeing of critical reason from the prejudices contained in the naive and uncritical religion of "facts" which he
challenged in its psychological form. It is this element of Husserl's
philosophy in which I see even today its "truth".'[13] Adorno thinks
that Husserl too believes that 'thoughts without content are empty,
intuitions without concepts are blind', yet that, like Adorno himself, Husserl is not entirely content with the attempt methodologically to separate out the contributions made by concept and
intuition respectively for further analysis. Adorno sees Husserl as
pursuing, like himself, a thinking which would be non-dogmatic
yet substantive.

Husserl's phenomenology had its origin in his attempt to criticize psychologistic accounts of logic. In such accounts the law of
non-contradiction, for example, could be grounded psychologically, in the inability of the human mind simultaneously to entertain
two contradictory propositions. Husserl found this account inadequate. In his *Logical Investigations* he argued that if logical
axioms were to be objectively true, true in themselves rather than
merely reflecting the way a particular kind of being happened to
think, their truth could not be grounded simply in an account of
the causal laws of human psychology, even supposing such laws to
be available. Logical principles are true regardless of whether they
have ever been thought.[14] Husserl concedes that there can be no
thought without someone to think it: otherwise we should be
subscribing to a kind of logical Platonism (of the kind which many
of Husserl's opponents took him to be promoting) in which logical
axioms are essences entirely removed from empirical existence. But

this fact about how a logical proposition comes about, its 'genesis', is quite irrelevant to the truth or otherwise of a logical proposition, its 'validity'.

Husserl's own philosophical project, 'phenomenology', sought to give a binding account of the validity of logical truths without either grounding such truths in a naturalistic psychology or converting them into essences entirely removed from human cognition. In his mature work (including and after the publication of *Ideas towards a Pure Phenomenology and a Phenomenological Philosophy* in 1913) Husserl distinguished two main tasks for phenomenology. The first was that of providing a 'phenomenological psychology'. It was necessary to provide such a psychology so that the relationship of logical truths to experience could be presented, rather than Platonistically set aside. Unlike empirical psychology, however, phenomenological psychology was to concern itself not with particular data about the human mind in so far as it could be experimentally observed, but with the essential structures of consciousness, those features of consciousness without which experience would be unthinkable. In order to ensure that such a psychology did not simply present idiosyncratic features of an individual's experience as though they were essential, however, it was necessary to 'bracket' or suspend for the purposes of phenomenological investigation whatever related to external experience of particular objects. Husserl called this bracketing the 'eidetic reduction' or the 'phenomenological reduction'.[15]

The second main task of phenomenology was to provide a 'phenomenological philosophy'. Such philosophy must rest on absolutely apodictic first principles. For this reason, 'eidetic' reduction and a phenomenological psychology were by themselves insufficient, because although they had bracketed out external experience of particular objects they still presupposed the existence of the world. Phenomenological philosophy, however, could not presuppose the existence of the world, because philosophy must be absolutely without presuppositions. A further, more radical bracketing was thus required, in which judgement as to the existence of the world would be suspended. Husserl called this bracketing the 'transcendental reduction'. What remains after the transcendental reduction has been performed is that which performed the reduction, the 'transcendental ego' which is not part of the world, but rather presents us with the essential modes of appearance of any possible world whatever.[16]

By now it may already be clearer why despite his sympathy for some of the impulses propelling Husserl's work, Adorno could not regard it as successful, nor even as giving the lines along which future work must proceed. Adorno recognizes that it is the aim of Husserl's 'transcendental reduction' to suspend the residual dogmatism of any transcendental method which presupposes that synthetic a priori knowledge is possible. However, he does not regard Husserl as having succeeded in this aim. In his *Metacritique of Epistemology* he analyses in detail Husserl's accounts of a whole series of phenomenological topics so as to show how a set of problems which can be expressed in the Kantian language of concept and intuition, or in an idealist language of subject and object, tacitly recur in Husserl's thought despite Husserl's painstaking attempts to distinguish the terms and methods of phenomenology from those of criticism and idealism.

Central to each of Adorno's discussions is the claim that Husserl's laudable desire to criticize psychologism pushes him into that dogmatic rationalism which he wishes to avoid.[17] For Adorno, that is, Husserl is right to protest against a straightforward identification of the validity of logical truths with their genesis, but wrong in so far as he insists that genesis makes no difference to validity.[18] Husserl's concession that without a thinker there can be no logical truth at all does not suffice to repel the charge of dogmatism, because Husserl persists in regarding this fact as entirely contingent to the validity of logical truths. While Adorno fully agrees that logic cannot be grounded in an anthropology or a psychology, he regards the need for a thinker as inherent in logical validity itself, rather than as an accidental supplement.[19] Husserl's insistence on keeping genesis and validity uncontaminated leads to 'the expulsion of humanity from the kingdom of its own reason'.[20]

The consequence is that the positivism which Husserl's thought was in some measure devised against returns in Husserl's appeal to 'givenness'. Logical truths are presented as givens. The relation between thinking and logical truth comes to be modelled on the natural-scientific conception of the relation between a knower and given data, even though it is central to the anti-epistemological impulse of Husserl's thought to challenge this model.[21] For Adorno, by contrast, no logical truth can ever be an immediate given, because it is ineliminable to logic that logic demands to be thought and thus to be conceptually mediated. When Husserl treats the genesis of logical truth as contingent to its validity, he construes such validity precisely as something which is sheerly 'given' irrespective of that to which it is given.[22]

Adorno continues to regard phenomenology as the most significant philosophical attempt stringently to break out of idealism. Above all, what he takes to be the central utopian impulse of phenomenology – a non-classificatory cognition[23] – remains of central importance to his own thought. Husserl's attempt to carry this impulse through without contradiction must founder in the context of a natural-historical experience which remains antagonistically structured.[24] It is the attempt to exclude contradiction which leads to the reappearance of a series of inert separations between subject-poles and object-poles which are no more sustainable than the methodological separation between concept and intuition in Kant's thought.

Negative dialectic or de-struction?

Many of Adorno's analyses of Husserl raise, although in a language which could scarcely be more different, questions also raised by Husserl's most celebrated pupil and critic: Martin Heidegger. For Heidegger, and for much of the immense body of work influenced by him, western philosophy since Descartes has remained in the grip of a Cartesian ontology dividing the world between spirit and matter, *res cogitans* and *res extensa*. Even Hegelian speculation, despite its claims to have re-exhibited and overcome this dualism, still remains, for Heidegger, bound up in such an ontology,[25] and Adorno's continued (albeit negative) deployment of the language of subject and object would from any Heideggerian standpoint imply that Adorno is liable to the same charge.

Adorno's critique of Heidegger is therefore of special importance to his work.[26] Adorno's intense antipathy towards Heidegger is prompted in part by his awareness of deep convergences between his thought and Heidegger's.[27] Each wishes to insist on the temporal-historical character of truth without taking this as an excuse for relativism; each resists reducing philosophy either to a method or to a doctrine. Most importantly, each is deeply concerned with a critique or questioning of modernity – and especially of the conversion of production into an absolute – without offering any simple return to tradition. Yet these convergences are accompanied by ineradicable political differences. Once more, Adorno's critique of Heidegger is more than a polemical intervention, though it is also that. The clarification of its own 'relation to ontology' is a central task for negative dialectic itself.[28] Adorno must show that differences which might be seen principally as differences of terminology or presentation make all the difference between his thought and Heidegger's. This task takes on particular importance today because of the interest in the possible relations between negative dialectic and deconstruction, whose ineliminably Heideggerian inheritance makes Adorno's critique of Heidegger the necessary starting point for any such inquiry.[29]

In *Being and Time* Heidegger argued that the 'question of being' had merely been forgotten, rather than answered, in life and thought since Plato.[30] Although even the most elementary proposition depends on some sense of the meaning of being, the question had come to be regarded as a pseudo-problem. Being had come to be regarded as a classificatory concept denoting simply the sum total of entities, things which are. But this understanding of being left entirely opaque the question of what it means to say that entities *are*. The meaning of being, Heidegger suggested, was just what ontology would have to investigate. In Heidegger's view the forgetting of this fundamental question had contaminated all thinking about all other topics – not just overtly ontological topics but also such questions as the relation between theory and practice.

In the modern epoch, the forgetting of being took the form of an opposition between spirit and matter, *res cogitans* and *res extensa*.[31] The contamination of all modern philosophy by its particular kind of 'forgetting of being' was not just an intellectual mistake: it was inseparably bound up with the way in which modern humans related to each other and to the world. 'Man' acted not as the 'shepherd of Being' but as the 'lord of beings', exercising mastery over a world conceived of as a mere aggregate of entities.[32] The modern understanding of other humans was also vitiated: once the question of being had been forgotten, human beings could be thought of only as a special kind of entity, the thinking thing.

This left thinking with a problem, Heidegger believed. Modern language itself, and especially modern philosophical language, testified to the forgetting of being. How could such a language be used to awaken itself from this forgetting? Heidegger approached this difficulty in a number of ways. Firstly, he suggested that a destruction or dismantling [*Destruktion*] of the previous history of ontology was a necessary precondition of any new 'fundamental ontology'.[33] Such an ontology could not be built from scratch. It was inevitably implicated in the forgetting of being from which it sought to wake up. Yet, secondly, Heidegger began to develop a new set of terms peculiar to his work (an idiolect) which were designed to avoid remaining for ever stuck in the presuppositions of previous ontology. The terms were new not in the sense that they came from nowhere; they very often replaced the Latinate vocabulary of modern ontology with German compounds in which concrete reference is more visible (to a German or Anglo-Saxon reader, at least) than in a Latinate lexicon. Heidegger thus does not speak of 'the subject' but of *Dasein* ('existence'; literally, 'being-there'). But *Dasein* is not just another word for 'the subject'. Crudely, it is to allow us to think human being without turning it into the *res cogitans*, the thinking thing in which the term 'subject', Heidegger thinks, already imprisons us.

Heidegger's use of an idiolect does not mean that he thinks he has escaped previous ontology with a single leap. Instead he regards his thought as ambiguously placed, both inside and outside previous ontology. Heidegger acknowledges his implicatedness, but at the same time thinks of himself as inconspicuously sowing the seed of a more primordial (*ursprünglicher*) kind of thinking, 'an other thinking that abandons subjectivity'.[34] Such an other thinking would announce also a different set of practical relations to the world, one in which we might be the shepherds of Being rather than the masters of entities.

It is difficult to discuss Heidegger without employing his own terms. As soon as these are translated back into a more familiar philosophical language, his whole project can be misunderstood. Nevertheless, Heidegger has a range of different registers in which he approaches fundamental questions from different angles. Much of his work on the philosophical tradition especially shows how deeply marked is Heidegger's thought by a persistent engagement with what it would overcome.[35]

It is in this context that Adorno's critique can best be understood. Both Adorno's and Heidegger's philosophical programmes had their initial context in the attempt to go beyond neo-Kantian transcendental idealism without either embracing Hegel's speculative identification of subject and object or falling back into a subjectivistic or objectivistic dogmatism.

Heidegger's reflection on the question of the 'transcendence' of Being focuses this problem. In *Being and Time* Heidegger insists that 'Being and the structure of Being lie beyond every entity and every possible character which an entity may possess. Being is the *transcendens* pure and simple.'[36] Yet the question of the meaning of Being can only be approached on the basis of an analysis of the finite and temporal-historical character of *Dasein*, human being, because truth is truth for mortal and historical human beings. The truth of Being can therefore only be thought through human 'projection'. Yet this projection does not *create* Being. However, we are *not yet* able to think the truth of Being.[37] Our ability to do so would depend on a dismantling (in thought and in our relations to the world) of the history of previous ontology in which we remain entangled.

The structural similarities to Adorno's project are clear. But Adorno continues to use the language of subject and object. Access to truth is always subjectively and historically mediated for Adorno. Yet the subject does not *create* its object. However, we are *not yet* able to think the priority of the object. Our ability to do so would depend on a critique of the fallacy of the constitutive subject together with the demise of the world of absolutized production which this fallacy both reflects and sustains.

The implications of this account are for Adorno what differentiates a negative dialectic from Heidegger's work. Especially important is Adorno's contrast between Heidegger's interest in 'historicity' and that of negative dialectics in history. For Adorno Heidegger's insistence on *Dasein*'s historicity repeats the structure of the relation between the question of being and particular entities: histor*icity* is prior to and qualitatively distinct from any merely ontic *history*. Historicity thus becomes the opposite of what it was supposed to be. It becomes a *de facto* invariant, because any historical particular is just as far away from 'historicity' in general as it is from an invariant 'nature'.[38] Heidegger's history thus becomes an 'epochal history of Being'; for Heidegger, the succeeding ontologies testify to the structuring first principles (*archai*) of all life in the epochs which they govern. For Adorno, on the other hand, there can be no history of Being without a history of beings.

Yet how can materialism, even one which advertises itself as non-dogmatic, do without an ontology? That this question is a pressing one is startlingly marked in one of Adorno's observations in *Negative Dialectics*: 'The expression Being means something entirely different in Marx and Heidegger, yet not without any common ground: in the ontological doctrine of the priority of Being before thinking, of its "transcendence", a materialist echo can be heard as in the far distance.'[39] Can materialism at all dispense with such an 'ontological doctrine'? Some of Adorno's own characterizations of it might appear to suggest otherwise.[40] So decisive to the success of Adorno's materialism is the question of whether this programme is possible, of whether his thought does not, rather, displace critique in favour of ontology – and so persistent are the charges that it does just this[41] – that it requires further examination. The nature and limits of the 'ontological moment' in Adorno's metacritical thought can be clarified by comparing it with the earlier Heidegger's account of the first critique.

The parallels between Heidegger's discussion of the first critique in *Kant and the Problem of Metaphysics* and Adorno's account of it are suggestive. Heidegger gives a hermeneutically 'violent' reading of the first critique which discovers there intimations of a fundamental, non-dogmatic ontology which could be thought on the basis of a *finite* human reason. He wants to show that 'thinking and intuiting, although different, are not separated from each other like two completely dissimilar things.'[42] Like Adorno, Heidegger is deeply troubled by the way in which the methodological separation of concept from intuition hardens in Kant's thought, to the point where it appears to need a series of third terms to bridge the series of gulfs which it creates. Even more strongly than Adorno, Heidegger wishes to contest neo-Kantian readings of the first critique as simply an epistemology: 'the positive outcome of Kant's *Critique of Pure Reason* lies in what it has contributed towards the working-out of what belongs to any Nature whatsoever, not in a "theory" of knowledge'.[43] Heidegger emphasizes instead Kant's 'insight' into the possibility of a fundamental (and, we should add, non-dogmatic) ontology.

An unprecedented degree of emphasis is thus laid on Kant's schematism chapter. It becomes 'the central core of the whole voluminous work.'[44] For Heidegger, the idea that the transcendental imagination itself makes possible both understanding and sensibility – and that it does so through transcendental schema-images which are 'transcendental determinations of time' – is a radically new insight which Kant himself to a certain extent lost sight of and which has certainly been lost sight of by his successors. It is a deeply significant insight, for Heidegger, because it opens up the possibility of a fundamental ontology whose 'horizon' is time.[45] Both Adorno and Heidegger are interested in the schematism. Firstly, they take it to suggest that critical thinking

may itself already contain the resources for an ontology (or ontological moment, in Adorno's case) in which being need not be
transfigured into an invariant. Secondly, they take it to indicate an
awareness of the metaphysical presuppositions of epistemology. It
is to these metaphysical presuppositions that Heidegger refers
when he remarks that '[p]ossibility of experience is therefore
synonymous with transcendence.'[46]

The immediately striking difference is that *Kant and the Problem
of Metaphysics* wants to express this in terms of the priority of
(categorial) intuition over concepts. On Heidegger's account,
'knowing is primarily intuiting'; '[a]ll thinking is merely in the
service of intuition.' Kant's insistence on the reciprocal interdependence of concept and intuition is thus given a particular and
admittedly violent emphasis by Heidegger. This emphasis is
worrying for Adorno because it suggests that the mediation
through concepts which is necessary for our knowledge of objects
to be *knowledge* of objects is in some way a dependent or inferior
element, 'in the service' of what is given in intuition: as Heidegger
puts it, 'the new interpretation of knowledge as judging (thinking)
violates the decisive sense of the Kantian problem'.[47] Adorno sees
Heidegger's downgrading of the conceptual mediation of knowledge in Kant as a further instance of what he regards as an
'incapacitation [*Entmächtigung*] of the subject' in Heidegger's
work.[48] Although Heidegger attempts to think beyond the category of the subject altogether, Adorno regards the category of
Dasein as a placeholder for the subject which cannot really escape
from subjectivity.[49]

These differences bring us up against the relationship between
judgement and ontology itself. For Heidegger, Being is not an
entity, nor is it merely the concept classifying all entities. Nor,
however, is it simply the history of the ways in which it has been
misidentified as a being or a concept. Being cannot be pointed to or
thought, nor do we point to or think Being when we think the
history of mistaken attempts to do so. Being, then, is not only
neither a concept nor a being, it is neither immediate nor mediated.
It is that of which nothing can be predicated without leaving a
remainder. The convergence which appears here lies in a shared
conviction of the limits of the predicative judgement; and in a
shared scepticism about the finality of any distinction between
analyticity and syntheticity. Adorno agrees that Being cannot be
taken simply as a classificatory *Oberbegriff* or cover-concept:

It is undeniable that being is not simply the sum of what is, of what is the case. This antipositivistic insight allows justice to be done to the overshooting of the concept beyond facticity. No concept could be thought, none would even be possible, without the surplus that makes language language. What echoes in the word being, as opposed to *ta onta* – that everything is more than it is – means its entanglement in a context, not something transcendent to it. But this is just what it does become in Heidegger, something added to the entity.[50]

Adorno is quite aware that Heidegger himself would have been horrified by any idea that Being is merely added to the entity as though it were an extra quality just happening to be transcendent to it. But he thinks that the insistence on Being's transcendence nevertheless brings about just what Heidegger wishes to avoid:

> Any entity is more than it is; being, in contrast to the entity, reminds us of this. Because there is no entity that does not have need of another entity which is not itself, through which it is determined and determines itself – since it could not be determined through itself alone – it points beyond itself. Mediation is just another name for this. Heidegger, however, seeks to keep what points beyond itself and discard that which it points beyond as refuse.[51]

The element of polemical exaggeration here – it is hardly true to say that Heidegger is so unconcerned with entities that he merely discards them – should not blind us to the central point at issue. Adorno agrees that being is neither an entity nor the sum of entities; it is *more* than these. But this 'more' cannot be corralled in the idea of 'Being'. The 'is' which 'is more' cannot be isolated in the copula and referred to 'Being', but is also already in the subject and predicate themselves. If it were not, the copula really would be a merely external additive link between them. This is just the idea against which the ontological difference, between Being and beings, was itself formulated.[52] On the other hand, being cannot *do without* the copula of predicative judgement any more than the copula can do without a concept of being. That being is not a classificatory cover-concept, not the sum of entities, a point on which Adorno is in complete agreement with Heidegger, does not make it any the less a concept. Rather it is the nature of conceptuality as such for Adorno that the concept is always more and less than what can be subsumed under it, just as the object is always more and less than the concept which subsumes it. It is essential to the 'ontological moment' which Adorno regards as necessary to materialism that it should not be conceived either as the 'given' of epistemology or as the 'gift' of Heidegger's later thought.

For Heidegger the fact that Being is neither a being nor a cover-concept leads us to a different sense for 'thinking'. In this different sense thinking would be more than just another name for sub-sumptive judgement. (It is towards this more 'primordial' thinking that he takes Kant's schematism to be moving, because it asks about how subsumption itself is possible.) The question of the meaning of Being could thus only begin to be asked where attempts to make subsumptive judgements about Being end. Hei-degger's later thought, especially, increasingly uses judgements which must sometimes appear either merely analytic or merely opaque to allow the history of Being sedimented in language to speak for itself. What such a path risks is a holding-off from, a desire to *avoid*, subsumptive judgement.[53] The risk of tautology or ambiguity, the ascetic 'poverty' of thinking,[54] is the risk taken by thinking itself which does not wish to lapse into (unthinking) knowing.

For Adorno, by contrast, there is no way round false identifica-tion other than through it.[55] When Heidegger speaks of human thought as having 'strayed into subjectivity', subjectivity is re-garded precisely as an *error*, as a wandering from the true path of thinking's 'descent to the poverty of its provisional essence', despite the emphasis on the difficulty of this descent.[56] The con-sequence is a thought which for all the talk of its own implicated-ness and the necessity of a de-struction of previous ontology nevertheless repeatedly offers to *turn* away from subjectivity, to 'abandon' or 'renounce' it.[57]

If the purpose of Adorno's account of the miscarried attack on idealism is to show that a contradictory entanglement in the language and problems of idealism can only be liquidated, dis-placed or 'dismantled' at the cost of something worse, however, this by no means adds up to a sufficient defence of the specific character of his own 'aporetic' thinking. Such thinking, in order not to be simply sceptical, must be able to give at least some account of the conditions on which it might cease to be contra-dictory. If this account relies wholly on an appeal to historical experience and the sheer abstract possibility that such experience may change, it will be inadequate by virtue of simply falling into the historicist relativism against which the very idea of natural-historical experience was conceived in the first place. Important as the idea of a possible change in natural-historical experience is to Adorno, it is no less important to him not to regard this idea as an abstract split between an actual experience and the bare possibility of its alteration, the pious hope for a better world which can never be properly imagined, articulated or even (some would charge) thought, and so remains wholly abstract, a new 'bad infinity'.[58]

This is why it becomes so important to Adorno to give an account of the nature and limits of negativity in his thinking, an account which can show not only how his aporetic thinking differs from sceptical nihilism, but also how it differs from a purely abstract utopianism or messianism. The account is developed above all through a meditation on the nature of illusory being (*Schein*), and on what might be meant by the idea of 'redeeming' such illusion. This meditation, as we have seen, forms the central theme of Adorno's late aesthetic theory. Within Adorno's negative dialectic it is considered through an account of what has happened to metaphysics in the late twentieth century. Metaphysical speculation appears not so much conclusively dispelled or refuted as obsolete. It looks threatened less with refutation by the series of logical, epistemological and post-metaphysical assaults mounted on it – for why would something which is supposed to be dead need killing so often? – than with being exposed as consolatory ideology by the catastrophes of twentieth-century historical experience itself. Yet metaphysical presuppositions keep returning even (and especially) within the very terms of those who most matter-of-factly announce their final demise. It is to an attempt to show the centrality of these considerations to Adorno's aporetic materialism that we must now turn.

'Nihil ulterius'?

What, then, 'is' the metaphysical moment which Adorno thinks of as currently ineliminable from thinking? Adorno's account of this demands one final further examination of his encounters with the thinker who has dominated all modern discussion of the problem of metaphysics, Immanuel Kant.

Adorno recognizes that the *Critique of Pure Reason* itself already aimed at a critical rescue of certain aspects of metaphysical thinking, rather than a simple liquidation of metaphysics.[59] Although it is Kant's view, in Adorno's words, that the result of the antinomies is that certain questions 'may not really be asked', the very premise of Kant's attempt, in the transcendental dialectic, to set clear limits to the use of the pure concepts of the understanding, is an admission that reason is naturally transgressive of these limits.

Kant points to 'a natural and unavoidable dialectic of pure reason . . . inseparable from human reason . . . which, even after its deceptiveness has been exposed, will not cease to play tricks with reason and continually entrap it into momentary aberrations ever and again calling for correction'.[60] This element in Kant's work can prompt Adorno to speak of a 'metaphysical experience' which 'inspires' Kant's thought:

> In order to be spirit, spirit must know that it is not exhausted in that to which it extends; that it is not exhausted in the finitude which it is like. Thus spirit thinks what would be beyond it. Such metaphysical experience inspires Kant's philosophy, once it has been broken free of its armour-plated method. Any consideration of whether metaphysics is still at all possible must reflect the negation of the finite demanded by finitude. Its riddle-image [*Raetselbild*] animates the word 'intelligible'.[61]

Such a passage seems to raise more problems than it solves. How, in particular, can spirit's 'thought' of what would be beyond it be compared to 'metaphysical *experience*'? Surely Kant's idea of the intelligible as such depends on just this distinction between our capacity to *think* the intelligible and the restriction of our *experience* to what appears?[62] However, it is in turn just this gulf between thinking and knowing, between thinking and experiencing which Adorno has in his sights when he refers to freeing criticism from transcendental method. Freeing Kant's thought from the armour of its method is what Adorno takes the metacritiques of transcendental inquiry (chapter 6) and practical reason (chapter 7) to have accomplished.

Kant's antinomies arise in the course of illegitimate attempts to use the pure concepts of the understanding as though they could by themselves yield knowledge of objects. Adorno, however, regards the concept of intelligibility itself as aporetic. To Kant's antinomies, as we saw in chapter 6, he adds a further antinomy which, as Albrecht Wellmer puts it, 'places not only the knowability, but also the *thinkability* of the intelligible world in question. The antinomy consists in the fact that objective reality cannot be attributed to the transcendental ideas, and yet if they are to be the expression of a meaningful thought, reality *must* be attributed to them.'[63]

Adorno's critique of Kant's 'block', then, is motivated by the attempt to criticize the separation between our real experience and a really possible future experience through a philosophical interpretation of the former. In this criticism it is not *cognition* of external metaphysical *entities* which is at stake. The loss of meta-physical dogmas is irreversible, and all hope for such knowledge already testifies in the terms expressing it to its own impossibility. What is at stake is how the moment of freedom in thinking testifies to the real possibility of a future experience not bound to self-preservation, a future experience in which spirit could relinquish its infinite postponement of material satisfaction.

As Albrecht Wellmer has remarked, in a lucid discussion of this aspect of Adorno's thought, for Adorno it is as though with this idea 'a thin crack had opened up through which a weak glimmer of light might fall from redemption upon the darkened world, enough to contest the right of Kant's metaphysical agnosticism to have the last word. Instead of "we cannot know": "we do not yet know".'[64] But Wellmer goes on to raise an important objection to Adorno's line of argument: 'We can *already* know that what we cannot even consistently think as actual, we cannot anticipate as actual either.'[65]

This objection by no means exhausts the issue, however. For Wellmer, Adorno becomes a pre-critical dogmatic metaphysician when he helps himself to a speculative Hegelian argument – the argument that the prohibition on the misemployment of pure concepts of the understanding is dogmatically formulated.[66] But this argument, if accepted, means that the very distinction between pre-critical and critical thinking which Wellmer, like almost all second-generation critical theorists, takes as a benchmark, cannot be taken as absolute. Indeed the whole point of this argument is that transcendental inquiry has not managed, and could not in principle manage, *radically* to separate itself from pre-critical 'meta-physics'. It is in fact quite central to Adorno's reflection on the demise of metaphysics, and part of the point of his 'metacritique', that transcendental inquiry was never as distinct from rationalism as it has sometimes subsequently been painted.

The motive for this argument is not to suggest that therefore it is legitimate to go back to pre-critical rationalism as though Kant had never happened, but rather to suggest that metaphysics may be ineliminable from thinking in a different way than was supposed by Kant. It need not be the case that, as Wellmer objects, this argument asks us to anticipate as actual what we cannot even consistently think as actual. Such a demand clearly would con-stitute a decisive objection to Adorno's account of his relation to metaphysics. The argument, instead, is a negative one. It points out that we cannot liquidate as chimerical what we cannot even consistently think as chimerical: the transcendence in thinking.

Adorno described Kant's statement that 'the critical path [in philosophy] alone remains open' beyond dogmatism and scepticism as 'one whose truth-content is incomparably greater than what it means in its particular context'.[67] Indeed critical thinking, for Adorno, may almost be defined as that thinking which manages in fact rather than merely in intention to take this path. It is in this context that Adorno's difficult remarks in the closing lines of *Negative Dialectics* on the 'solidarity' between his own thinking and metaphysics are finally to be understood.[68] Materialism and metaphysics alike violate both the Kantian prohibition on the misemployment of transcendent concepts and what Adorno sees as Hegel's total 'context of immanence'. Materialism and metaphysics are both untrue wherever they claim access to immediate givenness. But they are both true where they show how the prohibition on dogmatism is itself dogmatically formulated. This is the basis upon which Adorno can argue that 'materialism is not the dogma which its shrewdest opponents accused it of being, but rather the dissolution of something which has for its part been seen through as dogmatic. Hence materialism's rights [*Recht*] within critical philosophy.'[69] Kant's prohibition on the misuse of transcendent concepts is true to aspects of our present and past experience, but untrue in so far as it seeks to legislate for all future experience:

> Socially, it may be suspected with good reason that this block, the limitation on the absolute, is one with the need to work, which really does hold humans in the same spell which Kant transfigured into philosophy. The captivity in immanence to which he, with brutal honesty, confines spirit, is a captivity in self-preservation . . . if this beetle-like natural-historical care were broken through, the positioning of consciousness with respect to truth would be changed.[70]

The prohibition is 'honest' about natural-historical experience. It is only 'brutal' in so far as it confines such experience within supposedly immutable conditions of its possibility and to this extent prohibits experience from changing. Brutal honesty becomes brutally dishonest, Adorno suggests, by this appeal to invariance: The critical 'block' which prohibits experience of transcendence relies on a presentation of experience as invariably the pure work of conceptual forms upon the content of intuition. The block cannot be thought away. But thought can show how the experience on which the block rests is both real and changeable. A changed experience would change whatever are taken as the conditions of its possibility. A society in which our experience itself was no longer identitarian might be one in which the prohibition on the experience of transcendence would no longer apply.[71]

Negativity against nihilism

Adorno's account of the entanglement between materialism and metaphysics, then, depends centrally on this double move. To liquidate the possibility of experiencing transcendence would make thinking impossible; yet this does not of itself mean that immediate access to such experience has thereby been secured. This is why Adorno takes care to refer to his thinking on this topic as 'solely negative'.[72] The magical, mystical and theological terms which Adorno uses to designate the possibility of an escape from pure immanence or from self-preservation – as where he talks of 'breaking the spell' of the context of immanence or of a 'salvation' or 'redemption' of natural-historical life – need to be understood in the context of this negative thinking. Such expressions are, instead, a twofold 'anamnesis', thought's attempt to recollect, instead of suppressing, what it depends on. They recollect both instrumental reason's own history of pre-instrumental rationality, its inability to rid itself of the magical and mythical thinking which it has suppressed, and the concealed transcendence of prohibitions on transcendence. They are determinate negations of these prohibitions which make visible the experience implicitly sedimented in them.

How far does Adorno, then, appeal to negativity itself as a panacea? When Adorno and Horkheimer discussed the possibility of a materialist dialectic in 1939, Horkheimer was on one occasion driven to an exasperated outburst: 'So all we can do is just say "no" to everything!'[73] Adorno's reply does not attempt to conceal the extent to which he identifies thought itself with determinate negativity: 'There is no other measure of truth than the specificity of the dissolution of illusion.'[74] We need, finally, to consider in more detail just what Adorno means by negativity, as well as some of the more cogent amongst the many counter-arguments which have been offered to his conception.

Michael Theunissen has given a critical account of 'Negativity in Adorno' which is all the more powerful for its engagement with the philosophical tradition from which Adorno emerges. Theunissen argues that unlike most philosophers Adorno does not use negativity to refer to non-being (das Nicht*seiendes*), but rather to something which is existent, which negates, and which ought not to be (das Nichtsein*sollendes*): the existing negativity of identificatory thinking and the domination which it accompanies and makes possible.[75] The point of negative thinking, in this sense, is not a limitless scepticism which will negate any positive content whatever, but a negation of this existing negativity. Its point, that is, is the reverse of scepticism. It is conceived of as a negation of sceptical negativity which will overcome the prohibition on the experience of transcendence. Theunissen goes on to distinguish two primary conceptions of negative dialectic. On the one hand, he suggests, negative dialectic is conceived of as (1) a 'consistent "consciousness of non-identity" ',[76] on the other as (2) an 'ontology of the wrong state of things'.[77] Negativity means something different in each case. The non-identical is not itself negative, except from the standpoint of identificatory thinking. In sense (1), then, the negativity is, as it were, within quotation marks. In this sense, negative dialectic is not really negative. In sense (2), by contrast, the negativity referred to is the negativity of that which should not be, the 'wrong state of things'. In this sense, negative dialectic is not really dialectical. The result, for Theunissen, is that negative dialectic is 'a dialectic which transcends itself, as it makes a transition into metaphysics'.[78] A dialectic which was imagined as entirely self-sufficient would be making an entirely undialectical claim to exclusivity. Accordingly dialectic depends on an 'undialectical' moment. It is in invoking the ineliminability of this undialectical moment, in the raising of the non-identical to an absolute, Theunissen suggests, that Adorno's dialectic goes over into metaphysics.

The force of Theunissen's criticism, unusually, is that what he calls Adorno's 'negativism' is not, in a certain sense, negative *enough*.[79] It depends on a series of pre-negativistic or even anti-negativistic arguments. In particular, it depends on the argument that *total* despair is unintelligible, because as a minimal condition of the possibility of despairing determinately of the world as it is, consciousness must have a sense of some element which is not negative: 'When philosophy paints its grey in grey, a shape of life has grown old':[80] but '[c]onsciousness could not even despair over the grey, did it not harbour the notion of a different colour, whose dispersed traces are not absent in the negative whole.'[81] The negative is not the whole in the sense that there really is nothing positive – this would be the nihilism of 'all is nothing' against which Adorno sets himself – but in the sense that everything is shaped by negativity. The result, Theunissen argues, is that Adorno's negative thinking founders in contradictions which cannot be excused as the manifestation of historical antagonism but are, instead, of its own making: between insisting, for example, on the one hand that exchange is a distorted prolepsis of true reconciliation, and on the other that the work of art is a prolepsis of the thing which would no longer be mutilated by exchange;[82] or between insisting, on the one hand, that the world as it exists is 'false to its innermost core'[83] and insisting, on the other, that 'even in its most questionable state society is the epitome of the self-producing and reproducing life of mankind'[84] – 'that is', as Theunissen comments, 'for all its negativity, never *simply* negative.'[85] Only if negative thinking were to be able to free itself entirely from metaphysics could it avoid such 'bad contradiction'.

This is clearly a series of objections which goes to the heart of Adorno's work. Since negative dialectic so openly confesses its own aporetic quality, objections which merely point to contradiction are not addressing the decisive issue, which is, instead, to what extent and in which cases negative dialectic's claims that its moments of contradiction aporetically manifest real antagonism are justified. The question is partly a hermeneutic one which demands an examination of how to *read* a contradiction such as that between the claims of the type that (1) the existing world is false to its innermost core and claims of the type that (2) even in its most questionable state society is the epitome of the self-producing and -reproducing life of mankind. Claims of the first type, Adorno wants to suggest, cannot be made intelligible without already hearing claims of the second type sounding within them. Arguments to the effect that 'the existing world is false to its innermost core' can never be read as completely literal in Adorno's work, not at all because Adorno has in some way *decreed* that they should not be read literally, but because if taken with total literalness they are not thinkable. In the very act of thinking such a claim we provide ourselves with evidence of the extent to which it is untrue. That if we are to despair determinately we cannot make despair into an absolute – which Theunissen rightly emphasizes as what distinguishes Adorno's negative thinking from nihilism – also affects, rather than being a matter of indifference for, the hermeneutic status of Adorno's claims.

Here many may think that their worst fears have been confirmed. The problem of contradiction is to be evaded in favour of a

frankly aestheticized reason, which skips argument by an easy
appeal to context and removes contradiction by suggesting that
one limb of a contradictory pair was not meant literally. The
arguments raised here, however, are not simply aesthetic but
concern the extent to which Adorno's thought remains not only
dialectical but speculative. The model for what the 'speculative
moment' in thinking *means* for Adorno is provided by the idea that
we are already unable not to hear claims of the second type
sounding in claims of the first type. A moment of unliteralness is
non-liquidable from such claims to despair, because if they were
meant with absolute literalness they could not even be thought.
For Hegel, speculative thinking was famously able to see 'the rose
in the cross of the present'. Adorno's thinking is speculative to the
extent that this motif can be reread in the light of his own thesis
about the unthinkability of complete despair. Every line which if
read with sheer literal-mindedness speaks despair, *be*speaks hope.
What philosophical argument bespeaks, as well as what it speaks,
cannot in Adorno's view simply be reassigned to the aesthetic, and
used as the basis for a charge of an aestheticization of reason, as
though it were the place of strictly philosophical argument only
ever to read what is written with absolute literalness, because
absolute literalness is itself a chimera.

None of these arguments brings forward considerations of
which a series of objections like Theunissen's is unaware. Rather,
the weight resting on an argument such as the claim that complete
despair is not fully thinkable is just what Theunissen means by
arguing that Adorno's negative dialectic transcends itself in so far
as it goes over to metaphysics. What the perspective outlined
above would want to question, however, is Theunissen's suggestion that there *can* be a negative thinking which is fully freed from
metaphysics without becoming a nihilism. Theunissen's own work
has drawn attention to what he calls 'the critical function' of parts
of Hegel's logic – 'the logic of being exposes positivism as metaphysics; the logic of essence exposes metaphysics as positivism.'[86]
On Adorno's account the condition of such a critical logic, which,
despite Theunissen's criticisms of Adorno, remains very close to
the intentions of a negative dialectic, would be an acknowledge-
ment of the impossibility of liquidating metaphysical speculation.
It could not be expounded as a negativism absolutely free from
metaphysics without delusively making just the kinds of claim to
exclusivity which Theunissen himself regards as the reason for
negative dialectic's own 'transition to metaphysics'.

Kant protested that any thought which, like Adorno's, wanted to resist both dogmatism and the procedure of a critique of pure reason could only have the sceptical aim of 'changing work into play, philosophy into philodoxy'.[87] For Adorno, the work of thought is negativity. Positivity is where thought comes to rest, comes to a halt. The negativity of Adorno's thought represents its unceasing labour, its refusal to come to rest in a posited standpoint or fact or method. But the manual labour which 'smooths the path' for this 'labour of the concept' continues, and thought continues to live off it. For this reason, to come to rest in invariant positivity whilst work goes on all around is indeed 'to change work into play, philosophy into philodoxy'. Adorno does want to change work into play, but really to change it, not in thought alone, nor for thinkers alone. Only on this condition can negative thinking be distinguished from nihilism.

The hope of Adorno's negative thinking, then, is not to protect its own negativity but, in truth, to bring negativity to an end. Hegel referred to the course of thought as a self-correcting or 'self-perficient' scepticism.[88] Adorno's negativity too would be self-perficient, yet could not regard such self-perficience as guaranteed, nor as satisfactorily to be accomplished in thought alone:

> If thought . . . gropes beyond itself in such a way that it names the other as something simply incommensurable with it, which it yet thinks, it will find no shelter but in the dogmatic tradition. In such a thought thinking is alien to its content, unreconciled with it, and finds itself once again condemned to two separate kinds of truth, which would be irreconcilable with the idea of truth itself. Metaphysics rests on whether it is possible to escape from this aporia without any sleight of hand. To this end dialectic, at once the impression [*Abdruck*] of the universal context of delusion and its critique, must in one final movement turn itself even against itself.[89]

Adorno's 'non-identical', as he has emphasized throughout, is not 'simply incommensurable' with thought. Any statement of such 'simple incommensurability' is already a thought, after all. Dialectic 'turns against itself', not by exhaustedly lurching into a dogmatism it has managed to stave off until the last, but by making visible its own conditionedness. Adorno suggests, indeed, that charges of dogmatism will fall on any attempt to think the conditionedness of thought: 'Whatever convicts the subject of its own arbitrariness, whatever convicts the subject's *prius* of aposteriority, will always sound to the subject like a transcendent dogma.'[90] The two apparently opposed complaints most often addressed to Adorno's thought, that he makes an inadmissible leap into sociology, and that he takes flight into metaphysics or mysticism, are in truth deeply related. Both take Adorno as dogmatic in just the sense to which he here refers.[91]

But the statement also indicates just why it is so important to Adorno to contest the prohibition on the experience of transcendence. The impulse to thematize an ineliminably metaphysical moment in thinking is not the impulse once and for all to liberate spirit from its body: quite the reverse. The possibility of the experience of transcendence is *at once* that of the experience of freedom *and* that of thought's ability to think its own conditionedness. Without such a possibility thought will be unable to think what it lives off. Thought which fails to think what it lives off is not thinking. The reproach of dogmatism or of contradictoriness addressed to the idea of the non-identical – as though from blessed islands where these hydras have long been slain – does not succeed in eliminating either dogmatism or contradiction. The life of negative dialectic lies in contradiction; it does not aim to eradicate contradictions in thought, but to understand the possibility of reconciling antagonism. 'Nur wenn, was ist, sich ändern läßt, ist das, was ist, nicht alles': 'only if "that which is" can be changed is "that which is" not *all* there is.'[92]

Conclusion

What is living and what is dead in Adorno's thought? Benedetto Croce first asked this question about Hegel, and it is an obvious question to ask about Adorno.[1] It asks for a rational reconstruction separating out what might still be useful or relevant from what is obsolete. It is hardly easier to answer, however, than Croce's question about Hegel. As Adorno himself pointed out, the living and the dead can rarely be so neatly separated. The attempt to delete whatever has been deemed bad or dispensable can easily carry away with it just what is supposed to be salvaged.[2] This is especially so when this kind of reconstruction is performed upon any philosopher for whom form and style are integral to content rather than a mere vehicle for it. Attempts to rescue Hegel's social and political thought from his supposedly obsolete speculative logic have sometimes culminated in such insights as that 'human affairs are complex and beset with ambiguity.'

None the less, this kind of question will not go away, for attempts to argue that Adorno's work is all dead or all living have been unconvincing. The most ambitious attempt at reconstructing a 'critical theory' which would draw on the strengths of Adorno's work (and of that of other first-generation critical theorists) whilst abandoning its indefensible elements, is that of Jürgen Habermas and the group of philosophers concerned with 'discourse ethics' associated with Habermas, such as Karl-Otto Apel and Herbert Schnädelbach. A full account of their work cannot be given here, but consideration of the contemporary significance of Adorno's thought needs to reflect on the questions which they raise.[3]

The communicative turn

Adorno's thought would expect and hope to be in need of criticism. Any thinking which can describe itself as 'the rebellion of experience against empiricism'[4] necessarily concedes, indeed wishes for, its own mutability along with that of the experience in whose name it speaks. It could be claimed that in certain respects the social experience which critical theory addresses has not changed so greatly since Adorno's death as might superficially appear. The global expansion of the commodity form as the primary relation of production which is at the centre of Adorno's social theory continues; it remains a central topic of social-scientific debate. Adorno's lack of sympathy for Soviet Marxism means that his own thought appears more, not less relevant, after the demise of Marxism-Leninism. Since 1989 it has become easier, rather than more difficult, to see that capitalism cannot be understood through any political economy modelled on the idea of a natural or providential harmony between consumption and production.

The utopian element of Adorno's thought has appeared to some to have weathered less well. Utopianism in general has in some quarters been identified as the characteristic ideology of totalitarianism; and an anti-utopian and modest muddling through as the characteristic procedure of humane government. A utopia so negatively conceived as Adorno's, however, can hardly be written off as a totalitarian blueprint. Siegfried Kracauer once declared that the idea of utopia in Adorno was 'quite simply a regulative concept [*Grenzbegriff*]': a concept which never could be, and was never really intended to be, realized, but rather to act as a perennial corrective against any claim that a natural or equitable social order had been finally achieved.[5] Few aspects of Adorno's thought have attracted more qualification from second-generation critical theorists than his utopianism. Where a utopian moment remains in second-generation critical theory it is as a regulative ideal whose significances differ widely from anything envisaged by Adorno.

Jürgen Habermas's 'universal pragmatics', the attempt to reconstruct 'the general presuppositions of communicative action' is a good example.[6] For Habermas, 'the utopian perspective of reconciliation and freedom is ingrained in the conditions for the communicative sociation of individuals.'[7] Because Habermas has in mind communicative action, rather than explicitly discursive communication alone, his is not merely an epistemologically, but also a socially regulative ideal. Like Adorno's aporetic thought, it thus implies that overcoming logical contradiction is not merely a matter of logic but also rests on the reconciliation of social antagonism. The thrust of Habermas's criticisms and revisions of Adorno addresses both epistemological and political aspects of his work. Habermas takes as the centre of his 'programme' a problem that owes much to Adorno: how can thinking understand its own history and its own locatedness in a 'lifeworld', yet without lapsing into a relativism from which any possibility of normative moral and political judgement would have to be surrendered? Like Adorno, Habermas takes normative universalism to have emerged historically in modernity; like Adorno, he thinks that a norm's historical origin need not destroy its effectively normative character.[8] It has been argued here that it was always a distinctive feature of Adorno's Marxism that the central concepts of liberal political and legal thought were to be turned against what had taken place in their name, not written off as sheer ideology. Habermas emphasizes the universalist moment in the dialectic of enlightenment still more strongly than did even the late Adorno.

Habermas remains a genuinely 'critical' theorist in the sense of Horkheimer's opposition between critical and traditional theory, that critical theory is not an attempt simply to adequate itself to pre-given facts, but to criticize – by understanding – that 'state of facts' itself. But Habermas's critical theory also differs very strikingly from Adorno's philosophical compositions. Habermas believes that the earlier interdisciplinary programme of critical theory is abandoned in the later 1930s in favour of a critique of instrumental reason which is still tied to the presuppositions of classical philosophy of consciousness from Descartes to Kant.[9] Adorno and Horkheimer's attempt to criticize such philosophy of consciousness from within leads only to an aporia in which no rational foundation for the critique of instrumental reason can be secured. For Habermas this is not, as Adorno thought, because in an objectively antagonistic society critical theory must necessarily be aporetic. He thinks instead that Adorno and Horkheimer misguidedly abandoned the earlier interdisciplinary programme of critical theory in favour of philosophical composition. This later work, for Habermas, overemphasizes the aesthetic moment in cognition,[10] loses the necessary relation to specialist disciplines,[11] and remains trapped in the philosophy of consciousness.[12]

Habermas's criticisms are brought together in the charge that Adorno's aporetic thought cannot but founder in scepticism: 'like historicism, [Adorno and Horkheimer] surrendered themselves to an uninhibited scepticism regarding reason, instead of weighing the grounds that cast doubt on this scepticism itself.'[13] Habermas argues instead for a shift of paradigm to a 'communications-theoretic' paradigm. Such a paradigm insists that norm and description need to be procedurally separated, but also that this procedural separation does not imply a metaphysical or ontological separation.[14]

Habermas believes that these considerations necessitate a wholesale revision of critical theory. The universally valid norms governing communicative action can be isolated and stated, and critical theory should get on with this task. Without such a procedure, there can be no secure standard against which communicative action can be judged.[15] That there can be no normative presupposition without particular communicative actions in which norms are presupposed is fully admitted. The separation which Habermas proposes is not ontological, but procedural.[16]

It will be clear by this stage that Habermas's revisions affect (as Habermas is well aware) far more than questions of presentation. The notion that philosophical thinking and writing are dialectical makes fewer and fewer appearances in Habermas's work as it progresses, perhaps because it appears to Habermas tied either to speculative totality (Hegel) or to a fragile hope for the redemption of sceptical negativity (Adorno). Adorno's aporetic discontent with either an identification of, or a radical separation between, description and prescription is regarded as disabling. If norms cannot be separated from experience at least sufficiently to say what they are, in what sense is 'theory' any longer 'critical'?

Because of this normative and linguistic turn taken by second-generation critical theory certain problems connected with Adorno's critique of philosophy and metaphysics drop out of its social theory. In particular the problem of how a materialist thinking is possible is now of less central interest because the regulative ideal against which social theory is to be measured is intersubjective. The task of explicating universal pragmatics is procedurally separated from the task of the 'reconstruction of historical materialism'.[17] Habermas has little interest in that aspect of Adorno's thought which seeks to understand the possibility not merely of a reconciliation of autonomous subject with autonomous subject, but the end of subjectivity itself – and of inter*subject*ivity too – through a reconciliation of culture and nature. The end of domination always centrally implies, for Adorno, the end not only of direct social injustice, but the end of that internal self-mastery and self-slavery which characterizes the autonomous subject.

Adorno's thought, unlike Habermas's, thematizes happiness, including bodily delight and an end to material suffering, as strongly as it does free and rational intersubjectivity. That happiness and freedom are inextricably connected is a motif Adorno shares with Benjamin, who insisted that we could not speak of a 'happy fate': happiness would be freedom from fate.[18] This motif survives in Adorno's thought as the idea of release from endless self-preservation, the 'context of nature' (*Naturzusammenhang*): a release which would only be possible, by the central paradox of Adorno's thought, if we could stop acting and thinking as though we were self-made, as though human subjectivity and inter-subjectivity were pure culture. From an Adornian viewpoint, Habermas's thought risks recapitulating the cultural idealism which was the central target of the *Dialectic of Enlightenment*. For Adorno, ideally successful communicative action, realized and transparent intersubjectivity, would not necessarily be utopian, since the condition of an end to the domination of nature would be the ability to recognize that society is not pure culture, not subjectivity and not (only) intersubjectivity.

Habermas can point to the place left for a reconstruction of historical materialism in his theory of communicative action, and can reply that his separation between universal pragmatics or discourse ethics and such a reconstruction is not ontological but procedural. Kant similarly insisted that although concepts and intuitions could never be found in sheer isolation from each other, they had to be methodologically separated to determine the contribution made to knowledge by each.[19] But this innocuously methodological separation, like Kant's, cannot forestall its own hardening into a full-blown gulf between 'is' and 'ought' of just the kind against which Hegel's critique of Kant is directed.[20] We are again left in the predicament of 'always having to suppose' just what we never find to be fully true in any particular case, that 'only the unforced force of the better argument comes into play.'[21]

The impulse behind this kind of doubt about second-generation critical theory is not 'anti-humanist'. It is no more adequate to file Adorno's thought under this heading than it is to dismiss it as a

variety of 'Marxist humanism'.[22] Adorno aims at a 'true humanism' which would recognize how inhuman most 'humanism' is.[23]
That humanity which can glory only in its own work is not human.
Love is not simple, something which, as it were, was always there
all along but was sadly suppressed or misrecognized by organized
society, or by reification, or by alienation; rather it is known to us
only as the most fragile, transient and complex cognitive and social
achievement, an intimation of a possible freedom from sheer self-
preservation. When it is asserted that Adorno 'adheres to a sensualist concept of happiness',[24] then, this is mistakenly formulated:
the important truth that Adorno strongly resists a notion of
happiness which would somehow have freed itself from the
somatic and erotic is allowed to lead into the notion that his
concept of happiness is a sheerly sensualist one. Adorno's dissatisfaction with any notion of brute facticity runs right the way
through to his concept of happiness. Sheer sense-pleasure is no
more adequate to his concept of happiness than are sheer sense-
data to his concept of cognition.

If this notion of utopia is indeed a 'regulative idea' as Kracauer
suggested, it is clearly unusually internally differentiated for such
a concept. Nevertheless, the truth in Kracauer's remark is this: that
Adorno's utopianism, if it can properly be called such, is utopian
negativity. Unlike what is usually called utopianism, it in no way
seeks to assure us that the great day must come, nor even that it is
likely to. Instead its perennial aim is to resist the liquidation of the
possibility of really new experience. All Adorno's work attempts,
not to give stupid assurances that reconciliation must inevitably be
realized, but to resist the liquidation of this possibility by sciences
which legislate for the future in the image of the past. This is not so
mystical a thought as it has been painted. It does not take refuge
from the actual in the merely possible; instead, Adorno pursues
throughout the attempt announced in 'The Idea of Natural History', 'to criticize the separation of the actual and the possible from
out of the actual'.[25] I consider below how far such an attempt can
be characterized as 'speculative' in a Hegelian sense.

Negative dialectic and deconstruction

The possible criticisms of Habermas which could be mounted from
the perspective of a negative dialectic are in some respects not so
far from some of the objections raised by deconstructive thinkers to

aspects of Habermas's work. Might Derrida's deconstruction, in particular, share more with Adorno's critical theory than do the latter's own pupil-critics? There are clearly affinities between deconstruction's concern for an irreducible non-external heterogeneity which makes thought possible and cannot be exhaustively and transparently grasped by thought, on the one hand, and Adorno's formulation of the non-identical, on the other. Derrida's authorship is no less complex than Adorno's and any attempt to address this question in summary will be reductive. Nevertheless some affinities and differences can be indicated. Negative dialectic, like deconstruction, is neither a method, nor a world-view. It is the experience of thought's implicatedness with what is not thought.

This last characterization, however, marks the point at which the parallel between negative dialectic and deconstruction must end. For deconstruction any dialectic must implicitly depend on some notion of processual totality. Such a totality is always set in motion by some donative moment, a 'gift', outside this totality, which gives rise to it and which it cannot think.[26] Even Adorno's negative dialectic, which insists that non-identity, more radically than identity, makes the experience of thinking possible, would still fall foul of this objection. Adorno's insistence that cognition of the non-identical is only possible as the collapse of subjective misrecognition of it must mean, for deconstruction, that it is already inscribed in a dialectical relation. Adorno's 'non-identical' is not fully comparable to the irreducible alterity which is so often Derrida's concern.

The implications of these differences between deconstruction and negative dialectic extend to social and political thought. As we saw earlier, Adorno has some doubts about complete social transparency as a regulative utopia, because it threatens to restore a cultural idealism and to forestall any reconciliation of culture and nature. Yet he is closer to this view than to any implication that opacity is an irreducible feature of sociality as such. Such a view is implicit, despite all apologias, in Derrida's insistence – informed by Nietzsche, Heidegger and, recently, Benjamin – that we cannot dispense with the notion of legality as an irreducible 'gift' which constitutes in advance the possibility of sociation,[27] a 'yes, yes' which is the condition of all negation.[28] For Derrida, particular laws may be social products but this 'law, before any particular law' cannot be a social product. It is, rather, an irreducible violence, an imposition which is always already the precondition for any sociality whatever.[29] For a negative dialectic it is just the quasi-transcendental status of these kinds of gestures – 'law before any particular law', 'friendship before any particular friendship' – which is problematic.[30] They recapitulate the gulf pointed to earlier in Heidegger's work between 'historicity' and any particular history. The illusory concretion which Adorno took as a characteristic of Heidegger's quasi-transcendental thought is an equally marked feature of deconstruction. Law 'before' law, friendship 'before' friendship, are instances of this, because the priority referred to, the 'before', is not temporal or historical but quasi-transcendental.

The difference between negative dialectic and de-struction of previous ontology over the relationship between philosophy and the human sciences, then, is recapitulated in the case of deconstruction. Deconstructive writers deny that they claim any priority for deconstruction over the human sciences. Such a priority keeps returning in their written practice because a questioning of the metaphysical presuppositions of empirical inquiry is always what deconstruction must attend to first. The result is that the gulf between thinking and knowing keeps opening up as unbridgeably – and keeps being as arbitrarily leapt over – for Derrida as it did for Heidegger. Questioning of the tacit metaphysical presuppositions of syncretic or comparative work in the social sciences, for example, is thus allowed to disqualify such work. Deconstruction of syncretic social science itself falls into much more abstract formulations of the supposed shape of sociality 'itself' before any particular social action.

Relation to empiricism

Nevertheless, as we have seen, Adorno himself understands this fissure between thinking and knowing as real, if not absolute, and does not think that its halves can mechanically be glued together again.[31] In the early days of the Institute for Social Research, Horkheimer envisaged the Institute's project as one which would require the collaborative and interdisciplinary reunification of philosophy with science.[32] Adorno and Marcuse persuaded Horkheimer during the 1930s that this was a still more problematic aim than he had initially thought, because divided intellectual labour was not only mutilated by the division between its various disciplines. These disciplines themselves were also internally mutilated by their own methodologism. The critique of positivism becomes so central to the critique of instrumental reason towards the end of the 1930s that such a reunification is scarcely any longer imaginable.[33] Nevertheless there has recently been a resurgence of interest in Horkheimer's earlier interdisciplinary programme, together with a belief in various quarters that Adorno was one of the last 'one-man philosophers' and that the age when such moon-calves walked the earth is now for ever past. From such a stand-point, Adorno's emphasis on philosophy as composition can be taken as a consequence of the status of his work as an obsolete singular authorship.

The moment of truth in such reflections can be seen by consider-ing the work of those disciples of Adorno who have angrily rejected the revisions of second-generation critical theory and have pointed to what is lost in the revision.[34] They are surely correct in their argument that important features of critical theory as Adorno understood it have been lost in Habermas's critical revision. None the less, it is equally clear from their own efforts that negative dialectic, when protected by the faithful, is itself not immune from freezing to an idiolect which provides an *insulation* from new knowing and experiencing – as always already compromised by unacceptable epistemological or metaphysical presuppositions – rather than resisting the liquidation of the possibility of new experience. Negative dialectic as a creed can harden to a device by which experience can always already be discounted.

'One-person philosophy' cannot simply be stuffed, mounted and forgotten about, however, because what drives such singular authorships is a persisting criticism of the division of intellectual labour. It was already evident to Adorno in 1932 that the division between philosophy and individual disciplines could no longer simply be overcome by the genius or diligence of an individual; indeed, like Max Weber, he saw that the consequences of such a pretended overcoming were potentially disastrous. Yet this divi-sion cannot possibly be taken as read by any thinking worthy of the name. When the division of intellectual labour is misrecog-nized as an invariant and unchallengeable given rather than as a mutable process, many assertions to the effect that 'these are no longer properly sociological questions' or that 'it is not up to philosophers' to solve problem x, y, or z which is 'purely empirical' can be heard. Such disclaimers are by no means accidental but rather mark the point where inquiry threatens to address 'what something is, rather than that of which it is an instance or example, and which therefore it is not itself'. Theory must think what thinking's task is, not just read it off the contract.

Habermas is right to suggest that the future of critical theory remains closely connected with the question of the relation between critique and individual disciplines – and it is clear enough that this relation is what has been lost by keepers of the faith – but wrong to imply that this relation has been suppressed in Adorno's work by an aestheticization of reason. When Habermas suggests that the turn to the critique of instrumental reason in the late 1930s has 'the practical consequence of relinquishing a connection to the social sciences' it is as though the wartime and later social-critical essays had been entirely forgotten.[35] Critical theory does indeed become empty without this connection. But it is just as liable to lose it by innocent procedural separations of normative from substantive inquiry, separations which structure second-generation critical theory. Artless 'programmes' for reunification find what they hoped to add together coming apart at the seams. Adorno's attention to philosophical composition is motivated not by a wish to evade the demand for a relation to substantive inquiry but by the wish to answer it. What has recently struck second-generation critics as an aestheticization of reason is closely tied to the speculative moment of Adorno's thinking.

Speculative thinking: relation to the Absolute

The claim that negative dialectic retains a 'speculative moment'[36] requires a further examination of the vexed question of the relation of a dialectic to its sources in German idealism, not least because many of the arguments which can be marshalled against Adorno's critics are essentially Hegelian. With what right can Adorno deploy such arguments whilst insisting, aporetically, on the non-identical? This question has been forcefully turned against Adorno by his Hegelian critics. For some such critics, Adorno's talk of non-identity betrays a relapse from speculative thinking into a Schellingian invocation of the non-identity of thought and being which must become dogmatic in spite of itself.[37] Objections of this kind raise again the central question of whether, and in what sense, Adorno remains a speculative thinker as well as the related but not identical question of his relation to metaphysics.

Some illuminating recent commentaries have addressed this problem by describing Adorno's thought as a 'negative metaphysics'.[38] Yet Adorno seems rarely to have used this phrase himself, and it is doubtful whether, of itself, the label does more than displace the problem it is intended to solve, because Adorno introduces the idea that a moment of metaphysical speculation is ineliminable just where he wants to *question* the limits and nature of negativity. Indeed, it appears at first sight almost incomprehensible that a self-declaredly *negative* dialectic could think to have any connection whatsoever to speculative thinking, because such a dialectic at first appears precisely to insist on what Hegel called the dialectical moment of thinking, the negative, and to renounce the speculative moment as a 'positive negation', as the betrayal of dialectical to identificatory thinking. That one section from the introduction to *Negative Dialectics* is headed 'The speculative moment', however, should give us pause, not only because Adorno was rather careful in his choice of such terms, but because his account of such a moment is clearly linked to the meditations on the impossibility of liquidating metaphysical speculation which we have seen to be, for Adorno, the very condition of negative dialectic's possibility. Adorno is reluctant to surrender speculation as the sole property of a dialectic conducted along Hegelian lines. He writes of 'the speculative moment' as:

> whatever does not let its law be laid down by the given facts, yet transcends them in the closest feeling with the objects [*Gegenständen*] and in the renunciation of sacrosanct transcendence. That wherein thought is beyond that to which it resistingly binds itself, is its freedom. It follows the subject's drive for expression. The need to let suffering become eloquent is the condition of all truth. For suffering is objectivity with which the subject is burdened [*die auf dem Subjekt lastet*]: what it experiences as its most subjective element, its expression, is objectively mediated.[39]

This complex account of what the 'speculative moment' might mean for Adorno's thought needs careful consideration. Speculative thinking, for Adorno, 'does not let its law be laid down by the given facts'. We have seen throughout this book that a refusal to allow description, a replication of the given facts, to be tacitly turned into prescription, a law for thinking, is a central thread of Adorno's thought. But if thinking allows itself to go beyond the given facts in some way, will this not be just the kind of claim to an immediate access to transcendence which Adorno has wanted to resist? In just what way may thinking allow itself to go 'beyond the given facts' without becoming sheer fantasy? Adorno's initial answer here, that thought 'yet transcends them in the closest feeling with the objects', appears obscure. But it is given a more direct statement later in the passage: 'The need to let suffering become eloquent is the condition of all truth.' The centre of Adorno's notion of speculative thinking might be formulated thus: to allow what thinking lives off to speak in thinking. Thinking is always to remember its own indebtedness – *lasten* can refer to financial as well as literal burdens – yet, equally emphatically, it is not to transfigure that debt into fate, but to seek its dissolution.

It is here that some central incompatibilities between negative dialectic and speculation in its Hegelian form come into focus. In some respects Hegel's most celebrated speculative identification – his exposition of the failure of all attempts radically to separate 'ought' from 'is', the rational from the actual – is no less central to Adorno's than to Hegel's thought. All normative thinking is contaminated with reference to experience, and indeed must be so contaminated to have any normative force. Yet Adorno insists equally, and once more with Hegel, that this does not imply the simple disappearance of prescription into description, a theodicy in which whatever is, is right. When combined these positions might appear to lead inexorably to Hegel's speculative identification of 'is' and 'ought': an identification which, it will be remembered, exhibits the repeated breakdown of all attempts to shore up a radical separation between 'is' and 'ought'. For so long as speculative identification is understood in this way – as the exposition of the collapse of supposed radical separations – Adorno can be understood as a speculative thinker. For Adorno, thinking speculatively itself lies in this tireless renunciation (*Absage*) both of a radical separation of 'is' and 'ought' and of their abstract identification.

For Hegel, certainly, it is incoherent to want to help oneself to this negative aspect of speculation, this renunciation, without its identificatory moment. The only possible result of the collapse of any attempt radically to separate 'ought' from 'is' is their speculative – not abstract –identification. It is not difficult to see why several recent commentators should have chosen to express the difference between Hegelian dialectic and negative dialectic as a rejection of speculative thinking as such.[40] Speculation, 'speculative' identity, and 'speculative' thinking, are terms which Adorno uses infrequently, and with good reason. Speculation can never be used as a means to criticize those who fall short of it, because in this very employment it falls apart again into those elements which it is supposed to think together – and such would be the fate of any demand that Adorno 'ought' to be a more speculative thinker. This is because what, on Hegel's own account, differentiates speculative from sheer abstract identity is its restless return to the experience of non-identity. Genuinely speculative thinking, for Adorno, is precisely absent there where the thesis of speculative identity is most unyieldingly defended, where its name is most often made free with. Speculative thinking is not always most in evidence where it is most loudly invoked. The idea of seeing off all challenges to speculative thinking is absurd, because speculative thinking is least of all concerned with defending a correct 'position' against all comers; instead speculation continually recognizes the truth in distorted form in the misrecognitions of its opponent.

A negative dialectic which liquidated its speculative moment, however, would be a nihilism, not a dialectic. The speculative moment in Adorno's thought concerns not the identity of identity and non-identity but the (differentiating) reconciliation of the identical and the non-identical. Hence the philosophical syntax of Adorno's speculative thinking is not identical with that of Hegel's. Hegel's speculative propositions declare that the actual is the rational – or that substance is subject – but only out of the exposition of their diremption. They thus declare the identity of terms that are, also, non-identical. There are no such propositions as 'the actual is the rational' in Adorno's work. Nevertheless, since Adorno will not rewrite Hegel simply by settling into the sententious security of redundance – that, say, 'what is actual is not yet rational, but it ought to be' – he is accordingly in need of a different kind of speculative writing. This speculative writing could not invert Hegel's; nor is it any case simply a question of a form or a style. What, then, finally, is speculative about Adorno's thought?

Speculation suspends the abstract antithesis between prescription and description. In this sense, every line of Adorno's work – in which, to be sure, there are no positive prescriptions, but in which there is also no sheer description, nothing at all whose status is sheerly constative – is speculative, even though there are no speculative identifications in it. This is another way of understanding the importance of artifice to every aspect of Adorno's thought. That which has so often prompted the charge of an aestheticization of reason in his work is in truth the speculative element in which it moves, the more and less than literal status of its assertions. Of course this element has no accidental relation to the aesthetic, because wherever a suspension of the antithesis between prescription and description is attempted, thinking must become conscious of its own artifice of articulation. There is no artless cognition. This is not an aestheticization of reason but an account of what reason is like. To understand it we need to remember how negative dialectic wished to distinguish itself from idealist dialectic. If for Hegel only the identity of identity and non-identity makes (dialectical) thinking possible, for Adorno it is more radically the non-identity of identity and non-identity that makes (dialectical) thinking possible. Hegel's speculative propositions declare the identity of their terms out of the experience of their non-identity. Adorno's speculative compositions articulate the reconciled difference of terms which cannot yet be experienced as reconciled – *which cannot yet even, fully, be experienced as different*. Reconciled non-identity – between art and cognition or between culture and nature, between subject and object as well as between subject and subject – cannot be stated in a single proposition, however speculative, because the terms would no longer be self-identical in a reconciled state. The ineliminability of the thought of reconciled non-identity is the speculative moment which animates each of Adorno's works. Without speculation in this sense – as articulation of the real possibility of reconciled non-identity, not as the declared identity of identity and non-identity – there is no dialectic for Adorno, not even a negative one, but rather abstract negations which push its aporetic 'neither/nor' towards a nihilist 'all is nothing.' But because Adorno's speculative thinking is animated not by identity but by a really possible reconciled non-identity, it shows up not only how what has been thought of as fixatedly separate must be thought together, but also, and originally, how what cannot yet be properly experienced as non-identical might be so experienced. Life without self-preservation, reconciliation without sacrifice, happiness without power: these as yet barely imaginable differentiations are no less speculatively thought by Adorno than is the identification of the actual and the rational by Hegel. These are Adorno's speculative differentiations to Hegel's speculative identifications. They are not propositions – they have no copula and no main verb – but are negatively articulated by constellations of propositions.

The full weight which Adorno places on ineliminability, on hopes, wishes, desires and contents which cannot be deleted from thinking 'if thinking is to remain thinking' thus comes into view. The real possibility of reconciled non-identity is the condition of intelligibility of his very utterances and texts. In the work of any thinker the appeal to what is utterly irreducible, indestructible or non-interrogable risks standing as an unthematized placeholder for a tabooed absolute. In one respect it is correct to understand Adorno's appeal to what is ineliminable from thinking as a place-holder for the absolute: in the sense that his work is fully alive to the weight which is placed on the ineliminable and to its kinship with the absolute, rather than falling accidentally into them. Adorno was capable of closing a letter, disconcertingly, with the words: 'Max: the unconditional. There is nothing else!'[41] In print he insisted, less positively, that '[t]he authority of the Kantian concept of truth became terroristic with the prohibition on thinking the absolute.'[42] What makes Adorno's appeal to the ineliminability of the real possibility of reconciled non-identity different from an unconditioned absolute is, precisely, its conditionality: *if* thinking is to remain thinking, or, better, if thinking is first to become true, this possibility is ineliminable. There is no guarantee that thinking will remain thinking or become true thinking. Negative dialectic's enduring interest lies not in any otherworldly self-insulation but in its renewed return to experience – as to something which is, but may change. It is not utopian in the bad sense that it just hopes for the best, but in its relinquishment of any radical or methodological separation of the question 'what can we hope for?' from 'what can we know?' A hope with no cognitive content is not a hope but a sententious cipher. There is no hope which is not also in part a memory. Yet a thought which was utterly empty of desire, which did not wish for anything, would not be like anything, would not be a thought at all.[43] The wish in thinking cannot be deleted by labouring towards indifference; rather it will be at work anyway but not properly thematized. If reason is ever to become more than a court

> Where passions have the privilege to work
> And never hear the sound of their own names

then this much 'utopianism' at least will never be liquidable from thinking.

Notes

Introduction

1 Carlo Pettazzi, *Th. Wiesengrund Adorno. Linee di origine e di sviluppo del pensiero (1903–1949)* (Firenze: La nuova Italia, 1979), p. 16.

2 Ibid., p. 17. For a recent study of this period see Heinz Steinert, *Adorno in Wien: Über die (Un-) Möglichkeit von Kunst, Kultur und Befreiung* (Vienna: Verlag für Gesellschaftskritik, 1989). Adorno was still attempting to secure a favourable Viennese reception for his music in 1935. Adorno to Krenek, 10 March 1935, in Theodor W. Adorno and Ernst Krenek, *Briefwechsel*, (FfM: Suhrkamp, 1974), p. 72.

3 Hans Cornelius, *Transcendentale Systematik* (Munich: Ernst Reinhardt, 1916), pp. 28–44.

4 'Der Begriff des Unbewußten in der transzendentalen Seelenlehre', in *GS 1*, pp. 79–322, p. 81.

5 In a letter to Leo Löwenthal (16 July 1924), quoted in Löwenthal, *Mitmachen wollte ich nie: ein autobiographisches Gespräch mit Helmut Dubiel* (FfM: Suhrkamp, 1980), p. 247, Adorno comments that his Husserl dissertation is 'less authentic than it ought to be . . . it is Cornelian'. Cornelius wrote to the College of the Faculty of Philosophy (8 January 1928) that 'The concept of the unconscious' hardly went beyond 'a simple repetition of what he knows from my own lectures and books, although it is embellished with a great many words.' Quoted in Rolf Wiggershaus, *The Frankfurt School*, tr. Michael Robertson (Cambridge: Polity Press, 1993), p. 82.

6 What remained of lasting significance to him, however, was Cornelius's criticism of what he took to be the metaphysical presuppositions in Kant's concept of *Erfahrung*, experience. As late as 1956 Adorno could still occasionally be found quoting Cornelius (*ME*, p. 89; Domingo, p. 82).

7 Wilhelm Dilthey, *Der Aufbau der geschichtlichen Welt in den Geisteswissenschaften*, ed. B. Groethuysen (Leipzig: B. G. Teubner, 1927); Georg Simmel, *The Problems of the Philosophy of History: An Epistemological Study*, tr. Guy Oakes (New York: Free Press, 1977); Wilhelm Windelband, 'History

and Natural Science', tr. Guy Oakes, *History and Theory* 19 (1980), 169–85, p. 175.

8 'Der wunderliche Realist. Über Siegfried Kracauer', in *NzL*, pp. 388–408, p. 389; Nicholsen, pp. 58–75, p. 59.

9 'Die Aktualität der Philosophie', in *GS* 1, pp. 325–46; 'The Actuality of Philosophy' (1931), *Telos* 31 (1977), 120–33.

10 Wiggershaus, *The Frankfurt School*, p. 94.

11 Ibid., pp. 12–13.

12 *Archiv für die Geschichte des Sozialismus und der Arbeiterbewegung.*

13 Pettazzi, *Th. Wiesengrund Adorno*, pp. 89–90.

14 Ernst Bloch, *Geist der Utopie* (FfM: Suhrkamp, 1971), pp. 278, 25, 252, 254.

15 Ibid., p. 260.

16 Ibid., pp. 152–3.

17 Georg Lukács, *History and Class Consciousness*, tr. Rodney Livingstone (London: Merlin Press, 1971), pp. 1–24.

18 Ibid., p. 100.

19 Ibid., pp. 197–209.

20 Horkheimer, 'Bemerkungen in Sachen der Habilitation Dr. Wiesengrund', February 1931, in Theodor Adorno file (1924–68), Philosophy Faculty of the University of Frankfurt am Main. Quoted in Wiggershaus, *The Frankfurt School*, p. 93.

21 Max Horkheimer, 'The Present Situation of Social Philosophy and the Tasks of an Institute of Social Research' in *Between Philosophy and Social Science: Selected Early Writings*, tr. G. Frederick Hunter, Matthew S. Kramer and John Torpey (Cambridge, Mass.: MIT Press, 1993), pp. 3–14.

22 Max Horkheimer, 'Materialism and Metaphysics', in *Critical Theory: Selected Essays*, tr. Matthew J. O'Connell et al. (New York: Continuum, 1982), pp. 10–46, p. 34.

23 *The Origin of German Tragic Drama*, tr. John Osborne (London: New Left Books, 1977), p. 175.

24 Ibid., p. 79.

25 Ibid., p. 53.

26 Ibid., p. 216.

27 Adorno to Ernst Krenek, 7 October 1934, in Adorno and Krenek, *Briefwechsel* (FfM: Suhrkamp, 1974), p. 43.

28 Ibid., p. 44; Pettazzi, *Th. Wiesengrund Adorno*, p. 160.

29 Adorno to Krenek, 10 March 1935, *Briefwechsel*, p. 64.

30 Wiggershaus, *The Frankfurt School*, p. 237.

31 'Diskussionsprotokolle', in Max Horkheimer, *Gesammelte Schriften*, ed. Gunzelin Schmid Noerr and Alfred Schmidt (15 vols, FfM: Fischer, 1987), vol. 12, pp. 431–605.

32 Wiggershaus, *The Frankfurt School*, pp. 241–2.

33 Ibid., p. 370.

34 'Wissenschaftliche Erfahrungen in Amerika', *GS* 10.2, pp. 702–38; 'Scientific Experiences of a European Scholar in America', tr. Donald Fleming, *Perspectives in American History* 2 (1968), 338–70; repr. in Donald Fleming and Bernard Bailyn, eds, *The Intellectual Migration* (Cambridge, Mass.: Belknap Press / Harvard University Press), pp. 338–70. Cf. Martin Jay, 'Adorno in America', *New German Critique* 31 (Winter 1984) 157–82, p. 162.

35 Wiggershaus, *The Frankfurt School*, pp. 431–659.

36 Cf. 'Zum Klassizismus von Goethes Iphigenie', in *NzL*, pp. 495–514; Nicholsen, ii, pp. 153–70.

Chapter 1 The Dialectic of Enlightenment

1 Rolf Wiggershaus, *The Frankfurt School*, tr. Michael Robertson (Cambridge: Polity Press, 1993), p. 264.
2 'Einleitung zum "Positivismusstreit in der deutschen Soziologie" ', in *GS* 8, pp. 280–353, pp. 317–18. 'Statement of fact' is in English in the original text.
3 *DA*, p. 16; Cumming, p. xvi.
4 *DA*, p. 60; Cumming, p. 42. For Bacon: *DA*, pp. 20, 60; Cumming, pp. 4, 42. For misconstructions of Nietzsche: *DA*, p. 62; Cumming, p. 44.
5 *DA*, p. 13; Cumming, p. xiii.
6 *DA*, pp. 93–4; Cumming, pp. 74–5.
7 *DA*, p. 149; Cumming, pp. 127–8.
8 *DA*, pp. 34–5, p. 24; Cumming, pp. 18–19, p. 8.
9 *DA*, p. 32; Cumming, p. 16.
10 *DA*, p. 44; Cumming, p. 27; Introduction to *The Positivist Dispute in German Sociology*, pp. 5–6.
11 *DA*, p. 34; Cumming, pp. 17–18.
12 *DA*, p. 26; Cumming, p. 10.
13 *DA*, pp. 49–52; Cumming, pp. 32–4.
14 *DA*, p. 56; Cumming, p. 38.
15 *ND*, pp. 315–17; Ashton, pp. 321–3.
16 *DA*, p. 62; Cumming, p. 44.
17 Since some suspicion has recently been voiced of supposedly Klagesian elements in the *Dialectic of Enlightenment* (Axel Honneth is cited to this effect in Albrecht Wellmer, 'Wahrheit, Schein, Versöhnung. Adornos ästhetische Rettung der Modernität' in *Zur Dialektik von Moderne und Postmoderne* (FfM: Suhrkamp, 1985), pp. 9–47, p. 45, n.4), it is worth emphasizing the extent to which the work was conceived against Klagesian ideas from the outset.
18 Ludwig Klages, *Der Geist als Widersacher der Seele*, 4th edn (Bonn and Munich: Bouvier and Johann Ambrosius Barth, 1960), p. 69.
19 Ibid., p. 1409.
20 *DA*, p. 73; Cumming, p. 55.
21 *DA*, p. 26; Cumming, p. 10 (my emphasis).
22 *DA*, p. 67; Cumming, p. 49.
23 *DA*, p. 69; Cumming, p. 51.
24 *DA*, p. 94; Cumming, p. 75.
25 *DA*, pp. 15–16; Cumming, pp. 31–2.
26 *DA*, p. 26; Cumming, p. 10.
27 'The Psychological Technique of Martin Luther Thomas's Radio Addresses', *GS* 9.1: *Soziologische Schriften II: Erste Hälfte*, pp. 57–9; 'Freudian Theory and the Pattern of Fascist Propaganda', in *The Culture Industry*, ed. J. M. Bernstein (London: Routledge, 1991), pp. 114–35, p. 126.

28 *DA*, p. 76; Cumming, p. 57.

29 *ND*, p. 232; Ashton, p. 233.

30 Joel Whitebook, *Perversion and Utopia: A Study in Psychoanalysis and Critical Theory* (Cambridge, Mass.: MIT Press, 1995). For an account of the psychoanalytic aspects of Adorno's thought, cf. ch. 3 below.

31 Marcuse, *Eros and Civilization: A Philosophical Enquiry into Freud* (Boston: Beacon Press, 1966), p. 191.

32 Josef Früchtl, *Mimesis: Konstellation eines Zentralbegriffs bei Adorno* (Würzburg: Königshausen und Neumann, 1986), especially pp. 219ff: 'Zum Begriff der Synthesis bei Adorno'.

33 Cf. 'Der Essay als Form', in *NzL*, pp. 9–33, p. 13; Nicholsen, i, pp. 3-23, p. 6: 'A consciousness for which intuition and concept, image and sign would be one and the same – if such a consciousness ever existed – cannot be magically restored; and its restitution would constitute a regression to chaos. Such a consciousness is conceivable only as the completion of the process of mediation, as utopia, conceived by idealist philosophy ever since Kant under the name of intellectual intuition, something that broke down whenever actual knowledge appealed to it.'

34 As *Perversion and Utopia* itself partially concedes: p. 262.

35 *Perversion and Utopia*, p. 79.

36 Axel Honneth, *The Critique of Power: Reflective Stages in a Critical Social Theory*, tr. Kenneth Baynes (Cambridge, Mass.: MIT Press, 1991), p. 52; Gillian Rose, *The Melancholy Science* (London: Macmillan, 1978), p. 50.

37 Jean-Jacques Rousseau, *The Social Contract*, tr. G. D. H. Cole, revised J. H. Brumfitt and John C. Hall (London: Dent, 1973), pp. 190–3.

38 Friedrich Nietzsche, *The Genealogy of Morals*, tr. Francis Golffing (New York: Doubleday, 1956), part II, § xvii, pp. 219–20.

39 G. W. F. Hegel, *Phenomenology of Spirit*, tr. A. V. Miller (Oxford: Oxford University Press, 1977), pp. 111–19.

40 Honneth, *The Critique of Power*, p. 52.

41 Ibid. Honneth has since conceded that in the first edition of *The Critique of Power* he himself 'let the aspect of the social relation to the natural world remain too far in the background': ibid., p. xxi.

42 Ibid., p. 95.

43 Ibid., p. xxi.

44 Ibid., p. xiii.

45 'Zu Subjekt und Objekt', in *GS* 10.2, pp. 739–58, p. 743.

46 This is one of the complaints of Stefano Cochetti, *Mythos und 'Dialektik der Aufklärung'* (Meisenheim: Verlag Anton Hain, 1985), p. xvi.

47 Cf. 'World-Spirit and Natural History: An Excursus on Hegel'.

48 'Spengler after the Decline', in *Prisms*, tr. Samuel and Shierry Weber (Cambridge, Mass.: MIT Press, 1981), pp. 53–72, p. 61. G. W. F. Hegel, *The Philosophy of History*, tr. J. Sibree (New York: Dover, 1956), p. 21.

49 Karl Marx and Friedrich Engels, *Die Heilige Familie*, cited in *ND*, p. 299; Ashton, p. 304.

50 As Adorno notes, this is in its turn a Marxian insight. *ND*, pp. 299–300; Ashton, pp. 304–5.

51 *ND*, p. 314; Ashton, p. 320.

52 Ibid.

53 For a critical account of the idea of 'cultures' as windowless monads in twentieth-century social thought, cf. Tim Ingold, *Evolution and Social Life* (Cambridge: Cambridge University Press, 1986).
54 *ND*, p. 315; Ashton, p. 321.
55 Ibid.
56 Cited in Josef Früchtl, 'Radikalität und Konsequenz in der Wahrheitstheorie. Nietzsche als Herausforderung für Adorno und Habermas', *Nietzsche-Studien* 19 (1990), 431–61, p. 433.
57 Willem van Reijen, Jan Bransen, 'Das Verschwinden der Klassengeschichte in der "Dialektik der Aufklärung". Ein Kommentar zu den Textvarianten der Buchausgabe von 1947 gegenüber der Erstveröffentlichung von 1944', in Max Horkheimer, *Gesammelte Schriften*, vol. 5, ed. Gunzelin Schmid Noerr (FfM: Fischer, 1987), pp. 453–7. For a consideration of the extent to which class history does 'disappear' from Adorno's work, see ch. 2 below.
58 *ND*, p. 351; Ashton, p. 358. This is a textual variant which appears only in the fuller edition of *The German Ideology* in the *Marx-Engels Gesamtausgabe*, vol. 5, part 1 (Berlin: 1932), p. 567, not in the Berlin 1953 edition which was used as the basis for the English translation. Cf. Alfred Schmidt, *The Concept of Nature in Marx*, tr. Ben Fowkes (London: New Left Books, 1971), p. 49n.
59 *ND*, p. 351; Ashton, p. 358.
60 Herbert Schnädelbach, 'Die Aktualität der Dialektik der Aufklärung', in Harry Kunnemann and Hent de Vries, eds, *Die Aktualität der Dialektik der Aufklärung* (FfM: Campus Verlag, 1989), pp. 15–35.
61 Ibid., p. 31.
62 Ibid., pp. 20, 29.
63 Ibid., p. 22.
64 Ibid, p. 23.
65 Ibid., p. 25.
66 Ibid., pp. 25, 27.
67 Ibid., p. 30.
68 *DA*, pp. 9–10; Cumming, p. x.

Chapter 2 A Critical Theory of Society

1 Introduction to *The Positivist Dispute in German Sociology*, tr. Glyn Adey and David Frisby (London: Heinemann, 1976), p. 8.
2 Ibid., p. 15.
3 'Gesellschaft', in *GS* 8, pp. 9–19, pp. 11–12.
4 'Einleitung zu Emile Durkheim, "Soziologie und Philosophie" ', in *GS* 8, pp. 245–79, p. 278.
5 Ibid., pp. 255, 248.
6 Ibid., pp. 246–7, 258.
7 Ibid., p. 257.
8 *The Positivist Dispute*, pp. 15, 40, 106. For a qualified defence of one aspect of this distinction, however, see 'Kultur und Verwaltung', *GS* 8, pp. 122–46, p. 128. 'Culture and Administration' in *The Culture Industry*, ed. J. M. Bernstein (London: Routledge, 1991), pp. 93–113, p. 98.

9 'Einleitung zu Durkheim', pp. 265, 267. Durkheim's *The Division of Labour in Society*, tr. W. D. Halls (London: Macmillan, 1984) argued that such a division had replaced the merely 'mechanical' solidarity of more primitive social arrangements with a more powerful 'organic' solidarity.

10 'Science as a vocation', in *From Max Weber: Essays in Sociology*, ed. H. H. Gerth and C. Wright Mills (London: Routledge, 1991), pp. 129–56; *The Methodology of the Social Sciences*, tr. and ed., Edward A. Shils and Henry A. Finch (New York: Macmillan, 1949).

11 'Einleitung zu Durkheim', p. 258.

12 *The Methodology of the Social Sciences*, p. 20.

13 Ibid., p. 9.

14 *Vorlesung zur Einleitung in die Soziologie* (FfM: Junius, 1973), p. 87.

15 'Einleitung zu Durkheim', p. 259. See, for example, Weber, *On the Methodology of the Social Sciences*, p. 36.

16 Karl Marx, *Capital*, vol. 1 (Harmondsworth: Penguin, 1976), p. 102.

17 Ibid., p. 103.

18 *K*, p. 151; Hullot-Kentor, p. 106.

19 'Diskussionsprotokolle' in Max Horkheimer, *Gesammelte Schriften*, vol. 12: *Nachgelassene Schriften 1931–49*, ed. Gunzelin Schmid Noerr (FfM: Fischer, 1985–), pp. 349–605; pp. 399–522.

20 The subtitle of *Capital* is 'A Critique of Political Economy'.

21 'Diskussionsprotokolle', p. 438. For a similar argument cf. 'Spätkapitalismus oder Industriegesellschaft?', p. 368.

22 Cf. Introduction to *The Positivist Dispute in German Sociology*, p. 25.

23 *MM*, p. 281; Jephcott, p. 247.

24 *ND*, pp. 16–18; Ashton, pp. 4–6.

25 For an account of Adorno's Marxism as a 'morality of method' see Gillian Rose, *Hegel contra Sociology* (London: Athlone, 1981), pp. 31–3; for a related account of it as a 'search for style', see Rose, *The Melancholy Science* (London: Macmillan, 1978), especially pp. 11–26.

26 Marx, *Capital*, vol. 1, pp. 164–5.

27 Ibid., p. 165.

28 Georg Lukács, *History and Class Consciousness*, tr. Rodney Livingstone (London: Merlin Press, 1971), p. 85.

29 Ibid., pp. 88–92. Max Weber, *Economy and Society*, ed. Günther Roth and Claus Wittig (2 vols, Berkeley: University of California Press, 1978), vol. 1, pp. 161–4.

30 Lukács, *History and Class Consciousness*, p. 89.

31 Ibid., pp. 110–49.

32 Ibid., p. 166.

33 Ibid., p. 165.

34 Ibid., pp. 205–6.

35 Ibid., p. 206.

36 *ND*, pp. 301–2; Ashton, p. 307.

37 'Reflexionen zur Klassentheorie', in *GS* 8, pp. 374–91.

38 Marx, *Capital*, vol. 3, tr. David Fernbach (Harmondsworth, Penguin, 1981), pp. 349–59, 911.

39 Rudolf Hilferding, *Finance Capital*, ed. Tom Bottomore, tr. Morris Watnick and Sam Gordon (London: Routledge, 1981), p. 241.

40 Henryk Grossmann, *Die Akkumulations und Zusammenbruchsgesetz des kapitalistischen Systems* (Leipzig: Hirschfeld, 1929). Cf. Henryk Grossmann, *The Law of Accumulation and Breakdown of the Capitalist System*, tr. and abr. Jairus Banaji (London: Pluto Press, 1992), pp. 67–72.
41 Rosa Luxemburg, *The Accumulation of Capital: An Anti-critique* (London: Monthly Review Press, 1972), p. 61.
42 Grossmann, *The Law of Accumulation*, pp. 59–77.
43 Friedrich Pollock, 'Die gegenwärtige Lage des Kapitalismus und die Aussichten einer planwirtschaftlichen Neuordnung' [1932] ('The Current Situation of Capitalism and the Prospects for a New Planned Economic Order'), in *Stadien des Kapitalismus*, ed. Helmut Dubiel (Munich: C. H. Beck, 1975), pp. 22–38, p. 33.
44 Ibid., p. 28.
45 For a useful account of Adorno's relationship to the political economists, see Giacomo Marramao, 'Political Economy and Critical Theory', tr. Ray Morrow, *Telos* 24 (Summer 1975), pp. 56–80, esp. pp. 75–6.
46 'Spätkapitalismus oder Industriegesellschaft?', in *GS* 8, p. 355; ibid., p. 358.
47 *Vorlesung zur Einleitung in die Soziologie*, p. 24.
48 'Reflexionen', p. 380.
49 'The Schema of Mass Culture', tr. Nicholas Walker, in *The Culture Industry*, ed. J. M. Bernstein (London: Routledge, 1991), p. 83: 'They [the technicized forms of modern consciousness] transform culture into a total lie, but this untruth confesses the truth about the socio-economic base with which it has now become identical.'
50 'Reflexionen', p. 377.
51 Ibid., p. 385.
52 *Vorlesung zur Einleitung in die Soziologie*, p. 91.
53 'The Schema of Mass Culture', pp. 53–84, p. 77.
54 'Spätkapitalismus', p. 362.
55 'Spätkapitalismus', p. 363; *Vorlesung zur Einleitung in die Soziologie*, pp. 14–15.
56 'Spätkapitalismus', p. 365; ibid., pp. 368–9.
57 Ibid., p. 369.
58 Ibid., p. 361.
59 Michael Wilson, *Das Institut für Sozialforschung und seine Faschismusanalyse* (FfM and New York: Campus Verlag, 1982), p. 9.
60 Friedrich Pollock, 'State Capitalism: Its Possibilities and Limitations', *Studies in Philosophy and Social Science* 9 (2) (1941), pp. 200–25; repr. in Andrew Arato and Eike Gebhardt, eds, *The Essential Frankfurt School Reader* (Oxford: Blackwell, 1978), pp. 71–94.
61 Franz Neumann, *Behemoth: The Structure and Practice of National Socialism* (London: Gollancz, 1942), pp. 183, 239.
62 Ibid.
63 Adorno to Horkheimer, 8 June 1941. Cited in Rolf Wiggershaus, *The Frankfurt School*, tr. Michael Robertson (Cambridge: Polity Press, 1994), p. 282.
64 *Vorlesung zur Einleitung in die Soziologie*, p. 48.
65 'Scientific Experiences of a European Scholar in America', in Donald Fleming and Bernard Bailyn, eds, *The Intellectual Migration: Europe and*

America, 1930–1960 (Cambridge, Mass.: Belknap Press / Harvard University Press, 1969), pp. 338–70, pp. 367–8.

66 Neumann, *Behemoth*, pp. 85–110; *DA*, pp. 192–234; Cumming, pp. 168–208.

67 Neumann, *Behemoth*, pp. 90, 94.

68 'Freudian Theory and the Pattern of Fascist Propaganda', in *The Culture Industry*, pp. 114–35, 128–32.

69 *DA*, p. 225; Cumming, p. 199.

70 *DA*, p. 10; Cumming, p. x.

71 Neumann, *Behemoth*, p. 39. For an account of the influence of Schmitt on Neumann's and Kirchheimer's early work, and their subsequent break with him, see William E. Scheuerman, *Between the Rule and the Exception: The Frankfurt School and the Rule of Law* (Cambridge, Mass.: MIT Press, 1994).

72 In Neumann's sense: *Behemoth*, p. 382: 'there is no law in Germany, although there are thousands of technical rules that are calculable.'

73 For an account emphasizing the Nietzschean elements in *Dialectic of Enlightenment*, cf. Jürgen Habermas, 'The Entwinement of Myth and Enlightenment: Max Horkheimer and Theodor Adorno', in *The Philosophical Discourse of Modernity: Twelve Lectures*, tr. Frederick G. Lawrence (Cambridge: Polity Press, 1987), pp. 106–30.

74 Cf. Norbert Rath, 'Zur Nietzsche-Rezeption Horkheimers und Adornos' in *Vierzig Jahre Flaschenpost. 'Dialektik der Aufklärung' 1947–1987*, ed. Willem van Reijen and Gunzelin Schmid Noerr (FfM: Fischer, 1987), pp. 74–100.

75 'Diskussionsprotokolle', p. 570.

76 'The Schema of Mass Culture', p. 81; 'Diskussionsprotokolle', p. 566.

77 'Beitrag zur Ideologienlehre', in *GS 8: Soziologische Schriften I*, pp. 457–77, p. 472.

78 Ibid., p. 474.

79 Ibid., p. 473.

80 *ND*, p. 153; Ashton, p. 150.

81 'The Sociology of Knowledge and its Consciousness', in *Prisms*, tr. Samuel and Shierry Weber (Cambridge, Mass.: MIT Press, 1981), pp. 37–49, p. 39.

82 'Beitrag zur Ideologienlehre', p. 476.

83 Cf. Moritz Schlick, *Allgemeine Erkenntnislehre*, 2nd edn (Berlin: Julius Springer, 1925), pp. 214–24.

84 Introduction to *The Positivist Dispute*, p. 5.

85 *Thus Spoke Zarathustra*, tr. R. J. Hollingdale (Harmondsworth: Penguin, 1969), pp. 58–61.

86 Introduction to *The Positivist Dispute*, p. 12; G.W.F. Hegel, *Science of Logic*, tr. A. V. Miller (London: Allen & Unwin, 1969), p. 479.

87 *ND*, pp. 171–2; Ashton, pp. 169–70. See also Herbert Marcuse, 'The Concept of Essence', in *Negations* (Boston: Beacon Press, 1968), pp. 44–83.

88 'Diskussionsprotokolle', p. 522.

89 Jacques Derrida, *Specters of Marx* (London: Routledge, 1994), p. 170.

90 Michel Henry, *Marx* (2 vols, Paris: Gallimard, 1976).

91 Erich Fromm, *The Crisis of Psychoanalysis: Essays on Freud, Marx and Social Psychology* (London: Jonathan Cape, 1971), pp. 190–2.
92 Marx, *Capital*, vol. 1, p. 270; pp. 317, 326–7.
93 Ibid., pp. 772–81.
94 'Spätkapitalismus', p. 359.
95 Ibid.
96 'Thesen über Bedürfnis', in *GS* 8, pp. 392–6, pp. 392–4.
97 'Diskussionsprotokolle', p. 568.
98 Theodor W. Adorno and Arnold Gehlen, 'Ist die Soziologie eine Wissenschaft von Menschen? Ein Streitgespräch', in Friedemann Grenz, *Adornos Philosophie in Grundbegriffen* (FfM: Suhrkamp, 1974), pp. 225–51, p. 228.
99 Adorno uses this phrase before the publication of Ulrich Sonnemann's *Negative Anthropologie* (FfM: Suhrkamp, 1969) in *MM*, p. 188; Jephcott, p. 167.
100 *DA*, p. 17; Cumming, p. xvii.
101 *MM*, p. 260; Jephcott, p. 229.
102 Cf., despite disclaimers, Erich Fromm, 'The Method and Function of an Analytic Social Psychology' [1932] in *The Crisis of Psychoanalysis* (London: Jonathan Cape, 1971), pp. 135–62.
103 *DA*, p. 176; Cumming, p. 153.
104 For a useful account of Adorno's 'dialectical anthropology', see Stefan Breuer, 'Adorno's Anthropology', tr. John Blazek, *Telos* 64 (1985–6), 15–31.

Chapter 3 The Culture Industry

1 'The more iceboxes, the less Huxley'. 'Diskussionsprotokolle', in Max Horkheimer, *Gesammelte Schriften*, vol. 12: *Nachgelassene Schriften 1931–49*, ed. Gunzelin Schmid Noerr (FfM: Fischer, 1985), p. 561.
2 'Culture Industry Reconsidered', in *The Culture Industry*, ed. J. M. Bernstein (London: Routledge, 1991), pp. 85–92, p. 85.
3 *DA*, p. 157; Cumming, pp. 135–6.
4 'On the fetish character in music and the regression of listening', *The Culture Industry*, pp. 26–52, p. 31.
5 Adorno to Benjamin, 18 March 1936, in *Aesthetics and Politics*, ed. F. Jameson (London: New Left Books, 1977), p. 123.
6 'On the fetish character in music', pp. 40–1; 'How to look at television', in *The Culture Industry*, pp. 136–53, p.138.
7 On pseudo-individuality cf. *DA*, pp 144–5, 177–9; Cumming, pp. 123, 154–55.
8 Cf. Daniel Miller, *Material Culture and Mass Consumption* (Oxford: Blackwell, 1987).
9 *DA*, p. 191; Cumming, p. 167.
10 'The schema of mass culture', tr. Nicholas Walker, in *The Culture Industry*, pp. 79–80.
11 *DA*, p. 179; Cumming, p. 156.
12 *DA*, pp. 158–9; Cumming, p. 137. Cf. 'Free time', in *The Culture Industry*, pp. 162–70, p. 168.

13 'The schema of mass culture', pp. 71–4.
14 Ibid., pp. 77–8.
15 'Commodity Music Analysed', in *Quasi una Fantasia*, tr. Rodney Livingstone (London: Verso, 1992), pp. 37–52, p. 52.
16 Georg Lukács, *History and Class Consciousness*, tr. Rodney Livingstone (London: Merlin Press, 1971), p. 89; cf. ch. 7.
17 'Novissimum Organum', *MM*, pp. 259ff; Jephcott, pp. 228ff.
18 Adorno's epigraph from Kürnberger. *MM*, p. 20; Jephcott, p. 19.
19 'Freizeit', in *GS* 10.2, pp. 645-55, p. 655; 'Free time', in *The Culture Industry*, pp. 162–70, p. 170.
20 Immanuel Kant, 'Was ist Aufklärung?' in *Was ist Aufklärung? Aufsätze zur Geschichte und Philosophie*, ed. Jürgen Zehbe (Göttingen: Vandenhoeck & Ruprecht, 1985), p. 55.
21 Theodor Adorno and Hellmut Becker, 'Education for Autonomy', tr. David J. Parent, *Telos* 55–6 (Summer 1983), 103–10.
22 Walter Benjamin, *Illuminationen* (FfM: Suhrkamp, 1977), p. 141; cf. 'The Work of Art in the Age of Mechanical Reproduction', in *Illuminations*, tr. Harry Zohn (London: Fontana, 1973), pp. 211–44; p. 215 (tr. altered).
23 *Illuminationen*, p. 143; *Illuminations*, p. 218.
24 *Illuminationen*, p. 154; *Illuminations*, p. 224 (tr. altered).
25 *Illuminationen*, p. 159; *Illuminations*, p. 227 (tr. altered).
26 *Illuminationen*, p. 167; *Illuminations*, pp. 233–4.
27 *Briefwechsel*, p. 172.
28 *Briefwechsel*, pp. 171–2.
29 *Briefwechsel*, pp. 172–3.
30 *Illuminationen*, p. 144; *Illuminations*, p. 218.
31 Albrecht Wellmer, 'Wahrheit, Schein, Versöhnung. Adornos ästhetische Rettung der Modernität', in *Zur Dialektik von Moderne und Postmoderne* (FfM: Suhrkamp, 1985), pp. 9–47, p. 40.
32 Ibid., p. 42.
33 Ibid.
34 Erich Fromm, 'The Method and Function of an Analytic Social Psychology', in *The Crisis of Psychoanalysis* (London: Jonathan Cape, 1971), pp. 135–62.
35 *The Crisis of Psychoanalysis*, p. 154.
36 Ibid., p. 155.
37 Erich Fromm, 'Psychoanalytic Characterology and its Relevance for Social Psychology', in *The Crisis of Psychoanalysis* (London: Jonathan Cape, 1971), pp. 163–89, pp. 182–9.
38 'Die revidierte Psychoanalyse', in *GS* 8, p. 37.
39 Ibid., p. 27.
40 'Die revidierte Psychoanalyse', p. 38. From such a perspective it can be seen how unsympathetic Adorno would be to charges that his concepts of love and domination are insufficiently grounded in intersubjectivity (cf. Jessica Benjamin, 'The end of internalization', *Telos* 32 (Summer 1977), 42–64). Adorno's theory of society is not grounded in intersubjectivity alone. He regards such theories as idealist.
41 Benjamin, 'The End of Internalization: Adorno's Social Psychology', *Telos* 32 (1977), 42–64, p. 60.

42 'Zum Verhältnis von Soziologie und Psychologie', in *GS* 8, pp. 42–85, p. 62; pp. 56–7, pp. 44, 51.
43 For an especially direct formulation of the relationship between the increasing concentration of capital and ego-weakness, cf. *DA*, pp. 228–30; Cumming, pp. 202–4.
44 *ND*, p. 130, pp. 340–43; Ashton, p. 124, pp. 347–9.
45 Cf. Adorno's letter to Horkheimer (21 March 1936) in which he complains that Fromm 'takes the easy way out with the concept of authority'. 'I would strongly advise him to read Lenin.' Quoted in Rolf Wiggershaus, *The Frankfurt School*, tr. Michael Robertson (Cambridge: Polity Press, 1993), p. 266.
46 Lothar Düver, *Theodor W. Adorno. Der Wissenschaftsbegriff der kritischen Theorie in seinem Werk* (Bonn: Bouvier, 1978), p. 138ff. has a serviceable account of this aspect of Adorno's thought.
47 Cf. *MM*, p. 34; Jephcott, p. 32; *DA*, p. 216; Cumming, p. 191.
48 'Totalität und Homosexualität gehören zusammen.' *MM*, p. 51; Jephcott, p. 46. Jephcott translates this remark, not without justification from the context, as 'Totalitarianism and homosexuality belong together.'
49 Cf. *DA*, p. 217; Cumming, pp. 192–3.
50 Adorno, Introduction (with Else Frenkel-Brunswick, Darren J. Levinson and R. Nevitt Sanford) to *Studies in the Authoritarian Personality*. In *GS* 9.1: *Soziologische Schriften II* (FfM: Suhrkamp, 1975), pp. 143–509, p. 149.
51 Ibid., p. 185.
52 Ibid., p. 186.
53 Ibid., p. 182.
54 'Diskussionsprotokolle', pp. 474, 485, 528.
55 *Vorlesung zur Einleitung in die Soziologie*, p. 56.
56 *DA*, p. 39; Cumming, p. 23.
57 Alfons Söllner, *Geschichte und Herrschaft. Studien zur materialistischen Sozialwissenschaft 1929–1942* (FfM: Suhrkamp, 1979); Helmut Dubiel, *Theory and Politics: Studies in the Development of Critical Theory*, tr. Benjamin Gregg (Cambridge, Mass.: MIT Press, 1985).

Chapter 4 Art, Truth and Ideology

1 *AT*, p. 544; Hullot-Kentor, p. 366.
2 *AT*, p. 248; Hullot-Kentor, p. 166.
3 Cf. Howard Caygill, *Art of Judgement* (Oxford: Blackwell, 1989).
4 Immanuel Kant, *Critique of Judgement*, tr. Werner S. Pluhar (Indianapolis: Hackett, 1987), §8, p. 59.
5 Ibid., §6, p. 54.
6 Ibid., §5, p. 52.
7 Ibid., §4, pp. 48–51.
8 Ibid., §45, p. 174.
9 Ibid., §39, p. 159.
10 Ibid., §22, pp. 87–8.
11 Ibid., §34, p. 149.
12 For an account of the significance of *Vorstellung* in the *Critique of Judgement*, cf. ibid., p. 44, n. 4.

13 Ibid., §51, p. 190.
14 Ibid., §44, p. 172.
15 Ibid., §46, p. 175.
16 Ibid.
17 Ibid., §17, p. 84.
18 *AT*, p. 23; Hullot-Kentor, p. 10. For an account of Adorno's relationship to transcendental thought as a whole, cf. ch. 6.
19 *AT*, pp. 336–7; Hullot-Kentor, p. 227. Cf. 'Ist die Kunst heiter?', in *NzL*, pp. 599–606, p. 600 (Nicholsen ii. 248); 'Die Kunst und die Künste', in *GS* 10.1: *Kulturkritik und Gesellschaft I*, pp. 432–53, p. 435.
20 *AT*, p. 245; Hullot-Kentor, pp. 164, 10. Cf. also *AT*, p. 22.
21 *AT*, p. 24; Hullot-Kentor, p. 11.
22 *AT*, p. 25; Hullot-Kentor, p. 11.
23 *AT*, p. 24; Hullot-Kentor, p. 11.
24 *AT*, p. 25; Hullot-Kentor, p. 11. Kant, *Critique of Judgement*, tr. Pluhar, §15, p. 75.
25 *AT*, p. 148; Hullot-Kentor, p. 97.
26 *AT*, p. 248; Hullot-Kentor, p. 166.
27 *AT*, p. 23; Hullot-Kentor, p. 10.
28 Ibid.
29 Ibid.
30 G. W. F. Hegel, *Introductory Lectures on Aesthetics*, tr. Bernard Bosanquet (Harmondsworth: Penguin, 1993), p. 66.
31 G. W. F. Hegel, *Hegel's Aesthetics: Lectures on Fine Art*, tr. T. M. Knox (2 vols, Oxford: Clarendon Press, 1975), pp. 427–611. For a discussion of this distinction, cf. p. 119.
32 Cf. 'Voraussetzungen', in *NzL*, pp. 431–46, p. 432; 'Presuppositions', Nicholsen, pp. 95–108, p. 96.
33 *AT*, p. 166; Hullot-Kentor, p. 109.
34 Hegel, *Aesthetics*, tr. Knox, pp. 143–52: 'Deficiency of Natural Beauty'.
35 *AT*, pp. 102–3; Hullot-Kentor, p. 65.
36 *AT*, p. 105; Hullot-Kentor, p. 66.
37 *AT*, p. 115; Hullot-Kentor, p. 74.
38 *AT*, p. 107; Hullot-Kentor, p. 68.
39 *AT*, p. 98; Hullot-Kentor, p. 62.
40 *AT*, p. 26; Hullot-Kentor, p. 12.
41 *AT*, p. 198; Hullot-Kentor, p. 131.
42 *AT*, pp. 166–7; Hullot-Kentor, p. 109.
43 Kant, *Critique of Judgement*, tr. Pluhar, §311, p. 179.
44 *AT*, p. 160; Hullot-Kentor, p. 104.
45 *AT*, p. 86; Hullot-Kentor, pp. 53–4.
46 *AT*, p. 87; Hullot-Kentor, p. 55.
47 G. W. F. Hegel, *Hegel's Phenomenology of Spirit*, tr. A. V. Miller (Oxford: Oxford University Press, 1977), p. 39.
48 *AT*, pp. 171, 249; Hullot-Kentor, pp. 112, 166.
49 *Quasi una Fantasia*, tr. Rodney Livingstone (London: Verso, 1992), p. 146.
50 *AT*, p. 189; Hullot-Kentor, p. 188.
51 *AT*, p. 108; Hullot-Kentor, p. 69.
52 'Die Kunst und die Künste', p. 437; Wassily Kandinsky, *Concerning the Spiritual in Art*, tr. M. T. H. Sadler (New York: Dover, 1977).

53 Deryck Cooke, *The Language of Music* (Oxford: Oxford University Press, 1989).
54 *AT*, p. 37; Hullot-Kentor, p. 20.
55 *AT*, p. 193; Hullot-Kentor, p. 127.
56 *AT*, p. 194; Hullot-Kentor, p. 128.
57 *AT*, p. 198; Hullot-Kentor, p. 131.
58 *AT*, p. 199; Hullot-Kentor, p. 131.
59 *AT*, p. 194; Hullot-Kentor, p. 128.
60 *AT*, p. 200; Hullot-Kentor, p. 133.
61 *AT*, p. 37; Hullot-Kentor, p. 20. Cf. *Beethoven*, ed. Rolf Tiedemann (FfM: Suhrkamp, 1993), p. 32: 'music is the logic of synthesis without a judgement.'
62 *PnM*, p. 40.
63 *PnM*, pp. 40–1.
64 *AT*, p. 273; Hullot-Kentor, p. 183.
65 'Vienna' in *Quasi una Fantasia*, tr. Livingstone, pp. 201–24, p. 216. For further discussion of this problem.
66 *AT*, p. 266; Hullot-Kentor, p. 178.
67 *AT*, p. 222; Hullot-Kentor, p. 148.
68 *AT*, p. 358; Hullot-Kentor, p. 241.
69 *AT*, p. 12; Hullot-Kentor, p. 3.
70 *AT*, pp. 11, 12; Hullot-Kentor, p. 3.
71 *AT*, p. 82; Hullot-Kentor, pp. 50–1.
72 *AT*, p. 9; Hullot-Kentor, p. 1.
73 *AT*, p. 280; Hullot-Kentor, p. 188.
74 Albrecht Wellmer, 'Truth, Semblance, Reconciliation. Adorno's Aesthetic Redemption of Modernity', *Telos* 62 (1984–5), 89–115, p. 110.
75 Ibid., p. 103.
76 Ibid., pp. 102–3.
77 Ibid., p. 109.
78 Ibid., p. 106.
79 Ibid.
80 Ibid., p. 109.
81 Ibid.
82 Ibid., p. 110.
83 Rüdiger Bubner, 'Über einige Bedingungen gegenwärtiger Ästhetik', *Neue Hefte für Philosophie* 5 (1973), 38–73; cf. Wellmer, 'Truth, Semblance, Reconciliation', p. 109.
84 *ND*, p. 397; Ashton, pp. 405-6.
85 *AT*, p. 199; Hullot-Kentor, p. 132.
86 Ibid.
87 *PhT*, ii, p. 162 (8 January 1963); G. W. F. Hegel, *Science of Logic*, tr. A. V. Miller (London: George Allen & Unwin, 1969), p. 469.
88 *AT*, p. 196; Hullot-Kentor, p. 130.
89 *AT*, p. 164; Hullot-Kentor, p. 107.
90 *AT*, pp. 334–8; Hullot-Kentor, pp. 225–8.
91 *AT*, p. 338; Hullot-Kentor, p. 228.
92 *AT*, p. 337; Hullot-Kentor, p. 227.
93 Ibid.

94 Kant, *Groundwork of the Metaphysic of Morals*, tr. H. J. Paton (New York: Harper & Row, 1964), p. 102.
95 *AT*, p. 335; Hullot-Kentor, p. 226.
96 *AT*, p. 351; Hullot-Kentor, p. 236.
97 'Zur gesellschaftlichen Lage der Musik' [1932], in *Musikalische Schriften V*, *GS* 18, p. 757.
98 *AT*, p. 351; Hullot-Kentor, p. 236.
99 Ibid.
100 Ibid.
101 Ibid.
102 *AT*, p. 358; Hullot-Kentor, p. 241.
103 *AT*, p. 351; Hullot-Kentor, p. 236.
104 *AT*, p. 347; Hullot-Kentor, p. 234.
105 G. W. F. Hegel, *Aesthetics*, tr. Knox, vol. 1, p. 504.
106 Ibid., pp. 517–29.
107 Ibid., p. 576.
108 Cf. Gillian Rose, *Hegel contra Sociology* (London: Athlone, 1981), pp. 121–48.
109 'Die Kunst und die Künste', p. 436.
110 *Beethoven*, p. 72.
111 'Zemlinsky', in *Quasi una Fantasia*, tr. Livingstone, pp. 111–29, p. 113.
112 *AT*, p. 19; Hullot-Kentor, p. 8.
113 'Engagement', in *NzL*, pp. 409-30, p. 417; Nicholsen, ii. 83.
114 *AT*, pp. 54–5, 123; Hullot-Kentor, pp. 32, 79.
115 *AT*, p. 358; Hullot-Kentor, p. 241.
116 Ibid.
117 *AT*, pp. 358–9; Hullot-Kentor, p. 241.
118 *AT*, p. 342; Hullot-Kentor, p. 230.
119 *AT*, p. 53; Hullot-Kentor, p. 31.
120 *AT*, p. 342; Hullot-Kentor, p. 230.
121 *AT*, pp. 137–8; Hullot-Kentor, p. 89.

Chapter 5 Truth-Content in Music and Literature

1 'Die Kunst und die Künste', in *GS* 10.1: *Kulturkritik und Gesellschaft I: Prismen, Ohne Leitbild*, pp. 432–53, p. 432.
2 *AT*, pp. 141–4; Hullot-Kentor, pp. 91–3.
3 *Versuch über Wagner*, in *GS* 13, pp. 7–148, pp. 92–108; *In Search of Wagner*, tr. Rodney Livingstone (London: New Left Books, 1981), pp. 97–113.
4 'Die Kunst und die Künste', p. 437.
5 *AT*, p. 262; Hullot-Kentor, p. 175.
6 *Versuch über Wagner*, p. 26; Livingstone, p. 28.
7 'Die Kunst und die Künste', p. 433.
8 Cf., in particular, 'Zur gesellschaftlichen Lage der Musik' [1932], in *Musikalische Schriften V, GS* 18, pp. 729–77; 'On the Social Situation of Music (1932)', *Telos* 35 (1978), 128–64.
9 For more comprehensive accounts, see Lucia Sziborsky, *Adornos Musikphilosophie* (Munich: Wilhelm Fink, 1979), and Max Paddison, *Adorno's Aesthetics of Music* (Cambridge: Cambridge University Press, 1993).

10 Cf. 'Der Essay als Form', in *NzL*, pp. 9–33, p. 17; Nicholsen, i. 10.
11 *Beethoven*, ed. Rolf Tiedemann (FfM: Suhrkamp, 1993), pp. 36, 45, 99–100.
12 Cf. *Mahler. Eine musikalische Physiognomik*, in *GS* 13, pp. 149–319, p. 192; Jephcott, p. 43.
13 Rüdiger Bubner, 'Kann Theorie ästhetisch werden?', in Burkhardt Lindner and W. Martin Lüdke, eds, *Materialen zur ästhetischen Theorie Theodor W. Adornos* (FfM: Suhrkamp, 1985), pp. 108–37.
14 'Music and Language: A Fragment', in *Quasi una Fantasia*, tr. Rodney Livingstone (London: Verso, 1992), pp. 1–6, p. 1.
15 Ibid.
16 Ibid., p. 2.
17 *ND*, p. 44; Ashton, pp. 33–4.
18 *Beethoven*, p. 39.
19 *PhT*, I, pp. 21–8 (10 May 1962).
20 *Beethoven*, p. 31.
21 *DS*, p. 124; Nicholsen, p. 136.
22 *Beethoven*, p. 61.
23 Ibid., p. 87.
24 Ibid., p. 50.
25 Ibid., pp. 99–100.
26 Ibid., p. 40.
27 Ibid.
28 Ibid., p. 26. Cf. 'Beethovens Spätstil', in *Moments musicaux: neu aufgedruckte Aufsätze*, *GS* 17, pp. 13–17.
29 Cf. 'Der getreue Korrepetitor', in *GS* 15, pp. 251–368; *Alban Berg*, tr. Juliane Brand and Christopher Hailey (Cambridge: Cambridge University Press, 1991), pp. 35–135.
30 *AT*, p. 269; Hullot-Kentor, p. 180.
31 *AT*, p. 270; Hullot-Kentor, p. 180.
32 'Der Essay als Form', in *NzL*, p. 24; Nicholsen i, p. 16.
33 'Bach gegen seine Liebhaber verteidigt', in *GS* 10.1: *Kulturkritik und Gesellschaft I*, pp. 138–51, p. 138; Weber, p. 135.
34 'Bach', p. 139; Weber, p. 136.
35 'Bach', pp. 144–7; Weber, pp. 142–5.
36 'Bach', p. 142; Weber, p. 140.
37 'Bach', p. 143; Weber, p. 139.
38 'Bach', p. 144; Weber, p. 140.
39 Adorno never completed his planned 'Theory of Musical Reproduction', which was to have given his theory of performance; cf. however, 'Zur gesellschaftlichen Lage der Musik', in *GS* 18: *Musikalische Schriften V* (1932), pp. 729–77: 'II. Reproduktion, Konsum' (pp. 753–77).
40 Horkheimer to Adorno, 28 August 1941, quoted in Rolf Wiggershaus, *The Frankfurt School*, tr. Michael Robertson (Cambridge: Polity Press, 1993), p. 298; *PnM*, p. 11.
41 H. H. Stuckenschmidt, 'Das Zwölftonsystem', *Der neue Rundschau* 45 (1934), 301–11.
42 Theodor Adorno and Ernst Krenek, *Briefwechsel* (FfM: Suhrkamp, 1974), pp. 52–6.

43 'Schönbergs Bläserquintett', in *GS* 17: *Musikalische Schriften IV*, pp. 140–4, p. 140.
44 *PnM*, p. 70.
45 *PnM*, pp. 65–8.
46 *PnM*, p. 63.
47 Ibid.
48 Ibid.
49 Cf., especially, 'Vers une musique informelle', in *Quasi una Fantasia*, tr. Livingstone, pp. 269–322.
50 'Bach', p. 144; Weber, p. 140.
51 *PnM*, pp. 70–1.
52 *PnM*, pp. 171–4.
53 *PnM*, pp. 150–1.
54 *PnM*, pp. 187–9.
55 Cf. especially, 'Stravinsky: A Dialectical Portrait', in *Quasi una Fantasia*, tr. Livingstone, pp. 145–75.
56 'Zur gesellschaftlichen Lage der Musik', p. 743.
57 *PnM*, p. 191.
58 *PnM*, pp. 154–7.
59 For a partially parodic example of such grid-criticism, see Bernard Sharratt, *Reading Relations: Structures of Literary Production. A Dialectical Text/Book* (Brighton: Harvester, 1982), pp. 57–92.
60 'Der Essay als Form', in *NzL*, pp. 9–33, p. 17; Nicholsen, i, p. 10.
61 'Der Essay als Form', p. 17; Nicholsen, i, p. 9.
62 'Der Essay als Form', p. 22; Nicholsen, i, p. 14.
63 'Der Essay als Form', p. 24; Nicholsen, i, p. 16.
64 'Zu einem Porträt Thomas Manns', in *NzL*, pp. 335–44, p. 336; 'Toward a Portrait of Thomas Mann'; Nicholsen, ii, p. 13.
65 'Bach', p. 149; Weber, p. 144.
66 'Henkel, Krug und frühe Erfahrung', in *NzL*, 556–66, p. 556; 'The Handle, the Pot and Early Experience', Nicholsen, ii, p. 211.
67 'Parataxis. Zur späten Lyrik Hölderlins', in *NzL*, pp. 447–91; Nicholsen, ii, pp. 109–49.
68 'Parataxis', p. 451; Nicholsen, ii, p. 112.
69 'Parataxis', p. 452; Nicholsen, ii, p. 113.
70 'Parataxis', p. 459; Nicholsen, ii, p. 119.
71 'Parataxis', p. 462; Nicholsen, ii, p. 122.
72 'Parataxis', p. 455; Nicholsen, ii, p. 116.
73 'Parataxis', p. 468; Nicholsen, ii, p. 128.
74 'Parataxis', p. 464; Nicholsen, ii, p. 124.
75 'Parataxis', p. 466; Nicholsen, ii, p. 126.
76 Ibid.
77 'Parataxis', p. 465; Nicholsen, ii, p. 128.
78 'Parataxis', p. 466; Nicholsen, ii, p. 126.
79 'Parataxis', pp. 468–9; Nicholsen, ii, p. 128.
80 'Parataxis', p. 476; Nicholsen, ii, p. 135.
81 'Parataxis', pp. 476–7; Nicholsen, ii, p. 136.
82 'Parataxis', p. 475; Nicholsen, ii, p. 135.
83 'George', in *NzL*, pp. 521–35, p. 529; Nicholsen, ii, pp. 178–92, p. 185.

84 'Die beschworene Sprache', in *NzL*, pp. 536–55, p. 549; Nicholsen, ii, pp. 193–210, p. 205.
85 *AT*, p. 274; Hullot-Kentor, p. 184.
86 *AT*, p. 187; Hullot-Kentor, p. 123.
87 Ibid.
88 *AT*, pp. 186–8; Hullot-Kentor, pp. 122–3.
89 *AT*, p. 97; Hullot-Kentor, p. 61.
90 Walter Benjamin, 'Theses on the Philosophy of History', in *Illuminations*, ed. Hannah Arendt, tr. Harry Zohn (London: Fontana, 1973), pp. 245–55, p. 248.
91 'Erpreßte Versöhnung', in *NzL*, pp. 251–80, p. 271; Nicholsen, ii, pp. 216–40, p. 233.
92 Georg Lukács, *The Meaning of Contemporary Realism*, tr. J. and N. Mander (London: Merlin, 1962), p. 32.
93 'Erpreßte Versöhnung', pp. 272–3; Nicholsen, i, p. 234.
94 *AT*, p. 272; Hullot-Kentor, p. 182.
95 *AT*, p. 271; Hullot-Kentor, p. 182.
96 Cf. S. Jarvis, 'Soteriology and reciprocity', *Parataxis: Modernism and Modern Writing* 5 (1993), 30–9.

Chapter 6 Negative Dialectic as Metacritique

1 Wilfrid Sellars, 'Empiricism and the Philosophy of Mind', in *Minnesota Studies in the Philosophy of Science*, vol. 1: *The Foundations of Science and the Concepts of Psychology and Psychoanalysis*, ed. Herbert Feigl and Michael Scriven (Minneapolis: University of Minnesota Press, 1956), pp. 253–329, p. 253.
2 Cf. John McDowell, *Mind and World* (Cambridge, Mass.: Harvard University Press, 1994).
3 G. W. F. Hegel, *Phenomenology of Spirit*, tr. A. V. Miller (Oxford: Oxford University Press, 1977), pp. 351–2.
4 The 'crisis' was referred to as such by German thinkers from about 1920, and by Adorno himself in discussions with Horkheimer's Frankfurt circle: 'the crisis in science proceeds essentially from the incapacity of the individual disciplines to give an epitome of the whole of actuality, providing instead only partial cognitions which are without relations to the whole of our existence' ('Protokolle und Diskussionen', in Max Horkheimer, *Gesammelte Schriften*, 12: *Nachgelassene Schriften 1931–49*, ed. Alfred Schmidt and Gunzelin Schmid Noerr (FfM: Fischer, 1985), p. 358. The crisis for German intellectuals was an economic as well as an intellectual one: Fritz. K. Ringer, *The Decline of the German Mandarins: The German Academic Community, 1890–1933* (Cambridge, Mass.: Harvard University Press, 1969), pp. 295, 61–80, 254–434.
5 *ND*, p. 64; Ashton, p. 54.
6 Compare another version of this question in 'Thorstein Veblens Angriff auf die Kultur', in *Prismen* (FfM: Suhrkamp, 1955), p. 110: 'How is something new possible as such?' and 'Einleitung zu Emile Durkheim, "Soziologie und Philosophie" ', in *GS 8: Soziologische Schriften I* (FfM: Suhrkamp, 1972), pp. 245–79, p. 274.

7 Cf. Josef Früchtl, 'Zeit und Erfahrung. Adornos Revision der Revision Heideggers', in *Martin Heidegger: Innen- und Außenansichten*, ed. Forum für Philosophie Bad Homburg (FfM: Suhrkamp, 1989), pp. 291–312, pp. 294–5.

8 'Über Tradition', in *GS* 10.1: *Kulturkritik und Gesellschaft I* (FfM: Suhrkamp, 1977), pp. 310–20, pp. 314–15.

9 *ND*, p. 10; Ashton, p. xx.

10 *ND*, p. 64; Ashton, p. 55.

11 *ND*, p. 9; Ashton, p. xix.

12 'Spätkapitalismus oder Industriegesellschaft?' Einleitungsvortrag zum 16. Deutschen Soziologentag, in *GS* 8, pp. 354–70, pp. 364–5.

13 *ND*, p. 66; Ashton, p. 56.

14 *ND*, pp. 197–8; Ashton, pp. 197–8.

15 *ND*, p. 198; Ashton, p. 198. For one of the earliest arguments for a distinction between a sociology of knowledge and critical theory's interest in 'truth-content', see H. Marcuse, 'Philosophy and Critical Theory' (1937) in *Negations: Essays in Critical Theory*, tr. Jeremy J. Shapiro (Boston: Beacon Press, 1968), pp. 134–57, pp. 147–8.

16 *ND*, p. 139; Ashton, p. 135.

17 *ND*, p. 381; Ashton, p. 388.

18 *ME*, pp. 49–51; Domingo, pp. 42–4. *DA*, pp. 279–81; Cumming, pp. 242–4. *ND*, p. 263; Ashton, p. 266. Cf. Max Horkheimer, 'The Present Situation of Philosophy', in *Between Philosophy and Social Science: Selected Early Writings*, tr. G. Frederick Hunter, Matthew S. Kramer and John Torpey (Cambridge, Mass.: MIT Press, 1993), pp. 1–14, pp. 8–10.

19 Max Weber, *The Protestant Ethic and the Spirit of Capitalism*, tr. Talcott Parsons (London: Harper Collins, 1991), p. 29.

20 *ND*, p. 10; Ashton, p. xx.

21 *ND*, p. 205; Ashton, p. 205.

22 The German title of the work translated as *Against Epistemology* is *Zur Metakritik der Erkenntnistheorie* (*Towards a Metacritique of Epistemology*). Adorno, however, had initially wanted the work to be called *The Phenomenological Antinomies*; Adorno was planning in 1935 to subtitle the work 'Prolegomena to a Dialectical Logic': *Briefwechsel*, p. 47. The final title was a compromise with the publisher. *GS* 5, 386. For a discussion of the title of this book see *VEET*, p. 18.

23 J. G. Hamann, 'Metakritik', in *Sämtliche Werke*, ed. J. Nadler (Vienna: Herder, 1949-57), vol. 3. The work was written in 1784, but not published until 1800.

24 Kemp Smith, p. 283; *KrV* A 271/B 327.

25 Ibid.

26 Friedrich Nietzsche, *Beyond Good and Evil: Prelude to a Philosophy of the Future*, tr. R. J. Hollingdale (Harmondsworth: Penguin, 1990), p. 51: 'It is we alone who have fabricated causes . . .'

27 Kemp Smith, p. 27; *KrV* B xxvi.

28 *ND*, p. 383; Ashton, p. 391. *VEET*, p. 50. 'Der Essay als Form', in *NzL*, pp. 9–13, p. 17; Nicholsen i, p. 10.

29 *ND*, p. 379; Ashton, p. 386. *PhT*, ii, p. 98 (4 December 1962).

30 Cf. Anke Thyen, *Negative Dialektik und Erfahrung. Zur Rationalität des Nichtidentischen bei Adorno* (FfM: Suhrkamp, 1989).

31 *ND*, p. 189, pp. 379–80. Ashton, pp. 188, 387.
32 *PhT*, ii, p. 48 (20 November 1962).
33 Ibid.
34 *ND*, p. 382; Ashton, p. 389.
35 Cf. Ludwig Pongratz, 'Zur Aporetik des Erfahrungsbegriffs bei Theodor W. Adorno', *Philosophisches Jahrbuch 93* (1986), 135–42, p. 142.
36 *VEET*, pp. 185–320. An edition of this text overseen by the Theodor W. Adorno Archiv is to appear shortly as section 4, volume 1 of the *Nachgelassene Schriften* (*Posthumous Works*), published by Suhrkamp. Adorno's 1959 lectures on the *Critique of Pure Reason* will appear as section 4, volume 4 of the same series.
37 For whom see J. Alberto Coffa, *The Semantic Tradition from Kant to Carnap: To the Vienna Station*, ed. Linda Wessels (Cambridge: Cambridge University Press, 1991).
38 *VEET*, p. 187. Cf. Kemp Smith, p. 128; *KrV* B 127–8.
39 *ND*, p. 384; Ashton, p. 392.
40 Kemp Smith, p. 128; *KrV* B 128.
41 Kemp Smith, p. 28; *KrV* B xxviii.
42 Kemp Smith, p. 27n; *KrV* B xxvi n.
43 *ND*, p. 139; Ashton, p. 135.
44 *ME*, p. 84; Domingo, p. 78.
45 Kemp Smith, pp. 120–2; *KrV* A 84–7/B 116–19.
46 *ND*, p. 78; Ashton, p. 71. Cf. G. W. F. Hegel, *Science of Logic*, tr. A. V. Miller (London: George Allen & Unwin, 1969), pp. 412–16.
47 *VEET*, p. 288.
48 'Pure forms of intuition': Kemp Smith, p. 67; *KrV* B 36/A 22. 'Pure intuitions': Kemp Smith, p. 69; *KrV* B 39/A 24.
49 *ME*, p. 151; Domingo, p. 146.
50 *ME*, p. 151; Domingo, pp. 146–7.
51 *ME*, p. 151; Domingo, p. 146.
52 Cf. Carl Braun, *Kritische Theorie versus Kritizismus* (Kantstudien: Ergänzungshefte, 115) (Berlin: de Gruyter, 1983), passim.
53 *VEET*, p. 215. Cf. *VEET*, p. 182.
54 Kemp Smith, p. 161; *KrV* B 145–6.
55 *VEET*, p. 225.
56 Cf., e.g., Dieter Henrich, *Fluchtlinien: Philosophische Essays* (FfM: Suhrkamp, 1982), p. 144; Henrich, 'Gedanken zur Dankbarkeit', in R. Löw, ed., *Oikeiosis. Festschrift für R. Spaemann* (Weinheim: Acta Humaniora, 1987), pp. 69–86.
57 For a useful attempt at a synoptic account of Henrich's thought, cf. Richard Velkley, Introduction to Henrich, *The Unity of Reason: Philosophical Essays on Kant* (Cambridge, Mass.: Harvard University Press, 1993).
58 *ND*, p. 152; Ashton, p. 149.
59 G. W. F. Hegel, *Logic*, tr. William Wallace (Oxford: Oxford University Press, 1975), p. 237.
60 *ND*, p. 17; Ashton, p. 5.
61 Hegel, *Phenomenology of Spirit*, tr. A. V. Miller (Oxford: Oxford University Press, 1977), pp. 58–79.
62 Ibid.
63 *ND*, p. 152; Ashton, p. 149.

64 This would be a principal difference between Adorno's understanding of identity-thinking and any reformulation of it as 'a critique of a particular *way of using* language' or as an attempt to 'bid farewell to an "hypostasizing", "identificatory" use of language' as praised by Adolf Polti in Albrecht Wellmer's work: Polti, 'Ontologie als "Inbegriff der Negativität". Zu Adornos Interpretation der Philosophie Heideggers', in *Martin Heidegger: Innen- und Außenansichten*, ed. Forum für Philosophie Bad Homburg (FfM: Suhrkamp, 1989), pp. 273–90, p. 286.

65 *ND*, pp. 149–50; Ashton, pp. 146–7; 'Spätkapitalismus oder Industriegesellschaft?', in *GS* 8, pp. 361–2.

66 *ND*, pp. 149–50; Ashton, pp. 146–7. 'Zum Klassizismus von Goethes Iphigenie', in *NzL*, pp. 495–514, p. 508; Nicholsen ii, pp. 153–70, p. 165.

67 *DA*, pp. 19–60; Cumming, pp. 3–42.

68 *ND*, p. 148; Ashton, p. 144. 'Einleitung zum "Positivismusstreit in der deutschen Soziologie" ', in *GS* 8, pp. 280–353, p. 288; Introduction to *The Positivist Dispute in German Sociology*, tr. David Frisby and Glyn Adey (London: Heinemann, 1976), p. 9; cf. Helga Gripp, *Theodor W. Adorno. Erkenntnisdimensionen negativer Dialektik* (Paderborn: Schöningh, 1986), pp. 66–7.

69 Hegel never used this schema to refer to his own work, and criticized it as a 'lifeless schema'; its popularity is the work of a later summarizer, H. M. Chalybaeus. See G. E. Müller, 'The Hegel Legend of "Thesis–Antithesis–Synthesis" ', *Journal of the History of Ideas* 19 (1958), pp. 411–14.

70 G. W. F. Hegel, *Werke* (20 vols, FfM: Suhrkamp, 1969), vol. 5: *Wissenschaft der Logik I*, p. 51. Cf. Hegel, *Science of Logic*, p. 55.

71 Karl Marx, *Capital*, vol. 1, tr. Ben Fowkes (Harmondsworth: Penguin, 1976), p. 103.

72 *ND*, p. 183; Ashton, p. 182; Karl Marx, 'A Contribution to the Critique of Hegel's Philosophy of Right', in *Early Writings*, tr. Rodney Livingstone and Gregor Benton (Harmondsworth: Penguin, 1975), p. 247.

73 For a detailed examination of this relationship, see S. Jarvis, 'The "Unhappy Consciousness" and Conscious Unhappiness: On Adorno's Critique of Hegel and the Idea of an Hegelian Critique of Adorno', in G. K. Browning, ed., *Hegel's Phenomenology of Spirit: A Reappraisal* (Amsterdam: Kluwer Academic Publishers, 1997), pp. 57–72.

74 *DS*, p. 8; Nicholsen, p. xxxvi.

75 *DS*, p. 10; Nicholsen, pp. 2–3.

76 As Gillian Rose notes: *The Melancholy Science: An Introduction to the Thought of Theodor W. Adorno* (London: Macmillan, 1978), p. 58.

77 *DS*, pp. 12–13; Nicholsen, p. 5.

78 G. W. F. Hegel, *Elements of the Philosophy of Right*, ed. Allen Wood, tr. Barry Nisbet (Cambridge: Cambridge University Press, 1991), p. 20.

79 Hegel, *Logic*, tr. Wallace, pp. 9–10.

80 See especially *Science of Logic*, tr. Miller, pp. 131–6.

81 Ibid., pp. 440–1.

82 *DS*, pp. 33–4; Nicholsen, pp. 29–30. Hegel, *Elements of the Philosophy of Right*, tr. Nisbet, p. 267.

83 See Karl Löwith, *From Hegel to Nietzsche*, tr. D. E. Green (London: Routledge, 1964).

84 *ND*, p. 379; Ashton, p. 386.

85 Hegel, *Science of Logic*, tr. Miller, p. 439.
86 Ibid., pp. 440–1.
87 *ND*, p. 149; Ashton, p. 146.
88 *ND*, p. 151; Ashton, p. 148.
89 Cf. Michael Rosen, *Hegel's Dialectic and its Criticism* (Cambridge: Cambridge University Press, 1982), pp. 153–78: 'A Negative Dialectic?'
90 Vittorio Hösle, *Hegels System* (2 vols, Hamburg: Felix Meiner, 1988), vol. 1, p. 157.
91 Hegel, *Phenomenology*, tr. Miller, p. 11. *MM*, p. 55; Jephcott, p. 50.
92 *DS*, p. 71; Nicholsen, p. 74; *DS*, p. 60; Nicholsen, p. 62.
93 *DS*, pp. 31–5; Nicholsen, pp. 27–32.
94 *Science of Logic*, tr. Miller, pp. 54–6.
95 Ibid., p. 414.
96 *ND*, pp. 160–3; Ashton, p. 158–61.
97 *ND*, p. 163; Ashton, pp. 160–1.
98 *ND*, p. 397; Ashton, p. 406. Cf. Josef Früchtl, 'Zeit und Erfahrung. Adornos Revision der Revision Heideggers', in *Martin Heidegger: Innen- und Außenansichten*, ed. Forum für Philosophie Bad Homburg (FfM: Suhrkamp, 1989), pp. 291–312, pp. 294–5.

Chapter 7 Constellations: Thinking the Non-identical

1 Walter Benjamin, *Ursprung des deutschen Trauerspiels* (FfM: Suhrkamp, 1963), p. 16; *The Origin of German Tragic Drama*, tr. John Osborne (London: New Left Books, 1977), p. 34 (tr. altered).
2 *ND*, p. 62; Ashton, p. 53.
3 *ND*, p. 166; Ashton, p. 164.
4 *ND*, p. 167: 'In contrast to current scholarly practice . . . Weber was as clearly aware of the difficulty of defining historical concepts as previously only philosophers – Kant, Hegel, Nietzsche – had been.' Ashton, p. 165. Max Weber, *Gesammelte Aufsätze zur Religionssoziologie* (3 vols, Tübingen: J. C. B. Mohr (Paul Siebeck), 1934), vol. 1, pp. 1–206, p. 30; *The Protestant Ethic and the Spirit of Capitalism*, tr. Talcott Parsons (London: HarperCollins, 1991), p. 47 (tr. altered). *ND*, 167; Ashton, p. 165.
5 *ND*, p. 164; Ashton, p. 162.
6 Compare *ND*, p. 66 (Ashton, p. 56) where Adorno characterizes dialectic itself as 'language as the organon of thought'.
7 *DA*, p. 34; Cumming, pp. 17–18. Cf. 'Der Essay als Form', in *NzL*, pp. 9–33, p. 13; Nicholsen, i, pp. 3–23, p. 6: 'A consciousness for which intuition and concept, image and sign would be one and the same – if such a consciousness ever existed – cannot be magically restored; and its restitution would constitute a regression to chaos. Such a consciousness is conceivable only as the completion of the process of mediation, as utopia, conceived by idealist philosophy ever since Kant under the name of intellectual intuition, something that broke down whenever actual knowledge appealed to it.'
8 *ND*, pp. 266–7, p. 66; Ashton, p. 270, p. 56. Cf. Hauke Brunkhorst (1990), *Theodor W. Adorno. Dialektik der Moderne* (Munich: Piper, 1990), p. 240.

9 Thomas Hobbes, *Leviathan*, ed. Richard Tuck (Cambridge: Cambridge University Press, 1991), p. 28.
10 *ND*, p. 377; Ashton, p. 384.
11 As Ulrich Müller notes, *Erkenntniskritik und negative Metaphysik bei Adorno. Eine Philosophie der dritten Reflektiertheit* (FfM: Athenäum, 1988), p. 10. Contrast Albrecht Wellmer, *Zur Dialektik von Moderne und Postmoderne. Vernunftkritik nach Adorno* (FfM: Suhrkamp, 1985), pp. 48–114; 'On the Dialectic of Modernism and Post-modernism', *Praxis International* 4 (January, 1985), pp. 337–62; Jürgen Habermas, *Theorie des Kommunikativen Handelns* (2 vols, FfM: Suhrkamp, 1981), 1, p. 514. *AT*, pp. 86–90; *DA*, pp. 19–60; Cumming, pp. 3–42.
12 *ME*, p. 148n.; Domingo, p. 143n.
13 *ND*, p. 267; Ashton, p. 270.
14 *ME*, p. 148n; Domingo, p. 143n.
15 Kemp Smith, pp. 180–7; *KrV* A 137–47/B 176–87.
16 I translate 'ein Drittes' as 'a third element' rather than as 'a third thing' (Kemp Smith, p. 181) because its epistemological and ontological status is precisely what is in question in the following discussion.
17 Kemp Smith, p. 184; *KrV* A 143/B 183.
18 Kemp Smith, p. 180; *KrV* A 141/B 180.
19 Cf. Henry Allison, *Kant's Transcendental Idealism* (New Haven, Conn.: Yale University Press, 1982), p. 174.
20 *VEET*, pp. 315–16: 'although if Kant had heard these arguments in the form in which I have delivered them to you, he would doubtless have hounded me from my chair, something which would have been well within his official powers at that time'.
21 *ND*, p. 74; Ashton, p. 66.
22 'Der wunderliche Realist', in *NzL*, pp. 388–408, pp. 388–9; Nicholsen, ii, pp. 58–75, p. 59.
23 G. W. F. Hegel, *Science of Logic*, tr. A. V. Miller (London: George Allen & Unwin, 1969), p. 479.
24 *DS*, pp. 17, 20–1; Nicholsen, pp. 11, 15.
25 *ND*, p. 37; Ashton, p. 26, where this aspect of Kant's thought is called a 'formal recognition of the non-identical'.
26 *ND*, p. 184; Ashton, p. 183.
27 *ND*, pp. 173–4; Ashton, pp. 171–2.
28 *ND*, p. 182; Ashton, p. 181.
29 *ND*, p. 186; Ashton, p. 185.
30 *ND*, p. 233; Ashton, p. 234.
31 *ND*, p. 186; Ashton, p. 185.
32 *ND*, p. 10; Ashton, p. xx.
33 Karl Marx and Friedrich Engels, *The German Ideology*, tr. W. Lough (London: Lawrence & Wishart, 1974), p. 47. For Marx and dogmatism, see *K*, pp. 151–2; Hullot-Kentor, pp. 106–7.
34 *Critique of Pure Reason*, tr. Kemp Smith, pp. 409–15; *KrV* A 444–51/B 472–9.
35 Kant, *Critique of Practical Reason*, tr. Lewis White Beck (New York: Macmillan, 1956), p. 3. Cf. Kemp Smith, p. 26 (*KrV* B xxviii): 'Although I cannot *know*, I can yet *think* freedom.'
36 Ibid., p. 30.

37 Cf. Henry E. Allison, *Kant's Theory of Freedom* (Cambridge: Cambridge University Press, 1990), pp. 230–49.
38 *Critique of Practical Reason*, tr. Beck, p. 49; for a discussion of this claim see Allison, *Kant's Theory of Freedom*, pp. 243–5.
39 *ND*, p. 230; Ashton, p. 231.
40 Cf. Immanuel Kant, 'Idea for a Universal History with a Cosmopolitan Purpose', in *Political Writings*, ed. Hans Reiss, tr. H. B. Nisbet (Cambridge: Cambridge University Press, 1991), pp. 41–53.
41 Hegel first developed these criticisms in 'The Spirit of Christianity and its Fate', in *Early Theological Writings*, tr. T. M. Knox (Philadelphia: University of Pennsylvania Press, 1971), pp. 182–301, p. 211. For 'asymptotic convergence' – the approximation of one line to another to infinity without the two lines ever touching – cf. Kant, *Critique of Practical Reason*, tr. Beck, p. 33.
42 Cf. Adorno's 1963 lecture course, *Probleme der Moralphilosophie* (FfM: Suhrkamp, 1996), pp. 162–3.
43 Cf. Max Scheler, *Formalism in Ethics and Non-formal Ethics of Values: A New Attempt Toward the Foundation of an Ethical Personalism*, tr. M. S. Frings and R. L. Funk (Evanston: Northwestern University Press, 1973). *ND*, pp. 234–5; Ashton, p. 236.
44 Cf. 'Conclusion', below.
45 *ND*, pp. 236–9; Ashton, pp. 237–40.
46 Kant, *Critique of Judgement*, tr. Werner S. Pluhar (Indianapolis: Hackett, 1987), p. 52. *ND*, p. 231; Ashton, p. 232.
47 *PhT*, ii, p. 34 (15 November 1962). Cf., for example, G. W. F. Hegel, *Natural Law: The Scientific Ways of Treating Natural Law, its Place in Moral Philosophy, and its Relation to the Positive Science of Natural Law*, tr. T. M. Knox (Philadelphia: University of Pennsylvania Press, 1975), pp. 89–92. For an instance of a priori Fichtean politics, cf. *Der geschloßne Handelsstaat*, in *Ausgewählte politische Schriften*, ed. Zwi Batscha and Richard Saage (FfM: Suhrkamp, 1977), pp. 59–168.
48 *ND*, p. 236; Ashton, p. 237.
49 *ND*, p. 226; Ashton, p. 227.
50 *ND*, pp. 211–13; Ashton, pp. 211–14.
51 *MM*, pp. 13–14; Jephcott, p. 15.
52 Georg Lukács, *History and Class Consciousness*, tr. Rodney Livingstone (London: Merlin Press, 1971), p. 89.
53 'Falsche Praxis ist keine'. 'Marginalien zu Theorie und Praxis', in *GS* 10.2, pp. 759–82, p. 766.
54 Lukács made this charge in a later (1962) preface to his early *Theory of the Novel*, tr. Anna Bostock (London: Merlin Press, 1971), p. 22.
55 Cf. 'Marginalien zu Theorie und Praxis', p. 761.
56 *ND*, pp. 235, 294; Ashton, pp. 236, 299.
57 *ND*, p. 226; Ashton, p. 227. Kant, *Critique of Practical Reason*, tr. Beck, pp. 124–6. *ND*, p. 242: 'Marx took over the thesis of the primacy of practical reason from Kant and German idealism and sharpened it into an insistence upon changing the world rather than merely interpreting it. He thereby underwrote the programme of an absolute mastery over nature, an arch-bourgeois programme . . . [but] The telos [goal] of the praxis which Marx

considered appropriate was the abolition of the primacy of praxis in the form which had ruled bourgeois society. Contemplation would be possible without inhumanity as soon as productive forces had been unfettered to the extent that human beings would no longer be stuck in a praxis extorted from them by lack, a praxis which then becomes automatic in them.'

58 *ND*, pp. 228, 233; Ashton, pp. 229, 234.
59 *ND*, p. 242; Ashton, p. 245.
60 *ND*, p. 382; Ashton, p. 390.
61 'Beitrag zur Ideologienlehre', in *GS* 8, pp. 457–77, p. 474.
62 *ND*, p. 384; Ashton, p. 392.
63 *ND*, p. 242; Ashton, p. 244.
64 'Labour is *not the source* of all wealth. *Nature* is just as much the source of use-values (and it is indeed of such that material wealth consists!) as labour, which is itself only the manifestation of a natural force, human labour power.' Karl Marx, *Kritik des Gothaer Programms* in Karl Marx / Friedrich Engels, *Werke* (42 vols in 44, Berlin: Dietz, 1960–83), vol. 19, pp. 15–32, p. 15; *Critique of the Gotha Programme* (London: Lawrence & Wishart, 1939), p. 3 (tr. altered). *DS*, pp. 28–9; Nicholsen, pp. 23–4; *ND*, pp. 179, 301–2; Ashton, pp. 177–8, 307.
65 *ND*, p. 191; Ashton, p. 190. Adorno's primary target here is Lukács, *History and Class Consciousness*, but he also has in mind what he takes to be a related 'protest against objectification' in Heidegger's work: *ND*, pp. 96–9; Ashton, pp. 89–92. Cf. Hans-Hartmut Kappner, *Die Bildungstheorie Adornos als Theorie der Erfahrung von Kultur und Kunst* (FfM: Suhrkamp, 1984), p. 160.
66 *ND*, pp. 190, 192; Ashton, pp. 189, 191.
67 *ND*, p. 191; Ashton, p. 190.

Chapter 8 Materialism and Metaphysics

1 Rudolf Carnap, 'Pseudoproblems in Philosophy: The Heteropsychological and the Realism Controversy', in *The Logical Structure of the World*, tr. Rolf A. George (London: Routledge, 1967), pp. 301–43.
2 *K*, pp. 99–100; Hullot-Kentor, p. 68.
3 *K*, p. 13; Hullot-Kentor, p. 6.
4 *K*, pp. 40, 48; Hullot-Kentor, pp. 26, 32. However, Kierkegaard's thought does proceed surreptitiously towards such a restoration in Adorno's view: *K*, p. 152; Hullot-Kentor, p. 106.
5 *K*, p. 104; Hullot-Kentor, p. 71.
6 Despite the title of a central section of the *Concluding Unscientific Postscript*: 'Truth is subjectivity'. Søren Kierkegaard, *Concluding Unscientific Postscript to the Philosophical Fragments*, tr. David F. Swenson and Walter Lowrie (Princeton: Princeton University Press, 1941), pp. 169–224. *K*, p. 104; Hullot-Kentor, p. 71.
7 Adorno's later work on Kierkegaard is more favourable, although still critical, in its tone: see especially 'Kierkegaard noch einmal', in *GS* 2, pp. 238–58.

8 *K*, p. 151; Hullot-Kentor, p. 106.

9 *K*, p. 110; Hullot-Kentor, p. 76. The expression 'empty *and* blind x' plays on Kant's dictum quoted earlier: 'thoughts without content are empty, intuitions without concepts are blind'; Kemp Smith, p. 93; *KrV* A 51/B 75.

10 *K*, p. 56; Hullot-Kentor, p. 37.

11 *K*, p. 151; Hullot-Kentor, p. 106.

12 'Husserl and the Problem of Idealism', in *GS* 20.1 (1986), pp. 119–34, p. 120.

13 Ibid., p. 124.

14 Edmund Husserl, 'Prolegomena to Pure Logic', in *Logical Investigations*, tr. J. N. Findlay (2 vols, London: Routledge, 1970), vol. 1, pp. 53–246.

15 Edmund Husserl, 'Phenomenology: Edmund Husserl's Article for the *Encyclopaedia Britannica* (1927)', tr. Richard E. Palmer, in *Husserl: Shorter Works*, ed. Peter McCormick and Frederick Elliston (Brighton: Harvester, 1981), pp. 21–35, pp. 24–5.

16 Husserl, 'Phenomenology', pp. 29–31.

17 *ME*, pp. 138, 171; Domingo, pp. 132, 167.

18 *ME*, p. 85; Domingo, p. 78.

19 *ME*, p. 74; Domingo, p. 67.

20 *ME*, p. 91; Domingo, p. 84.

21 Husserl, *Logical Investigations*, tr. Findlay, vol. 2, p. 783: 'As the sensible stands to sense perception so the state of affairs stands to the "becoming aware" in which it is (more or less adequately) given . . .' *ME*, p. 205; Domingo, p. 202.

22 *ME*, p. 140; Domingo, p. 135.

23 *ME*, pp. 212–13; Domingo, p. 210.

24 *ME*, p. 196; Domingo, p. 193.

25 For a convincing defence of Hegel against the charge of hyper-Cartesianism, see David Kolb, *The Critique of Pure Modernity: Hegel, Heidegger and After* (Chicago: University of Chicago Press, 1986), pp. 201–36.

26 The critique is most rigorously developed in *ND*, pp. 69–136; Ashton, pp. 61–131.

27 Cf. Adorno's letter to Horkheimer on Heidegger of 26 November 1949, quoted in Rolf Wiggershaus, *The Frankfurt School*, tr. Michael Robertson (Cambridge: Polity Press, 1993), p. 593. For the most detailed study of the Adorno–Heidegger relationship to date, see Hermann Mörchen, *Adorno und Heidegger. Untersuchung einer philosophischen Kommunikationsverweigerung* (Stuttgart: Klett-Cotta, 1981); Mörchen's findings are discussed in ch. 2 of Fred R. Dallmayr, *Life-World, Modernity and Critique* (Cambridge: Polity Press, 1991).

28 The whole of part one of *ND* is headed 'Relation to Ontology'.

29 See, for examples, Peter Dews, *Logics of Disintegration: Post-structuralist Thought and the Claims of Critical Theory* (London: Verso, 1987); Drucilla Cornell, *The Philosophy of the Limit* (London: Routledge, 1992); Helga Gripp, *Theodor W. Adorno* (Paderborn: Schöningh, 1986), pp. 132–44. For a deconstructive account of Adorno and Heidegger, cf. Alexander Garcia Düttmann, *Das Gedächtnis des Denkens. Versuch über Adorno und Heidegger* (FfM: Suhrkamp, 1991).

30 *SZ*, pp. 1–4; *BT*, pp. 19–24. The divergences between Heidegger's earlier and his later thought cannot be discussed here. Although Adorno is sensitive to this divergence he does not value Heidegger's work before 1929–30 more highly than his later work (unlike, for example Jürgen Habermas: cf. 'The Undermining of Western Rationalism through the Critique of Metaphysics: Martin Heidegger', in *The Philosophical Discourse of Modernity*, tr. Frederick Lawrence (Cambridge: Polity Press, 1987), pp. 131–60.

31 *SZ*, pp. 89–112; *BT*, pp. 112–48.

32 Heidegger, 'Letter on Humanism', in *Basic Writings*, tr. D. F. Krell (San Francisco: Harper, 1977), pp. 193–242, p. 221.

33 *SZ*, pp. 19–27; *BT*, pp. 41–9.

34 Heidegger, 'Letter on Humanism', p. 207.

35 As Adorno recognizes: *PhT*, i, p. 157 (12 July 1962).

36 *SZ*, p. 38; *BT*, p. 62. 'Letter on Humanism', pp. 216–17.

37 Heidegger, 'Letter on Humanism', p. 216.

38 *ND*, pp. 134–6; Ashton, pp. 128–31. See also 'Die Idee der Naturgeschichte', in *GS* 1, pp. 349–52; and Adorno's review of Herbert Marcuse, *Hegels Ontologie und die Grundlegung einer Theorie der Geschichtlichkeit*, in *Zeitschrift für Sozialforschung* 1 (1932), pp. 409–10, repr. in *GS* 20.1; *ME*, p. 191; Domingo, p. 188.

39 *ND*, p. 200; Ashton, p. 200.

40 *ND*, p. 186.

41 For two examples, cf. Braun, *Kritische Theorie versus Kritizismus* (Berlin: de Gruyter, 1983) and, ultimately, Albrecht Wellmer, ' "Metaphysik im Augenblick ihres Sturzes" ', in *Metaphysik nach Kant? Stuttgarter Hegel-Kongreß 1987*, ed. Dieter Henrich and Rolf-Peter Horstmann (Stuttgart: Klett-Cotta, 1988), pp. 767–83, p. 774.

42 *KPM*, p. 101.

43 *SZ*, p. 10; *BT*, p. 31.

44 *KPM*, p. 60.

45 *KPM*, p. 74.

46 *KPM*, p. 80.

47 *KPM*, p. 15.

48 *ND*, pp. 74–6; Ashton, pp. 66–8.

49 *ND*, pp. 130–1; Ashton, pp. 125–6.

50 *ND*, p. 112; Ashton, p. 106.

51 *ND*, p. 109; Ashton, p. 102.

52 *ND*, pp. 107–8; Ashton, pp. 101–2.

53 Heidegger, 'On the Essence of Truth', in *Basic Writings*, pp. 117–41, p. 140; cf. *Vom Wesen der Wahrheit* (FfM: Vittorio Klostermann, 1949), p. 26: 'Er ist überhaupt kein Satz im Sinne einer Aussage'.

54 Heidegger, 'Letter on Humanism', p. 239.

55 *ND*, p. 152; Ashton, p. 149.

56 Heidegger, 'Letter on Humanism', p. 231.

57 Ibid., pp. 207–8.

58 For the idea of a 'bad' infinity, cf. G. W. F. Hegel, *Hegel's Logic*, tr. William Wallace (Oxford: Oxford University Press, 1975), p. 137, §94.

59 *ND*, p. 374; Ashton, p. 381.

60 Kemp Smith, p. 300; *KrV* A 298/B 355.

61 *ND*, p. 384; Ashton, p. 392.
62 See, for example, Kemp Smith, p. 28; *KrV* B xxviii: 'Though I cannot *know*, I can yet *think* freedom; that is to say, the representation of it is at least not self-contradictory, provided due account be taken of our critical distinction between the two modes of representation, the sensible and the intellectual, and of the resulting limitation of the pure concepts of understanding and of the principles which flow from them.'
63 Albrecht Wellmer, ' "Metaphysik im Augenblick ihres Sturzes" ', in *Metaphysik nach Kant? Stuttgarter Hegel-Kongreß 1987*, ed. Dieter Henrich and Rolf-Peter Horstmann (Stuttgart: Klett-Cotta, 1988), pp. 767–83, p. 767.
64 Ibid., p. 773.
65 Ibid., pp. 773–4.
66 Ibid., p. 773.
67 Kemp Smith, p. 668; *KrV* A 856/B 884. 'Über Tradition', in *GS* 10.1, pp. 310–20, p. 315.
68 *ND*, p. 400; Ashton, p. 408.
69 *ND*, p. 197.
70 *ND*, pp. 381–2; Ashton, p. 389.
71 Ibid.
72 *ND*, p. 384; Ashton, p. 392.
73 'Diskussionsprotokolle' in Max Horkheimer, *Gesammelte Schriften* 12, p. 490.
74 Ibid.
75 Michael Theunissen, 'Negativität bei Adorno', in *Adorno-Konferenz 1983*, ed. Ludwig von Friedeburg and Jürgen Habermas (FfM: Suhrkamp, 1983), pp. 41–65.
76 *ND*, p. 17; Ashton, p. 5.
77 *ND*, p. 22; Ashton, p. 11.
78 Theunissen, 'Negativität', p. 46.
79 Ibid., p. 61.
80 G. W. F. Hegel, *Elements of the Philosophy of Right*, ed. Allen Wood, tr. Barry Nisbet (Cambridge: Cambridge University Press, 1991), p. 23.
81 *ND*, p. 370; Ashton, pp. 377–8.
82 *AT*, p. 337; Hullot-Kentor, p. 227.
83 *ND*, p. 41; Ashton, p. 31.
84 *AT*, p. 335; Hullot-Kentor, p. 226.
85 Theunissen, 'Negativität', p. 53.
86 Theunissen, *Sein und Schein. Die kritische Funktion der Hegelschen Logik* (FfM: Suhrkamp, 1980), p. 33.
87 Kemp Smith, p. 33; *KrV* B xxxvii.
88 G. W. F. Hegel, *Phenomenology of Spirit*, tr. A. V. Miller (Oxford: Oxford University Press, 1977), §78.
89 *ND*, p. 397; Ashton, pp. 405–6.
90 *ND*, p. 183; Ashton, p. 181.
91 For an account aware of the link between these two charges, see Michael Theunissen, *Hegels Lehre vom absoluten Geist als theologisch-politischer Traktat* (Berlin: de Gruyter, 1970), pp. 27–40.
92 *ND*, p. 391; Ashton, p. 398. On the persistence of dogmatism, cf. especially lecture 23 from *PhT*, ii, pp. 44–55 (20 November 1962).

Conclusion

1 Benedetto Croce, *What is Living and what is Dead of the Philosophy of Hegel*, tr. Douglas Ainslie (London: Macmillan, 1915).
2 *DS*, pp. 9–16; Nicholsen, pp. 1–9.
3 For an important discussion of Habermas's thought from a viewpoint strongly informed by Adorno, cf. J. M. Bernstein, *Recovering Ethical Life: Jürgen Habermas and the Future of Critical Theory* (London: Routledge, 1995). See also Claudia Rademacher, *Versöhnung oder Verständigung? Kritik der Habermasschen Adorno-Revision* (Lüneburg: zu Klampen, 1993) and Peter Moritz, *Kritik des Paradigmenwechsels: mit Horkheimer gegen Habermas* (Lüneburg: zu Klampen, 1992).
4 *VESoz*, p. 56.
5 Cited in Hauke Brunkhorst, *Theodor W. Adorno: Dialektik der Moderne* (Munich: Piper, 1990), p. 230.
6 'What is universal pragmatics?', in Habermas, *Communication and the Evolution of Society*, tr. Thomas McCarthy (London: Heinemann, 1979), pp. 1–68.
7 Habermas, *The Theory of Communicative Action*, vol. 1: *Reason and the Rationalization of Society*, tr. Thomas McCarthy (Boston, Mass.: Beacon Press, 1984), p. 398.
8 Habermas, 'Historical Materialism and the Development of Normative Structures', in *Communication and the Evolution of Society*, pp. 95–129.
9 Habermas, *Theory of Communicative Action*, vol. 1, pp. 366–99, p. 399.
10 Axel Honneth, 'Communication and Reconciliation: Habermas' Critique of Adorno', *Telos* 39 (Spring 1979), 45–61; Habermas, *Theory of Communicative Action*, vol. 1, p. 385.
11 Habermas, *Theory of Communicative Action*, vol. 1, p. 385.
12 Ibid., p. 386.
13 Jürgen Habermas, *The Philosophical Discourse of Modernity: Twelve Lectures*, tr. Frederick G. Lawrence (Cambridge: Polity Press, 1987), p. 129.
14 Ibid., p. 130.
15 Ibid., p. 129.
16 Ibid., p. 130.
17 Habermas, *Communication and the Evolution of Society*, pp. 1–68, 130–77.
18 Walter Benjamin, 'Fate and character', in *One Way Street*, tr. Edmund Jephcott and Kingsley Shorter (London: New Left Books, 1979), pp. 124–31, p. 126.
19 *KrV* A 52/B 76; Kemp Smith, p. 93.
20 For Habermas's defence against such charges, cf. Habermas, 'Morality and Ethical Life: Does Hegel's Critique of Kant apply to Discourse Ethics?' in *Moral Consciousness and Communicative Action*, tr. Christian Lenhardt and Shierry Weber Nicholsen (Cambridge: Polity Press, 1990), pp. 195–211.
21 Habermas, *Philosophical Discourse of Modernity*, p. 130.
22 Göran Therborn, 'The Frankfurt School', *New Left Review* 63 (1970), 65–96; Martin Jay, 'The Frankfurt School's Critique of Marxist Humanism', *Social Research* 39 (1972), 285–305.
23 For an important discussion of humanism, cf. 'Zum Klassizismus von Goethes Iphigenie', in *NzL*, pp. 495–514; Nicholsen, ii, pp. 153–70.

24 Albrecht Wellmer, 'Wahrheit, Schein, Versöhnung. Adornos ästhetische Rettung der Modernität', in *Zur Dialektik von Moderne und Postmoderne. Vernunftkritik nach Adorno* (FfM: Suhrkamp, 1985), pp. 9–47, p. 19. 'Truth, Semblance, Reconciliation', tr. Maeve Cooke, *Telos* 62 (1985), pp. 90–115.

25 'Die Idee der Naturgeschichte', in *GS* 1, pp. 345–65, p. 354; 'The Idea of Natural History' (1932), *Telos* 60 (1984), 111–24, p. 117.

26 Jacques Derrida, *Given Time*, vol. 1: *Counterfeit Money*, tr. Peggy Kamuf (Chicago: University of Chicago Press, 1992), pp. 6–33; *Glas*, tr. John P. Leavey Jr. and Richard Rand (Lincoln: University of Nebraska Press, 1986), pp. 242ff; *The Truth in Painting*, tr. Geoffrey Bennington and Ian McLeod (Chicago: University of Chicago Press, 1987), pp. 291–2; *Specters of Marx*, tr. Peggy Kamuf (London: Routledge, 1994), p. 27.

27 Derrida, 'The Politics of Friendship', *The Journal of Philosophy*, vol. 85, no. 11 (November 1988), 632–44.

28 Derrida, *Psyche: Inventions de l'Autre* (Paris: Galilée, 1987), p. 163.

29 'The Politics of Friendship', 632–4.

30 Ibid.

31 *ND*, p. 263; Ashton, p. 266.

32 Max Horkheimer, 'Materialism and Metaphysics', in *Critical Theory: Selected Essays*, tr. Matthew J. O'Connell et al. (New York: Continuum, 1982), pp. 10–46.

33 Cf. 'Diskussionsprotokolle' in Max Horkheimer, *Gesammelte Schriften*, vol. 12, ed. Gunzelin Schmid Noerr and Alfred Schmidt (FfM: Fischer, 1985), pp. 476–83.

34 Cf. *Das Unerhört Moderne: Berliner Adorno-Tagung*, ed. Frithjof Hager and Hermann Pfütze (Lüneburg: zu Klampen, 1990).

35 Habermas, *Theory of Communicative Action*, vol. 1, p. 385.

36 *ND*, pp. 27–9; Ashton, pp. 15–18.

37 Gillian Rose, 'From Speculative to Dialectical Thinking' in *Judaism and Modernity: Philosophical Essays* (Oxford: Blackwell, 1993), pp. 53–63; Michael Theunissen, *Hegels Lehre vom absoluten Geist als theologisch-politischer Traktat* (Berlin: de Gruyter, 1970), p. 32. Other commentators have regarded the affinity with Schelling as redounding to Adorno's credit: cf. Andrew Bowie, *Schelling and Modern European Philosophy* (London: Routledge, 1993), p. 183.

38 Cf. Anke Thyen, *Negative Dialektik und Erfahrung. Zur Rationalität des Nichtidentischen bei Adorno* (FfM: Suhrkamp, 1989); Ulrich Müller, *Erkenntniskritik und negative Metaphysik bei Adorno. Eine Philosophie der dritten Reflektiertheit* (FfM: Athenäum, 1988).

39 *ND*, p. 29; Ashton, pp. 17–18.

40 Thyen, *Negative Dialektik und Erfahrung*, p. 165.

41 Adorno to Horkheimer, 20 October 1952. Quoted in Rolf Wiggershaus, *The Frankfurt School*, tr. Michael Robertson (Cambridge: Polity Press, 1993), p. 456.

42 *ND*, p. 381; Ashton, p. 358.

43 *ND*, p. 100; Ashton, p. 93. For the verses quoted, see William Wordsworth, *The Prelude: A Parallel Text*, ed. J. C. Maxwell (pp. 446–8) (1805–6 text, book x, ll. 813–14).

Bibliography

This bibliography is selective. It includes only books and articles cited in the text and a few other works which may be of further help. For larger bibliographies see René Görtzen, 'Theodor W. Adorno. Vorläufige Bibliographie seiner Schriften und der Sekundärliteratur', in Ludwig von Friedeburg and Jürgen Habermas, eds, *Adorno-Konferenz 1983* (FfM: Suhrkamp, 1983), pp. 402–71; Klaus Schultz, 'Vorläufige Bibliographie der Schriften Theodor W. Adornos' in Hermann Schweppenhäuser, ed., *Theodor W. Adorno zum Gedächtnis* (FfM: Suhrkamp, 1971), pp. 177–242; Peter Christian Lang, 'Commentierte Auswahlsbibliographie 1969–1979', in Burkhardt Lindner and W. Martin Lüdke, eds, *Materialien zur ästhetischen Theorie Theodor W. Adornos* (FfM: Suhrkamp, 1980), pp. 509–56.

Works by Adorno

Gesammelte Schriften (23 vols, FfM: Suhrkamp, 1970–). Volumes are edited by Rolf Tiedemann except where otherwise indicated. The date of first publication (or completion for previously unpublished works) is given in square brackets.
1 (1973) *Philosophische Frühschriften*
'Die Transzendenz des Dinglichen und Noematischen in Husserls Phänomenologie' [1924]
'Der Begriff des Unbewußten in der transzendentalen Seelenlehre' [1927]
'Die Aktualität der Philosophie' [1931]
'Die Idee der Naturgeschichte' [1932]
'Thesen über die Sprache des Philosophen' [early 1930s]
2 (1979) *Kierkegaard. Konstruktion des Ästhetischen* [1933]
3 (1981) (with Max Horkheimer) *Dialektik der Aufklärung* [1944]
4 (1980) *Minima Moralia. Reflexionen aus dem beschädigten Leben* [1951]
5 (1971) *Zur Metakritik der Erkenntnistheorie. Studien über Husserl und die phänomenologischen Antinomien* [1956]
Drei Studien zu Hegel [1963]

6 (1973) *Negative Dialektik* [1966]
Jargon der Eigentlichkeit. Zur deutschen Ideologie [1964]
7 (1970) *Ästhetische Theorie* [1970]
8 (1972) *Soziologische Schriften I* [various]
9.1 (1975) *Soziologische Schriften II. Erste Hälfte*
'The Psychological Technique of Martin Luther Thomas's Radio Addresses' [1943]
Studies in the Authoritarian Personality [1950]
9.2 (1975) *Soziologische Schriften II. Zweite Hälfte*
The Stars down to Earth [1957]
Schuld und Abwehr [1955]
10.1 (1977) *Kulturkritik und Gesellschaft I*
Prismen [1955]
Ohne Leitbild. Parva Aesthetica [1967]
10.2 (1977) *Kulturkritik und Gesellschaft II*
Eingriffe [1963]
Stichworte [1969]
11 (1974) *Noten zur Literatur* [1958; 1961; 1965]
12 (1975) *Philosophie der neuen Musik* [1949]
13 (1973) *Die musikalischen Monographien*
Versuch über Wagner [1952]
Berg. Der Meister des Kleinsten Übergangs [1968]
Mahler. Eine musikalische Physiognomik [1960]
14 (1973) *Dissonanzen* [1956]
Einleitung in die Musiksoziologie [1962]
15 (1976) *Komposition für den Film* [1944; 1969]
Der getreue Korrepetitor [1963]
16 (1979) *Musikalische Schriften III*
Klangfiguren [1959]
Quasi una Fantasia [1963]
17 (1982) *Musikalische Schriften IV*
Moments Musicaux [1964]
Impromptus [1968]
18 (1984) *Musikalische Schriften V* [various]
19 (1984) *Musikalische Schriften VI* [various]
20.1 (1986) *Vermischte Schriften I* [various]
20.2 (1986) *Vermischte Schriften II* [various]

The following texts of lecture courses, correspondence and unfinished works are those so far available:

Beethoven: Philosophie der Musik. Fragmente und Texte, ed. Rolf Tiedemann (FfM: Suhrkamp, 1993)
Erziehung zur Mündigkeit. Vorträge und Gespräche mit Hellmut Becker, 1959–69, ed. Gerd Kadelbach (FfM: Suhrkamp, 1970)
Philosophische Terminologie (FfM: Suhrkamp, 1973–4)
(with Walter Benjamin) *Briefwechsel 1928–1940*, ed. Henri Lonitz (FfM: Suhrkamp, 1994); translation forthcoming (Cambridge: Polity Press)
(with Alfred Sohn-Rethel) *Briefwechsel 1936–1969*, ed. Christoph Godde (Munich: Edition Text und Kritik, 1991)

(with Ernst Krenek) *Theodor W. Adorno und Ernst Krenek. Briefwechsel*, ed. Wolfgang Rogge (FfM: Suhrkamp, 1974)

Vorlesungen zur Ästhetik 1967–8 (Zurich: H. Mayer Nachfolger, 1973)

Vorlesung zur Einleitung in die Erkenntnistheorie 1957–58 (FfM: Junius, n.d.)

Vorlesung zur Einleitung in die Soziologie (FfM: Junius, 1973)

Translations and Publications in English

Aesthetic Theory, tr. C. Lenhardt (London: Routledge, 1984) (This translation is unreliable and has been withdrawn by the publishers)

Aesthetic Theory, tr. Robert Hullot-Kentor (London: Athlone, 1997)

Against Epistemology, tr. Willis Domingo (Oxford: Blackwell, 1982)

Alban Berg: Master of the Smallest Link, tr. Juliane Brand and Christopher Hailey (Cambridge: Cambridge University Press, 1991)

Aspects of Sociology, tr. John Viertel (Boston: Beacon Press, 1972)

(with Else Funkel-Brunswik, Daniel J. Levinson and R. Nevitt Sanford, in collaboration with Betty Aron, Maria Hertz Levinson and William Morrow) *The Authoritarian Personality* (New York: Harper, 1950 (Studies in Prejudice, vol. 1))

(with Hanns Eisler) *Composing for Films*, ed. Graham McCann (London: Athlone, 1994)

The Culture Industry: Selected Essays on Mass Culture, ed. J. M. Bernstein (London: Routledge, 1991)

(with Max Horkheimer) *Dialectic of Enlightenment*, tr. John Cumming (New York: Seabury Press, 1972)

Hegel: Three Studies, tr. Shierry Weber Nicholsen (Cambridge, Mass.: MIT Press, 1993)

In Search of Wagner, tr. Rodney Livingstone (London: Verso, 1981)

Introduction to the Sociology of Music, tr. E. B. Ashton (New York: Seabury Press, 1976)

The Jargon of Authenticity, tr. Knut Tarnowski and Frederic Will (London: Routledge, 1973)

Kierkegaard: Construction of the Aesthetic, tr. Robert Hullot-Kentor (Minneapolis: University of Minnesota Press, 1989)

Mahler: A Musical Physiognomy, tr. E. F. N. Jephcott (Chicago: University of Chicago Press, 1992)

Minima Moralia, tr. E. F. N. Jephcott (London: New Left Books, 1974)

Negative Dialectics, tr. E. B. Ashton (London: Routledge, 1973)

Notes to Literature, tr. Shierry Weber Nicholsen (2 vols, New York: Columbia University Press, 1991–2)

The Philosophy of Modern Music, tr. Anne G. Mitchell and Wesley V. Blomster (New York: Seabury Press, 1973)

The Positivist Dispute in German Sociology, tr. Glyn Adey and David Frisby (London: Heinemann, 1976)

Prisms, tr. Samuel and Shierry Weber (Cambridge, Mass.: MIT Press, 1981)

Quasi una Fantasia: Essays on Modern Music, tr. Rodney Livingstone (London: Verso, 1992)

The Stars down to Earth and other Essays on the Irrational in Culture, ed. Stephen Crook (London: Routledge, 1994)

Articles in English and Translations into English

Only those articles which are not more conveniently available in collections are listed here.

'The Actuality of Philosophy', *Telos* 31 (1977), 120–33

'Alienated Masterpiece: The *Missa Solemnis*' (1959), *Telos* 28 (1976), 113–24

'Contemporary German Sociology', in *Transactions of the Fourth World Congress of Sociology* (London: International Sociological Association, 1959), vol. 1, pp. 33–56

'Education for Autonomy' (1969) (with Hellmut Becker), *Telos* 55–6 (1983), 103–10

'Functionalism Today', *Oppositions* 17 (1979), 31–41

'Goldmann and Adorno: To Describe, Understand and Explain' (1968), in Lucien Goldmann, *Cultural Creation in Modern Society*, tr. Bart Grahl (Oxford: Blackwell, 1976), pp. 129–45

'The Idea of Natural History' (1932), *Telos* 60 (1984), 111–24

'Is Marx Obsolete?', *Diogenes* 64 (1968), 1–16 (tr. of 'Spätkapitalismus oder Industriegesellschaft?')

'Jazz', in *Encyclopaedia of the Arts*, ed. Dagobert D. Runes and Harry G. Schrickel (New York: Philosophical Library, 1946), pp. 511–13

'Music and Technique' (1958), *Telos* 32 (1977), 79–94

'Music and the New Music: In Memory of Peter Suhrkamp' (1960), *Telos* 43 (1980), 124–38

'New Music and the Public: Some Problems of Interpretation' (1957), in *Twentieth-Century Music*, ed. Rollo H. Myers (London: Calder and Boyars, 1968), pp. 63–74

'Of Barricades and Ivory Towers: An Interview with T. W. Adorno', *Encounter* 33 (3) (1969), 63–9

'On Popular Music' (with George Simpson), *Studies in Philosophy and Social Science* 9 (1949), 17–48

'On the Historical Adequacy of Consciousness' (with Peter von Haselberg), *Telos* 56 (1983), 97–103

'On the Question: "What is German?" ' (1965), *New German Critique* 36 (1985), 121–31

'On the Social Situation of Music' (1932), *Telos* 35 (1978), 128–64

'Progress', *The Philosophical Forum* 15 (1983–4), 55–70

'The Radio Symphony: An Experiment in Theory', in *Radio Research 1941*, ed. Paul F. Lazarsfeld and Frank N. Stanton (New York: Duell, Sloan and Pearce, 1941), 110–39

'Resignation', *Telos* 35 (1978), 165–8

Review of Jean Wahl, *Études Kierkegaardiennes*; Walter Lowrie, *Kierkegaard*; and *The Journals of Soren Kierkegaard*, *Studies in Philosophy and Social Science* 9 (1941), 167–78

'Scientific Experiences of a European Scholar in America', tr. Donald Fleming, *Perspectives in American History* 2 (1968), 338–70; repr. in Donald Fleming and Bernard Bailyn, eds, *The Intellectual Migration: Europe and America, 1930–1960* (Cambridge, Mass.: Belknap Press/Harvard University Press), pp. 338–70

'Society' (1966), *Salmagundi* 10–11 (1969–70), 144–53

'Sociology and Psychology', *New Left Review* 46 (1967), 63–80; 47 (1968), 79–97

'The Sociology of Knowledge and its Consciousness', in Andrew Arato and Eike Gebhardt, eds, *The Essential Frankfurt School Reader*, pp. 452–65

'Spengler Today', *Studies in Philosophy and Social Science* 9 (1941), 305–25

' "Static" and "Dynamic" as Sociological Categories' (1956), *Diogenes* 33 (1961), 28–49

'Subject and Object' (1969), in Andrew Arato and Eike Gebhardt, eds, *The Essential Frankfurt School Reader*, (New York: Urizen Books, 1978), pp. 497–511

'Theses against Occultism', *Telos* 19 (1951), 7–12

'Theses on the Sociology of Art' (1967), *Working Papers in Cultural Studies* 2 (Birmingham, 1972), 121–8

'Wagner, Nietzsche and Hitler' (review), *Kenyon Review* 9 (1) (1947), 165–72

General Bibliography

Ahlers, Rolf, 'Endlichkeit und absoluter Geist in Hegels Philosophie', *Zeitschrift für philosophische Forschung* 29 (1975), 63–80

——, 'The Overcoming of Critical Theory in the Hegelian Unity of Theory and Praxis', *Clio* 8 (1) (1978), 71–96

Allison, Henry, *Kant's Transcendental Idealism* (New Haven, Conn.: Yale University Press, 1982)

——, *Kant's Theory of Freedom* (Cambridge: Cambridge University Press, 1990)

Arato, Andrew, and Eike Gebhardt, eds, *The Essential Frankfurt School Reader* (New York: Urizen Books, 1978)

Arlt, Gerhard, 'Erkenntnistheorie und Gesellschaftskritik', *Philosophisches Jahrbuch* 90 (1983), 129–45

Arnold, Heinz-Ludwig, ed., *Theodor W. Adorno* (Munich: Text und Kritik, 1983)

Barth, Karl, *The Epistle to the Romans*, tr. Edwyn C. Hoskyns (Oxford: Oxford University Press, 1933)

Beier, Christel, *Zum Verhältnis von Gesellschaftstheorie und Erkenntnistheorie. Untersuchungen zum Totalitätsbegriff in der kritischen Theorie Adornos* (FfM: Suhrkamp, 1974)

Benhabib, Seyla, *Critique, Norm and Utopia: A Study of the Foundations of Critical Theory* (New York: Columbia University Press, 1986)

Benjamin, Andrew, ed., *The Problems of Modernity: Adorno and Benjamin* (London: Routledge, 1991)

——, Wolfgang Bonß and John McCole, eds, *On Max Horkheimer: New Perspectives* (Cambridge, Mass.: MIT Press, 1993)

Benjamin, Jessica, 'The End of Internalization: Adorno's Social Psychology', *Telos* 32 (1977), 42–64

Benjamin, Walter, *Ursprung des deutschen Trauerspiels* (FfM: Suhrkamp, 1963)

——, *Briefe*, ed. Gerschom Scholem and Theodor W. Adorno (2 vols, FfM: Suhrkamp, 1966)

——, *Illuminations*, ed. Hannah Arendt, tr. Harry Zohn (London: Fontana, 1973)

——, *The Origin of German Tragic Drama*, tr. John Osborne (London: New Left Books, 1977)

——, *One Way Street*, tr. Edmund Jephcott and Kingsley Shorter (London: New Left Books, 1979)

Berman, Russell A., 'Adorno, Marxism and Art', *Telos* 34 (Winter 1977–8), 157–66

——, 'Adorno's Radicalism: Two Interviews from the Sixties', *Telos* 56 (1983–4), 94–7

Bernstein, J.M., *The Fate of Art: Aesthetic Alienation from Kant to Derrida and Adorno* (Cambridge: Polity Press, 1991)

——, *Recovering Ethical Life: Jürgen Habermas and the Future of Critical Theory* (London: Routledge, 1995)

Bloch, Ernst, *Geist der Utopie* (Munich and Leipzig: Duncker and Humblot, 1918 (facs. FfM: Suhrkamp, 1971))

——, *Briefe 1903–1975*, ed. Karola Bloch et al. (2 vols, FfM: Suhrkamp, 1985)

Bockelmann, Franz, *Über Marx und Adorno. Schwierigkeiten der spätmarxistischen Theorie* (FfM: Makol, 1972)

Bowie, Andrew, *Schelling and Modern European Philosophy* (London: Routledge, 1993)

——, *From Romanticism to Critical Theory* (London: Routledge, 1997)

Braun, Carl, *Kritische Theorie versus Kritizismus* (Kantstudien Ergänzungshefte, 115) (Berlin: de Gruyter, 1983)

Breuer, Stefan, 'Adorno's Anthropology', tr. John Blazek, *Telos* 64 (1985–6), 15–31

Brunkhorst, Hauke, 'Adorno, Heidegger and Postmodernity', *Philosophy and Social Criticism* 14 (1988), 411–24

——, *Theodor W. Adorno. Dialektik der Moderne* (Munich: Piper, 1990)

Bubner, Rüdiger, 'Über einige Bedingungen gegenwärtiger Ästhetik', *Neue Hefte für Philosophie* 5 (1973), 38–73

——, 'Kann Theorie ästhetisch werden? Zum Hauptmotiv der Philosophie Adornos', in Burkhardt Lindner and W. Martin Lüdke, eds, *Materialien zur ästhetischen Theorie Theodor W. Adornos* (FfM: Suhrkamp, 1980), pp. 108–37

Buck-Morss, Susan, *The Origin of Negative Dialectics: Theodor W. Adorno, Walter Benjamin, and the Frankfurt Institute* (Hassocks: Harvester, 1977)

Cahn, Michael, 'Subversive Mimesis', in *Mimesis in Contemporary Theory*, ed. Mihai Spariosu (Philadelphia: John Benjamin's Publishing Company, 1984)

Carnap, Rudolf, 'Pseudoproblems in Philosophy: The Heteropsychological and the Realism Controversy', in *The Logical Structure of the World*, tr. Rolf A. George (London: Routledge, 1967), pp. 301–43

Caygill, Howard, *Art of Judgement* (Oxford: Blackwell, 1989)

Cochetti, Stefano, *Mythos und Dialektik der Aufklärung* (Meisenheim: Verlag Anton Hain, 1985)

Coffa, J. Alberto, *The Semantic Tradition from Kant to Carnap: To the Vienna Station*, ed. Linda Wessels (Cambridge: Cambridge University Press, 1991)

Connerton, Paul, *The Tragedy of Enlightenment: An Essay on the Frankfurt School* (Cambridge: Cambridge University Press, 1980)

Cooke, Deryck, *The Language of Music* (Oxford: Oxford University Press, 1989)

Cornelius, Hans, *Transcendentale Systematik. Untersuchungen zur Begründung der Erkenntnistheorie* (Munich: Ernst Reinhardt, 1916)

Cornell, Drucilla, *The Philosophy of the Limit* (London: Routledge, 1992)

Croce, Benedetto, *What is Living and What is Dead of the Philosophy of Hegel*, tr. Douglas Ainslie (London: Macmillan, 1915)

Dahlhaus, Carl, 'Adornos Begriff des musikalischen Materials', in Hans Heinrich Eggebrecht, ed., *Zur Terminologie der Musik des 20. Jahrhunderts* (Stuttgart: Musikwissenschaftliche Verlags-Gesellschaft, 1974), pp. 9–21

——, 'Soziologische Dechiffrierung von Musik. Zu Theodor W. Adornos Wagner-Kritik', *The International Review of the Aesthetics and Sociology of Music* 1 (1979), 137–47

Dallmayr, Fred R., *Life-World, Modernity and Critique* (Cambridge: Polity Press, 1991)

de Vries, Hendrich and H. Kunnemann, eds, *Die Aktualität der 'Dialektik der Aufklärung'* (FfM: Campus, 1989)

de Vries, Hent, 'Moralität und Sittlichkeit. Zu Adornos Hegelkritik', *Hegel-Jahrbuch* (1988), 300–7

Derrida, Jacques, *Glas*, tr. John P. Leavey Jr and Richard Rand (Lincoln: University of Nebraska Press, 1986)

——, *Psyche. Inventions de l'Autre* (Paris: Galilée, 1987)

——, *The Truth in Painting*, tr. Geoffrey Bennington and Ian McLeod (Chicago: University of Chicago Press, 1987)

——, *Given Time*, vol. 1: *Counterfeit Money*, tr. Peggy Kamuf (Chicago: University of Chicago Press, 1992)

——, *Specters of Marx*, tr. Peggy Kamuf (London: Routledge, 1994)

——, 'The Politics of Friendship', *Journal of Philosophy*, vol. 85, no. 11 (November 1988), 632–44

Dews, Peter, *Logics of Disintegration: Post-Structuralist Thought and the Claims of Critical Theory* (London: Verso, 1987)

——, *The Limits of Disenchantment* (London: Verso, 1996)

Dilthey, Wilhelm, *Der Aufbau der geschichtlichen Welt in den Geisteswissenschaften*, ed. B. Groethuysen (Leipzig: B. G. Teubner, 1927)

Dubiel, Helmut, *Wissenschaftstheorie und politische Erfahrung. Studien zur frühen Kritischen Theorie* (FfM: Suhrkamp, 1978)

——, *Theory and Politics: Studies in the Development of Critical Theory*, tr. Benjamin Gregg (Cambridge, Mass.: MIT Press, 1985)

Durkheim, Émile, *The Division of Labour in Society*, tr. W. D. Halls (London: Macmillan, 1984)

Düttmann, Alexander García, *Das Gedächtnis des Denkens. Versuch über Adorno und Heidegger* (FfM: Suhrkamp, 1991)

Düver, Lothar, *Theodor W. Adorno. Der Wissenschaftsbegriff der Kritischen Theorie in seinem Werk* (Bonn: Bouvier, 1978)

Edgar, Andrew, 'An Introduction to Adorno's Aesthetics', *British Journal of Aesthetics* 30 (1) (1990), 46–56

Fichte, J. G., *Ausgewählte politische Schriften*, ed. Zwi Batscha and Richard Saage (FfM: Suhrkamp, 1977)

Fink, Eugen, 'Husserl's Philosophy and Contemporary Criticism', in R. D. Elveton, ed., *The Phenomenology of Husserl* (Chicago: Quadrangle, 1970), pp. 73–147

Forum für Philosophie Bad Homburg, eds, *Martin Heidegger: Innen- und Außenansichten* (FfM: Suhrkamp, 1989)

von Friedeburg, Ludwig and Jürgen Habermas, eds, *Adorno-Konferenz 1983* (FfM: Suhrkamp, 1983)

Fromm, Erich, *The Crisis of Psychoanalysis* (London: Jonathan Cape, 1971)
Früchtl, Josef, *Mimesis. Konstellation eines Zentralbegriffs bei Adorno* (Würzburg: Königshausen und Neumann, 1986)
——, 'Unparteiische Vernunft und interesseloses Wohlgefallen. Zu Adornos Transformierung des Kantischen Modells', *Zeitschrift für philosophische Forschung* (41) (1987), 88–99
——, 'Radikalität und Konsequenz in der Wahrheitstheorie. Nietzsche als Herausforderung für Adorno und Habermas', *Nietzsche-Studien* 19 (1990), 431–61
——, ' "Moral begründen ist schwer". Die Rolle der Mitleidsethik bei Adorno und Habermas', *Schopenhauer Jahrbuch* 72 (1991), 36–44
Galeazzi, Umberto, 'Kant e Husserl nei primi lavori filosofici di Adorno', *Rivista Filosofica Neoscolastica* 75 (1983), 263–87
Gans, Herbert J., 'Popular Culture in America: Social Problem in a Mass Society or Social Asset in a Pluralist Society?', in *Social Problems: A Modern Approach*, ed. Herbert S. Becker (New York: Wiley, 1966)
Geuss, Raymond, *The Idea of a Critical Theory: Habermas and the Frankfurt School* (Cambridge: Cambridge University Press, 1981)
Grenz, Friedemann, *Adornos Philosophie in Grundbegriffen. Auflösung einiger Deutungsprobleme* (FfM: Suhrkamp, 1974)
Gripp, Helga, *Theodor W. Adorno. Erkenntnisdimensionen negativer Dialektik* (Paderborn: Schöningh, 1986)
Grossmann, Henryk, *Das Akkumulations- und Zusammenbruchsgesetz des kapitalistischen Systems* (Leipzig: Hirschfeld, 1929)
——, *Marx, die klassische Nationalökonomie und das Problem der Dynamik* (FfM and Vienna: Europäische Verlagsanstalt and Europa Verlag, 1969)
——, *The Law of Accumulation and Breakdown of the Capitalist System*, tr. and abr. Jairus Banaji (London: Pluto Press, 1992)
Günther, Klaus, 'Dialektik der Aufklärung in der Idee der Freiheit. Zur Kritik des Freiheitsbegriff bei Adorno', *Zeitschrift für philosophische Forschung* 39 (1985), 229–60
Guzzoni, Ute, 'Hegels "Unwahrheit". Zu Adornos Hegel-Kritik', *Hegel-Jahrbuch* (1975), 242–6
Habermas, Jürgen, *Communication and the Evolution of Society*, tr. Thomas McCarthy (London: Heinemann, 1979)
——, *Theorie des kommunikativen Handelns* (2 vols, FfM: Suhrkamp, 1981)
——, *The Philosophical Discourse of Modernity: Twelve Lectures*, tr. Frederick G. Lawrence (Cambridge: Polity Press, 1987)
——, *The Theory of Communicative Action*, tr. Thomas McCarthy (2 vols; Boston: Beacon Press, 1984 and Cambridge: Polity Press, 1987)
——, *Moral Consciousness and Communicative Action*, tr. Christian Lenhardt and Shierry Weber Nicholsen (Cambridge: Polity Press, 1990)
Hager, Frithjof and Hermann Pfütze, eds, *Das unerhört Moderne. Berliner Adorno-Tagung* (Lüneburg: zu Klampen, 1990)
Hamann, J. G., *Metacritik* (1800), in *Sämtliche Werke*, ed. J. Nadler (Vienna: Herder, 1949–57), vol. 3
Hegel, G.W.F., *The Philosophy of History*, tr. J. Sibree (New York: Dover, 1956)
——, *Hegel's Science of Logic*, tr. A. V. Miller (London: George Allen & Unwin, 1969)
——, *Werke* (20 vols, FfM: Suhrkamp, 1969)

——, *Early Theological Writings*, tr. T. M. Knox (Philadelphia: University of Pennsylvania Press, 1971)

——, *Hegel's Aesthetics: Lectures on Fine Art*, tr. T. M. Knox (2 vols, Oxford: Clarendon Press, 1975)

——, *Hegel's Logic*, tr. William Wallace (Oxford: Oxford University Press, 1975)

——, *Natural Law: The Scientific Ways of Treating Natural Law, Its Place in Moral Philosophy, and Its Relation to the Positive Science of Natural Law*, tr. T. M. Knox (Philadelphia: University of Pennsylvania Press, 1975)

——, *Hegel's Phenomenology of Spirit*, tr. A. V. Miller (Oxford: Oxford University Press, 1977)

——, *Elements of the Philosophy of Right*, ed. Allen Wood, tr. Barry Nisbet (Cambridge: Cambridge University Press, 1991)

——, *Introductory Lectures on Aesthetics*, tr. Bernard Bosanquet (Harmondsworth: Penguin, 1993)

Heidegger, Martin, *Vom Wesen der Wahrheit* (FfM: Vittorio Klostermann, 1949)

——, *Being and Time*, tr. John MacQuarrie and Edward Robinson (Oxford: Blackwell, 1962)

——, *Basic Writings*, tr. D. F. Krell (San Fransisco: Harper, 1977)

——, *The Question concerning Technology*, tr. William Lovitt (New York: Harper, 1977)

——, *Sein und Zeit*, 16th edn (Tübingen: Max Niemeyer, 1986)

——, *Kant and the Problem of Metaphysics*, tr. Richard Taft (Bloomington and Indianapolis: Indiana University Press, 1990)

Held, David, *Introduction to Critical Theory: From Horkheimer to Habermas* (London: Hutchinson, 1980)

Henrich, Dieter, *Fluchtlinien. Philosophische Essays* (FfM: Suhrkamp, 1982)

——, 'Gedanken zur Dankbarkeit', in R. Löw, ed., *Oikeiosis. Festschrift für R. Spaemann* (Weinheim: Acta Humaniora, 1987)

Henry, Michel, *Marx* (2 vols, Paris: Gallimard, 1976)

Hilferding, Rudolf, *Finance Capital*, ed. Tom Bottomore, tr. Morris Watnick and Sam Gordon (London: Routledge, 1981)

Hobbes, Thomas, *Leviathan*, ed. Richard Tuck (Cambridge: Cambridge University Press, 1991)

Hölderlin, Friedrich, *Poems and Fragments*, tr. Michael Hamburger (Cambridge: Cambridge University Press, 1980)

Honneth, Axel, 'Communication and Reconciliation: Habermas' Critique of Adorno', *Telos* 39 (Spring 1979), 45–61

——, 'Foucault and Adorno: Two Forms of the Critique of Modernity', *Thesis Eleven* 15 (1986), 48–59

——, *The Critique of Power: Reflective Stages in a Critical Social Theory*, tr. Kenneth Baynes (Cambridge, Mass.: MIT Press, 1991)

Horkheimer, Max, 'Traditionelle und kritische Theorie', *Zeitschrift für Sozialforschung* 6 (1937), pp. 245–92

——, ed., *Zeugnisse. T. W. Adorno zum 60. Geburtstag* (FfM, Institut für Sozialforschung, 1963)

——, *Critical Theory: Selected Essays*, tr. Matthew J. O'Connell et al. (New York: Continuum, 1982)

——, *Gesammelte Schriften*, ed. Alfred Schmidt and Gunzelin Schmid Noerr (15 vols, FfM: Fischer, 1985–)
——, *Between Philosophy and Social Science: Selected Early Writings*, tr. G. Frederick Hunter, Matthew S. Kramer and John Torpey (Cambridge, Mass.: MIT Press, 1993)
Hösle, Vittorio, *Hegels System* (2 vols, Hamburg: Felix, Meiner, 1988) -
Husserl, Edmund, *Logical Investigations*, tr. J. N. Findlay (2 vols, London: Routledge, 1970)
——, *Husserl: Shorter Works*, ed. Peter McKormick and Frederick Elliston (Brighton: Harvester, 1981)
——, *Ideas towards a Pure Phenomenology and a Phenomenological Philosophy: First Book*, tr. F. Kersten (The Hague: Martinus Nijhoff, 1983)
Ingold, Tim, *Evolution and Social Life* (Cambridge: Cambridge University Press, 1986)
Jameson, F., ed., *Aesthetics and Politics* (London: New Left Books, 1977)
Jarvis, Simon, 'Soteriology and Reciprocity', *Parataxis: Modernism and Modern Writing* 5 (1993), 30–9
——, 'The "Unhappy Consciousness" and Conscious Unhappiness: On Adorno's Critique of Hegel and the Idea of an Hegelian Critique of Adorno', in G. K. Browning, ed., *Hegel's Phenomenology of Spirit: A Reappraisal* (Amsterdam: Kluwer Academic Publishers, 1997), pp. 57–72
Jaspers, Karl, *Die Idee der Universität* (Berlin: Julius Springer, 1923)
Jay, Martin, 'The Frankfurt School's Critique of Marxist Humanism', *Social Research* 39 (1972), 285–305
——, *The Dialectical Imagination: A History of the Frankfurt School and the Institute of Social Research, 1923–50* (London: Heinemann, 1973)
——, 'The Concept of Totality in Lukács and Adorno', *Telos* 32 (1977), 117–37
——, *Adorno* (London: Fontana, 1984)
——, 'Adorno in America', *New German Critique* 31 (Winter 1984), 157–82
——, *Permanent Exiles: Essays on the Intellectual Migration from Germany to America* (New York: Columbia University Press, 1985)
Kandinsky, Wassily, *Concerning the Spiritual in Art*, tr. M. T. H. Sadler (New York: Dover, 1977)
Kant, Immanuel, *Kritik der reinen Vernunft*, 1st edn (Riga, 1781)
——, *Kritik der reinen Vernunft*, 2nd edn (Riga, 1787)
——, *Kritik der reinen Vernunft*, ed. Albert Görland (Berlin: Bruno Cassirer, 1913)
——, *Critique of Pure Reason*, tr. Norman Kemp Smith (London: Macmillan, 1933)
——, *Critique of Practical Reason*, tr. Lewis White Beck (New York: Macmillan, 1956)
——, *Groundwork of the Metaphysic of Morals*, tr. H. J. Paton (New York: Harper & Row, 1964)
——, *Was ist Aufklärung? Aufsätze zur Geschichte und Philosophie*, ed. Jürgen Zehbe (Göttingen: Vandenhoeck & Ruprecht, 1985)
——, *Critique of Judgement*, tr. Werner S. Pluhar (Indianapolis: Hackett, 1987)
——, *Political Writings*, ed. Hans Reiss, tr. H. B. Nisbet (Cambridge: Cambridge University Press, 1991)
Kappner, Hans-Hartmut, *Die Bildungstheorie Adornos als Theorie der Erfahrung von Kultur und Kunst* (FfM: Suhrkamp, 1984)

Kierkegaard, Søren, *Concluding Unscientific Postscript to the Philosophical Fragments*, tr. David F. Swenson and Walter Lowrie (Princeton: Princeton University Press, 1941)

Klages, Ludwig, *Der Geist als Widersacher der Seele*, 4th edn (Bonn and Munich: Bouvier and Johann Ambrosius Barth, 1960)

Kluke, Paul, *Die Stiftungsuniversität Frankfurt am Main, 1914–1932* (FfM: Kramer, 1973)

Kolb, David, *The Critique of Pure Modernity: Hegel, Heidegger and After* (Chicago: University of Chicago Press, 1986)

Kroner, Richard, *Von Kant bis Hegel* (2 vols, Tübingen, 1921)

Leske, Monika, 'Das Totalitätskonzept von Th. W. Adorno', *Deutsche Zeitschrift für Philosophie* 28 (1980), 1090–1102

Lindner, Burkhardt, and W. Martin Lüdke, eds, *Materialien zur ästhetischen Theorie Theodor W. Adornos* (FfM: Suhrkamp, 1985)

Link, Thomas, *Zum Begriff der Natur in der Gesellschaftstheorie Theodor W. Adornos* (Cologne: Bohlau, 1986)

Löbig, Michael, and Gerhard Schweppenhäuser, eds, *Hamburger Adorno-Symposion* (Lüneburg: zu Klampen, 1984)

Löwenthal, Leo, *Mitmachen wollte ich nie. Ein autobiographisches Gespräch mit Helmut Dubiel* (FfM: Suhrkamp, 1980)

——, *An Unmastered Past: The Autobiographical Reflections of Leo Löwenthal* (Berkeley: University of California Press, 1987)

Löwith, Karl, *From Hegel to Nietzsche*, tr. D. E. Green (London: Routledge, 1964)

Lukács, Georg, *The Meaning of Contemporary Realism*, tr. J. and N. Mander (London: Merlin Press, 1962)

——, *History and Class Consciousness*, tr. Rodney Livingstone (London: Merlin Press, 1971)

——, *Theory of the Novel*, tr. Anna Bostock (London: Merlin Press, 1971)

Luxemburg, Rosa, *The Accumulation of Capital: An Anti-critique* (London: Monthly Review Press, 1972)

McDowell, John, *Mind and World* (Cambridge, Mass.: Harvard University Press, 1994)

Marcuse, Herbert, 'Transzendentaler Marxismus', *Die Gesellschaft* 7 (1930), 304–26

——, 'Zum Problem der Dialektik', *Die Gesellschaft* 7 (1930), 15–30

——, *Reason and Revolution: Hegel and the Rise of Social Theory*, 2nd edn (London: Routledge, 1955)

——, *Eros and Civilization: A Philosophical Enquiry into Freud* (Boston: Beacon Press, 1966)

——, *Negations: Essays in Critical Theory*, tr. Jeremy J. Schapiro (Boston: Beacon Press, 1968)

——, 'On the philosophical foundation of the concept of labor in economics', *Telos* 16 (1973), 9–37

——, *Hegel's Ontology and the Theory of Historicity*, tr. Seyla Benhabib (Cambridge, Mass.: MIT Press, 1987)

Marramao, Giacomo, 'Political Economy and Critical Theory', tr. Ray Morrow, *Telos* 24 (Summer 1975), 56–80

Marx, Karl, *Early Writings*, tr. Rodney Livingstone and Gregor Benton (Harmondsworth: Penguin, 1975)

——, *Capital*, vol. 1, tr. Ben Fowkes (Harmondsworth: Penguin, 1976)

——, *Capital*, vol. 2, tr. David Fernbach (Harmondsworth: Penguin, 1978)

——, *Capital*, vol. 3, tr. David Fernbach (Harmondsworth: Penguin, 1981)

——, and Engels, Friedrich, *Critique of the Gotha Programme* (London: Lawrence & Wishart, 1939)

——, and Engels, Friedrich, *Werke* (42 vols in 44, Berlin: Dietz, 1960–83)

——, and Engels, Friedrich, *The German Ideology*, tr. W. Lough (London: Lawrence & Wishart, 1974)

Mauss, Marcel, *The Gift: The Form and Reason for Exchange in Archaic Societies*, tr. W.D. Halls (London: Routledge, 1990)

Migdal, Ulrike, *Die Frühgeschichte des Frankfurter Instituts für Sozialforschung* (FfM: Campus, 1981)

Miller, Daniel, *Material Culture and Mass Consumption* (Oxford: Blackwell, 1987)

Mittelstraß, J., 'Kant und die Dialektik der Aufklärung', in J. Schmidt, ed., *Aufklärung und Gegenaufklärung in der europäischen Literatur* (Darmstadt: Wissenschaftlische Buchgesellschaft, 1989), 341–63

Mörchen, Hermann, *Macht und Herrschaft im Denken von Heidegger und Adorno* (Stuttgart: Klett-Cotta, 1980)

——, *Adorno und Heidegger. Untersuchung einer philosophischen Kommunikationsverweigerung* (Stuttgart: Klett-Cotta, 1981)

Moritz, Peter, *Kritik des Paradigmenwechsels: mit Horkheimer gegen Habermas* (Lüneburg: zu Klampen, 1992)

Müller, G. E., 'The Hegel Legend of "Thesis–Antithesis–Synthesis" ', *Journal of the History of Ideas* 19 (1958), 411–14

Müller, Ulrich, *Erkenntniskritik und negative Metaphysik bei Adorno. Eine Philosophie der dritten Reflektiertheit* (FfM: Athenäum, 1988)

Neumann, Franz, *Behemoth: The Structure and Practice of National Socialism* (London: Gollancz, 1942)

Nietzsche, Friedrich, *The Genealogy of Morals*, tr. Francis Golffing (New York: Doubleday, 1956)

——, *Beyond Good and Evil: Prelude to a Philosophy of the Future*, tr. R. J. Hollingdale (Harmondsworth: Penguin, 1990)

Ollig, Hans-Ludwig, ed., *Neukantianismus. Texte der Marburger und der Südwestdeutschen Schule, ihrer Vorläufer und Kritiker* (Stuttgart: Reclam, 1982)

Paddison, Max, *Adorno's Aesthetics of Music* (Cambridge: Cambridge University Press, 1993)

Pettazzi, Carlo, *Th. Wiesengrund Adorno. Linee di origine e di sviluppo del pensiero (1903–1949)* (Florence: La nuova Italia, 1979)

Pollock, Friedrich, *Stadien des Kapitalismus*, ed. Helmut Dubiel (Munich: C. H. Beck, 1975)

Pongratz, Ludwig, 'Zur Aporetik des Erfahrungsbegriffs bei Theodor W. Adorno', *Philosophisches Jahrbuch* 93 (1986), 135–42

Pütze, Peter, 'Nietzsche and Critical Theory' (1974), *Telos* 50 (1981–2), 103–14

Rademacher, Claudia, *Versöhnung oder Verständigung? Kritik der Habermasschen Adorno-Revision* (Lüneburg: zu Klampen, 1993)

Rath, Norbert, 'Zur Nietzsche-Rezeption Horkheimers und Adornos', in *Vierzig Jahre Flaschenpost. 'Dialektik der Aufklärung' 1947–1987*, ed. Willem van Reijen and Gunzelin Schmid Noerr (FfM: Fischer, 1987), pp. 73–110

Reijen, Willem van and Gunzelin Schmid Noerr, eds, *Vierzig Jahre Flaschenpost.* *'Dialektik der Aufklärung' 1947 bis 1987* (FfM: Fischer, 1987)

Rickert, Heinrich, *Die Grenzen der naturwissenschaftlichen Begriffsbildung* (Verlag von J. C. B. Mohr: Tübingen, 1929)

——, *The Limits of Concept Formation in Natural Science*, abr. and tr. Guy Oakes (Cambridge: Cambridge University Press, 1986)

Ringer, Fritz K., *The Decline of the German Mandarins: The German Academic Community, 1890–1933* (Cambridge, Mass.: Harvard University Press, 1969)

Rose, Gillian, *The Melancholy Science: An Introduction to the Thought of Theodor W. Adorno* (London: Macmillan, 1978)

——, *Hegel contra Sociology* (London: Athlone, 1981)

——, *The Broken Middle* (Oxford: Blackwell, 1992)

——, *Judaism and Modernity: Philosophical Essays* (Oxford: Blackwell, 1993)

Rosen, Michael, *Hegel's Dialectic and its Criticism* (Cambridge: Cambridge University Press, 1982)

Rosenzweig, Franz, *Der Stern der Erlösung* (FfM: Suhrkamp, 1988)

Rousseau, Jean-Jacques, *The Social Contract*, tr. G. D. H. Cole, rev. J. H. Brumfitt and John C. Hall (London: Dent, 1973)

Scheler, Max, 'Universität und Volkshochschule', in Leopold von Wiese, ed., *Soziologie des Volksbildungswesens: Schriften des Forschungsinstituts für Sozialwissenschaften in Köln, 1* (1921), 153–91

——, *Formalism in Ethics and Non-formal Ethics of Values: A New Attempt toward the Foundation of an Ethical Personalism*, tr. M. S. Frings and R. L. Funk (Evanston: Northwestern University Press, 1973)

Scheuerman, William, E., *Between the Rule and the Exception: The Frankfurt School and the Rule of Law* (Cambridge, Mass.: MIT Press, 1994)

Schlick, Moritz, *Allgemeine Erkenntnislehre* (Berlin: Julius Springer, 1925)

Schlüter, Carsten, *Adornos Kritik der apologetischen Vernunft* (2 vols,Würzburg: Königshausen und Neumann, 1987)

Schmidt, Alfred, *The Concept of Nature in Marx*, tr. Ben Fowkes (London: New Left Books, 1971)

——, *Die Kritische Theorie als Geschichtsphilosophie* (Munich: Carl Hanser, 1976)

Schmidt, Friedrich W., 'Hegel in der Kritischen Theorie der "Frankfurter Schule"', in Oskar Negt, ed., *Aktualität und Folgen der Philosophie Hegels* (FfM: Suhrkamp, 1971)

Schmitt, Carl, *The Concept of the Political*, tr. George Schwab (New Brunswick, NJ: Rutgers University Press, 1976)

Schnädelbach, Herbert, 'Dialektik als Vernunftkritik. Zur Konstruktion des Rationalen bei Adorno', in *Vernunft und Geschichte: Vorträge und Abhandlungen* (FfM: Suhrkamp, 1987), pp. 179–206

——, 'Die Aktualität der Dialektik der Aufklärung', in Harry Kunnemann and Hent de Vries, eds, *Die Aktualität der Dialektik der Aufklärung* (FfM: Campus Verlag, 1989)

Schürmann, Reiner, *Heidegger on Being and Acting: From Principles to Anarchy*, tr. Christine-Marie Gros (Bloomington: Indiana University Press, 1987)

Schweppenhäuser, Hermann, ed., *Theodor Adorno zum Gedächtnis. Eine Sammlung* (FfM: Suhrkamp, 1971)

Sellars, Wilfrid, 'Empiricism and the Philosophy of Mind', in *Minnesota Studies in the Philosophy of Science*, vol. 1: *Foundations of Science and the Concepts of*

Psychology and Psychoanalysis, ed. Herbert Feigl and Michael Scriven (Minneapolis: University of Minnesota Press, 1956)

Sharratt, Bernard, *Reading Relations: Structures of Literary Production. A Dialectical Text/Book* (Brighton: Harvester, 1982)

Shils, Edward, 'Daydreams and Nightmares: Reflections on the Criticism of Mass Culture', *Sewanee Review* 65 (Autumn 1957), 487–508

Simmel, Georg, *The Problems of the Philosophy of History: An Epistemological Study*, tr. Guy Oakes (New York: Free Press, 1977)

Sohn-Rethel, Alfred, *Intellectual and Manual Labour: A Critique of Epistemology*, tr. Martin Sohn-Rethel (London: Macmillan, 1978)

Söllner, Alfons, *Geschichte und Herrschaft. Studien zur materialistischen Sozialwissenschaft, 1929–1942* (FfM: Suhrkamp, 1979)

Sonnemann, Ulrich, *Negative Anthropologie* (FfM: Suhrkamp, 1969)

Sorel, Georges, *Reflections on Violence*, tr. T. E. Hulme (London: Allen & Unwin, 1916)

Stahl, Joachim, *Kritische Philosophie und Theorie der Gesellschaft. Zum Begriff negativer Metaphysik bei Kant und Adorno* (FfM: Peter Lang, 1991)

Steinert, Heinz, *Adorno in Wien. Über die (Un-)Möglichkeit von Kunst, Kultur und Befreiung* (Vienna: Verlag für Gesellschaftskritik, 1989)

Stuckenschmidt, H. H., 'Das Zwölftonsystem', *Der neue Rundschau* 45 (1934), 301–11

Sziborsky, Lucia, *Adornos Musikphilosophie. Genese-Konstitution-Pädagogische Perspektiven* (Munich: Wilhelm Fink, 1979)

Tertulian, Nicolae, 'Lukács, Adorno and the German Classical Philosophy', *Telos* 63 (1985–6), 79–96

Therborn, Göran, 'The Frankfurt School', *New Left Review* 63 (1970), 65–96

Theunissen, Michael, *Gesellschaft und Geschichte. Zur Kritik der kritischen Theorie* (Berlin: de Gruyter, 1969)

——, *Hegels Lehre vom absoluten Geist als theologisch-politischer Traktat* (Berlin: de Gruyter, 1970)

——, *Sein und Schein. Die kritische Funktion der Hegelschen Logik* (FfM: Suhrkamp, 1980)

Thyen, Anke, *Negative Dialektik und Erfahrung. Zur Rationalität des Nichtidentischen bei Adorno* (FfM: Suhrkamp, 1989)

Tichy, Matthias, *Theodor W. Adorno. Das Verhältnis von Allgemeinem und Besonderem in seiner Philosophie* (Bonn: Bouvier, 1977)

Tomberg, Friedrich, 'Utopie und Negation. Zum ontologischen Hintergrund der Kunsttheorie Theodor W. Adornos', *Das Argument* 26 (1963), 36–48

Velkley, Richard, Introduction to Dieter Henrich, *The Unity of Reason: Philosophical Essays on Kant* (Cambridge, Mass.: Harvard University Press, 1993)

Weber, Max, *Gesammelte Aufsätze zur Religionssoziologie* (3 vols, Tübingen: J. C. B. Mohr (Paul Siebeck), 1934)

——, *The Methodology of the Social Sciences*, tr. and ed. Edward A. Shils and Henry A. Finch (New York: Macmillan, 1949)

——, *Economy and Society*, ed. Günther Roth and Claus Wittig (2 vols, Berkeley: University of California Press, 1978)

——, *From Max Weber: Essays in Sociology*, ed. H. H. Gerth and C. Wright Mills (London: Routledge, 1991)

——, *The Protestant Ethic and the Spirit of Capitalism*, tr. Talcott Parsons (London: HarperCollins, 1991)

Wellmer, Albrecht, *Kritische Gesellschaftstheorie und Positivismus* (FfM: Suhrkamp, 1969)

——, 'Truth, Semblance, Reconciliation: Adorno's Aesthetic Redemption of Modernity', *Telos* 62 (1985), 89–115

——, *Zur Dialektik von Moderne und Postmoderne. Vernunftkritik nach Adorno* (FfM: Suhrkamp, 1985)

——, "Metaphysik im Augenblick ihres Sturzes", in *Metaphysik nach Kant?*, ed. Dieter Henrich and Rolf-Peter Horstmann (Stuttgart: Klett-Cotta, 1988), pp. 767–83

Whitebook, Joel, *Perversion and Utopia: A Study in Psychoanalysis and Critical Theory* (Cambridge, Mass.: MIT Press, 1995)

Wiggershaus, Rolf, *The Frankfurt School*, tr. Michael Robertson (Cambridge: Polity Press, 1993)

Wilke, Sabine, *Zur Dialektik von Exposition und Darstellung. Ansätze zu einer Kritik der Arbeiten Martin Heideggers, Theodor W. Adornos und Jacques Derridas* (Stanford German Studies, 24) (New York: Peter Lang, 1988)

Wilson, Michael, *Das Institut für Sozialforschung und seine Faschismusanalyse* (FfM and New York: Campus Verlag, 1983)

Windelband, Wilhelm, 'History and Natural Science', tr. Guy Oakes, *History and Theory* 19 (1980), 169–85

Wohlfart, Günther, 'Anmerkungen zur ästhetischen Theorie Adornos', *Philosophisches Jahrbuch* 83 (1976), 370–91

Wolin, Richard, *Walter Benjamin: An Aesthetic of Redemption* (New York: Columbia University Press, 1982)

Wood, Allen, *Hegel's Ethical Thought* (Cambridge: Cambridge University Press, 1990)

Zuidervaart, Lambert, *Adorno's Aesthetic Theory: The Redemption of Illusion* (Cambridge, Mass.: MIT Press, 1991)

Index